Greenhill Books

Bayonets for Hire

Other books by William Urban include:

MEDIEVAL MERCENARIES
The Business of War

THE TEUTONIC KNIGHTS
A Military History

TANNENBERG AND AFTER
Lithuania, Poland and the Teutonic Order in Search of Immortality

THE LIVONIAN CRUSADE

THE SAMOGITIAN CRUSADE

Bayonets for Hire
Mercenaries at War, 1550–1789

by

William Urban

Foreword by William H. McNeill

Greenhill Books, London
MBI Publishing, St Paul

Greenhill Books

Bayonets for Hire
Mercenaries at War, 1550–1789

First published in 2007 by Greenhill Books, Lionel Leventhal Limited,
Park House, 1 Russell Gardens, London NW11 9NN
www.greenhillbooks.com
and
MBI Publishing Co., Galtier Plaza, Suite 200, 380 Jackson Street, St Paul,
MN 55101-3885, USA

British Library Cataloguing-in Publication Data
Urban, William L., 1939–
Bayonets for hire : mercenaries at war, 1550–1789
1. Mercenary troops – Europe – History – 16th century
2. Mercenary troops – Europe – History – 17th century
3. Mercenary troops – Europe – History – 18th century
4. Europe – History, Military – 1492–1648
5. Europe – History, Military – 1648–1789
I. Title
355.3'54'094'09032

ISBN-13: 9781853677427

Library of Congress Cataloging-in Publication Data available

For more information on our books, please visit www.greenhillbooks.com, email
sales@greenhillbooks.com or telephone us within the UK on 020 8458 6314.
You can also write to us at the above London address.

Edited and typeset by Palindrome
Maps drawn by Palindrome

Printed and bound in Great Britain by
Creative Print and Design (Wales), Ebbw Vale

Contents

Illustrations

Charles V, Holy Roman Emperor. Portrait by Bartel Beham, 1531.

A *Landsknecht*, the professional infantryman of the era. From a drawing by Hans Holbein the elder.

Saint Anthony and the City, by Albrecht Dürer (1519).

Albrecht Dürer's *Four Horsemen of the Apocalypse*.

View of Reval in the nineteenth century.

Coins from Livonia.

Gustavus Adolphus, the 'Lion of the North', King of Sweden.

The battle of Lützen in 1632.

Polish Nobleman by Rembrandt von Rijn painted in 1637.

View from the heights of the Vienna Woods, showing the Christian forces advancing on the Ottoman army besieging Vienna.

Banquet of the Amsterdam Civic Guard in Celebration of the Peace of Münster, by artist, Bartholomeus van der Helst (1613–70).

Louis XIV, the Sun King.

The Duke of Schomberg.

The walls of Ypres, destroyed in the First World War.

John Churchill, later Duke of Marlborough.

Recruiting poster for the duke of Penthievre's dragoons.

Troops on the march to Spain in a French calendar for 1720.

French officers recruiting troops and paying the enlistment bonus.

Eugene of Savoy meets with his old enemy, Marshal Villars, to negotiate peace at Rystatt.

Peter the Great 'incognito' at the court of Louis XIV.

View of Moscow.

The stronghold at Kaminets in Podolia (modern Ukraine).

The Battle of Poltava (1709) by Denis Martens the Younger, painted in 1726.

Nineteenth-century view of Riga.

Hungarian nobles pledging their loyalty to Maria Theresa 11 September 1741.

Cartoon from 1739, when Britain was about to go to war with Spain.

Cartoon from 1749, after the Peace of Aix-la-Chapelle ended the War of the Austrian Succession.

Madame de Pompadour.

Coins from Austria and Prussia.

Winter Scene by Isaac van Ostade, painted in 1645.

Marshal Maurice de Saxe, son of Augustus the Strong.

'Old Fritz', Frederick the Great of Prussia.

Cartoons from 1756–7.

Preface

Why a book on early modern mercenaries from the Wars of Religion to the French Revolution? First of all, because it was a natural continuation of my earlier book, *Medieval Mercenaries* (Greenhill, 2006). Second, because mercenaries represented an early aspect of modernisation.*

In the mid-sixteenth century all armies were composed of mercenary soldiers, usually led by a professional captain, but often with the territorial ruler in command of the army. In time the rulers came to realise that this could not continue, because the size of the state had become too large – medieval principalities were being consolidated into great empires; perhaps it was because the rulers came to realise that they lacked the time and expertise to manage large armies, or from an awareness that war was dangerous, and a state in chaos from losing its ruler in combat was not likely to survive.

Warfare had likewise become too complicated to rely on individual soldiers or units to provide their own weapons. It eventually became possible to provide each soldier with a dozen to three dozen paper cartridges containing powder and shot, to be kept in the cartridge case slung over the left shoulder and resting on the right hip for ready access while reloading. Just before 1700 flintlocks began to replace matchlocks; the bayonet appeared about the same time; later iron ramrods replaced those made of hard wood. Soldiers wore thick overcoats in battle, but they were too heavy to march in – this put a new burden on the supply services, to carry these along with the troops so that they could be donned when combat seemed imminent. Each innovation was expensive.

In addition, the rulers began to realise that commoners were too valuable to allow foreigner recruiters to lure them abroad. Later, commoners began to understand more fully that they were citizens of a

---

* Most forceful of scholars endorsing this sometimes controversial concept is Geoffrey Parker, *The Military Revolution* and *The Army of Flanders and the Spanish Road*.

nation, not just subjects of a ruler; as Germans or Frenchmen or Irish-men, they preferred to fight for employers who advanced the cause of their nation and their religion.

Though common soldiers and the rulers were coming more and more to represent their nation, the officer corps remained thoroughly international. In fact, rulers clearly preferred to entrust their armies to foreigners who would not aspire to replace them as would be the case if they selected family members or prominent local nobles. Also, they wanted the best men with experience and training. Such men were less likely to be found at home than in the wider European talent market.

Some successful rulers built their states around their armies. Many a nation has been created by its military elite, and more than a few are governed by these elites today. Creating such an elite, one might conclude, might be an essential part of nation-building. One has only to read the inside pages of good newspapers to see how important military specialists are today for turning courageous but half-armed tribesmen into soldiers, or for routing undisciplined gangs which pass themselves off as armies. Usually these specialists work for national armies. But not always. When weak nations prove themselves ineffective at maintaining law and order, and public opinion in advanced nations becomes disillusioned with the costs of intervention, local power-brokers turn to mercenaries to do the fighting. This is most obvious in post-colonial Africa, where small bodies of European mercenaries have defended or overthrown gangster regimes; and perhaps some that might not have been so bad. In Latin America, too, local hired guns, sometimes supported by drug money, have both supported and threatened governments.*

Then there are those so committed to an ideology – religion most often – that they leave their homeland to fight in sometimes hopeless struggles against ancestral enemies and perceived foes. Such men – they are almost always men – are not quite mercenaries, but not quite freedom fighters, either. They may be patriots, or terrorists, or start out as one and end up as the other. Or be both.

There are also those dragged unwillingly into a brutal system. Most pitiable were those pressed by crop failures or whose farms had been destroyed by plunderers or stripped by commissary sergeants. The enlist-

---

* Tilly warns against the 'intellectual colonial' belief that the European experience in state development will be followed by Third World states today. An alternative to the nation-state is necessary, but he cannot imagine what it will be. Boot disagrees. Interstate war is less likely than before, but warfare by non-state entities is a present reality. There is no formula for success – too much change can fail as completely as too little; and new weapons never made old ones obsolete. Superiority in military prowess has always been fleeting, but states which did not make the adaptations necessary to meet military challenges – adaptations which still today require changes throughout society and especially in thinking – have failed to protect their borders, their people, even their very existence.

ment bonus was small – in England famously called the King's Shilling – but it might save a family from starvation. If the wages were minimal, and often not paid at all, at least there was one less mouth at home to feed.

Next were those coerced into military service, often as teenagers, and who remained in arms so long that they knew no other occupation. They were certainly not volunteers, often not exactly draftees, but as soldiers for life they had to find employers. This was more true for common soldiers, less so for noble officers, but both had some freedom about the choice of army and of moving from one employer to another.

It is often said, usually correctly, that most conscripts were the communities' undesirables – the unemployed, the unemployable, the criminal – but recruiting officers were usually more interested in meeting their quota than in following a ruler's guidelines; besides, armies needed blacksmiths, carpenters, bakers and boot-makers. Officers wanted servants, and military bands had to have musicians. There was even the occasional need for a clerk who could read and write.

A few must have seen a military career as an opportunity to leave home – to escape an oppressive father or a boring, purposeless existence, or – the old cliché – a failed love affair; or a shrewish wife and demanding children. Certainly some wanted to earn fame and honour – a necessary achievement for young nobles, even the boys of prominent houses.

Last, we must never forget the lure of adventure. Young boys want to see the world, and sometimes even old men of thirty or so feel the same urge.

In a complicated world, it is too simple to reduce every decision to its simplest motives, especially economic motives. Sometimes people just say, 'what the hell' and do stupid things. Money was important, but if Karl Marx could reject simple-minded economic determinism, we should be able to do the same.*

Since varied motives lay behind the individual choices that led to military service, it is difficult to draw a clear line between volunteers and mercenaries. Perhaps the latter look more carefully at the money, perhaps the former are inspired by appeals to their religion and defending their homeland, but in the course of time all come to seem pretty much alike. Hard experience coarsens men, and war is the hardest experience of all.†

---

* Marx provided us with the most negative description of those who make up a dysfunctional class below the workers. Those who defy the social order, and those who enforce it, belong to the *Lumpenproletariat*. Lacking a social conscience, they would anything for money; they are society's natural bullies, the enemies of order and progress. But, like Lenin's 'useful idiots', they can be useful. Any government that does not shrink from using coercion and fear can make them into fine soldiers – up to a point. When opportunities for rape and rapine appear, they seize them; and when the fighting gets hot, they think more of survival than victory.

† Maurice Keen warns us in his authoritative work, *Chivalry*, 'In terms of motivation, calculation and conduct the line between gentlemen and mercenary was simply too difficult to draw with precision.'

The European political world of early modern times often appears impossibly complicated. This may be less so if we make a minor adjustment to our mental image of the players in great power politics. We are accustomed to focusing on one state at a time – English-language readers naturally having more interest in Britain and France than other regions. That causes us to lose sight of Italy and Spain, even of Germany, and certainly of the vast stretches of territory from Livonia in the north to the Balkans in the south. This is understandable: life is short, schools have limited time and other subjects to teach, until recently travel there was difficult, and, most fundamentally, that isn't 'our history'. Of course, it is 'our history' in a most fundamental way: whatever contributes to making our modern world is our history. We must look at it in a broader context. This could be religion, popular culture or economics, but here let it be mercenaries.

Few medieval rulers could hire mercenaries as a permanent force, nor did they want to. They recruited professionals only for short periods and at need, did what they could to control them, and ultimately dismissed them (hopefully with a bonus, on the condition that they disperse quietly). There was a general consensus that such warriors should not become rulers themselves (though that rule was obviously ignored when necessary, especially when nobles began to hire their talents to the highest bidder).

Subsequently, the periphery of Europe became more important. This was seen in the wars of religions, but the process was then assisted by the heartland of Europe being divided for a generation into two parallel universes at war, each with mercenary armies. The first is the most familiar, that of the western half of Europe – France versus Spain, Austria and Britain. The second is the eastern – Sweden versus Russia and Poland, with Turkey occasionally involved. These two great conflicts touch, but they never overlap. Before those wars it appeared that Austrian and Russian armies would march south, reversing the Turkish expansion of recent centuries; afterward, there was a long stagnation.

In the middle of the eighteenth century there was a great reordering of power relationships in the heart of the Continent – the traditional Continental powers believed it was necessary to curb the ambitions of Prussia and reverse a tendency of Germans to look to Prussia for leadership; France saw opportunities in this internal German conflict for territorial gain and the recovery of lost prestige; Russia saw an opportunity to advance westward. These were the last great wars that involved large numbers of mercenaries.

By the outbreak of the French Revolution an international class of officers had come to dominate the profession of war. And then, almost overnight, they vanished.

Preface

If our modern world seems precariously balanced between what was and what might be, so it always was. Parallels can be easily (if somewhat inaccurately) drawn. Before there was a United Nations, there was the Holy Roman Empire and, perhaps, Christendom. Before post-colonial Africa, there were the Balkan territories of the Ottoman Turks. There were regional warlords in China, and up-and-coming dynasties in Germany and Italy. There is a clear line linking the medieval world to the early modern, a less distinct line coming right to our own times, but history does not have a single message for all people or all nations.

Why the title, *Bayonets For Hire*, when no officer would ever lower himself to handle one? Partly because the bayonet symbolises the process of modernisation – it combines two traditional military functions (the spear and the missile weapon), and it is best produced and employed by a large state apparatus. But also because there is something very personal about using a bayonet. Two men look one another in the eyes. One of them dies. It's something very different from the impersonal nature of modern war.

No one likes mercenaries. Yet everyone has used them. Perhaps the awareness of the past and present use of mercenaries is justification enough for another book on them and the business of war.

William Urban
Lee L. Morgan Professor of History
and International Affairs
Monmouth College (Illinois)

Foreword

Mercenaries have a long history and a bad reputation which is not undeserved. This book shows why. Their history is part of the human proclivity for violence that reaches back to pre-human times, when defence of territory against neighbouring human and proto-human bands was just as essential to group survival as defence against the big cats and other animal predators who preyed on our remote ancestors.

Defence of territory against human neighbours probably resembled what happens today among chimpanzee bands. Among chimps, all adult males fight against outsiders, hand to hand, face to face, and often inflict lethal wounds. Yet cross-border intrusions by small companies of males sporadically test the boundaries that ordinarily limit where each band can feed. Elastic boundaries reflecting the rise and fall of numbers within adjacent bands result; and the same sort of elasticity probably drove the expansion of humankind around the earth when our ancestors' increasing formidability began to lift them to the top of the food chain. Coordinated action sustained by language and by using ever improving weapons explains their extraordinary success.

After small agricultural villages started to spread, about 11,000 years ago, the exercise of violence against neighbours slowly assumed a different form that lasted as long as agrarian society outweighed old-fashioned hunters and gatherers, on the one hand, and modern urban, industrial ways of life on the other. To put the change in a nutshell: effective village defence required specialised well-equipped warriors, supported by rents and taxes collected from farming villagers, who thereby gave up major responsibility for their own defence.

Differentiation between specialised fighting men and ordinary farmers was an earmark of early civilisations. As long as tax and rent receivers and tax and rent payers coexisted more or less peaceably, larger numbers of persons could in fact survive in agricultural landscapes, and over time elaborated all the diverse forms of art, religion and literary culture that we associate with the term civilised. But persistent instabilities remained as the harsh record of European warfare between 1550 and 1789, that this book surveys, makes all too clear.

The most intractable problem was that a few years of peace and good harvests allowed villagers to raise more children than could find enough land to live on as their parents had done. Whenever local cultivable land was already fully exploited, a plurality of sons and daughters meant that most of them had to go elsewhere and try to make a living by working for hire, or, perchance, by resorting to violence and seizing what they could not earn peaceably. For millennia, therefore, young unpropertied villagers filled the ranks of varied protest and revolutionary movements, and readily accepted mercenary employment when opportunity offered.

As far as I know, the first literary record of this sort of social-political instability is preserved in the biblical account of the rise of the Hebrew kingdom under Saul and David (1020–961 BCE). According to the Books of Samuel, ecstatic wandering bands of prophets constituted the kernel around which first Saul and then David formed their armies; and the story of how King David betrayed Uriah the Hittite shows how, in a single lifetime, local volunteers were supplemented (at least sometimes) by foreign mercenaries.

Whenever a new state, like King David's kingdom, faced internal strains, monarchs were impelled to hire foreign mercenaries who had no personal ties to discontented local groups. Only so could obedience to the royal will be more nearly assured. David must have acted on that principle when he hired Uriah; and Urban's account of the innumerable foreign adventurers who scattered across central and eastern Europe in the sixteenth to the eighteenth centuries shows how vigorous that practice remained toward the close of the agrarian era.

There was, however, another ancient military tradition – local self-defence by a citizen army of propertied farmers, commanded by elected magistrates. City states in ancient Greek exemplified this ideal, so did republican Rome. When a handful of Greek cities defeated the imperial army of Persia in 480–479 BCE, Herodotus concluded that because they fought of their own free will, citizen soldiers fought better and could therefore defeat soldiers who obeyed a king whose will was not their own.

Other factors undoubtedly were in play in 480–479 BCE, most notably Persian dependence on supply from the rear. But the notion that free citizens fought better than subjects flattered the Greeks and Romans and pervades the classical literary tradition. Persians, too, found much to admire in Greek fighting men, as is shown by the fact that they began to hire large numbers of Greek mercenaries soon after 479 BCE.

Xenophon's *Anabasis* tells how one such band, 10,000 strong, enlisted in the service of a pretender to the Persian throne and penetrated almost to Babylon. Then, after their employer died in battle, the soldiers elected new leaders (of whom the Athenian Xenophon was one) and made their way safely back to Greece in 400 BCE.

Later, to be sure, in the time of the Roman empire, the imperial patterns of military organisation, long at home in the Near East, prevailed throughout the Mediterranean coastlands. But memory of civic freedom and past glories lingered long after paid soldiers displaced citizen-farmers in the Roman army. That memory revived later in Europe when city states in Italy and elsewhere reproduced some of the characteristics of antiquity.

After some dramatic initial victories by citizen militias in Italy beginning about 1100, however, a new golden age for mercenaries dawned when citizens opted out of their military responsibilities, preferring to hire experts from afar and often only for a single campaign. The Hundred Years War (1337–1453) between France and England, and recurrent fighting among rival Italian states gave ample employment for mercenaries, as Urban's earlier book, *Medieval Mercenaries*, explains. Here its successor pursues the tangled record of mercenary warfare in Europe to a climax during the Thirty Years War (1618–48) that devastated much of Germany, and sets forth its subsequent diminution (but not extinction) down to 1789.

Over this period of time, tactics and weapons became more complex; combined arms – infantry, cavalry and artillery – learned to coordinate their movements on battlefields; and, above all, warfare became more and more expensive. When in 1494 a French army, equipped with newly mobile siege guns, invaded Italy and captured previously impregnable fortresses with ease, Italian engineers quickly responded by inventing cannon-proof forms of fortification.

But the Florentine statesman, Niccolò Machiavelli (1469–1527), blamed Italian failures on the half-heartedness of mercenary captains, who fought to live another day, mayhap under a different paymaster. Machiavelli sought instead to revive the Florentine militia, believing citizens could match the military successes citizen-soldiers of republican Rome had so gloriously exemplified.

His condemnation of professional mercenaries coloured the republican ideal thereafter, bearing fruit both among the founding fathers of the United States, and among French revolutionaries who made military service obligatory for young male citizens in 1792, and actually did save the republic in the next few years with the much enlarged French armies that conscription created.

A lively nationalism among Frenchmen made revolutionary conscription practicable. In the course of the nineteenth century, rival nationalisms, most notably in Germany, set the scene for other European states to introduce universal military training, even in peacetime; and conscription filled the ranks of the vast armies that fought World Wars I and II. Yet the U.S. went over to voluntary recruitment of its armed services in 1973, and in the decades after World War II many other countries did the same.

No one calls the professional fighting men waging the most recent American wars mercenaries. We prefer to speak of national service and self-sacrifice. Nearly all U.S. service men and women are in fact patriotic American citizens. Yet pay matters far more for professional armed forces than it did for temporary conscripts who counted on a civilian career after discharge.

I conclude that the age-old divergence of interest between civilian paymasters and professional fighting men, that gave mercenaries such as bad reputation, is still safely hidden, but may flare again into angry confrontation in time to come. For the age of mercenaries is not a thing of the past. It is instead a growing reality among us, not solely in the United States, but around the world.

William H. McNeill
Professor of History, emeritus
University of Chicago

Timeline

1500	*Ferdinand and Isabella* ruling united Spain; Austria, Spain and France fighting in Italy
1513	Machiavelli writes *The Prince*
1517	Luther challenges the doctrine of indulgences
1519	Leonardo da Vinci dies; *Charles V* elected German king (later crowned Holy Roman Emperor)
1521	Luther confronts Charles V at Reichstag in Worms
1525	Protestant Reformation spreading; peasant rebellion in Germany Battle of Pavia (Charles V captures Francis I of France)
1526	Battle of Mohacs (Hungary falls to Turks)
1527	Charles V's army sacks Rome
1529	First Turkish siege of Vienna
1530	Augsburg Confession (definition of Protestant beliefs) read to Charles V at Reichstag
1545	Council of Trent (start of the Counter-Reformation)
1546	Battle of Mühlberg (Charles V defeats German Protestants)
1550	A pause in the Empire's wars with France and Turkey Nostradamus writes his first almanac
1556	Charles V divides Habsburg possessions between Austria and Spain
1555	Peace of Augsburg: Princes of Holy Roman Empire to choose religion (*cuius regio, eius religio*)
1558	Livonian War begins; *Ivan the Terrible*
1559	*Elizabeth I* of England crowned
1564	Michelangelo dies
1571	Battle of Lepanto (Holy League defeats Ottoman navy)
1575	Sweden and Poland opposing Russia in Livonian War
1576	Death of Titian (painter)
1580	Death of Palladio (architect)

	Religious war in France between Catholics and Protestants (Huguenots)
1583	Sweden and Poland defeat Ivan the Terrible (Livonian War ends)
1588	The Spanish Armada defeated by Elizabeth's navy (beginning of Spain's decline)
1594	Death of Palestrina (master of polyphonic Renaissance music)
1600	Time of Troubles in Russia; Bourbon dynasty begins in France
	Chocolate drinks become popular with nobility; pipe tobacco smoked widely
1618	Thirty Years War begins in Bohemia
1625	Denmark enters the Thirty Years War; Protestants defeated in France; *Richelieu, Wallenstein, Gustavus Adolphus*
1632	Battle of Lützen (Gustavus Adophus defeats Wallenstein, but falls in battle)
1635	Battle of Nördlingen (Imperial Army defeats Swedes)
1640	Death of Peter Paul Rubens (baroque art)
	Louis XIV becomes king of France
1641	Death of Monteverdi (popularises baroque music) dies
1642	English Civil War begins (Parliament against Charles I)
1645	Battle of Naseby (New Model Army defeats Charles I)
1646–48	Treaty of Westphalia ends Thirty Years War
1648–53	Civil War in France (*Fronde*)
1649	Charles I beheaded
1650	*Cromwell* conquers Ireland and Scotland; Jews allowed back into England and France; death of Descartes (philosopher)
1655	Poles break Swedish siege of Czestochowa
1558	Death of Cromwell
1660	Restoration in England (*Charles II* returns from exile)
1666	Great Fire of London
1669	Rembrandt dies; Louis XIV starts building Versailles
1675	Louis XIV expands into Low Countries and crosses the Rhine
1683	Siege of Vienna by Ottoman Turks; relief army led by Charles of Lorraine and *Jan Sobieski*
1688	The Glorious Revolution in England (*William and Mary* replace *James II*)
1689	War of the League of Augsburg begins (Germans, Spanish, Dutch and English against France)
1690	Introduction of the bayonet
	Battle of the Boyne (William III defeats James II in Ireland)
1691	*Türkenlouis* defeats Turks in Balkans

1697	Peter the Great tours western Europe; end of War of the League of Augsburg
1700	Beginning of the War of the Spanish Succession and the Great Northern War; *Eugene of Savoy, Marlborough, Charles XII* Tea and coffee introduced into France; flintlock muskets replacing matchlocks
1703	*Peter the Great* begins construction of St Petersburg
1707	Act of Union (Scotland and England united)
1709	Battle of Poltava (Peter the Great defeats *Charles XII*)
1710	Augustus II begins construction of the Zwinger in Dresden and porcelain manufacture in Meissen
1713	Peace of Utrecht ends War of the Spanish Succession
1714	Eugene of Savoy starts work on Belvedere Palace
1715	Karlskirche started in Vienna by Charles VI; death of Louis XIV
1721	Peace of Nystadt ends Great Northern War
1725	Decline of Austria and Poland
1733	War of the Polish Succession
1735	William Hogarth draws *The Rake's Progress*
1740	Start of the War of the Austrian Succession; *Maria Theresa, Frederick the Great*
1741	Death of Vivaldi (transforms baroque music into classical)
1745	Frederick the Great starts Sanssouci Palace in Potsdam
1750	Enlightenment era; death of J. S. Bach; Jean-Jacques Rousseau and Voltaire writing; Handel (musician) in Britain
1754	*Elizabeth of Russia* begins the Winter Palace in St Petersburg
1756	Seven Years War begins (Austria, France and Russia attack Prussia)
1757	Battle of Plassey (Clive establishes Britain as the major foreign power in India)
1759	Joseph Wedgwood begins manufacturing porcelain; France creates the first division in army (combined arms under one command)
1760	*George III* becomes king of Great Britain
1762	Death of Elizabeth of Russia; *Catherine the Great* seizes power
1765	Hennessy founds company in Cognac
1767	*Sturm und Drang* movement (beginning of romanticism)
1768	Royal Academy founded
1770	Death of François Boucher (rococo painter)
1771	Goethe (philosopher, poet, scientist) writes *Götz von Berlichingen* (romantic tragedy about a sixteenth-century soldier of fortune)
1772	First Partition of Poland (Russia, Prussia and Austria take lands)

1774	*Louis XVI* becomes King of France
1775	American Revolution begins; *George Washington;* Christopher Wren designs St Paul
1776	Hessian Mercenaries in America
1778	French enter American War for Independence
1781	Battle at Yorktown (Americans and French capture Cornwallis's army)
1783	Treaty of Paris recognises American Independence Catherine conquers the Crimea
1785	*Napoleon Bonaparte* graduates from royal military academy
1788	Death of Gainsborough (portrait artist)
1789	French Revolution begins
1791	Death of Mozart
1792	Battle of Valmy (French turn back armies intent on overthrowing the Revolution)
1793	Louis XVI beheaded; Napoleon drives British from Toulon 2nd Partition of Poland
1795	3rd Partition of Poland

Maps

Europe 1550–1789

500 miles

European battles 1550-1789

500 miles

Note on currencies

European coinage throughout the medieval and early modern periods comprised a variety of denominations and standards. The influx of new silver supplies in the early medieval period had brought about a system of accounting based on 12 *denarii* (pennies) to the *solidus* (*soldo, sou,* shilling) and 20 *solidi* to the *librum* (*livre,* pound). Multiples of the penny later appeared, usually in a form derived from the Italian *grosso denaro* (groat, *groschen, gros*). Gold denominations included the *florin, gulden* (guilder) and *ducat.* These were later replaced by large silver coins, such as the *thaler* (whence came dollar).

In 1524 Emperor Charles V attempted to establish a common money standard: 1 guilder/thaler = 24 groschen, 72 kreuzer, 288 pfennigs or about 3 livres.

As an indication of value, in the 1520s a Landsknecht in Germany was paid four florins a month (in England those in the service of Henry VIII in 1544 received 12s 14d per month).

This may be contrasted with an anecdote from 1637: when a well-off Dutch merchant apparently earned 3,000 guilders a year, one of the newly introduced tulips went for 5,200 guilders! The tulip bubble burst, of course – speculation frenzies were common in eras of expansion, uncertainty and inflation.

Chapter 1

Mercenaries Medieval to Modern

The End of the Middle Ages

It is not easy to mark the moment that the Middle Ages became the Modern World, because that moment did not occur everywhere at the same time. It is like trying to identify when an individual becomes mature – for some people it is at an early age, for others it is 'any day now'. The Russians are widely considered the last major European power to enter the modern age, the Italians the first.

Today we call this new world the Renaissance, but that term would have meant nothing to the humanists and artists we think of as typifying the era. What educated men and women understood was that the world they knew was changing, and that nothing demonstrated the changes more than developments in the military arts. The traditional city-state or small kingdom could not afford to equip and maintain large armies, re-build ageing castles, or to ask vassals and militias to travel far from home. Only the richest kings could stay in the competition for greatness, and even then only by hiring professionals.

That, perhaps, is the moment when we know the Middle Ages have passed – the moment when professionals take over everywhere – in art, music, education, architecture, medicine, commerce . . . and war. We call many military professionals of this era mercenaries. They will be the heart and soul of the first royal armies, the armies that crush the small states in Renaissance Italy, the armies that hold together and protect the new national state.*

---

* The influence of humanism, with its secular attitudes and values, led more educated people to read history, especially ancient history. The word 'Renaissance' means rebirth and signifies the revival of interest in ancient thought, and the study of the classical period later influenced the military arts. Parker, *The Military Revolution*, emphasises the significant increase in the size of armies, which in turn required much great outlays of money, heavier taxes, increased borrowing, and more recruiting of men from other countries.

But that is to hurry the story. It took 300 years for the concept of nation-hood to mature. Until then loyalty to a lord, not a nation, remained the dominant ethos. As Jacques Barzun noted in *From Dawn to Decadence, 500 Years of Western Cultural Life*, common men were 'subjects', not 'citizens', and with provinces being passed around according to the whims of war, marriage and inheritance, there was no reason for any ambitious and capable man to limit his employment to the ruler of the land of his birth.

Nowhere was this clearer than in Germany.

Germany in the Reformation Era

Erasmus of Rotterdam (1466–1536) repeatedly criticised princes for making wars and civilians for approving them; soldiers, he said, joined armies to take booty (going away like Mercury, coming home like Vulcan – that is, flying off in search of profit, limping back). In his essay *Dulce Bellum Inexpertis*, written in 1515, he criticised Vegetius' then popular military manual *De Re Militari*. He once commented that *milites ad odorem pacis peiora moliuntur quam in bello** (soldiers get up to worse things at the smell of peace than they do in war), meaning that mercen-aries always preferred war to unemployment. This certainly applied to the class of free knights in the Holy Roman Empire, many of whom served in mercenary armies.

These knights were mostly descendants of that class of German warrior-administrators called *Ministeriales*. Originally, many were called serf-knights because their lords had selected outstanding commoners to perform military service. This emphasis on ability rather than birth is a major distinction between German knights and their neighbours on all sides. But how many were originally peasants? Many must have been free farmers; some were burghers, young men accustomed to bearing arms while transporting goods from one city to another.

In the course of time these knights came to think of themselves as noble, and they were extremely sensitive to any implication that they were not. As a result, when the massive political, economic and social changes of the early sixteenth century began to bear down on them, they hired themselves out as mercenaries in order to afford the expenses associated with their claims to be free, independent and noble knights.

This claim was supported by those few of their members who had been educated in classical studies – that is, younger sons who had been sent to a university to prepare for a clerical career but did not feel the calling as much as their parents wished. Ulrich von Hutten, the most

---

* This in a letter recounting Erasmus's meeting with Cardinal Canossa, who had been charged with negotiating peace between England and France in 1514.

famous of these humanist scholars, delved back into Tacitus to show that all Germans had once been free warriors, men and women who refused to bow to Roman servitude.* Their descendants were unwilling to give up their rights and properties to the Holy Roman Emperor. This meant that this class of knights was likely to find the Protestant Reformation more agreeable than bending to the demands of a Roman Catholic Church that tended to support imperial rights.

Germany was fragmented into a small number of duchies (the most important ruled by the *electors* who served as imperial councillors and who voted in imperial elections), counties (whose noble rulers had the right to attend the sessions of the German equivalent of parliament, the *Reichstag*) and free cities (which sent representatives to the Reichstag); there were also archbishops (three of whom were electors), bishops and abbots (also represented in the Reichstag; many were called prince-bishops because of their secular life styles) and the free knights. All of these states were independent. Most were hereditary, except the cities and ecclesiastical states, which in practice tended to be dominated by the same families generation after generation.

There was much less peace and order than everyone desired, but there was even more fear of anyone who acquired enough power to enforce the rulings of the *Reichstag* and the imperial council.

If this was a problem for maintaining order at home, it was even worse for efforts to develop a coherent foreign policy.

German Knights

Ulrich von Hutten's famous letter to Pirckheimer in the autumn of 1518 is often quoted to illustrate the declining status of the free knights in Germany. He depicted harried men trying to protect their forest-bound estates from attack, unable to raise more revenues from their poverty-stricken and ignorant peasants, and seeking a protective association with some powerful lord who would not simply dispossess them at the first opportunity.

Life was squalid in the lofty but crowded fortifications atop isolated hills; visits from bandits and robbers outnumbered those from merchants and churchmen. There was fear of a peasant uprising, as did soon occur, and appeals to chivalry brought more wry smiles than sympathetic nods. German society was in desperate need of reform, but the knights' influence

---

* Hutten (1488–1523) was educated in Germany and Italy, concentrating on the study of law. His *Epistolae obscurorum virorum* (*Letters of Obscure Men*), mocking ignorant churchmen, made him famous, even earning him appointment as court poet by Emperor Maximilian. An early supporter of Luther, his effort to lead the free knights of Germany against the Roman Catholic Church failed – ending the knights' role in imperial politics; he died in exile in Switzerland of syphilis.

31

was reduced to two areas – their role as administrators of church property and their willingness to serve as officers of mercenary units.*

The Habsburg emperor Charles V came to power in Germany from 1519 until 1556. He would become wealthy thanks to the silver mines in his American possessions. However, faced by hostile powers – the Ottoman Turks, France and then German Protestants – he would be unable to bring his forces to bear on more than one crisis at a time, thus allowing earlier opponents time to recover from their defeats.†

In addition, Charles's Spanish subjects insisted on his seeing to their interests, too, which meant defending their commercial interests in the Low Countries (the Netherlands and Belgium). The famous 'Spanish Road' across the Holy Roman Empire was created by using silver from the Americas to hire mercenaries in Italy and Switzerland, then marching them through Germany to the Low Countries.

Austria, Spain and the Low Countries

Charles V's grandfather Maximilian I (1493–1519) had been a cautious ruler who followed his own father's example of doing little, but doing it very well. His leadership in rallying resistance to French encroachment on German frontiers made him popular, but he talked more than he acted. When Germans in distant Livonia appealed to him for help against the grand duke of Moscow, he sent sweet words of encouragement, but no money or troops.

His Austrian and Czech lands made a compact, if landlocked, economic unit, and merchants there were in easy contact with their counterparts in wealthy Italian and German cities. But the economic heart of the Holy Roman Empire was in the Low Countries. That trade with England and Scotland, Germany, Scandinavia and the Baltic, Spain, Portugal and the Mediterranean caused treasure to flow into the Habsburg coffers long before it was supplemented by the rich stream of gold and silver from the New World.

The New World was one of the attractions for a marriage between Maximilian's son, Philip the Handsome, and Juana (Joanna), the daughter of Ferdinand and Isabella. But there was more than a combination of looks and money – instead of fighting over the Low Countries and Italy, they joined forces. Their two sons, Charles and Ferdinand, would successively become Holy Roman emperors, each

---

* Black, *European Warfare, 1494–1660*, notes that the roles slowly merged as 'martial elite culture', transformed by princes and administrators.
† Braudel in *The Structures of Everyday Life* calls the armies of this era 'miniature', a reality that limited everyone's options.

founding a Habsburg dynasty, the former in Spain, the latter in Austria.

The other attraction was to form a united front in Italy to defend their possessions from the French; they succeeded, temporarily, only to find their allies then wished them to leave as well.

To make matters worse, the Ottoman conquest of most of Hungary and the Protestant Reformation in Germany distracted Charles V from his efforts to deal with the French.† By the time religious peace was reached, temporarily, at the Peace of Augsburg in 1555 – allowing each prince to determine his subjects' religion – the old problems had been supplanted by new ones. The new Holy Roman Emperor, Ferdinand (1556–64) essentially stood on the defensive on every front. Doing little once again seemed the safest policy.

Italy

The Italian peninsula was politically divided even before the French invasion of 1494. After that date it was a battlefield, with French and Spanish armies unsetting the balance of power that had long kept the level of violence at an acceptable level.

Machiavelli, the author from this era most widely read today, tried to make sense of this new situation. Spanish armies, led first by Ferdinand of Aragon (1479–1516) and Maximilian of Austria, then by their grandson, Charles, fought French armies led by Louis XII (1498–1515) and Francis I (1515–47). The popes and other minor rulers tried to maintain a balance of power by siding with whomever was the weaker at any given point in time, but it was a game that they inevitably lost.

The story of these wars, told in *Medieval Mercenaries: the business of war*, is complex, somewhat interesting, and inconsequential. Italy was so rich, Italians were so creative, the pope so central to religious life, that no great power could afford to withdraw from the contest. But none was sufficiently powerful to prevail. Italy became the black hole of the pre-Copernican European political universe, sucking into it everyone who approached.

Just off-stage lurked the Ottoman Turks, a menacing presence perhaps familiar to those who remember Shakespeare's and Verdi's versions of *Otello*. To us it may seem strange that a black man commanded the Venetian fleet, but to Shakespeare's contemporaries it was no surprise – mercenaries came in every guise and colour. Most Turkish slaves were white – especially the skilled warriors of the Janissary Corps, selected as

---

† McNeill says that the dissolution of King Matthias Corvinus's mercenary army led directly to the Hungarian disaster. The nobility refused to defend the border at the very moment they were provoking peasant uprisings by increasing taxes and services.

children from the sultan's Christian subjects – but the Ottoman territories stretched across northern Africa, with trade connections across the Sahara and down the East African coast; moreover, Turkish slavery was not an immutable condition, and more than a few slaves rose to high positions in the Ottoman civilian and military ranks. For a black mercenary to offer his services to the greatest maritime power of the era was entirely plausible.

As for the tragedy, Shakespeare's audience might believe that Iago was a reference to Santiago, the patron saint of Spain; and Spain was England's greatest enemy.

France

The kingdom of Francis I was more or less surrounded by Habsburg lands. The goal of Francis, of his successors, and of countless talented royal advisors, was to break that iron ring. This meant first opposing the Habsburgs in Italy, then encroaching on the frontiers of the Low Countries and Germany.

Although many historians suggest that the horseman had been partially supplanted by mercenary infantry, it might be more accurate to say that he had been *supplemented*; certainly, proud French knights were reluctant to abandon their high social status – for good reasons they were envied by nobles throughout Europe – and fighting on foot was a step too far in that direction. Cavalry remained important for the royal invasions of Italy. A king could not command effectively except from horseback; and he needed cavalry for scouting, sudden attacks and pursuit. Daring horsemen remained indispensable.

France had no overseas possessions yet, so no need for a large navy. When Louis XII invaded Italy in 1499, it was simply a matter of controlling the Alpine passes – hence the emphasis on acquiring Savoy. He seemed to have good chances for success in both Lombardy and Naples, but he fled the peninsula in 1513, defeated in every way. Francis I attempted to retake Milan, only to be defeated by Charles V and captured. He eventually gave in to the unique Habsburg method of torture – the emperor encouraged all the ladies of the court to flirt with him, but warned them that dire consequences would follow if any dared to give him sexual satisfaction.

Francis was a true Renaissance prince, with fine tastes in art and architecture, also in women and wine. He spent money freely, squandering the reserves left by his father, dispersing his assets and increasing taxes. He left his nation bankrupt.

In addition, by the mid-century there was a growing Protestant community in France, the Huguenots, who – like many Protestants in northern Europe – tended to have commercial rather than agricultural interests. All too quickly France became embroiled in a religious civil war, a conflict marked by acts of terrible brutality; this war was worse than the German wars of religion because important members of the royal family were involved on either side, and many believed that the victor would impose his beliefs upon the entire country.

No matter what the religious persuasion of the would-be kings of France were, all lusted after the Low Countries, which had been a goal of French expansionists for centuries now, and which appeared once again vulnerable – thanks to the Dutch Protestants having divided local resources and resolve.

The British Isles

England, ruled by Henry VII until his death in 1509, was a minor power; and Englishmen were more concerned about preventing another War of the Roses than anything else. The last English foothold in France was the port of Calais, a poor but proud reminder of the great victories of the Hundred Years War, and the French king, Louis XII, was determined to take it. Henry had joined the Holy League (the pope and the Habsburg emperor) in hopes of saving Calais and perhaps of even recovering some of his family's ancient possessions in France.

The French queen, Anne of Brittany, sought to relieve the English pressure on the French northern lands by encouraging the Scottish monarch, James IV (1488–1513), to create a diversion. James invaded England in the late summer of 1513, bringing a very large army – sometimes estimated at 60,000 men – to plunder the borderlands. His two limited goals – to enrich his followers and to annoy his English enemy – were forgotten while he tarried with an attractive captive until it was too late to escape an English army under the Earl of Surrey.

James had already sent many of his men home with the booty, but he still had about 30,000 men on hand. His plan, it appears, was only to prevent the English for making a reprisal raid into the Scottish borderlands – thus, he stood on the defensive. The armies were about equal in size, with the Scots holding the high ground above Flodden Field – the name apparently referring to the marshes there. The English, not daunted, found a bridge, then formed up at the base of the heights and went forward.

The first moments of combat ended with the Scots routing the English right wing, but James unwisely sought to exploit this success by sending his pikemen into the English centre; his attack slowed as his men encountered an unseen bog. As order broke down, the English closed in. Tens of thousands of Scots perished, James among them. This day, 9 September 1513, was a decisive moment in the history of the British Isles.

In the following decades England became Protestant – with the king as the head of the national church. Scotland, in contrast, adopted a more democratic form of Protestantism – Presbyterian. However, there were many Roman Catholics in each land, Catholics willing to endure persecution and even exile. This was even more so in Ireland. Moreover, few issues were based solely on religion.*

The borderlands were always unruly, whether between Scots and English, between Scot clans, or in Ireland between clans and between all Irish and all immigrants. Whichever faction was defeated in the unpredictable wars of the next centuries, its leaders often went into exile, exercising the only skill they knew – fighting – in Continental armies.

Poland

In 1500 the future of the Polish–Lithuanian Commonwealth seemed assured. The Jagiellonian dynasty had defeated its ancestral enemy, the Teutonic Knights, and made half of Prussia part of its kingdom; it was in the process of humbling Ivan III (the Great, 1462–1505) of Russia, and the Tatars, thus expanding its frontiers east, south-east and south, then sprinkling those regions with towns and peasant settlements.

The Polish problems were space and tradition. Poland–Lithuania was a gigantic land, with only one formidable mountain barrier – in the south, on the Hungarian border. Open to invasion on three sides, lacking a diverse economy, its population growth had failed to keep pace with that of its neighbours. There was one exception, however – the number of nobles was far greater than the peasants could support. Hence, when possible, the peasants moved off to the even emptier lands of the east. The nobles, logically, sought to make the peasants into serfs in order to keep them on their estates. The result was to discourage individual initiative, to resist change, and – for the nobles, who saw only the surface of the brilliant Polish Renaissance – to believe that living as a rural aristocrat was the only possible career for a real man. Polish nobles, with their magnificent costumes, great moustaches, their striking chivalric gestures and their lavish spending habits, were the envy of their peers elsewhere. Proudly lacking any trace of education other than in hunting and boozing,

---

* Here, as elsewhere, religious differences tended to screen from view more basic disputes over power. While religion was important, sometimes religion served principally as a rallying point for national or ethnic identity, sometimes to solidify family or clan leadership, and sometimes as resistance to change. One might wonder, for example, how the Irish would have behaved if the England had not become Protestant. To what extent was the Irish devotion to their Church a way to say that they were 'Not English'? For Poles to say that they were 'Not Russians'? Tanner notes how eagerly the Irish obeyed the 1572 papal bull forbidding them to attend Protestant services, how they sent their children overseas for education, and how – in effect – the Counter-Reformation arrived there ahead of the Reformation.

they were the models for many nobles in Russia, Lithuania and the German lands; and their almost unchallenged social supremacy was a slap at those upward striving classes of lawyers and clerics who urged reforms upon the king, a king whom the nobles reminded that they had elected.

The clergy, fearing that the Reformation would sweep their lands and traditions away, supported the nobles; and both insisted on electing a weak king who would not threaten any of their powers and privileges.

It was only when the Polish–Lithuanian Commonwealth was hard pressed that it selected a powerful ruler, but even then, it preferred a foreigner. Some connection to the royal family was desirable but not essential. Stephen Batory of Transylvania came to the throne in 1576, then Jan Sobieski of Lithuania almost a century later. In between lay a vast wasteland of political chaos and military defeat.

Russia

Russia had long been a geographic term, but by 1500 the grand duke of Moscow, Ivan the Great, had made himself master of the many scattered city-princedoms. He faced tremendous problems – his was a primitive rural state with few cities and little industry or commerce, surrounded by enemies – but his land was rich in people and resources. The principal problem was outside invaders, especially the Tatars. In Fernand Braudel's words, the Tatars would eat the countryside right down to the root. Worse, they carried away entire communities for sale in Moslem slave markets.*

Then the Tatars began to lose momentum – many of their allies had ridden off to the east, to take advantage of better opportunities for plunder in China and India.

Ivan the Terrible (1530–84) crushed two of the great Tatar states in 1551 and 1556, thus making it possible for peasants to move safely onto the steppe and for soldiers and merchants to enter Siberia. He saw no limit to the potential expansion of his state.†

Scandinavia

Two Scandinavian states were major powers, with an influence far beyond what the numbers and wealth of their inhabitants would lead one

---

* William McNeill reminds us that Ottoman slavery was not nearly as onerous as that of the New World; and transportation to the exciting cities of the Ottoman world was, for many of those who survived, an improvement over rural poverty and monotony.

† Parker, *The Military Revolution*, reports that the first Streltsy unit was created about 1500 to use handguns. In the 1630s there were 17,000 foreign troops employed, then dismissed. In 1663 there were 60,000; in 1681 there were 80,000.

to expect. If the one-eyed man is king of the land of the blind, then it is not surprising that the relatively weak monarchs of Denmark and Sweden had relatively powerful armies and extraordinary ambitions.

The Lutheran Reformation had taken firm root everywhere. Perhaps that reflects the northern character, perhaps the interests of the kings and nobles in restricting the ability of churchmen to continue the mischief-making of the recent past, and perhaps the sheer distance from any Roman Catholic state.

The important province of Livonia was unstable, thanks to the advance of Moscow toward the Baltic coast, and to the economic developments taking place in the sparsely populated lands along that sea – grain production was increasing, thanks to the ruthless suppression of the peasantry by powerful noblemen. Lords were making the formerly free farmers on their estates into serfs, a process made easier by ravaging armies impoverishing vast regions and by a *de facto* population swap – armies from all sides carrying away farmers and using prisoners-of-war to replace the people stolen from their lands.

Three points were of strategic importance for commerce and taxation. First the straits (the Sound) between the Danish islands and Scania (today's southern Sweden). Second, the port of Danzig, which controlled the mouth of the Vistula river. Third, the eastern end of the Gulf of Finland, with the Narva river leading to Dorpat and Pskov, and the Neva river leading to Novgorod (and later St Petersburg).

It had appeared that Denmark would remain the dominant power of the region forever. The Union of Kalmar, 1397, had brought Norway, Denmark and Sweden together under one dynasty, and Christian II (1513–23) seemed ready to make himself an absolute ruler. But, with unerring bad judgement, he overplayed his hand. Sweden broke away, his nobles drove him into exile (summoning the duke of Holstein to be king), and the Hanseatic League revived, once again becoming an important political and economic force.

The Evolution of Warfare

The landsknechts of Germany, like the Swiss phalanxes they were modelled on, began to lose dominance on European battlefields after 1500. The Spanish *tercio*, with shorter pikes, more firearms, and mobile arquebusiers on the corners, were both smaller and more deadly, thanks to the front-rank firing and turning to the rear to reload while the next ranks were firing. The French introduced horse-drawn artillery, and the arquebus (a matchlock firearm) replaced the bow and arrow, but the advantage still lay with defending forces that could easily withdraw into remodelled fortresses that could not be taken except by long sieges.

By the 1590s the Dutch were experimenting with units yet smaller and shallower, and more manoeuvrable – the emphasis on drill transforming the process of getting each unit into line quickly, with minimum confusion. The Dutch being renowned for their knowledge of optics, they made the first field glasses; their doughty navigational exploits made it easier for them to improve maps, and being well off from trade, they paid their soldiers more promptly.*

Later the musket, with a heavier ball that could inflict more damage, replaced the arquebus, and new cavalry tactics emphasising speed and agility rather than the power of a charge employed pistols effectively.†

Why Rulers Preferred Mercenary Armies

Europeans and North Americans today think of peace as the normal condition of life. Their ancestors knew better, especially those ancestors who lived in the sixteenth and seventeenth centuries. People living then were also aware of the changing nature of warfare – the replacement of traditional feudal armies by more flexible and deadly professional forces, so that half-trained knights and militias stood little chance against confident phalanxes of landsknechts, experienced cavalry and thunderous artillery. Rulers who had formerly been limited to armies of 30,000 or so men – a number they could command effectively on the battlefield and feed during a campaign – now felt compelled to raise double or treble that many troops, and to pay them more.‡ This led to the development of

---

* Black (in both volumes) disagrees with the 'Robert's Thesis', particularly as elaborated by Parker, in *The Military Revolution*, preferring to emphasise new weapons such as the bayonet and the rifle, also looking at military developments in Africa and Asia. He sees stability as the essential characteristic of the time. However, he concedes that if military force is not seen as playing a crucial role in state formation, then an alternative theory has to be put forward. How does change occur? Punctuated equilibrium? The development of bureaucracies? Economic growth? He gives more emphasis to the spread of ideas through print. Also a cultural openness to innovation. Thus, there was no one 'military revolution', but a series of small ones that became most apparent in a global context, when European armies using firearms confronted non-Europeans without them. Parker defends himself in *The Military Revolution*. See also his *The Army of Flanders and the Spanish Road* for the importance of fortresses, with raiders creating a no-man's land; many more men were needed, both to take these strongholds and to defend them; bringing troops from Italy to Flanders along 'the Spanish Road' could only be accomplished if Lorraine remained out of French hands.

† Roberts in *Gustavus Adolphus* describes the cavalry caracole as horsemen approaching infantry, turning to the right, firing one pistol, then turning to the left to fire with another, then retiring to reload; the lance almost disappeared.

‡ Richard Bonney reminds us that the size of these armies was often fictitious – so many troops deserting, so many funds pocketed by commanders, and so many communities complaining about the 'contributions' they were forced to make (and no complaint was ever

a more sophisticated command structure, a seemingly simple idea that neither feudal armies nor non-western ones were willing to adopt.

As important, perhaps, was the intricate drill. Soldiers could master the commands only after extensive training under the watchful eye and thundering voice of a new class of sub-officer – the NCO.* Max Boot summarises this process as transforming warriors into soldiers. Warriors emphasised individual prowess, soldiers worked as a unit.

The consequences of battlefield defeat being so serious, no one readily took any risks unless having the advantages of numbers, firepower and position – which meant taking hardly any risk at all. The weaker party, logically enough, withdrew into prepared defensive positions and dared the attackers to storm their fortification. In time Louis XIV's talented minister of war, Vauban, made the construction of fortresses into a science, and siege operations became the specialty of engineers; but this was an evolutionary process, not a revolution.

The drawbacks to mercenary armies were obvious. Our ancestors may have been more superstitious (an assertion that any perusal of today's tabloids should keep us from exaggerating), but they were not stupid. Anyone could see that mercenary commanders were not only reluctant to risk defeat, but that they drew wars out as long as possible; commanders who won wars were soon unemployed. Mercenary troops were more likely to mutiny over back pay than to assault an enemy; in fact, the protest mutiny seems to have been made into a fine art, especially by the businesslike Walloons in the Spanish armies in the Netherlands – Spain having more money than anyone else. The cold, hard financial facts limited the possession of mercenary armies to states which were both comparatively wealthy and sufficiently organised to tax that wealth.

In short, as historians and political scientists have noted, the future belonged to those rulers who 'modernised' their states by developing central administrations that simplified laws, taxes and tariffs, reduced the independence of nobles and cities, and gathered power into their own hands.† These 'absolutist' rulers – most importantly France and Spain – understood well the opportunities for territorial expansion that lay before them, and the danger of watching idly while rivals seized those opportunities. It was this perception that lay behind so many wars: greed and fear combined, and if a ruler had any sincere concern for his citizens, their

---

strengthened by underestimating the number of troops a region had to house and feed). Thus, in effect, the size of the armies did not increase significantly; and in that sense, there was perhaps no significant military revolution other than the greater firepower provided by better muskets and cannon.

* Roberts, *Gustavus Adolphus*, attributes much of this to a careful study of classical warfare. Parker, *The Military Revolution*, points to importance of recruiting veterans, who would require less training and be steadier in combat.

† Black, *European Warfare, 1660–1815*, questions which was the cause and which the effect.

local traditions, and their interests, he had to protect them from by his own absolutist rivals.

Not every ruler was absolutist or even desired to be an absolutist ruler (or perhaps even understood what the concept meant), but each understood the realities of political life. Unless they protected their borders, their citizens' commerce, and their religious beliefs, they would not be rulers long. European courts were littered with nobles possessing once-impressive names; such 'pretenders', as men without lands to match their titles were often called, were useful for rulers who desired to take those very lands for themselves. Besides, men having more to fight for than money often made very good mercenary commanders.

The most basic problem that rulers faced, according to Richard Bonney, was financial. Tax collection was geared for peacetime conditions, with little ability to collect the large sums needed in wartime, or to collect and transport the foodstuffs needed by troops. This reflected the nature of the economy – so primitive was commerce and industry still, that there was little surplus left to tax; we think of the early modern era as relatively advanced in commerce and industry, which is true when comparing it to the medieval situation, but there was still too little flexibility to provide large sums of money at critical moments during the campaigning season – for recruiting in the spring, for the summer campaigns, and in the fall for troops being dismissed or sent into winter quarters.*

Feudal armies were cheaper, but in addition to their fundamental inferiority to the new armies, they were beholden to local nobles whose interests seldom coincided completely with those of the ruler. Therefore, kings and emperors preferred to hire dependable (and competent) generals and recruit foreign mercenaries over summoning their own nobles and subjects to war. Foreign troops might be exceptionally brutal and completely unreliable when the tide of battle ran against them, but they could not easily desert and hide among the local population. Mercenaries also did not consider religion as important as did regional troops – while German Protestants obviously enjoyed sacking Rome in 1527, they justified their actions as an alternative means of collecting the pay the emperor owed them; they might serve a Roman Catholic Holy Roman emperor, but if he didn't pay on time, he shouldn't complain about a few looted churches.

---

* Turberville describes the problems involved in finding quarters for troops in peacetime. Dividing regiments into small units and stationing them in small towns was both cheaper and less likely to result in a mutiny, but the townsmen complained and the officers grew too bored to supervise them. But the public never wanted the army to disappear. In an age without organised police forces, the troops were the only guarantee of law and order. The legendary outlaw was no legend. Parker, *The Military Revolution*, describes vividly the problems associated with the increase in the size of armies—paying the soldiers, equipping them, feeding them, even providing clothes and shelter. He goes into more detail in *The Army of Flanders and the Spanish Road.*

Local forces were quite willing to fight in defence of their homeland – narrowly defined, usually, as their region, not a national entity – but any suggestion that they would be deployed abroad would result in massive desertion.

Similarly, as soon as rulers gave evidence that their tyrannical instincts stood a chance of being realised, resistance appeared. Not just among rivals, but among nobles and clerics who had previously been allies in the local dynastic conflicts. With constitutionalism as a unifying motto, they managed to modify the ambitions of their rulers; or, in the case of Poland, almost to nullify it.

Guards

Every ruler had a bodyguard. Theoretically, every knight was bound to serve personally in garrisons and to accompany his lord on ceremonial occasions and at war. In practice, the duty of protecting the ruler fell to a small professional force of Life Guards (*Leibwache* in German). This name was extended to the most dependable infantry units when permanent armies became standard in the seventeenth century.

In addition, rulers had militias (*Heerbann*) and guild associations (*Schützengilden*) who were assigned specific portions of city walls (where they held shooting contests).

Where uniforms existed before 1600, the colours varied greatly from regiment to regiment. This was partly for ease of recognition, but certainly partly for *esprit de corps*. Also, some units dressed as Swiss Landsknechts and some as Turkish Janissaries. These were particularly common among the household watch – and the practice has continued in the Vatican to the present day, using real, live Swiss Catholics.

Knights resisted uniforms (and uniformity) as long as possible. Only in 1618 was the Elector of Saxony able to require that his nobles ex-change their old cuirasses for more easily identifiable new ones. These, like the handful of cannon that comprised the artillery, were kept in the armoury, which everywhere was among the most prominent buildings.

Power Shifts to the North ... and Rises in the East

It was perhaps inevitable that changing demographic and commercial realities would make northern Europe rather than the Mediterranean the future centre of political gravity. First of all, France, Germany, England and Scandinavia were recovering rapidly from the impact of the Black Death and the terrible wars of the fifteenth century (the Hundred Years War being the worst, followed by the Hussite Wars in and around

Bohemia). Second, the Ottoman Turks were making themselves masters of much of the Mediterranean.

Italy became the prey of the great powers. The Spaniards took the kingdoms in the south, the French Milan, and the Austrians the tiny principalities closest to the Tyrol. The popes became, for all practical purposes, political nonentities who supported the Catholic monarchs in their wars against Muslims and Protestants; the dynasties in Naples, Milan and Florence died off or became political nullities; the Venetians fought a rearguard action against the Ottoman Turks; and the ordinary citizens, aware that political and religious non-conformity was dangerous, began to confine their interests to science, music, art and architecture – subjects that were both safe and in demand all across Europe, later even in Istanbul and St Petersburg.

Denmark had long been the dominant power in the north, and its recent extension of royal authority over Norway and into Germany seemed to confirm its status. However, Sweden became a strong competitor after 1560, when the king, council and parliament approved intervention in the Livonian War. Later Sweden would strive for total domination of the Baltic Sea.*

As the northern European states became ever more important, so, too, did their armies. These armies were essentially mercenary forces.

---

* Roberts, *The Swedish Imperial Experience*, notes that Swedish historians give two different explanations for this. The 'Old School' stresses political necessity – Sweden, trapped between Denmark and Russia, has to fight for its existence. What Swedes saw as defensive wars, neighbours believed was aggression. The 'New School' stresses economic causes – first, control of the trade with Russia, then control of all Baltic commerce.

Chapter 2

The Periphery of Europe

Russia Expands West

The complex and strange Livonian War that lasted from 1558 to 1583 in the eastern Baltic is important for understanding the events discussed in this book. The small states in Livonia first sought to use mercenaries to offset the low quality and unimpressive numbers of their knights and militia, then the larger states of Poland–Lithuania, Sweden and Denmark brought more into the conflict. Russia made its first significant appearance on what western Europeans considered their part of the world stage, but only learned the value of mercenaries during the course of the war.

Before the war began every knowledgeable person in western and central Europe had heard of Russia, but few knew much more than the name of the land, that it was strange and wonderful, and that it was far away. A few could remember the 1502 victory of Wolter van Plettenberg, *Landmeister* of the Livonian Order, over Ivan III the Great in a great battle near Pskov. Though Russia soon fell back from the west, somewhat in disorder and confused, this retreat would not last long. When Ivan IV became grand duke of Moscow in 1547, he moved quickly to consolidate authority in his own hands, defeated two Tatar khans, assumed the title of tsar and made plans to expand his authority in all directions.

Already Russia was home to many foreign experts. Ivan IV would expand their numbers and responsibilities. Realising the implications of the 'gunpowder revolution', he sought to purchase guns and hire cannon-masters, but he was frustrated by his western neighbours' refusal to allow these weapons and specialists to travel through their lands to him.

Polish and Livonian reluctance to help Russia develop its military machine rested on sound observations – their own survival was at stake. But embargoes can usually be bypassed if enough money is offered; and though Ivan's subjects were poor, he felt entitled to tax them heavily.

Informed observers were aware that more centralised national states had significant advantages over feudal and multinational ones. Parliaments, by whatever name they went, were often reluctant to take necessary steps for defence – most significantly, to collect the taxes necessary for hiring well-trained *landsknechts* armed with pikes and halberds and supporting them with artillery and cavalry; but also to entrust command to an experienced general. That usually came at a price – the sacrifice of political independence.

There was the rub. The nobles and clerics in both Poland and Livonia were reluctant to sacrifice either their influence in politics or their social status; and merchants were unwilling to cut into what they considered fairly narrow profit margins. They read and discussed the most recent theories of warfare, but they refused to consider even basic changes.*

Livonian policies, such as the loose Livonian Confederation could devise, consisted largely of avoiding giving neighbours any pretext for war, of believing that military preparations were too expensive, and that ageing fortresses would give them sufficient time to respond to any aggression.

The Livonian Confederation could see that mercenary soldiers were becoming more important, especially in Saxony, Brandenburg and Prussia; also that the Scandinavian kingdoms of Denmark and Sweden were becoming more powerful, and to the east there was Ivan IV. But its members would not hire more than a handful of troops; nor could they see that their internal conflicts would draw the great powers into their country, to fight one another for control of the eastern shores of the Baltic Sea.†

Civil Conflicts in Livonia

The Livonian Confederation was so highly democratic that it hardly functioned. As was so common elsewhere, especially in the badly fractured Holy Roman Empire (the Confederation's much admired model), it was almost impossible to persuade the Livonian master (the elected head of a semi-autonomous branch of the Teutonic Order), the archbishop of Riga, the bishops of Oesel-Wiek, Dorpat (Tartu), Reval (Tallinn) and Courland (Kurland), the abbots of Padis, Falkenau and Dünamünde, and the cities of Riga, Dorpat, Reval, Pernau and others, and the knightly corporations, to pass necessary legislation; whatever benefited some, or even most, of the member states, almost necessarily harmed somebody's interests. There were some laws passed confirming the direction that class relationships were taking (for example, allowing landowners to reduce more of their workers to serfdom) and some efforts

---

* In Malcolm Vale's words: 'practical necessity, rather than awareness of classical precedent or contemporary theory, determined the structure of armies and the course of battles.'

† Kirby emphasises the balance of power that kept the great powers from aggression. Their 'curious caution and reluctance' came from each having more important enemies – the Tatars for both Russia and Poland–Lithuania, with the Ottoman Turks in the background. But the heart of the 'Baltic Question' was Russia's rise to dominance in Eastern Europe.

to limit currency manipulation (an impossible task in a time when silver prices were in flux, thanks to new mines opening in Germany, Mexico and Columbia). But taxation for national defence? That was impossible. Nor were the masters who followed Plettenberg able to persuade the prelates, nobles and burghers to follow their lead in international politics, or anybody's lead. Partly this was due to the Reformation, which had divided citizen against citizen, subject against ruler, and even the knights of the Livonian Order into feuding parties. Partly it was the traditional defence of individual and collective rights against tyranny.

This difference of opinion became a serious problem in 1556, when the aged Livonian master was determined to be incapable of governing alone. Two candidates for the office of *coadjutor* (to share his duties) presented themselves to the knights, sergeants and priests of the military order, to be voted upon at the next great assembly of the membership – Wilhelm von Fürstenberg (about 1500–68) represented the Catholics, Jasper von Münster (about 1500–77) the Protestants. A great comet presaged trouble, and with civil war apparently about to break out, first inside the military order, then with the archbishop of Riga, one of the prominent officers, Gotthard Kettler (1517–87), went to Germany to recruit mercenaries.

When these warriors arrived in Riga, the citizens stared in amazement. Or so wrote the best of the chroniclers of the era, Balthasar Russow of Reval:

> A mighty rumour arose that a mass of ships filled with horsemen and foot soldiers had been sent by the Archbishop and his brother, the Duke of Prussia, and were near at hand about to launch a surprise attack on Livonia. Therefore, letter after letter was sent both by day and by night to the landowners, instructing them to raise forces commensurate with the size of their holdings immediately upon receipt of the letter. They were to proceed to the harbours and beaches to meet the enemy attack. But at this time many of the Livonians, complacent and unaccustomed to war, had neither soldiers nor equipment befitting their holdings. In haste, therefore, they had to enlist non-German* stable boys and old, married two-bit lackeys who had already drunk themselves half to death and many of whom had scarcely fired a musket in their entire lives. They put on the old rusty armour, but before setting out, they first got roaring drunk, each swearing to stand by the other in life or death. After this a number of them were half dead as they mounted their horses and rode off to battle. The women, girls and children wept and howled as though these warriors were leaving never to return.

---

* That is, native. It would have been awkward to list all the various ethnic groups in the region; before the arrival of the crusaders Livonia had been inhabited by mutually hostile tribes, some of which occasionally paid tribute to the nearest Russian princes.

The daunting sight illustrated how unprepared the knights and gentry were for war. But it got worse:

> Now when they arrived at the harbours and beaches there was nothing threatening there, neither ship nor soldier, nothing but their own fear, and after they had lain idle for several weeks, consuming provisions and draining beer casks, they returned home, not, in their eyes, without honour and glory.

Nor did Russow spare the Protestant burghers. An eyewitness to the events in Reval and, like everyone else, an eager listener to reports and rumour, he wrote:

> In the Livonian cities there was at this time likewise no little complacency and ignorance of war. They also had to hastily raise troops. There was even a great shortage of drummers, but eventually they were able to find someone who could manage to beat one. All the inexperienced apprentice boys became seasoned warriors. In the evenings, at the changing of the watch, mobs of townspeople, young and old, would run to the market square, gawking at the soldiers' manoeuvres with such intense wonder that many missed their suppers on this account. In the middle of the service many would run out of the church whenever they heard the drum. Such was the novelty of war for them at that time. Towards autumn many horsemen and foot soldiers from Germany came to the aid of the Order and the cities. The nobles enlisted many fine horsemen and moved to Bauske in Courland in order to man the border against the King of Poland and the Duke of Prussia. And as the German soldiers moved through the regions of Livonia to join their lord, they passed with their women and pages through the villages and the noblemen's estates, asking for food and drink as was their custom. When they would enter a house, in their long leggings and tattered clothes, with their long pikes and battle-swords, the nobles, peasants, women, girls and servants would gape in astonishment as though seeing some great sea monster. Up to now they had been unaccustomed to such unusual guests, and, due to the haste in which the troops had been summoned, they had arrived quite unexpectedly.

When Fürstenberg's forces overwhelmed those of the archbishop, the king of Poland decided to intervene. The Livonian master freed the archbishop, returned his lands, and then dismissed his landsknechts; however, he was not required to relinquish his now re-established position at the head of the Livonian Confederation, as long as he made no efforts to impose his will on the other members. At a subsequent meeting with King Sigismund Augustus (1520–72) at Pozwol, Fürstenberg signed an alliance that made Livonia more or less a Polish satellite. The new emperor, Ferdinand, was not happy, but he was unwilling to commit any resources to aiding a faraway province that paid no taxes and provided no troops for his own wars.*

In distant Moscow, when Ivan IV, then just twenty-three years old, heard of this treaty, he concluded that he had better strike before the agreement turned into an effective alliance, and before Fürstenberg could restore order to Livonia. Ivan had been seizing formerly Russian lands from the Polish–Lithuanian state for several years now, and he desired to take more. There was peace at the moment, but everyone understood that there would be war again – there could be only one Russian power, and Poland–Lithuania, which was identified with the pope and the Roman Catholic Church, could not compete with the grand duke of Moscow for the allegiance of the *Pravo-Slavi* (true believers) of the Russian Orthodox Church. Moreover, Ivan was fresh from his triumph in Kazan, the subjugation of one of Russia's most feared oppressors. He was ready to take on the next enemy. Who could stand against his battle-tested troops, his engineers, his experienced generals? Certainly not the Livonians!

In addition, Ivan was already angry wirh the Livonian Confederation. At moments in the past war when he needed cannon and experienced cannonmasters, the Confederation had refused to allow them through its lands. Ivan was not enthusiastic about trade, but he did want access to the most modern weapons, and these could only be obtained over the Baltic Sea. Moreover, if Ivan could force the Livonians to pay him tribute, the revenge would be even sweeter – his tormentors would be paying for the cannon themselves.

Ivan also complained about the harassment of Russian merchants who visited or lived in Dorpat and other Livonian towns. Most importantly, the Orthodox churches were old and dilapidated, some perhaps since the temporary expulsion of the Russian inhabitants from Dorpat in 1470, or even from 1463, when, according to Russian tradition, seventy-two believers who had refused to join the Catholic Church had been thrust under the ice. Some churches had been despoiled of their icons – no rare occurrence in Catholic and Protestant churches during the disorders of the Reformation – and some had been turned into arsenals or privies. He insisted that new churches be provided for Orthodox worshippers.

Stories of other atrocities against Orthodox believers circulated in Russia, stirring up war fever. Quite likely, given the fevered religious climate of the times, some of these stories were true.

The question of whether the Protestants or Roman Catholics would dominate in Livonia was resolved for the time being, but everyone

---

* Kirby emphasises Polish reluctance to come to the aid of Protestants, Livonian nobles' fear of a peasant uprising, and the importance of Livonian grain to Dutch commerce. Nobody in the West wanted change.

understood that the issue would return. No contemporary could look toward the future with confidence. War was imminent. If not civil war, then foreign invasion.

Ivan the Terrible

According to the chronicler Johannes Renner, the Livonian master wrote to the bishop of Dorpat before the war began, offering to help defend his frontiers. The bishop, however, remembering long animosities with the Livonian Order, declined. But when the diplomatic efforts failed to persuade Ivan IV to abandon his effort to collect tribute from first Dorpat, then all of Livonia,

> Thereupon the master once again wrote to the Bishop of Dorpat and earnestly advised him to decline no assistance. If he alone were unable to provision the landsknechts, others would help him. He himself was ready to come to his aid with horsemen. The bishop had but to designate some place for his encampment. But the bishop's councillors and the noblemen opposed this and dissuaded the bishop with the argument that if these landsknechts and horsemen came into the diocese, they would plunder it and take all manner of liberties with their wives and children. This they could not endure. And if it were to be devastated, better by enemies than by friends. That, at least, they could understand. And so the bishop wrote to the master, kindly thanking him for his offer of assistance, but saying he was certain it would not be needed, since the emissaries would doubtlessly negotiate peace.

When the negotiations broke down – the Livonian Confederation could see nothing in the future but greater and more extravagant demands – Ivan sent raiders across the border as a demonstration of strength. Ivan's historical claims to sovereignty over all Livonia were largely imaginary, certainly antiquarian, but his army was very real.[*]

The bishop of Dorpat ordered a mobilisation, but his summons produced more panic and disorganisation than well-equipped knights, burghers and peasant militias. Belatedly, he informed the Livonian master that he was now interested in a military alliance. This while his peace commissioners were in Russia. Fürstenberg sent war warnings throughout the land, but the archbishop responded that he lacked sufficient men to garrison his castles and, in any case, the master had not returned the cannon which had been confiscated during the recent confrontation.

---

[*] In *The Teutonic Knights* I mention the mutual deceptions each side was practising in the negotiations, with Ivan seeking out long-forgotten precedents for demanding tribute and the Livonians making promises that they knew the Holy Roman emperor would nullify.

At first there were only light Russian probes along the frontier, but when resistance proved unexpectedly feeble, especially in Dorpat, raiders dashed into the interior. Perhaps Ivan had not seriously entertained the idea of conquering Livonia at this time, but intended only to frighten the Confederation into paying tribute. No matter. When Ivan's generals reported how heavily armed Livonian units, dragging their heavy cannons slowly behind them, were never able to catch up with the Tatar horsemen, and how small their numbers were, he decided to send larger armies into the country.

The War Comes

The Russian offensive began in January 1558, a good time of year for men accustomed to severe cold. Ivan's force was vastly larger than Fürstenberg's. The tsarist army numbered 64,700 – a figure obtained from the body of the Russian paymaster, whose books listed all the troops employed up and down the front. This figure frightened many of the landsknechts, who refused to sally out of Dorpat unless accompanied by the cavalry.

While the Livonian Order's commanders stayed in their castles, Russian raiders crossed the Narva river into Estonia almost unnoticed. Russow wrote that many of these commanders were completely incompetent:

> The last advocate and commander of the Order at Wesenberg was a blatant whore-monger, who openly committed fornication not only with common wenches but with married women as well. And the daily work of the commander's servants consisted of nothing but gluttonous feasting and love-making, which they regarded as nothing disgraceful, but rather as something honorable and virtuous.

No one suggested attacking Ivangorod, Ivan's powerful new fortress across from the antiquated castle at Narva. Designed on the most modern lines, Ivangorod was an impregnable base for raiders. Attacks into Pskov's territory were discussed, but not acted upon. The mentality of the Livonians was defensive. Plettenberg's offensive strategy would be mentioned, only to be dismissed as too risky. The philosophy was to hold out, to pray, and to ask the neighboring monarchs for help (but not too much help, lest they make themselves masters of the region).

Clearly, this was not a leadership likely to be effective in protecting the country. Nor was it. The troops, naturally, took after the example of the officers.

Fürstenberg was capable and honest, but he was an old man, with limited energy and even more limited imagination. He tried to intercept an army moving along the southern shore of Lake Peipus, but failed.

Meanwhile, there was a series of minor combats elsewhere in Estonia against other raiders. Western successes were few, and most efforts to drive the intruders away were total failures. But neither did the Russians settle down to stay. Herbertstein, an imperial observer of the Russian scene, remarked at this time that Russian attitudes were much like those of the Germans: a defiant attack at the beginning, followed by a collapse of morale; the motto was 'run, or we shall'.

In April the commander of the Narva garrison warned that a large Russian force had arrived at Ivangorod. Already he had received a warning to surrender, or else. Everything was lacking for a proper defence, he warned, adding that the Russians had to be hindered from commencing a siege.

When the marshal, Gotthard Kettler, arrived in May, he ordered his men not to enter Narva. He feared that the landsknechts there would not allow this perceived reinforcement to leave again – he had gone into the city once himself and barely managed to get out again. The garrison troops had originally come from Riga and Reval, but they had become very independent-minded – that is, arrogant and quarrelsome, greedy and dissolute. Kettler decided to make his camp twenty miles away, sufficiently distant that the attitudes of the garrison would not easily infect his own men.

The Russian Conquest Begins

On May 11 a house in Narva caught fire; it was later believed that the owner was cooking some alcoholic beverage – the Russians claimed that the brewer irreverently threw an icon onto the fire, thus causing an explosion; more likely, either the fire got out of control or the alcohol blazed up. Soon other houses were on fire, too. The blaze was so intense that it was visible in daylight even as far away as Kettler's camp, where some landsknechts noticed it. Kettler quickly rode toward Narva with sixty men, telling the rest of his force to follow behind as quickly as possible.

Two incompatible stories described what happened next. The first was that the vice-mayor of Narva met Kettler two miles outside the city and said that the fire had been extinguished. However, that was incorrect. The fire had become a conflagration. The second was that Kettler arrived in the neighbourhood of Narva only after sunset. Not knowing the twisting roads, he tried without success to find a guide. At length, fearful of an ambush, he decided to return to camp. By the time his exhausted men stumbled back into quarters at daybreak, the first refugees from Narva began to arrive. The city had fallen, and there was nothing he could do about it.

What seems to have happened was that when Russians living on the opposite bank saw the fire, they hurriedly found boats, planks and even doors, then crossed the river, paddling hard against the current. They had no difficulty entering the city, because most of the garrison had withdrawn into the castle. Soon Russian troops joined them, and when the garrison came down to drive them away, the Russians wheeled the cannon on the walls around toward them and fired away.

The landsknechts had resisted fiercely, house to house, and even cellar to cellar. But the garrison was eventually forced back into the castle. There they found themselves in an impossible position – one gate was so vulnerable to artillery fire that it would surely be blown down soon. On the Russian part, however, there was great reluctance to risk pitched combat. They had seen that the landsknechts were formidable warriors and they believed that Kettler, not far away, was approaching quickly. The Russian commander, therefore, offered the garrison very favourable terms: the landsknechts could leave freely with all their weapons and possessions.

The landsknechts asked for clarification and were told that they could take with them anything they could carry. That was enough to seal the bargain. The castle had contained a warehouse full of fine goods – cloth, silk, velvet. The landsknechts carried it all away.

The most important fortress on that border thus fell to Ivan's men. Since Narva controlled the river connecting Lake Peipus to the Gulf of Finland, the way was now open for tsarist armies to invade Estonia at will, and for western ships loaded with military goods to reach Russia. Also changing hands was an impressive store of firearms: two large cannon, two medium cannon, twenty-eight small cannon; three large guns, five swivel guns, seven medium guns; forty-two muskets and thirty-six hand-guns; with a huge store of shot and powder.

Morale collapsed across Livonia. The citizens of Dorpat, seeing that many of their landsknechts had been withdrawn to serve in the master's army, opened secret negotiations with the tsar. They offered to pay the tribute and, it was believed, were willing to submit totally. Local nobles captured early in the war went through the countryside, encouraging surrender.

Panic was setting in. The garrison in Dorpat fired on rioting citizens, restoring order temporarily. But the citizens became even more frightened when the border castle at Warbeck fell. The forty landsknechts who comprised that garrison had all become drunk; a townsman who had witnessed the party informed the Russians, who hurried there and set the gate afire. When the Russians broke into the castle, most of the Germans were still asleep in their beds. The captured commander was forced to accompany the Russians to Dorpat and plead with the citizens to surrender.

The landsknechts reacted with surprising initiative to these new dangers, sallying out to gather lumber, then burning all the surrounding buildings and fields to deny the invaders shelter and fodder. This in the middle of a heat spell so intense that knights stuffed inside warm armour fell unconscious from their horses.

When Ivan arrived personally before the city with a huge army, the nobles and landsknechts put up a good fight. Twice they drove the Russians back from the gun emplacements they were building, and once thirty-eight horsemen routed 500 enemy cavalry. But once Ivan's men had put up earthworks around the city, he persuaded the citizens to agree to a cease-fire; during that interval, he moved eight large cannon and two mortars on to a high hill overlooking the city.

When the Russian assault commenced, townspeople and Russian sympathisers set fires throughout the city. The bishop, ready to surrender, was prevented from doing so only by the landsknechts. But even they could see that the situation was hopeless. After three days they gave in. The mercenaries marched out, together with many citizens, bearing as much as they could on their backs. One Russian musketeer tried to seize a German's gun, but his commander ordered him to return it and had the soldier beaten.

Few of these landsknechts joined the master's army, despite his entries that they do so. Here as elsewhere the Russians made a list of the mercenaries' names, warning that anyone who was captured again would be put to death. With the military situation deteriorating, the chances of being taken prisoner again were too high. As for the Russians' motives, they did not want these formidable warriors to believe that they would be better off fighting to the end than making an honourable surrender. Ivan and his generals wanted the mercenaries out of the country more than they wanted their possessions.

Ivan was now in possession of one of the region's largest and richest cities. Livonian nobles who had gone over to Ivan (perhaps under duress, perhaps not) attempted to explain to him that if he treated the burghers and nobles well, they would become loyal vassals; Dorpat could be a model for a future united Livonia, ruled by local nobles, but subject to the tsar. Ivan did not take this advice long, but began to use them as he did his own subjects – he later ordered the bishop and many of the people who had remained taken to Moscow. The city's economy collapsed. Short-term, Ivan benefited greatly from the 700 firearms his men found in the city and the general panic among his enemies, but long-term he had shown what those who surrender to an irrational tyrant had to expect.

When the refugees from Dorpat reached Weissenstein, in central Estonia, the commander asked his landsknechts if they thought they could hold the fortress. They thought not. When the commander left, taking with him the cannon, the landsknechts sacked the castle, stealing guns, food, whatever they could, then marched to Reval, where they offered their services to the Danish representative.

The soldiers from Dorpat arrived later. Apparently, they had been delayed by the formalities connected with the surrender. When they arrived at Weissenstein, they found the castle empty. Empty everywhere except for the wine cellar, that is. Only after consuming the wine and beer did they proceed on to Reval.

Soon the citizens of Reval were complaining to Fürstenberg about the impositions – men and horses were everywhere, they wrote, and they were expected to feed and house them. And they had a point, that if the Russians had been properly driven away in the first place, this would not be necessary. Moreover, if the Livonian master could not defend them, perhaps they had better find a lord who could.

Now the Livonian Confederation raised the 60,000 thalers Ivan IV had demanded earlier, and an impressive delegation led by the archbishop took it to Moscow to present it to the tsar, but Ivan was no longer interested in a peace treaty. He wanted to see what he could win by force of arms – most likely he did not trust the Livonians to abide by any promises they made. When the tsar returned the money, Fürstenberg appropriated it to pay his troops.

Locally, the situation was chaotic; there was no cooperation, no coordination. As far as receiving assistance from abroad, ordinary citizens and even peasants could summarise it thus: no help from the Holy Roman Empire, no help from Sweden or Poland–Lithuania, and no help from Denmark.

Livonia was on its own. This would not necessarily be fatal, if the states of the Livonian Confederation could work together. However, as Renner described the situation:

> Although there were horsemen and landsknechts available, they refused to band together. The archbishop wanted to defend his territory; the bishops of Oesel and Reval, theirs, and so there was no united defence. The men of Harrien and Wierland had gone to Reval and now considered themselves Danish subjects. All this caused great division and discord among the people. The lords of the Order blamed the noblemen for not joining them in battle and helping defend their fatherland. The noblemen, in turn, blamed the Order for not recruiting landsknechts and bringing them into the country to defend it. The townsmen blamed the noblemen who would rather brag and pose and parade their horses at weddings and christenings than fight the enemy. The noblemen in turned blamed the townsmen for so treacherously surrendering their cities, Narva and Dorpat, for example. The peasants blamed the Order, the nobility and Germans in general, saying they were always around to rob them, to strip them of what they had, to make their lives wretched, but nowhere to be seen when it was time for them to defend them. Such was the pitiful state of affairs in Livonia at this time. It would have been easy then for the enemy to have brought his war to a conclusion.

Although Kettler found it difficult to pay his mercenaries, in October he prevailed over a Russian force of 5,000 men. He promoted subordinate officers who demonstrated competence, thereby making his cavalry more effective.

Kettler ordered the army to move against Ringen, a strong fort in central Livonia, where the Russians had built a blockhouse in front of the gate to prevent him from setting up cannons there. The landsknechts made two efforts to take the blockhouse, hoping either to capture it or to set it on fire, but they were repulsed with seven dead and many wounded; still, believing that they could take the place, they sent to Wenden, the master's main fortress, for two cannon, the 500 landsknechts stationed there, and several thousand peasants. It appeared that the siege of Ringen might be the decisive battle that Kettler wanted.*

When the artillery arrived at Ringen, its impact was immediate. The first shots killed the Russian commander as he stood at a window observing the besiegers' efforts. After many defenders had fallen, the survivors, among whom were many German mercenaries, asked for a parley. Assured that their lives would be spared, ninety-six surrendered and were imprisoned in Wenden. The rest of the garrison – forty-two Russians, five of whom were boyars – knew that Ivan would never forgive them for capitulating. They barricaded themselves in the blockhouse and defied their attackers; this worked until Kettler told his landsknechts they could plunder the castle if they captured it. This changed everything. The landsknechts understood that to get into the castle, they would have to take the blockhouse. They did so quickly. The only death they suffered was a landsknecht who fell into a well.

Among the prisoners was a German musketeer from Riga whose marksmanship had caused many casualties. He was executed by quartering.

The Germans then moved on to another castle, making camp so close to the walls that they could hear the Russians talking. That evening, when the artillery arrived, they began to shell the castle. The Russians fired back, killing three landsknechts. The mercenaries, deciding that their firepower was insufficient for the task, had the peasants assist them in placing a burning barrel of pitch against the gate, expecting that this would burn the doors down. However, the Russians opened the gate enough to pour beer over the fire, extinguishing it. Obviously, this was a desperate measure.†

On the third day the mercenaries broke camp and returned to Reval

---

* The war was getting serious now. Previously, atrocities had been reserved for the peasants – who were the chaff of war, blown this way and that by all sides. But this chaff consisted of Livonian taxpayers and Roman Catholics. Ketter had six raiders hanged from trees near Wenden for their criminal behaviour; in retaliation, the Russians in Dorpat flayed twenty-one Germans, then cut off their fingers and toes and finally decapitated them.

† Had the Germans thought about this, that Russians were unlikely to waste good beer if there had been water available, they would have continued the siege longer. But they were deceived by the Russian bravado, the efforts of the reorganised foragers to give the impression that a relief force had come to the rescue, and by the garrison hammering on beams to make it appear that they were strengthening the gate against assault.

with great numbers of livestock, mostly oxen, horses and cattle. Afterwards they learned that the Russians would not have been able to hold the castle much longer, for there was no water left.

The archbishop, feeling the necessity of contributing something more to the war effort, published an Articles of War in late December. First in importance was prayer and temperance in eating and drinking; second was to organise public ceremonies in which the most solemn oaths would be rendered; third, that both German and non-German (native) warriors would spare women, children and aged persons; fourth, no fighting among the troops. Other articles required every man of suitable age to perform military service – standing watch, for instance; he should not become drunk, nor plunder, nor sell weapons, and not just go home. It was a summary of the problems the Livonian leaders faced.

In 1559, Ivan, having become impatient with the strategy of winning over the nobles and burghers by persuasion, turned to terror. For this he had the perfect instrument, his own professional soldiers and his new Tatar subjects. First there were successes in Estonia, then central Livonia, where they committed atrocities that shocked witnesses and hearers almost beyond belief. As the raiders stormed through Courland, they ran into a small body of mercenaries. Renner described the ensuing battle:

> Twenty-four landsknechts, most of whom had muskets, were on their way from Prussia to Riga and had spent the night in the inn at Kaugern. The Russians attacked them, but they put up a resolute defence, three times driving the Russians out of the courtyard and killing over one hundred of them. But by then they were completely exhausted and the Russians had received reinforcements and set fire to the village. And so the landsknechts were forced out and then attacked from all sides. Twenty-one of them, along with the innkeeper Borchert and all his people, were killed. Two of the landsknechts were taken prisoner.

This campaign was not without its cost. Though the raiders had met relatively little resistance outside the castles and thus had been able to depopulate entire regions by frightening the people into wild flight, they lost about 2,000 Russians and 4,000 Tatars. Of course, one should always mistrust estimates of enemy loses, but in this case it probably reflects at least the proportion of ethnic troops among the raiders. Deep snow hindered the raiders, who had to break a path through the drifts in order to pass along the forest roads (though they often required captured peasants to walk ahead and trample down a path), while those same paths allowed pursuers to follow at full speed.

Danish and Polish–Lithuanian Intervention

It was at this low point in Livonian fortunes that Christopher von Münchhausen, an official of the prince-bishop of Oesel-Wiek, persuaded Magnus of Holstein (1540–83), the younger brother of the Danish king, that this would be an opportune moment to purchase the diocese and then acquire additional territories across Estonia; after all, Estonia had once been Danish. The bishop was willing, no, eager, to sell his lands on the coast and islands, though they were still relatively safe from Russian attack. Christopher suggested that Magnus could use Danish money to pay the bishop, then hire mercenaries and send them east. Münchhausen would use those troops to take first Riga, then all of Livonia, after which he would turn the region over to the Danish prince.

Magnus like the idea, modifying it slightly: he would divide the entire region between himself and the tsar. The tsar had been trying in vain to persuade Livonian nobles to come over to him, but even before he showed the signs of instability and insanity that gave him the nickname, Ivan the Terrible, the Livonians did not trust him. The Danish prince, in contrast, was a westerner, with Protestant values and familiar if somewhat flexible morals. Magnus explained that the nobles would swear allegiance to him – after all, he was the son of a king. All he needed was the tribute money the Livonians would pay the tsar; with that money he could hire mercenaries and make himself a great prince. A Russian vassal, of course, like the Tatar khans, but still a great prince.

At first, the King of Denmark mistrusted this plan and wanted nothing to do with it. However, his mother liked it. Hers was the decisive voice. Magnus made plans to sail east with enough money and men to establish himself in Oesel-Wiek, but it would not be until the end of the Dithmarschen campaign in the summer of 1559 that he could do anything.* Münchhausen's plans were put on hold.

Another stroke of luck for the Livonian Order was that Ivan was being pressed by the Crimean Tatars on his southern front. On 1 May he agreed to a six-month truce. The Livonian peace commissioners returned home expecting congratulations, only to learn that Kettler was very displeased. A large number of mercenaries had just arrived, a force large enough for a summer offensive. Now Kettler had to pay the landsknechts to lie about idle. That, Ivan surely knew, was the Livonians' weakest point – if they had to pay their expensive troops while he could allow his to return to their homes, the Livonians would exhaust their resources, making it more difficult to oppose him when the truce expired.

The mercenaries were dispersed across the countryside, both to feed

---

* Dithmarschen was a republic in north Germany. The defence of its liberty is described in my *Medieval Mercenaries, the business of war.*

them better and perhaps to keep them away from innocent civilians in Riga. A musketeer in one village shot at a pigeon, set the straw roof on fire and burned down all but three of the houses. In June the mercenaries in Fellin broke the truce by attacking the peasants belonging to the abbot of Falkenau. Their excuse was probably that the abbot's lands were under Russian occupation. Truce terms be hanged! They needed beef.

This was not their only plundering raid. Fürstenberg, who was commanding the great fortress at Fellin, probably believed that he had little choice but to allow his mercenaries to do as they wished. His fortress stood in the centre of the country and had the largest artillery part in the region. Without mercenaries he could not hold it, and, lacking money to buy supplies or pay them, he could hardly stop men trying to feed themselves. His warning that this garrison was unreliable was serious, but Kettler could not afford to replace those troops with better ones.

By summer Kettler's greatest worry was not money – he thought it safe to discharge some unneeded troops; it was enforcing the embargo on military supplies being sent to Russia. Hanseatic ships from Lübeck and Hamburg, and other cities were sailing into the Gulf of Finland, seeking to reach Russian ports such as Narva. Although Kettler persuaded the citizens of Reval to capture some of these vessels, that only benefited the English, who were delivering weapons around the tip of northern Norway and through the White Sea to Archangel. Still, most ships made their way safely through the Gulf of Finland, to the great profit of Hanseatic merchants. In addition, the Livonians feared that they would lose control of the narrow sea – Duke Johannes of Mecklenburg reported to the Reichstag that the Russian tsar had more than 800 carpenters working on a fleet, and that seven ships were manned and gunned; moreover, that he had experts from England and Germany directing the work. Privateers operating out of Reval attacked storage facilities in Finland, where supplies for Russia were awaiting transport. They also captured two Lübeck ships heading for Narva, laden with guns and armour; and they seized or sank English vessels filled with weapons.

In July the mercenary commander Joseph van Munden arrived in Riga with 800 landsknechts, most veterans of the Dithmarschen campaign. Fifty horsemen came at their own expense, confident that their services would be needed. And, as for pay, everyone knew that Livonian commissioners, led by Gotthard Kettler, were at the imperial court asking for help. Surely the emperor would at least contribute some money. After all, Ferdinand had promised to send a delegation to Moscow. He had no troops to send, but he had promised money. Some of this would have to make its way to Riga.

Thus, after months of depressing news, the Livonians had reasons for optimism. The Livonian Confederation at last agreed to tax its members and to unify, somewhat, their forces. Every lord in Livonia was to enlist one-third of his male subjects – meaning natives; each company would be commanded by a landsknecht who knew the recruits' language; each unit would have its own special banner, and even though most would serve only as garrison troops or scouts, that would free landsknechts and knights to join the main army. The archbishop and the Livonian master would command their own men, but they would cooperate in the field. Each promised that his men would not loot the property of the peasants.

The taxes would be heavy. Even the mercenaries were expected to pay 10 per cent. The cities would contribute supplies, so that, it was reiterated, the mercenaries would not have to live off the land. Strictest discipline would be maintained regarding looting.

There was some progress on the diplomatic front, when Kettler once again met the king of Poland–Lithuania. Negotiations had been long and seemingly repetitious, with the same proposals and the same objections coming up again and again; personal appearances tended to speed the process along. To win Polish support, Kettler agreed to relinquish the entire region south of the Daugava (Düna) river – Courland. This did not bring Polish and Lithuanian soldiers to his aid immediately – almost nothing happened immediately unless there was no choice – but it would allow him to transfer troops north as soon royal troops took their place.

A Tatar chief was present at that meeting. He promised that his khan would attack Russia from the south if the Livonians could keep the tsar busy in the north. That was the encouragement that Kettler needed to make an advance on a fort near Narva. Once there, however, he found his mercenaries unwilling to attack. Frustrated with the passive resistance of the troops, Kettler was sufficiently pleased with their commander to give him a complete suit of clothes, every piece made of expensive velvet.

The next day the landsknechts attacked, only to be repulsed again. The walls were so high that no one could get over them. That is, no one except the leader of the assault, who was shot just as he reached the parapet. When artillery was bought close enough to blow down sections of the wall, the Russians asked for a truce. At first the Russians claimed that they would never be able to face their grand duke if they surrendered, because he never tolerated any excuse for failure; then they asked for an honourable capitulation that allowed them to carry away their possessions. Kettler seems to have been tempted, but the captains of the mercenary companies objected – they could still take the castle, they argued (and the loot, which was not mentioned). In the meantime the Russians constructed earthworks in front of their breached walls.

The next day, when the mercenaries came on, they reported gunfire so intense that it appeared that the castle was on fire. After that, although the landsknechts formed up, they refused to attack. Then the peasants refused to stay; they demanded their pay and left. Many knights and landsknechts did not even wait to be paid – they just left. That was it. Of the 700 men Kettler had brought from Reval, he brought only 150 back.

In 1560 the situation became worse. When the powerful fortress at Marienburg surrendered, Kettler was furious. As soon officers and troops of the garrison appeared, he questioned them closely. Then he imprisoned the commander, leaving him jailed until his death not long afterward. He gave the troops until sunset to get out of his territories. They apparently complied.

By spring Kettler had no money. He could pay neither cavalry nor infantry, and he could promise landsknechts only two guilders apiece and musketeers one – a substantial cut. He owed one mercenary captain, Balthasar Fürstenberg, 2,000 thalers.* Kettler scattered his men across the country in small garrisons, perhaps as much to prevent their conspiring to demand payment as to avoid overburdening any one locality. Mutiny was mentioned frequently in his letters, though the number of actual incidents was smaller than expected.

Townspeople gave the mercenaries whatever they could to keep them from leaving, but since the countryside had been ravaged for three winters in a row, the peasants had lost almost all their grain stores. Nobles mortgaged or sold their land at half its value, not in order to flee the country, but to buy bread at the currently inflated prices. There was no money at all to buy imports, not even of foodstuffs. Everything went to the mercenaries.

But not all townspeople did this willingly. The citizens of Wenden wrote Fürstenberg, asking him to free them from the obligation to work on strengthening the city walls and to send the mercenaries somewhere else before the city was bankrupted. The master was stunned – and said so – that people could be so obtuse to the dangers that were practically at their gates. Moreover, Wenden was among the most important posts in the entire country. It had to be held. Yes, even cut down the trees in the city park!

This was the situation when Duke Magnus arrived in Oesel on 15 April with five ships and 400 landsknechts. The bishop greeted him and happily turned over the diocese. Christopher von Münchhausen arrived later with fifty landsknechts and assumed the actual direction of the duke's programme. Magnus may have been 'Bishop of Oesel and Wiek, heir to the Norwegian crown, duke of Schleswig, Holstein and Stormarn, Count of Oldenburg and Delmenholst', but he knew very little about his new possessions. Without Münchhausen's mercenaries, Magnus was a nobody; with them, he might become the next duke of Livonia, or even king.

Magnus and his campaign manager discovered that the mercenaries on the island, most of whom were local knights and gentry who had recently served in Kettler's army, had already taken the local Order commander hostage, demanding that he pay their back wages. Their captains had promised to get them their pay within a month, but had not

---

* Though von Fürstenbergs were plentiful in Livonian history, Balthasar had no known connection other than probably having come from Westphalia.

been able to do so. Magnus easily persuaded the rebels to join his forces.

In May Magnus received a letter that caused him to jump from his desk with joy and hurry to the dungeon to inform the captive officer that he would soon have company. He then read aloud, with obvious satisfaction, that a company of mercenary horsemen had taken Kettler prisoner. The officer was despondent, not being able to comprehend how this could all happen.

The story turned out to be false. Only Magnus's hatred of Kettler was real. He could not understand how that lowly monk (all Livonian knights were technically monks) could stand in his way. Kettler was not only refusing to acknowledge him as the new leader of the war, but he was standing in the way of his even taking possession of cities and castles that clearly belonged to the bishop of Oesel-Wiek; and Magnus, though not interested in celibacy or religious services, was bishop now. He had bought the title fair and square. Moreover, he was nineteen and in a hurry.

Joseph von Munden, meanwhile, having learned from a Russian captive that raiders were nearby, attacked the peasants who were guiding the enemy. As the chronicler Renner wrote: 'They plundered, burned and killed everything they could, causing great devastation far and wide. They seized a great booty in livestock and returned with it to Oberpahlen.' He then mounted some of his men on the captured horses and sent them ahead of his main body. There were not many landsknechts in this force, but he made a brave show of it. He mounted a strange banner depicting a rooster, a rat and a cross on a prominent tree where the enemy could see it. Though he left no men to guard the banner, the Russians were persuaded that another unit was hidden nearby, and therefore prudently retreated.

Meanwhile, the situation had become so desperate that the Polish king sent troops. Apparently, Kettler's representatives had persuaded him that unless he acted, the Russians would occupy the region, then use it as a base against Lithuania. When a small number of Poles and Lithuanians arrived in Courland, Kettler redeployed men from there to central Livonia.

From this moment the situation seemed to improve. Kettler, now in full command, sold a rich island in the Daugava and several hundred farms to the city of Riga for an unspecified sum and mortgaged the territory of Grobin, far to the south, to Albrecht of Prussia for 40,000 guilders; he sold the convent in Bremen to the city for 7,000 guilders. Then he announced to his men that they would be paid and ordered the national levy to assemble. He intended to meet the Russian invasion head on.

All he needed was additional Polish and Lithuanian reinforcements. They had been promised, but they did not arrive. June and July saw Kettler furiously trying to keep a deteriorating situation together.

To please the Polish monarch, he appointed Jasper von Münster to the castle at Ascheraden that guarded the Daugava crossing, then he had to admonish him to stop writing letters with false reports and slanders.

Letters and then more letters went to the Lithuanian commander, urging him to come quickly and, even more urgently, to send 40,000 thalers to pay the troops. Then letters went to the mercenaries, saying that Lithuanian and Polish coins would be just as good as the Order's. Then he sent warnings that he would not pay the troops for any time lost to their mutinies.

He sent letters about Duke Magnus, delegations to Sweden and Poland, and more promises to the troops that money would indeed be coming. At the end of July, as the Russian army approached, his letters to the Lithuanian commander became more frantic; and his pleas for money, too.

At length, when the Lithuanian commander slowly moved north, he made it clear that he expected to be welcomed into Riga and the other strongholds. This sent shivers through Protestant spines – they feared, with good reason, that as a pre-condition for assistance, Roman Catholicism be re-established. Kettler naturally resisted – the game of delay and prevaricate could be played by all sides – putting off every concession as long as he could. Meanwhile, there were the minutiae of daily business: orders concerning the proper exchange rate for thirty-seven different foreign coins, on the weight of small change, innumerable petitions, and more correspondence with the great powers. In free moments perhaps, he read letters from his brother about the varieties of Rhine wine he had purchased for him. But most of Kettler's time in 1560 was spent on diplomacy and organising his army.

The Battle at Ermes

In early August Kettler brought all his finest warriors together at Ermes in central Livonia. It was the best army he ever commanded, but until reinforcements arrived from Poland–Lithuania, he still did not dare risk battle with the Russian force just to the east. While he was away at one point, everything went wrong. No one planned to get into a fight. It just happened. What started as a skirmish drew more and more of the Livonian Order's fine little army into what became a gigantic trap. Russian numbers were far too great, and more and more arrived each minute. By the end of the day 500 of Kettler's cavalrymen had perished or been captured. Among that number were almost all of his best commanders; those who were taken prisoner survived only long enough to be paraded through the streets of Moscow, after which their heads were battered in with clubs. A tombstone of the most inspiring officer was later erected by the bishop of Dorpat in Moscow.

For Ivan the Terrible the battle at Ermes was a great triumph – his armies could now march into Central Livonia almost without resistance and with little warning. For Kettler it was an unqualified disaster.

Kettler's first thought upon hearing the news was that he should combine whatever forces he could still muster with the approaching Polish–Lithuanian army and hurry to the rescue of Fellin, where the Order's supplies and artillery were stored. But the Poles and Lithuanians still did not appear, nor was there any money forthcoming. He could do nothing but watch and pray.

As Kettler feared, Ivan immediately besieged Fellin, where the old master, Fürstenberg, was undaunted by Ivan's one hundred cannon (some brought from Russia, others captured at nearby castles). Fellin was a strong fortress, built atop a hill with a lake and a steep cliff protecting two sides; any approaching enemy would have to pass over two strongly defended bridges; the castle had a lead roof, and thus could not be set ablaze with incendiary missiles. The city below the castle had a high stone wall with ten gates; and the tallest tower, Long Herman, had a commanding view of the approaches so that snipers and guns could inflict terrible casualties on enemies attempting to dig trenches toward the fortifications. Fürstenberg's 250 landsknechts, together with the men of the town, seemed adequate to holding off the 15,000 Russians.

The old master proved to be a formidable warrior. Sending his men out to attack the Russian lines, he was able to spike two cannon. Still, on 17 August the Russian siege guns were in place, bombarding the town with stone shot that broke down entire houses, then following with fire balls. At first the defenders could extinguish the fires, but the fourth attack consisted of three volleys of fifteen fireballs coordinated with soldiers storming the walls. The conflagrations were more than the fire-fighters could handle, especially when the citizens had to give priority to fending off the Russians' efforts to break into the town. While the defenders threw back three attempts to force their way through a breach, the houses and commercial buildings burned. Although the Russians had lost 2,000, and the defenders only six landsknechts, one musketeer and one peasant, it was apparent that the citizens could no longer contribute significantly to their own defence.

Fürstenberg, recognising the seriousness of the situation, proposed withdrawing into the castle. Not having enough ready money to interest the mercenaries, he promised them his personal gold and silver. But the mercenaries rejected his offer. They wanted to accept Ivan's invitation to surrender honourably; they took seriously his warning that survivors of the next attack, should there be any, would be given no quarter. Why fight, when the inevitable outcome seemed death? The old master threw himself at their feet, tears in his eyes, and begged them not to surrender. But one of the landsknechts struck him down, seized the keys and opened negotiations.

The landsknechts were allowed to carry their weapons as far as a nearby manor, thus guaranteeing their safety from the irate enemy troops lining the road out of the castle, then they surrendered them. The next morning they were given white sticks to signify that they were non-combatants, and set free. The Russians took four wagonloads of firearms back to the castle, and later even larger amounts of armour and weapons.*

The old master, carried off to captivity in Moscow, never ceased to explain that the castle would never have been taken if the landsknechts had been willing to fight. Kettler made a list of the mutineers and later hanged or impaled every one he could find. He beheaded eleven he caught waiting at Dünamünde for a ship to take them back to Germany; others he kept in prison there for months before releasing them – by which time there were no more ships sailing. A few slipped away, probably overland through Courland and Prussia. Others perished from hunger and cold.

Magnus, hearing that Russians were approaching, sailed over to Oesel. His example – putting caution before courage – proved contagious. There was widespread panic and despair. For everyone, that is, except Kettler.

Kettler replaced the garrisons at three castles with Lithuanians, 600 of whom had finally come to assist him. He sent the mercenaries away in small bands, chiding them for having abused the peasants. The chronicler Renner says that the landsknechts would like to have banded together and paid Kettler back, but he carefully kept them dispersed until they took ship.

Not even Magnus was able to pay his landsknechts at this time. His brother's advisors were protesting against putting more Danish money into this vain enterprise. His soldiers, disgusted with their employer, went to Reval and enlisted there.

Swedish Intervention

Reval had meanwhile offered to put itself under the protection of the new king of Sweden. Erik (1533–68) declared himself willing to consider the offer, but before he could send an army, the citizens had prudently notified Kettler of their intentions, whereupon the Livonian master sent north a Polish–Lithuanian force called the *Praesidium*. Despite its impressive name, it was merely another mercenary company. Unfortunately for Kettler's plans, these troops could not work with German mercenaries. The city council paid them off and sent them away, then accepted the king of Sweden's generous offer.

Troops, artillery, supplies and ammunition flooded into Reval in amounts so impressive that Ivan offered a two-year truce. The Livonians seized the offer eagerly, even though it meant leaving half the country in

---

* One mercenary was recognised as a previous prisoner who had violated his parole (his word of honour). He was immediately flayed, then hanged from a tree and finally shot.

the tsar's hands. There was no alternative. Kettler had but 300 men and no money; the Livonian Confederation had ceased to exist.

Livonia was now well on the way to being divided up. By the start of 1561 Swedes and Danes held the northern coasts, Russians the eastern provinces, and Lithuanians the south. Riga, the centre of the last independent region, was visited by the Lithuanian commander, who paraded through the city with his army. The citizens stared not so much at the Lithuanians and Poles as at the strange costumes of Armenians, Turks, Tatars, Ukrainians, Russians and Rumanians. As Russow put it, 'They saw their own distress in the fact that such bizarre, strange and barbarian nations and people were in their fatherland, treading the streets of the Christian city of Riga. If the sight of these peoples, riding amiably through the city, brought sorrow and dismay to everyone, what dismay and terror would there be in one saw them at war, besieging, conquering and ruling a Christian city?'

Crowding so many troops and refugees into towns came at a price. In August over 2,000 Swedish troops in Reval died of a 'strange' disease. No citizen or peasant perished.

Livonia Carved Up by the Great Powers

The Livonian Order ceased to exist in 1562. Gotthard Kettler became the hereditary duke of Courland, a Protestant vassal to the Catholic king of Poland–Lithuania. His negotiations with the kings of Denmark and Sweden, Magnus of Holstein, the various interests in Livonia, the pope and the grand master of the Teutonic Knights in Germany, and the Holy Roman emperor, were complicated, but successful. Kettler gave fiefs to several of his closest advisers and generals and began looking for a proper wife who could deliver him sons. He quickly found Anna of Mecklenburg, whose father's small but strategically placed state on the south coast of the Baltic provided him access to German mercenaries and some hope of financial assistance.

Johan of Finland (1537–92), who favoured Swedish intervention in the war, married the sister of the Polish king and brought her home through Reval; this seemed a guarantee that the two major western powers would work in concert. However, King Erik, being less than sound in his mind and very jealous of his brother, would have none of it. Johan had married without royal permission and, therefore, soon found himself in prison.

Ivan's attack on Lithuania in 1563 took off some of the pressure. Moreover, Ivan was his enemies' best friend – when the Lithuanian campaign did not go well, his generals fled west. Ivan's reaction was to employ his secret police, the *Oprichniki*, striking fear into both internal friends and enemies alike and paralysing all initiative. Offensive operations in Livonia slowed and stalled.

Exchanges of territories occurred at a dizzying pace, as one claim was swapped for another. Kettler got Magnus's Courland possessions in return for the Order's territories in Oesel-Wiek. As the chronicler Solomon Henning wrote, the country was like 'a hay stack from which almost everyone plucked or pulled something. It was indeed the apple of Eris and the gold of Toulouse and everyone who tried to seize some of it almost all had their fingers smartly burned.'

The nobles in Livonia received grim confirmations that their claims on ancestral estates would be honoured, even though it was obvious that their future holdings would not resemble those of the past. As for the peasants, most were sinking rapidly into serfdom. Many were refugees, with little choice but to accept whatever work was available. That was better than starvation.

The war continued on other fronts, Poland–Lithuania succumbing slowly to Russian forces; and when the kings of Denmark and Sweden went to war with one another, the conflict spilled into to Estonia.

Unpaid Mercenaries Revolt

On 7 January 1570, Swedish mercenaries seized the castle in Reval, imprisoning the royal governor and his family, then sending word of their brave deed to Duke Magnus. The mercenaries seem to have been German-speaking Livonians led by Klaus Kurssel. Their complaint was about back pay, and while they were willing to wait, they said, their creditors were not. If the king would pay them, they would release the governor and turn the castle back over to him. Until they were paid, however, they would occupy the castle; if not paid, they would sell it to the highest bidder. The governor, having promised to do what he could, was allowed to take his family down into the city and find another residence.

On 4 February Magnus's representatives appeared at the city, asking for a safe conduct so that he could talk with the governor. Soon it became clear that Kurssel was considering turning the castle over to the Duke, a plan that was very unpopular among the citizens, and absolutely unacceptable to the Swedish garrison in the lower city.

On Good Friday, Swedish loyalists retook the castle by a ruse. They had noticed that the German mercenaries regularly held great feasts at which they drank themselves into a stupor and also that, because the castle walls facing away from the city were very high, situated on high crags, and lined with cannon, few men were on guard there. In contrast, the garrison watched carefully the walls facing the more gentle approach from the city. The trick to capturing the citadel, the Swedes had concluded, was to wait until the cavalry had ridden out into the countryside to round up food for the feasts, then to find some way of slipping into the heart of the fortress from the rear. Slipping into it is exactly what they did. They somehow made contact with three renegade Swedes who had joined the mercenaries after being charged with murder and assault. These renegades had made their way down the crag to negotiate with the besiegers, then suggested that for a proper bribe they would lower a rope and haul soldiers up to the crag, then pull them through a toilet shaft into the castle. The besieging Swedes immediately paid the first portion of the agreed sum, which the conspirators used – won gambling, they told the garrison – to throw a party. As Russow described it, 'There was mighty boozing and when the guests were dead drunk, they laid down and slept like swine.' Then the three renegades lowered themselves on a rope ladder down to the crag at the rear of the fortress and walked along the edge of the precipice in their woollen socks to a place they could signal the besiegers where to come up. One by one, they brought up 300 men, first to the base of the wall, then up the toilet shaft into the castle. The attack came as a complete surprise, then turned into a massacre.

A few mercenaries managed to slip, half-naked, down toilet shafts themselves and escape, but the others were either shot or captured. The renegades were rewarded with golden necklaces, silver daggers, silks and satins, and good horses.

The German mercenaries who were released on bail made their way to Russia and enlisted in Ivan's army. Among those who had escaped capture was Jürgen Farensbach, who became one of the most famous mercenaries of the following decades.

The Last Years of the War

Livonia was now flooded with mercenary troops. While many of these were foreigners, an increasing number were sons of Livonian nobles. These local boys had numerous advantages as warriors – they knew the regional languages and were familiar with the land, they had become skilled cavalrymen, and they were fighting for their country as well as for money. Moreover, surrender was no longer an option. The tsar had sent in his dreaded *Oprichniki*. These men, delighting in torture and murder, terrorised not only the inhabitants of Livonia and Lithuania, but even the highest-born boyars in Russia. Their goal was to crush all resistance to the tsar; their effect was to strengthen the resistance in Livonia.

In the years to follow there were desperate battles and sieges. After the mercenary commanders Boisman and Fürstenberg, the last great hopes that local autonomy could be saved, had been slain; and Magnus, a plausible alternative to direct tsarist rule, was held in virtual house arrest, in humiliating poverty, Livonia seemed totally doomed.

There were odd, almost unbelievable occurrences, such as the 1,500

Scottish mercenary infantry who in 1574 attempted to preach Presbyterianism in their lowland English dialect to the bewildered citizens of Reval. After quarrelling with the German mercenaries, they marched out of their camp in full battle array, captured the artillery and fired on German horsemen. Both sides appealed to the Swedes for help, but the Swedish commander wanted no part of their quarrels; similarly, the Scottish cavalry remained aloof, waiting to see how the affair would play out. When the Germans made a counter-attack, the Scots scattered, to be hunted down one by one by the Germans and local Estonian peasants. Prisoners were not taken.

The Scottish cavalry remained in Swedish pay. The infantrymen who survived the clash made their way to Russian lines and enrolled in Ivan's army, only to be arrested later and taken to Moscow, where seventy of them were executed.

At length, the Swedes and Poles began to drive Ivan's forces east. In 1581 the allies crossed into Russian territory, where Stephen Batory (1533–86) of Poland–Lithuania won a crushing victory at Pskov. Ivan, ill and mentally disturbed, his country defeated and impoverished, made peace. The victors then divided Livonia among themselves.

Mercenaries in the Baltic and Russia

The Polish and Swedish monarchs, unable to pay their mercenary leaders, gave them estates in the lands they had recovered from the tsar or which had belonged to owners recently slain or bankrupted. The new nobility often had connections to the past, often being sons or nephews or, by now, the grandchildren, of important families. Newcomers added to their numbers and intermarried with them. Known popularly as Baltic barons, they would now serve whatever lord held the land – Swedish, Polish or Russian. They were mercenaries at heart, though this sentiment would be gradually remodelled into personal loyalty, then patriotism – ultimately Russian patriotism. Baltic barons would achieve the highest positions in the tsarist army and government, serving their new masters until 1917 with the same skill and devotion that their ancestors had shown their employers in the Livonian War.

Latvians and Estonians noted, however, that they added to their original arrogance and greed the vices of mercenaries.

As for the mercenaries, Balthasar Russow had the last word, saying that the Russians would fight to the last man rather than surrender a fortress, since the tsar would execute them for cowardice. Nor would they consider accepting refuge in another country, or serving outside Russia. 'But it does not matter to a German where he stays as long as he has enough grub and booze.'

The Russians were also so accustomed to meagre rations that they could survive on next to nothing – that being water, flour, salt and brandy. Russow commented wryly, 'A German cannot do this.' While Russians were almost always loyal, Germans would follow anyone with money. (Well, perhaps not Ivan the Terrible. He had expectations of loyalty and self-sacrifice that ran contrary to long-established professional standards.)

Why had so few western mercenaries been able to hold out against such warriors? Russow's first answer was to the point: the Russians were 'incredibly ineffectual' in pitched battles, running from much smaller forces. His second was that the people of Livonia – nobles, burghers and native peasants – had learned the hard arts of war and now bore most of the fighting. While the kings of Sweden and Poland–Lithuania, who eventually wore the Russian tsar down and forced him to make peace, local people – knights, gentry, burghers, peasants – deserve credit for the ultimate victory.

Gotthard Kettler founded a dynasty in Courland – three of his seven children lived to adulthood. No longer having an active military command, he established a court in Mitau and busied himself with reforming the schools and churches.

Magnus was luckier than his wife's family, who were all murdered by the tsar. When Ivan released him, he escaped with his wife to the west. He exchanged war-torn Oesel-Wiek for a poor but safe territory in Courland, where he could live in relative comfort far from his father-in-law's irrational massacres of relatives and friends; this also saved him from a humiliating return to Denmark, to explain why his grand plans had gone so badly and expensively awry. But even his more limited ambitions could not be fulfilled – his northern garrisons quickly declared their allegiance to King Johan of Sweden.* When Magnus's life ended in his castle at Pilten in 1583, he was nothing more than a footnote in the history of the region; his lands went from hand to hand, eventually becoming Polish.

The war concluded with the original parties all out of the action. Within a few years, however, the Swedes and the Poles would fall out over the winnings, almost unconscious of the changes that had occurred in Russia, where the day of the mercenary would shine more brightly than elsewhere.

---

* The son of Gustav Vasa, he became king in 1568, when the nobles recognised that Erik was insane. His son, Sigismund III (1566–1632) was elected king of Poland in 1587, then joint king of Sweden, too, from 1592–99.

Chapter 3

The Periphery of Europe

Russia Expands South

Jürgen Farensbach, the First Great Mercenary in Russia

Jürgen Farensbach was a child of the Livonian War. His immigrant ancestor, Wilhelm Farensbach, had come east as the business manager of the bishop of Oesel-Wiek, in charge of all castles, incomes and local affairs; he arrived with only ten guilders, but since he was the bishop's nephew, he was not worried – quarrelling with neighbours and gathering in estates and money was a prominent family characteristic. His estate at Heimar was only the most impressive of several prosperous properties worked by Estonian peasants.

Jürgen Farensbach was born in 1551, the ninth of eleven sons of Wolmar Farensbach, a Lutheran nobleman sufficiently important to have been twice selected for delegations to the emperor and pope. Seven years later Ivan the Terrible invaded Livonia, overran the borderlands, smashed the army of the Livonian Order, and pressed right up to the largest city in Estonia, Reval. Had Ivan been less tyrannical, or perhaps less insane, he would either have achieved little or done much more – his subjects trembled with fear at his murderous whims, his generals obeyed without question or fled abroad, and enemies either resisted to the death or despaired. He turned Tatars and irregular troops loose in Livonia, to rob, rape, murder and burn. Clearly, he believed that a policy of terror alternating with offers of clemency and peace would bring unconditional surrender. Instead, it inspired a spirit of resistance among those who could fight, flight among those who could not.

As Oesel-Wiek was being flooded with refugees, mercenary soldiers and adventurers, the bishop sold his diocese to a teenaged Danish prince, Magnus of Holstein. But the great question was who would get possession of Reval, farther east on the coast. In January 1570 a body of unpaid mercenaries led by Klaus Kurssel seized control of the castle there, only to be dispossessed on Good Friday by Swedish forces.

Jürgen Farensbach was among the few Germans to escape. He was only nineteen, but he already had a life-time worth of adventures behind him.

France and Austria

Farensbach hardly remembered his father, who died young; only two of his brothers survived childhood. He must have been about ten when he was sent to Sweden for military training. This was not unusual for noble youths. Less common was his being given a command so quickly.

Soon afterwards he went to France, where a bloody civil war pitted Huguenots (Calvinist Protestants) against Catholics. Most likely, he served in a cavalry unit – landsknechts tended to be commoners.

He was a small man, thin but muscular, with piercing eyes, the kind that make reluctant men obey commands. Quick to see what had to be done, quick to do it, and never quitting any task while the slightest potential of success remained. Everyone who met him understood that they were face to face with a leader of men.

In 1566 he enlisted in Habsburg service because Suleiman the Magnificent (1520–66) was marching on Austria. The Turkish threat made even Protestants forget the crisis in France and the war in Livonia. The new emperor, Maximilian II (1564–76), was Catholic, but he was also a German, and Farensbach's patriotism was stronger than his Lutheran convictions. However, it was important for him that one of the issues of the war was possession of Transylvania, a mountainous region of Hungary long inhabited by Germans who had recently become Calvinists and, like the Romanians who dwelt around them, found Ottoman rule more tolerant of their religious non-conformism than the Counter-Reformation zeal of the Holy Roman emperor. Farensbach was also attracted by the emperor's promise of good wages.

The campaign culminated in the Turkish siege of Szigeth and ended on 8 September 1566, when the sultan died unexpectedly. With the Turkish threat temporarily receding, the emperor discharged his mercenaries. The peace settlement left Transylvania essentially independent, though technically an Ottoman province; in 1571 a Transylvania noble, Stephen Batory, became governor (*voivode*), performing so well that the Polish nobles and clergy elected him king five years later.

Farensbach missed his opportunity to accompany Batory north. He had gone to the Netherlands, where the Dutch were fighting for independence and religious freedom against the greatest power of the era – Spain. He apparently remained in Holland until 1569, when he returned home and enlisted in Klaus Kurssel's company.

Livonian Service

Farensbach escaped from the castle in Reval with nothing but the clothes on his back, which must have been in sad shape after he had slid down a toilet shaft. He could hardly complain, however, since he had managed to avoid imprisonment – the sentence handed out to most surviving Livonian nobles – or execution, the fate of Kurssel, three of his officers, and all foreign mercenaries.

When the Danish administrator of the diocese, Christopher von Münchhausen, learned that Farensbach had appeared at the family estate, he immediately asked him to join a diplomatic mission to the Russian tsar. Duke Magnus desperately needed Ivan's assistance, since Swedish troops were pushing toward his seat at Leal. As it happened, the Swedes were already been repelled before Russian help arrived, but as far as this help went, Magnus would have been better off without it – his rescuers drove away the last of the Swedes, but then plundered the countryside from end to end. It did lead, however, to an alliance with the tsar. Once he had the use of Russian troops, Magnus was proclaimed the 'King of Livonia', a title that his powers hardly justified.

Farensbach missed the sieges of Reval in 1570–1. When the mercenaries accompanying the delegation to Moscow seized several Russian castles, Ivan had them arrested and brought to him in chains. Fortunately for Farensbach, Ivan was insane. That meant that, in his particular combination of depression and paranoia, he was highly unpredictable. At the moment Farensbach most needed divine help, the tsar was in a mood to tolerate Farensbach's refusal to grovel – usually a fatal mistake.

It may be that the tsar saw in this proud nobleman a means of persuading prominent Livonians to surrender; he promised to respect their customs, their religion and their possession of family estates. That was, in fact, the program that Magnus of Holstein had been pursuing on the advice of two nobles from Dorpat, Johann Taube and Elert Kruse, but his plan was totally self-serving – he proposed to marry Ivan's extremely young niece, then to rule the country in the tsar's name. Rightly or wrongly, Taube and Kruse were forever damned as traitors – even though generations later their formula was the one by which Livonian nobles submitted to tsarist rule – while Farensbach became a hero.*

Russian Service

In May 1571 Ivan's army was routed by the Tatar army of Khan Girai –

---

* Kruse wrote an angry defence of their actions. See the appendix of *The Chronicle of Balthasar Russow.*

actually more outmanoeuvred than outfought. When his demoralised troops flooded back into Moscow, Ivan did not even trust the stout stone walls of the Kremlin to protect him, but fled all the way to Jaroslavl. It was probably good judgment – Moscow was burned, perhaps by accident rather than intent, and, according to rumour, 130,000 people perished in the flames, including all but 300 soldiers of his army.

When Ivan sent out a call for experienced men to form the backbone of a new army, Taube and Kruse recruited two companies of German cavalry led by Hans von Zeitz and Reinhold von Rosen. Those forces, however, did not get further east than Dorpat before being told to tarry there as garrison troops – there was no point in sending them against the Tatars until he had found a good commander. The tsar, who was shrewd even when he was mad, offered to spare Farensbach's life if he would lead this new army south.

Farensbach accepted. Soon he was joint commander of a force of 7,000 men (that somehow did not include the newly enlisted Livonian horsemen). On 1 August 1572, he repulsed the Tatars on the Oka river, preventing them from reaching Moscow again. He had ridden out between the two armies to challenge the enemy commander to single combat, killed him, and came away with a reputation for reckless courage and chivalry. A song celebrated his exploit:

Und als die Tatern haben verheert	After the Tatars sacked
Die Moschkaw und mit Feuer zerstört,	Moscow and burned it
Gab ihm der Moschkowiter groß Sold	The Tsar gave him money that
Gegen Tatern er sich brauchen wollt	he would need against the Tatars.
Da hat er deutscher Pferd ein Heer,	He had a German cavalry force
Geführt bis an das caspisch Meer,	That he led to the Caspian Sea
Den ersten Streit find er selbst an,	He opened the battle himself,
Erschoß aus stracks den ersten Mann;	Right away shooting the
	commander;
Die Tatern flohen all zurück,	The Tatars fled away,
Der Farensbach behielt den Sieg.	Farensbach won the day.

Meanwhile, Taube and Kruse betrayed him. Russow's chronicle described the attempted coup of October 1571 in Dorpat, where the mercenaries barely failed to take the city from its Russian garrison – Rosen had feared to take the other units into his confidence, so he was left alone to fight to the death. Taube and Kruse fled to Poland, and as Russow wittily remarked, 'Nor did Hans von Zeitz wish to wait for his pay, but rather departed.'

Magnus, hearing of this and remembering what happened to other prominent lords who had earned the tsar's displeasure, hurried to Oesel, putting as much distance and water between himself and Ivan as practical.

This left Jürgen Farensbach as the only prominent Livonian in the tsar's employ. In 1572 he returned to Russian-occupied Livonia to enlist cavalrymen for service against the Tatars and other enemies. He recruited one entire squadron immediately and many more later, but he was unwilling to lead them against his homeland, as the tsar desired. Instead, fearing that the *Oprichniki*, Ivan's ruthless secret police, would number him among their many victims, he slipped away to Austria, then to Denmark. His men were allowed to return to Livonia, to be criticised by the chronicler, Salomon Hennig, for not having put their talents to the service of their native land.

In April 1573 Magnus married the tsar's thirteen-year-old niece in a mixed Lutheran–Orthodox ceremony so strange that Hennig could only make a parody of it. He returned to Livonia with ample funds for hiring mercenaries. Among his new officials was Farensbach's brother, Dietrich, who became privy councillor and commander of Fellin, once the greatest fortress in Livonia.

Magnus's recruiting efforts prompted the Swedish king to send a large force under Pontus de la Garde into Livonia. De la Garde, a French-Swedish mercenary who would make his career in Estonia, had only one success in this campaign – capturing Dietrich Farensbach – but he disrupted the Dane's plans and persuaded Ivan that Magnus was incompetent. The 'King of Livonia', reduced to a tiny territory in the centre of the country, lived in poverty while his wife played with dolls.

In 1575, the duke of Saxony invaded Oesel from Sweden with a mercenary army. Fighting raged between Danish and Swedish garrisons on the island while Russian armies plundered Magnus's mainland possessions. In 1577 Ivan invaded central Livonia, his troops ravaging the country so terribly that subsequent generations could not think about that summer without shuddering. Several fortresses offered to surrender to Magnus rather than to Ivan, but this was not a situation the tsar approved of long. He became suspicious that Magnus was planning to make himself an independent potentate, as indeed he was – he had made secret offers to the citizens, promising them lenient treatment.

After Magnus obeyed orders to tell his garrisons to open their gates to Russian forces, one did – Kokenhausen – whereupon Ivan had the entire garrison slaughtered. Then, declaring that Livonia was 'God's little country', Ivan forbade any looting or burning on the march north to Wenden, where Magnus had taken refuge.

When Ivan arrived, the garrison of Wenden was, naturally enough, unwilling to allow the Russians entry. Magnus reluctantly went out to meet the tsar, but during the conference, just as Ivan was about to forgive Magnus for his 'disobedience', someone fired a shot at the tsar. Ivan was one of those men who never hesitated to order the murder of thousands or send them to their death in battle, but he was terrified of dying himself.

He arrested Magnus, then ordered the castle taken. The last 300 men, women and children blew themselves up rather than be taken prisoner; they had correctly inferred that the fate of those taken captive was to be roasted alive.*

The tsar held Magnus prisoner in deplorable conditions, then unexpectedly released him to rejoin his wife. Not long afterwards Ivan demanded a huge sum of money and all his jewellery. Magnus sent his gold chains and rings, but explained that he could only raise money if he were allowed to go abroad. Under this pretext he escaped to Courland, to the diocese of the last bishop. His pretence of being a bishop was ludicrous, but no more so than his claim to be king of Livonia.

Danish and Polish Service

Jürgen Farensbach, meanwhile, had become court marshal for King Fredrik II (1534–88) of Denmark. For eight years he was close to the king, who loved to hear the stories of his adventures. But Farensbach was bored. Although once it appeared that the king might intervene in the Livonian War – and use Farensbach's skills – it was at length apparent that he would not. Farensbach found employment in Poland, an unhappy country which had elected a young Valois prince as the successor of Sigismund Augustus, on the promise that he would marry the late king's elderly daughter. In 1574, however, king-elect learned that his elder brother had died; without hesitating, he fled Poland and became Henry III of France. The ensuing election was complicated. In 1576 a majority of the electors chose Maximilian of Austria, but most Poles did not want a German king, much less the Holy Roman emperor. Stephen Batory, prince of Transylvania, seized the moment and made himself king – it helped that he was willing to marry the jilted daughter; the election also made Batory grand duke of Lithuania.

Civil war broke out, with the Prussian cities declaring their allegiance to the emperor. When Batory sent Polish troops to take Danzig, the city council recruited mercenaries. Farensbach's defence of the city was so expert that Batory tried to win him over to his service.

When peace was concluded, King Fredrik gave Farensbach estates on Oesel and authority over all Danish territories in Estonia. Not that this meant much; with Magnus's defeat, Danish prospects in Livonia were dim. The tsar's last siege of Reval, in 1577, failed, with the loss of 3,000

---

* Sir Jerome Horsey, an English commercial agent in Moscow 1573–90, described (in *Rude & Barbarous Kingdom*) the sad condition of the many captives he saw. Many were sold into slavery in Persia and to the Tatars, but he was able to ransom some, and after he persuaded the tsar that Scots were not Swedes, Ivan allowed them to enlist in the Russian army for the campaign against the Tatars.

men, but he had come sufficiently close to success that Sweden and Poland had joined forces. In October 1578 a Swedish–Polish army routed the Russians, killing over 6,000 men and capturing all their artillery. This battle at Wenden was, as contemporaries punned on the German verb, the 'turning' point of the war.

Swedish forces moved east along the Finnish coast; in 1579 the royal army captured Narva, and in 1580 and 1581 retook important castles that had been in Russian possession for years. Stephen Batory occupied central Livonia, causing many nobles and clerics to fear he would annex the country to his kingdom and introduce the Counter-Reformation. But that was a matter to be worried about later; at the moment, everyone agreed that the Russians had to be expelled. Therefore, although Batory's Polish, Hungarian and German troops provoked stares of wonderment when they passed by Riga, they were very welcome. Batory had Lithuanians, too, but fewer, because they had to protect their own long border against Russian armies.

Batory understood the importance of having men who knew the country – its terrain, language and peoples. In 1580 he hired Farensbach – with one hundred cavalry and fifty musketeers – and assigned him joint responsibility for the van of the army, to be the first on the roads through the dense forests, the first to cross the rivers and swamps. In the royal council Farensbach argued persuasively to take the war into Russia itself, right to Pskov, but it was only in the third campaign that the king actually reached that strategic city.

The first campaign was directed at Polotsk, then Vielikii Luki, important towns on the Daugava River along the most direct route from Lithuania to Pskov. Farensbach wanted to lead the assault on the walls, but the king forbade that – he did not have experienced commanders to spare. Even so, once the fighting was underway, no one could stop Farensbach from riding forward in hopes of saving the last remnant of the heroic Russian garrison from massacre. It was in vain. Though he was able to hear the Russians pleading for their lives, he could not stop his enraged landsknechts from taking revenge for lost comrades; in fact, the soldiers pulled the Russian commander right out of Farensbach's arms and killed him.

Peace and Prosperity

Peace negotiations were led by the Jesuit priest, Possevino, whose memoirs are invaluable for understanding the moment. As Farensbach led his men home to Estonia, he had to take an indirect route back through Lithuania and then into Courland. There he met the widow of the recently deceased Thieß von der Recke, one of the most important and controversial figures of the era. Sophia was thirty-seven, ten years old than Farensbach, and had two sons and two daughters. Quite understandably, she saw in Farensbach not only a man who could save her and her family, but also a man who was considerably more attractive than her late husband. Marriage followed.*

Batory's 1581 offensive saw Farensbach at the head of 1,500 troops, some from Scotland. Riga had submitted to Polish rule in January of that year, with the king present personally in April to receive the oath of loyalty and to promise that the city's traditional rights and privileges would be observed. Batory began a siege of Pskov in August, then crushed Ivan in a great battle. He broke off the siege in January after a ten-year truce was signed.

The tsar used these months to divide his enemies. Ivan's commissioners wasted time in frivolous debates over rank and titles, knowing how difficult it would be for Batory to keep his expensive army mobilised. The tsar had been saved, given a period to recover his strength, perhaps even his sanity, and for his opponents to become distracted by other wars.

King Johan of Sweden did not join in this peace settlement, but continued his offensive until he had retaken all of Estonia, including Narva, and occupied the Russian coastline all the way to the Neva river. Only in 1583 did he sign the first of the three-year truces that brought peace.

During Lent in 1582 Batory's army paraded through the streets of Riga, and Jesuits occupied St James's church, to the horror of Lutherans. But such concessions could not be avoided – Polish authority was now totally dominant. The king was besieged by Livonian noblemen who wanted guarantees that their estates would be returned; they sensed that both the Polish and Swedish monarchs would reward mercenary leaders not with money, but with land. Batory, unwilling to make promises that would be difficult to keep, especially if the truce was broken, told everyone to come back to Riga in a year. At that time there would be a great conference to sort such matters out.

Early Retirement Comes to an Early End

Farensbach's career had been what every mercenary had dreamed of – adventure, honour, success, and a retirement to a country estate in the company of a wealthy and attractive wife. Unfortunately, as was often the case, the life of a warrior was war.

---

* Recke's career illustrated the unpredictability of life in this era. Until the age of sixty he was an officer in the Livonian Order, commander of the castle of Doblen in southern Courland. When the military order was dissolved in 1561, he accepted that castle as a fief from Gotthard Kettler and married a fifteen-year-old heiress, Sophia Fircks. In his later years he was kidnapped by passing mercenaries, his estates plundered, and the titles to his lands disputed. But he managed to hold on to his possessions until his death in 1580 at age eighty.

In early 1583 Batory was distracted by an uprising in Courland – when Magnus died that March, almost alone and in poverty, his lands were supposed to revert to Poland, but Gotthard Kettler had recently persuaded Magnus to accept the parts of Oesel once belonging to the Livonian Order in exchange for his Courland possessions. The citizens, to make the matter more complex, wanted to be subjects of the king of Denmark. Eventually the duke of Prussia bought the Danish claims.

This crisis must have involved Farensbach, because his wife's lands were threatened and because he owed allegiance to the Danish king for his own estates on Oesel, where he was the commander of the royal forces. Moreover, Farensbach was a Protestant, while the largest army in the region was Polish, and Batory's Jesuit advisors wanted Catholicism restored in the newly conquered lands. Wisely, Batory avoided provoking popular discontents – he appointed Farensbach administrator of Livonia, a post Farensbach must have accepted with mixed feelings. In fact, although in April 1583 King Fredrik had agreed to be godfather to Farensbach's son, when he heard of Farensbach's appointment as Polish administrator, he was furious; in March 1584, after six days of siege by Danish forces, Farensbach's mercenaries surrendered Arensburg, the largest castle on Oesel.*

Farensbach's wife had fled to Gotland – a centrally located island under Swedish control – then sailed to Livonia and joined him at Wenden. In 1585, the Polish king, happy to have Farensbach solely in his employ, endowed him with hereditary lands nearby. Unhappily, Batory died in December 1586, throwing Poland and Lithuania into another confused election. When Sigismund III (1587–1632, the son of Johan of Sweden) prevailed, the losing candidates threatened war, and it was expected that Russia and Turkey would take advantage of the confusion to steal borderlands. Moreover, everyone was afraid that the Swedish and Polish empires would be combined, creating a new superpower.

Farensbach raised Livonian troops and hastened to southern Poland, to the capital at Cracow. The swift mobilisation gave pause to the national enemies, who quickly assured everyone that they had no hostile intentions. This earned Farensbach the title of senator, but he could not remain in Poland long – efforts to restore Roman Catholicism in Livonia had provoked protests, and Farensbach was needed to restore peace and order. Also, it was necessary for him to sort out the hundreds of claims on property raised by dispossessed owners. Since many estates had been given to mercenary leaders, he had to arrange exchanges – usually giving

---

* The chronicler Hennig recorded that Farensbach did not take this amiss, but continued to do 'all a servant should and could do in speaking most loyally of his lord'. He added, 'The court cats who lick with one end and scratch with the other give an example of just the opposite'.

noble families vacant lands in the neighbourhood of their former estates; in any case it made little sense to give back the ancient manor houses, since so many had been burned.

In 1589, when King Sigismund decided to go to Reval to see his father, Johan of Sweden, he stopped in Riga to resolve matters there. Earlier he had ordered Farensbach to travel to the duke of Courland, to explain that the Diet in Warsaw had not yet decided how to handle the situation in Courland, but that he would like the duke to accompany him on his journey. They indeed met, but the size of the parties made it necessary for them to make their way north separately.

Livonia Between Sweden and Poland

When King Johan died in 1592, so, too, did joint rule in Livonia. The war of the Swedish succession – an unusually complicated dispute that drew all the neighbouring states into it – saw Farensbach land in Sweden with an army. He withdrew after suffering reverses, but his invasion helped persuade the Swedes to accept Sigismund as king – after giving promises to guarantee the nobles the same extensive rights as the Polish nobles enjoyed. This was a popular act – among the nobles. But the religious question remained open, no matter what the king promised the Protestants. After all, he had told the Livonians that he would respect their beliefs, then authorised the Jesuits to restore Roman Catholicism. Had the king kept his original resolutions, he might have succeeded in holding his empire together, but his regent in Sweden, another son of Gustav Vasa, Charles IX (1550–1612), led a Protestant rebellion in 1598.

Once again Farensbach crossed the Baltic. He rallied Swedish nobles, but was beaten at Stängebrö in September. Farensbach hurried to Poland to apologise for his failure, but the king only thanked him for his courageous efforts and sent him back to Livonia to continue military operations. Farensbach, hearing that his wife had died, made a short detour to see to his four sons and his daughter, but the interlude was short. Charles, aware that he could not remain on the defensive, invaded Estonia, then marched on Riga.

Farensbach had left his treasure at Karkus, guarded by a strong garrison. But he was absent when the Swedes attacked, whereupon his mercenaries had rebelled, slain their commanders and surrendered the fortress. He had been with the Lithuanian governor Chodkiewicz, defending Riga, which was the true key to the entire territory. Although the odds were against them, they repelled desperate Swedish assaults and forced the enemy to sail home in defeat.

Farensbach then went on the offensive, besieging the fortress at Fellin in mid May 1602. His men took the outer walls on the first attempt, but faced a greater challenge in taking the castle, which was protected on two sides by lakes and a double dry moat on the others, while powerful artillery-filled towers covered every approach. Farensbach, seeing his infantry assaults repulsed, dismounted his cavalry and led them forward. He scaled the first wall, but the second wall was just as formidable as the first, so that the assaults failed one after the other. Farensbach was prevented from putting himself at the head of the storming columns until he could no longer just watch; breaking free, he joined his men and charged forward. He fell, shot in the hand and through the body as he climbed the wall. But his example had worked its usual magic – the troops continued to press on until the last Swedish defenders had blown up the citadel to avoid having it fall into Polish hands. Farensbach heard news of the victory before he expired. He was still only fifty years of age.

Seven years later a biography appeared – *Vita illustris et magnifici herois Georgii Farensbach, Palatini olim Vendensis etc. quam David Hilchen, secretaries* . . . The German translation was, for the times, a best-seller.

He named his son Wolmar (9 February 1586–11 May 1633) in honour of his father. Wolmar became governor of Livonia in 1611, then fought in the Thirty Years War in Germany. Accused of planning to betray his employer, he was beheaded in Regensburg.

Sweden in Livonia

Charles IX brought stability and order to his kingdom and its Baltic possessions. In memory this was the beginning of the 'good old Swedish days'. Good for the nobility and commercial classes, at least. He lost a great battle at Kirchholm in 1605, overwhelmed by the spectacular winged hussars of the Polish–Lithuanian army, but when the Polish mercenaries refused to fight further without being paid, he was able to hold on to the Estonian coast. His son, Gustavus Adolphus (1594–1632), would renew the struggle for hegemony in Livonia.

Russia's Turkish Wars

It became apparent quickly that Ivan's successors were not as mad as he had been; moreover, with many men claiming to be the rightful tsar, the opportunities for employment were numerous. In ensuing years many Livonian nobles served as mercenaries in Russia's wars against the Turks. Most were served in the cavalry, or became officers of the newly formed musketeer units which had made the landsknechts outmoded.

The Ottoman state was no longer as strong as before, with sultan warriors and rigid morality. Murad III (1546–95) had followed tradition when he became sultan in 1574 – he had ordered his twenty younger half-brothers strangled (and six of his father's pregnant wives) to avoid their being used as figureheads by rebellious governors. His successor, Mehmet III, ended the practice of sending sons out to provinces as governors to gain experience, but instead confined them in the palace – a place of comfort and isolation known as the *harem* – which meant that they grew up ignorant of the world, unaccustomed to political discussions and disputes, and without much acquaintance even of one another. This may have seemed wise at the moment, when the Ottoman Empire was torn by widespread revolts, but it meant that future sultans would enter office completely unprepared for their manifold duties. When Ahmed I took power in 1603 at age thirteen, he spent more time trying to end the popular practice of drinking wine than he did resolving political problems. Perhaps it was just as well – for the next century and a half the Janissary corps – the elite infantry units – prevented the sultans from making any significant military reforms.

The Tsars Seeks Out Mercenaries

The Time of Troubles (1605–18) demonstrated the utter weaknesses of the traditional military practices of the newly formed tsarist state. Swedes and Poles invaded the country, imposters sat or the throne or tried to, and the boyars fought among themselves for dominance. Only after terrible sufferings was the crisis overcome in 1613 by Michael Romanov (1596–1645).*

The young tsar met relatively little opposition to his military reforms, partly because he had eliminated most potential dissidents, but also because most boyars and clerics could remember how small foreign armies had beaten some of their best forces. While it was clear that European-style armies were not suited to every military challenge the empire faced, it was necessary to introduce better firearms and more discipline. He named his father, the patriarch of Moscow, Feodor Nikitich Romanov (1553–1633), to oversee the reforms; the elder Romanov, in turn, in named his brother-in-law, Ivan Borisovich Cherkasskii, head of the various offices that supervised military affairs – the treasury, the musketeers chancellery and the foreign mercenary chancellery. Everything was in position by 1622, but it was not until 1631, when war with Poland over Smolensk demonstrated the inadequacy of existing forces, that there was a great effort to recruit foreigners; the experiences of the Time of Troubles had warned against giving foreigners too much power, but now

---

* McNeill demonstrates that Poland, and to a lesser extent Austria and the Ottoman Empire had a Time of Troubles, too from 1570–1650.

there was little choice. By the end of the year, 190 were in positions of command. Efforts to recruit infantry, however, were less successful; only Alexander Lesley was able to bring a sizeable force east (4,600 of the 7,500 he had hired, of whom 214 died in the next two years). The pay was an attractive inducement, set very high to counter the horrific stories circulating in the west about the debauched habits of the people, the superstitions (which far surpassed those of contemporary westerners, a feat not easily accomplished), and the dangers. Lesley had come from Scotland via Sweden. More influential even was Indrik van Dam, a Dutchman who trained the best of the new regiments in western tactics.*

The problem facing the Russian army was more complex than the westerners appreciated at first. It was one thing to train an infantry force to face Poles and Swedes, quite another to fight Tatars, raiders who could not be easily brought to battle – infantry were completely ineffective on the steppe. Also, the boyars, who considered themselves the traditional military class of Russia, refused to serve under foreign command. When the tsar's administrators attempted to enlist commoners, even Cossacks, the reputation of the new regiments sank to the point that almost no respectable man would enlist. The first draft of peasants came only in 1647, when every ten to twenty houses was to supply one recruit, mostly for non-combat duties, but also as soldiers.

The traditional approach to fighting the Tatars was to fortify the well-known traditional routes into Muscovy – guarding fords, patrolling the thousand-mile frontier, cutting down trees in the dense forests to create barriers (and forbidding woodcutting anywhere, so as to make it extremely difficult to bypass the obstacles), burning the grass to deprive the Tatar ponies of fodder, and digging moats. To prevent farmers from fleeing to safer areas, the tsars bound all peasants to their land and built frontier towns to serve as strongholds; they hired French Huguenots and Dutch engineers to design fortifications. This worked well enough that many peasants migrated south illegally, requiring the tsars to build yet newer frontier defences. But each advance south made it more difficult for the traditional armed forces to participate in defending the frontier.

The new regiments were eventually equipped with flintlock muskets, the matchlock having the disadvantage of being readied for firing only slowly (a great problem when faced by unexpected Tatar attacks); cavalry, of course, had flintlock pistols available, but generally relied on the sabre and bow. As for producing weapons, even at this early date a technologically backward Russia was able to turn them out in massive quantities, though it was necessary to purchase specialised parts, such as firing mechanisms, abroad. The tsars' specialists produced cannon in great numbers, but in a staggering variety of calibres, and no obsolete

---

* Details from Richard Hellie.

weapon was ever discarded. It was a logistical nightmare for the quarter-masters general.

Then, as in modern times, all decisions were made in Moscow; not even minor matters could be resolved locally. This led both to wise choices and disastrous ones.

After the Peace of Westphalia in 1648, more mercenaries made their way east. Some officers brought entire companies with them – Protestants came in 1661 from Germany, Denmark, England and Scotland, a logical choice for the tsar, considering the Orthodox Church's hostility towards Roman Catholics. These officers were occasionally less competent than they claimed to be – some forged papers, some of their military experience was imaginary, and some were merely escaping failures in life or criminal prosecution. Their pay was very generous, but some, not knowing Russian, did not realise that they were signing contracts for lifetime service! Few found it as easy to leave Russia as it was to enter. Those who converted to Orthodoxy and married Russian wives received additional pay.

Most western officers found it difficult to adjust to their new circumstances. Even in western armies discipline was strict, and failure to obey orders instantly was punished by death – often instantly. But all were struck by the brutality in the Russian army. This rested on an assumption that words have no power to inspire, and that leading by example is impossible; only a beating has the perverse effect of per-suading wives, girlfriends, peasants and soldiers that they were truly loved. Or so observed Casanova on his visit to Russia in 1764–5. Beatings and brandy together worked even better.

Thanks to these officers, whatever their skills might have been, the Russian army was both modernised (somewhat) and expanded (greatly). By 1681 there were 80,000 under arms. The numbers would have been even larger, Richard Hellie argues, if the officers accustomed to the bloodletting of the Thirty Years War had not led their men into similar massacres. While it might be argued that the Poles and Tatars had some say in the choice of whether to offer battle or not, and how desperately these battles were contested, there is no question that the Russian army suffered more defeats than it celebrated victories. However, since the tsar could replace his losses by conscripting more unhappy men into service than his enemies could, and could better afford to equip his armies and to hire mercenaries, the setbacks were only temporary. When the tax burden sparked peasant revolts, nobles resented their loss of authority, or Roman Catholic and Uniate* subjects objected to Russian Orthodox intolerance, the tsars used their new army to suppress every violent expression of the popular will.

---

* The Uniates kept the Orthodox rite but recognised the pope as the head of the Church.

The seemingly confusing wars of this era can be reduced to one principle: the tsars were determined to protect their territories. This could be done only by defeating the Tatars to the south, and the Tatars could be crushed only by employing the latest in military technology, tactics and strategy. Those could be provided only by hiring western experts – mercenaries. Especially mercenary officers. As a result, young Peter the Great was able to meet foreign officers. He came to the throne at the age of ten, but his elder sister, Sophia, made every decision. Bored, he would wander over to the foreigners' settlement just outside Moscow. There he made the acquaintance of men who were friendly, adventurous and well-informed. They taught the young tsar how to drink (not that Russians needed much instruction in that), introduced him to exciting women, and explained western weaponry and military practices. Russia was a strong country, he knew, but also weak. He saw in the ideas of the foreign officers the means of making Russia into a great empire.

Chapter 4

The Celtic Periphery of Europe
The Wild Geese

Scots and Irish who went into exile after English Protestants conquered their homelands became known as the 'Wild Geese'. More narrowly the term refers only to those Stuart loyalists (Protestant and Catholic) who fought on the losing side of the 'Glorious Revolution' of 1688. The following year James II (1633–1701) landed in Ireland and rallied Irish Catholics to his cause.

That conflict had begun when the English Whigs, disgusted with James's pro-Catholic policies, invited his eldest daughter, Mary (1689–94) and her husband, Prince William of Orange (1689–1702), from Holland, to become king and queen. James fled to France, then after the battle of the Boyne in 1690, returned there for good.* According to the Treaty of Limerick (1691), those Irish who swore allegiance to King William could keep their lands; those who refused the oath could leave the country safely. Many went overseas to enlist in the armies of France, believing that Louis XIV would soon place James Stuart back on his throne and that their sacrifices would be well rewarded.†

Some went to Spain, but others formed an Irish brigade that served in the French army; over the next century these men were joined by recruits from Ireland and the exile community. Their hopes of returning home dimmed, but not their anger or their courage.

These were not what we think of as typical mercenaries, though there were individuals who were primarily seeking adventure and booty. Most only wanted to fight England. In the course of time some joined armies as diverse as Protestant Sweden and Orthodox Russia. Others went to Austria, where exiles had actually been serving for many years. They also

---

* Baxter notes the awkwardness of James's position. He had not fought earlier, when he had a good chance of winning. In 1690, when the likely results of victory would be an independent Ireland and an England dominated by France, he did no better. In short, anyone loyal to the Jacobite cause, i.e., to James Stuart, was likely to be disappointed.

† Stay-at-home Jacobites referred to James as 'the king across the waters'.

took employment in Poland and the Holy Roman Empire.

Such diverse careers cannot be surveyed in a short narrative. The best we can do is look at a few of the most prominent exiles. And to remind ourselves *that these were far from the first exiles* from Ireland and Scotland.

William Stanley

Irish exile William Stanley (1548–1630) served under the notorious Duke of Alva in the Low Countries from 1567–70; despite the Spanish ability to draw on the wealth of the Americas, their mercenary armies were literally bogged down when the Dutch flooded their fields, surrounding their cities with shallow water. It was not a situation that offered much advantage to Stanley, who yearned to return home.

In 1570, having persuaded Queen Elizabeth that he was no longer committed to the Catholic cause, he went to England and was interviewed by the queen who sent him to Ireland to serve in the occupation forces. Undoubtedly, Stanley believed that he could be fairer and more just to his countrymen than any Englishman; and who knew what bigot might hold that post if he declined it? His actions ran contrary to a papal degree of that year that no loyal Catholic could serve Queen Elizabeth.

There were a series of rebellions in Ireland in the decade that followed, each ending with more confiscations of rebel lands, which, of course, provoked more rebellions. In 1579 Stanley was named captain and knight, then sent in pursuit of Gerald Fitzgerald, the fifteenth earl of Desmond, who had established a base in Limerick. The following year he recruited more troops in England, so that by 1583 he was able to suppress rebellions over wide stretches of Ireland, including in 1584 a Protestant uprising in Ulster. By this time he was an English hero and a royal favourite.

In 1585 the queen, wanting to assist the Dutch against the Catholic army operating out of the Spanish Netherlands, commissioned him to raise a regiment in Ireland to serve in the Low Countries; with 1,400 men, many of them followers of the earl of Desmond, he joined the army led by the queen's favourite, Robert Dudley. Already Stanley may have been contacted by Spanish agents and Jesuits who were eager to see Elizabeth removed from the throne by either assassination or force (God was not providing much assistance in removing her quietly). After the assassination plots failed, Stanley remained on the Continent, impatiently waiting for the next conspiracy – surely one had to be successful. When the king of Spain began building a great Armada to ferry his army from the Low Countries to England, Stanley's hopes revived.

To mask his true intentions, Stanley continued to fight valiantly for the queen, his men even distinguishing themselves in the capture of the strategic fort at Deventer. Not surprisingly, he was named governor and his Irish regiment was assigned garrison duty there. Immediately he made contact with the enemy, and in January 1587 delivered the post to the Spanish. Since other English officers joined in this conspiracy, the Dutch defensive lines were seriously imperilled.

This came as a shock to the queen and most Englishmen – in fact, the queen had been considering rewarding him handsomely. But Stanley had a greater prize in mind – leading the Spanish invasion and restoring Catholic rule. This would, of course, lead to Irish self-government; or at least to an end of Protestant oppression.

With the failure of the Armada, Stanley was stranded in the Low Countries. Though he often journeyed to Spain in efforts to persuade the king and royal council to raise another great fleet, eventually his passion exhausted his listeners – there was little or no chance of overthrowing Elizabeth. His unit was disbanded in 1600, and after Elizabeth's death in 1603 he again asked permission to return home. James I cautiously said no.* Stanley died in obscurity in 1630, too elderly to support the Catholic cause during the Thirty Years War.

His example was not forgotten. In 1607 Hugh O'Neill and Rory O'Donnell, Irish lords, left County Donegal in what was called the 'flight of the earls'. They had risen upon hearing of Elizabeth Tudor's death, but their effort was doomed when the English accepted James VI of Scotland as their king. James settled Scots on the confiscated lands in Ulster.†

The English Civil War

There were many Irish volunteers for the Spanish army in the Thirty Years War.‡ Most were stationed in the Low Countries, but some returned to Ireland in 1641, when the English Civil War seemed to provide another opportunity to win Irish independence. The roots of that bloody conflict lay in the efforts of Charles I (1600–49) to widen the range of royal authority after 1625. The king, having effectively overridden Puritan resistance in England, believed he could do the same in Ireland. However,

---

* James I (1566–1625) had been James VI of Scotland. His mother, Mary, Queen of Scots, had died as a loyal Catholic with a claim to the throne as good as Elizabeth's – and, in Catholic eyes, better.

† Tanner compares Ulster to the contemporaneous colonies in North America, none of which were guaranteed to succeed. Ulster, in fact, almost went under in 1641, when bloody wars began, the very facts of which cannot be agreed upon by Catholic and Protestant historians. Black, *European Warfare, 1494-1660*, emphasises the Irish lack of weapons, supplies and discipline.

‡ Strandling has much on this.

the Irish Catholics, having less to lose than the Puritans, rose in rebellion, slew about a third of the Protestant population in Ulster (perhaps 12,000 victims), and drove many more to seek refuge in strongholds such as Londonderry and Dublin. Charles sent the Earl of Strafford, no stranger to harsh methods, who quickly restored order of a sort.

Charles, whose incompetence frustrated even his most loyal followers, then attempted to force the Scots to use the Book of Common Prayer; that is, to follow the form of service prescribed by the Church of England. When rebellion followed, Charles ordered Strafford to raise another army, but for that he needed additional revenues. Calling Parliament into session, the king quickly found himself in conflict with the Puritan majority. Soon Strafford lost his head, literally, after which the crown's position in Ireland slipped – the army was unpaid, no reinforcements were sent, little encouragement given, and Ulster Presbyterians were as unhappy as the Catholics. The situation in Scotland was no better. Then Charles's foolish insistence that royal prerogatives trumped Parliament's, especially regarding control of the budget and foreign policy, led to Civil War. He lost. In 1649 Charles was led on to a special scaffold in Whitehall and beheaded. Out of this came a nursery rhyme based on his nickname:

Humpty Dumpty sat on a wall.
Humpty Dumpty had a great fall.
All the king's horses and all the king's men
Couldn't put Humpty together again!

While there are alternative explanations, the reference to the king's head and body are still the most satisfactory. Particularly if you know the name of the king's horse.

There was considerable international manoeuvring over Ireland's status, but with so many people pulling in different directions, Irish policy resembled another Humpty Dumpty. A decade later, when Cromwell led his battle-hardened Ironsides to Ireland, the result was almost foreordained – disciplined troops led by a talented general routed the quarrelling rabble. Irish courage could not make up for the lack of unity; as many as 34,000 patriots went into exile. Their lands went to English settlers, many Cromwell's veterans.

Some of those who entered Spanish service rose to positions of high command, and a few were posted to administrative and commercial posts in Mexico and South America. Several units were long designated as Irish, but in later years only the officers were Irish; the men were predominantly Spanish.

Many Catholic Scots followed the Irish exiles to Europe, and Protestant Scots, too. Three Scots became Swedish field marshals –

Alexander Leslie, who rose to become governor of Livonia, Patrick Ruthven, who was governor of Ulm, and Robert Douglas. Four became generals – James, Marquis of Hamilton, James Spence, George, earl of Crawford-Lindsay, and Andrew Rutherford. One became a lieutenant general – Alexander Forbes. Nine became major generals; forty-two became colonels; and many served as captains.

Patrick Sarsfield

Patrick Sarsfield (c. 1660–93) was an Irish rebel by inheritance – his maternal grandfather, Roy O'Moore, had organised the uprising of 1641. His prominent role in patriotic mythology came later, during the Restoration which brought Charles II (1630–85) to the throne in 1660. The Stuart king gave Irish Catholics reason to believe that they would be given important roles in local governance, and the Sarsfield family came out of the settlement well. In 1678, when Patrick's family purchased him a position in Donegal's Regiment of Foot, he joined an important pro-Catholic officer clique that was viewed with suspicion by Protestants who looked back longingly to the days of Cromwell. Not surprisingly, he served willingly in the forces Charles sent to assist his French benefactor, Louis XIV, in his German wars.

Parliamentary Protestants, who were now being called Whigs, were uncomfortable with the French advance to the Rhine (a similar provocation caused a later generation of Germans to respond enthusiastically to the martial hymn *Die Wacht am Rhein*) because it seemed to benefit only France and the Catholic cause. However, the Whigs did not want to oppose royal wishes, because that might lead to a political crisis with the new party gathering around the king – the Tories – or even provoke a new civil war. Though the Whigs suspected that the French king was secretly supplying Charles II with funds that Parliament refused to grant, proof came only years later. And, because the war got Tory officers out of the country, the Whigs took what comfort they could from that.

Patrick Sarsfield returned home after King Charles's death in 1685. He, and everyone else, understood that there would soon be a confrontation between Parliament and the new king, James II (1633–1701), who was openly Catholic and authoritarian. James wanted trustworthy officers nearby, a move that proved wise when Charles's illegitimate son, the duke of Monmouth, staged a march on London. Sarsfield's troops helped quell the uprising, then supervised the duke's execution. Sarsfield's reward was a promotion. As a colonel, Sarsfield was in a position to advance royal plans to replace Protestants with Catholics in other government offices; Whigs thought it suspicious that he was sent to Ireland as second in command to Richard Talbot, earl of Tryconnell.

In 1688, upon his elder brother's death, Sarsfield inherited the family estate, but he spent little time at home, since the king – on a collision course with Parliament – summoned him to England with his men to resist the impending invasion of the Protestant champion, William of Orange; however, once the Dutch king was in England, most of the army went over to him without fighting. Sarsfield's men put up some resistance, but when King James fled to France, Sarsfield followed. Soon he was back in Ireland with the Jacobite forces led by Richard Talbot; the French general Lauzen brought 6,000 French troops. James II thought less of Sarsfield's judgment than of his courage, but the Irish believed that there was no one equal to him.

The Battle of the Boyne (1 July 1690)

This great encounter of was seen at the time (and later in Irish mythology) as a heroic conflict between Catholicism and Protestantism. However, modern studies have shown that William of Orange's crack unit of Dutch Blue Guards contained many Catholics, while the 'Frenchmen' in the Jacobite ranks were often German Protestants; the pope even gave a papal banner to William's men because he feared the growth of French power more than he hated Protestant kings.

William's second in command was Frederick (Friedrich Hermann, 1616–90), duke of Schomberg, an aged professional soldier who had been a French marshal until 1685, when Louis XIV ordered all Protestants to leave the country. But that was late in Schomberg's career – Schomberg had been born in the Palatinate and trained in Holland; he subsequently served in Swedish forces in 1634, then, a year later, entered the service of Sweden's strongest ally – France; when a truce was signed, he retired to his family estate on the Rhine, only to return to Dutch service from 1639 to 1650. Subsequently, Schomberg served under Marshal Turenne in the long French civil war known as the *Fronde* – a period immortalised by *The Three Muskeeters* – and earned the rank of lieutenant general. Between 1659 and 1665 he was in Portugal, ostensibly as a military advisor for Charles II of England, but actually as a agent of Louis XIV, working to keep Portugal independent from France's main enemy of the moment – Spain. He returned to France laden with Portuguese honours, titles and incomes.

In 1673 Charles II asked him to take command of the royal army, but the officers were so mistrustful of French influence that the king had to withdraw the offer. Subsequently, Schomberg led the French invasion of Spain and in 1675 was made marshal, the highest honour Louis XIV had to bestow on capable and trustworthy officers.

After Louis revoked the Edict of Nantes in 1685, withdrawing the few remaining religious rights from French Protestants (Huguenots), Schomberg went to Brandenburg, along with thousands of other Frenchmen. Three years later William of Orange asked him to assist in the invasion of England, then the war in Ulster. Ireland was not a lucky assignment for an aged man. The duke of Schomberg discovered – according to Fortescue – that the 'boys' were unruly, the officers incompetent, the equipment either non-existent or impossible; only one man in four knew how to fire his weapon; and basic hygiene was ignored. Of the 10,000 men originally in his army, two-thirds died of disease. Fortunately for Schomberg, the Irish were no better off. When William arrived with Dutch and Danish reinforcements, the Irish could only fall back towards Dublin, fighting a series of rear-guard actions.*

Schomberg was too ill to lead his men when William ordered his army to cross the Boyne river and attack the Irish camp. Over a thousand Huguenots, exiles from their homeland, waded across the river under the command of Schomberg's son, Meinhardt, the water reaching their shoulders; they struggled through a marsh and up a steep incline, where the fighting became so intense that it appeared the attack would fail. Hearing that a disaster was in the making, the aged Schomberg rose hurriedly from his sickbed, but lacked the time to put on his armour; surrounded by Irish horsemen in the river, he fell in battle. His attack had been so successful, however, that James II diverted many troops to that front. William's Dutch Guards were able to deliver a decisive attack on the other flank, driving the Jacobites into flight.† Voltaire summarised the battle by saying that *the Irish, who fight so well abroad, do poorly at home.*

The battle of the Boyne provided the Continent with a new wave of Wild Geese to populate Continental armies; it also sent James II into what became permanent exile. The Treaty of Limerick allowed all Irish who swore allegiance to King William to keep their properties and rights; a secondary provision allowed the Irish soldiers who did not rejoin royal army to depart unhindered for France – as many as 19,000 left their

---

* Turner describes James as both irresolute and incompetent, not using his French money or distributing arms, unable to understand the feuding Irish factions, and – though blessed with moments of energy and enthusiasm, these did not last; his administration was usually in total disorder. He exchanged 6,000 Irish recruits for 6,000 French soldiers, then gave command to the Comte de Lauzun, whose only merit was a reluctance to point out James's mistakes. The multiple failures at the Boyne were partly due to James, partly to his undisciplined army.

† Black, *European Warfare, 1660–1815*, notes that William III had the heel of his boot shot off, and another hit his pistol. The outcome of the battle reflected the importance William III gave to the war in Ireland, while Louis XIV was concentrating on the Low Countries.

‡ Sarsfield had been given the title of the 1st lord of Lucan. He expired saying that he wished he had shed his last blood for Ireland. His widow married the illegitimate son of James II and Arabella Churchill. Parker, *The Military Revolution*, notes that allowing rebels to go into exile was not a particularly generous act—the 'wastage' of mercenary armies was so great that few would ever return to Ireland.

homeland forever. Their leader, Sarsfield, was mortally wounded at the battle of Landen in August 1693, fighting against William of Orange.‡

The Treaty of Limerick is among the most disappointing of the many failed efforts at peace in this era – it provided a basis for a settlement that, if it had been honoured by all sides, might have restored peace to a disordered land. But treaties are broken more easily than they are made.

Peter Lacy and Thomas Lally

Peter Lacy (1678–1751) was among the hundred or so European officers to whom Peter the Great of Russia offered commissions during his first tour of the west. Lacy joined the tsar at Narva in 1700, witnessing first-hand the disastrous performance of Peter's troops against the smaller army of the Swedish king. A lesser soul or one less desperate might have gone back to Limerick at that point, but the tsar was in such need of experienced and competent officers that he made extravagant payments to any foreigner who would serve him.

Lacy's youth notwithstanding, he was an experienced officer. His first military action came at the age of thirteen. He had fought against the English in 1691, then went to France to enlist in an Irish brigade.

By 1706 he was in command of the Polotsk regiment and entrusted with raising and training three more. In 1708 he led a daring attack on the headquarters of the Swedish king, and was rewarded with the command of an elite regiment of grenadiers. His recommendation at Poltava that the troops not fire until they were right upon the Swedes was widely considered the most important change in Russian tactics, and for the first time a Russian army beat a Swedish one.

Subsequently, Lacy was involved in the invasion of Sweden in 1719 and in 1725 was given command of all the armies and fortresses in the north of Russia. In 1727 he led an army into Courland, expelling the capable French field marshal, Maurice de Saxe, from that duchy. In 1733, in the War of the Polish Succession, he was decorated by the successful candidate for the crown, Augustus III of Saxony (de Saxe's half-brother), with the Order of the White Eagle, then named field marshal by the tsarina. Now having command of all imperial armies, he expanded Russia's boundaries in the south in 1737–8, into Finland in 1741.

Unfortunately, when Elizabeth became empress, she embarked on a programme of Russification that soon resulted in most foreign officers (except Lacy) being dismissed. Their departure from St Petersburg was not quiet, but in the midst of popular riots; only Lacy's intervention saved the officers and perhaps the capital itself from great harm.

One of Lacy's protégés was a Protestant Scot, James Francis Edward Keith, who had been a colonel in the Spanish army, but, being a

Protestant, he knew there were not only limits to his career, but that many were sceptical of his loyalties. In 1729 he went to Russia, where Lacy advanced him quickly to colonel of the Guards' regiment. He became lieutenant general during the War of the Polish Succession and distinguished himself in the Turkish war of 1737.*

Peter Lacy retired after one more successful campaign against the Swedes, living quietly on his estates near Riga. His family prospered. He sent his youngest son, Franz (1725–1801) to Austria in 1737, to learn the arts of command from Maximilian Browne; in 1740 his daughter Helene married another immigrant from Limerick, George Browne, a cousin of the Austrian general. This George Browne ultimately rose to the rank of field marshal in Russian service. Franz became the Austrian minister of war.

Another son, Maurice Lacy (1740–1820), became field marshal in Russia before also entering Austrian service.

Thomas Lally (1702–66) was born in France to Gerard Lally. When he was seven, his father presented him with a captain's uniform, a commission! Everyone assumed that it was an honorary award, but Thomas immediately accompanied the army to a siege, where he did not flinch at the sight of corpses. In 1714, after serving at the siege of Barcelona, he began his university studies. He was later offered a proper commission, but his father insisted that he wait until he was ready for the responsibilities. In 1720, at age eighteen, he became the captain of one of the Irish regiments, then four years later became its major. In the War of the Polish Succession his regiment fought in Germany for two years.

In 1737 Thomas Lally made an 'educational' tour of Scotland (actually scouting the potential for a Stuart uprising) and then of Russia, escorted by Peter Lacy, who must have been hoping to attract him to the imperial service. In 1741 he assumed command of an Irish regiment which fought

---

* George Keith (1693–1778, the 10th and last Marischal of Scotland) and James (1696–1757) had resigned from Queen Anne's army when George I became king, then participated in the failed Stuart uprising of 1715. After a period in France, George went first to Spain, then in 1745, after a short stay in Vienna, to Berlin; asked to lead the Jacobite forces in the Scottish uprisings of 1745, he refused, saying it was hopeless. In 1751 Frederick appointed him ambassador to France, but withdrew it later to appease the English crown; later, however, Frederick's intersession allowed him to return to the family estates in Scotland, but in 1764 Frederick recalled him to Potsdam, where he lived in a royal villa for the rest of his life. He was a close friend of Voltaire and an acquaintance of Rousseau – a wise distinction that shows his intelligence and discernment. James's life was even more adventurous, having served in the French, Spanish and Russian armies; he made a Swedish prisoner his mistress, then had several children by her; he was so badly wounded in 1737 fighting the Turks that his brother took him to France for medical attention. The two brothers then visited England, partly as a representative of the empress, partly to make their peace with the king. James returned to Russia, George to Spain. Frederick made James a Prussian field marshal in 1747, then governor of Berlin.

in Flanders the next two years. In October 1744, when all the Irish brigades were combined into one regiment, Thomas Lally became its colonel.

Ulysses Von Browne

Ulysses Freiherr von Browne (1659–1731) was among the most successful Irish exiles. His family could trace its origins to the Norman Conquest, and many of his forbearers had died in royal service; Ulysses's father had drowned in a shipwreck while on an expedition against Spain. When James II called upon Catholic Irishmen to assist him in bringing Protestant rebels in line, Ulysses and six of his seven younger brothers offered their services to the Stuart monarch – his brother George (1657–1729) was already in James's army. However, William of Orange struck before the new royal army could be organised – as the English clamorously welcomed the Dutch king and his Stuart wife, Ulysses Brown was among the loyalists who followed James to France.

It is assumed that Ulysses Browne served in one of the three Irish brigades in the French army. If so, he would have participated in some of the terrible massacres of French Protestants of the following years and in battles against William of Orange. When peace came in 1697, these units were disbanded as an economy measure, the officers and soldiers scattering, some settling down in French villages and cities, some becoming criminals, and others seeking employment in other mercenary armies.

Ulysses Browne went to Austria, where George had commanded the Irish brigade of 1,800 men that James II had sent to the emperor in 1689; although that unit, the Sapieha regiment, had been disbanded in 1693, George had remained in Austrian employ. Ulysses entered the service of Emperor Charles VI about 1700, and in 1716 was named a count (*Reichsgraf*) of the Holy Roman Empire; *Freiherr*, a title often insinuated into his name, translates roughly as nobleman, but in Germany had historical roots in the free nobles who had no lord except the emperor.

He married Annabella Fitzgerald in January 1699 and had one son, Maximilian, born in Basel in 1705; at age five or thereabouts he sent Max to Limerick for an Irish education (enrolling him, for lack of alternatives, in a Protestant school), where he remained until about ten. Ulysses Browne was active in the wars against Louis XIV and was acquainted with Marlborough, who hoped that he could lure some of Louis's Irish soldiers over to imperial service. It was on Marlborough's recommendation that in 1705 Ulysses was entrusted with the command of a cavalry regiment that had been originally in Prussian service. Afterwards Ulysses commanded garrisons in Germany and travelled to Britain in 1710 and 1711 – Austria and England had been allies, a connection that overcame any lingering doubts about his loyalties; When the war ended in 1713, he retired from the army, being kept on the books as a major general in case a mobilisation was declared; he was promoted to general in 1723, but it was an honour of only symbolic importance.

Ulysses Browne's inability to rise higher in rank illustrates how the practice of conferring command upon titled nincompoops assured that men like him, who possessed little more than talent, would be passed over. Late in life Ulysses made efforts to reconstruct an extensive genealogy, but it was too late to impress the Habsburg courtiers, who, in any case, looked down their long noses on outsiders – hiring foreigners for the difficult tasks of brigade and regimental command, where one might easily be shot, was good policy, but high command was reserved for blue blood. Maria Theresa's blind trust in her genial but mediocre cousin, Charles Alexander of Lorraine (1712–80, who was both her husband's brother and the future husband of her sister) being an obvious and long-lived example. Thus it was that the caretaker of the Browne family enterprise had always been, not Ulysses, but his brother George.

Thanks to George's prior service in the imperial army, he had sufficient seniority to qualify for service in the War of the Spanish Succession – the European effort that united Catholics and Protestants against Louis XIV's attempt to turn Spain from a perennial enemy to an ally, perhaps even to combine the two kingdoms. George Browne was given his first regimental command in 1705, fought in Italy and Catalonia until 1711, and in 1715 was given command of an Austrian infantry regiment.

Undoubtedly, his advancement owed much to a dual system of command. There was first the titular commander, who was usually a prominent noble who lived in dread of garrison duty and flying bullets; second, a professional officers with an almost identical title of colonel who did the work and ran the risks. George Browne was of the second variety.

In 1717 George wrote a lavishly illustrated and widely disseminated book of regulations, describing in detail not only the drills that soldiers had to master, but also the code of behaviour expected of officers. He stressed religious observations – requiring each soldier to go to confession at least three times a year! Such devotion won him great praise at court. Sermons, though regular, were short and simple. He designed a more comfortable uniform, relaxed the standards of physical preparedness, and set limits to the beatings officers could inflict. In short, he believed that soldiers were more than human fodder to be fed into the maw of the military machine.

Duffy uses the book of regulations to describe vividly life (and death) in an infantry regiment: most of the soldiers were musketeers, who would be drawn up in two lines opposite the enemy; on either flank were the grenadiers, who were armed with small bombs for hurling into forts but were better known for being tall and sturdy, and perhaps also, in order to live up to their appointed reputation, the most courageous and daring. The formation would advance against the enemy, the pace set by the fifes and drums, the colonel riding in front.

George Browne noted that few units could stand against a regiment which advanced within fifteen paces, even with muskets shouldered – the effect of a coordinated volley being too horrible to contemplate, most men threw themselves on the ground or fled. A bayonet charge against troops disorganised by a volley was seldom repulsed.

He later served under Prince Eugene in the Turkish campaigns of 1716–18. Luckily for him, he was assigned to defend the camp against the Turkish relief army rather than to lead the storm of Belgrade. Luckily for the Austrian empire, George Browne invited his nephew, Maximilian, to serve under him, to learn first-hand the hard arts of war. Maximilian became one of Austria's finest generals.

In early 1716, George and Ulysses had received imperial patents of nobility, accompanied by the grant of an estate in eastern Bohemia. Ironically, this estate had been confiscated by the Habsburgs from Protestants who now found themselves in the same situation as the Irish – serving in foreign armies in order to maintain their noble status.

In the autumn of 1718 George Browne led his regiment to Italy, to garrison duty in Lombardy – a region claimed by the Bourbon king of Spain. The progress of the unit through friendly lands was marked by howls of outrage from the peasants and villagers – the regiment's reputation for drunken and brutal behaviour never vanished, and too often the Lombards' complaints were directed at the Irish officers that George Browne had recruited into the regiment. Also, absenteeism was a problem that never seemed to go away. He died in Italy in 1729, leaving his fortune to his nephew, Maximilian, with instructions to care for his parents. Maximilian was helped along greatly by his wife's relatives at the Habsburg court.

A distant relative, George Browne (1698–1792), served in the Russian army, married a daughter of Peter Lacy, then switched to Austrian employ; in 1779 this George Browne, too, was made a *Reichsgraf*.

Although several Austrian regiments bore the name of Irish colonels, it is surprising that more Irish patriots did not migrate there. The emperor was very open to hiring foreign officers – far fewer than half his generals in the 1737–9 war against the Ottoman Empire were Austrians. The emperor was more loyal to the pope than the French king. Moreover, Vienna was an exciting multinational city, a cosmopolitan centre of the arts which attracted great artists and greater musicians; and even officers who failed to attain high rank could expect a pension sufficient for an honourable retirement. Last, anyone serving under Eugene of Savoy could take pride in the repeated triumphs of Habsburg arms. For individuals accustomed to defeat, the thrill of victory must have been especially sweet.

Chapter 5

Disaster in the Heart of Europe
The Thirty Years War

This was the war that should not have happened, the war that got out of hand, the war in which European mercenaries would burn countless hamlets, villages and towns in Germany, the Low Countries, the Czech lands and Poland; in some areas up to 30 per cent of the population would disappear between 1618 and 1648 – dead or fled.*

The tinder for this war had long been there – internal confusion in the Ottoman empire had temporarily removed that state as a common enemy, gold and silver from the Americas had strengthened the Habsburgs in Spain and Austria significantly and fostered new banking systems, while commercial growth had encouraged Protestant self-confidence – Protestantism being a common characteristic of the middle classes and northern gentry; there was also the Habsburg rivalry with the Bourbons over border territories and claims to Italian lands. Further, there were ambitious monarchs of middling authority and great imagination, religious enthusiasm and justified suspicion of opponents, and crises that often follow the deaths of important rulers.† Johannes Keppler, the court astronomer, observed three comets in 1618 – an event that contemporaries believed to be a warning of impending troubles.‡

David Maland calls the fragile peace 'the twelve years' truce' – but the

---

* Geoffrey Parker's analysis in *The Thirty Years War* suggests a population decline in the Holy Roman Empire of 15 to 20 per cent, with great variation from the lightly affected north to the southern battlegrounds. Disease and famine often followed in the path of marauding armies.

† Parker notes how the Habsburgs (including Matthias) were suppressing Protestants in their lands. Those, together with the generally increased intolerance by both sides, made Protestants fearful. Catholics, for their part, believed there was a general Protestant plot against their religion. As war seemed ever more likely, Protestant and Catholic princes constructed larger and more elaborate fortresses and built impressive walls around their cities.

‡ Keppler's most important activity was to prepare horoscopes, including the later famous one of Wallenstein, predicting his death.

flashpoint was expected to be in the Low Countries. It was, however, in the Czech lands, following the passing of Matthias, king of Bohemia and Holy Roman emperor. Between his election as Holy Roman emperor in 1612 and his death in 1619, Matthias had moved between Prague and Graz and other secure locations; but he was childless, and the imperial crown was expected to go to his nephew, Ferdinand II (1578–1637), who had had actually been elected king of Bohemia in 1617 to forestall opposition. However, Ferdinand's Counter-Reformation zeal had frightened the Czechs, who prided themselves on having had the first Reformation of the Church – the Hussite rising a century before Luther. The Council of Basel had guaranteed the Czechs the right to communion in both bread and wine, and to a married clergy, but nobody expected Ferdinand or his Jesuit advisors to honour the promises of a long-deceased pope and emperor – lacking the talent to persuade or cajole, he instinctively used raw power.

Ferdinand's rooting out of Protestants from Austria, Styria and Slovenia caused the Czechs to depart from custom and law.* Rather than accepting the Habsburg heir as their king, they first threw two of his officials from a high window of the Hradčany palace (the second Defenestration of Prague, which actually – perhaps miraculously – did not kill them), then offered the Bohemian crown to the nearby Calvinist elector of the Palatinate, Frederick V (Friedrich, 1596–1632). With Frederick then holding two of the nine votes necessary to win the imperial election, and the Protestant Saxon and Brandenburg electors likely to support him (the elector of Brandenburg also being his brother-in-law, and the Saxon elector had wisely turned down the crown himself), Frederick felt confident that he could prevent Ferdinand from being elected. He was mistaken.†

Ferdinand understood the limitations of his talents. But he had the backing of the Spanish Habsburgs who provided him with money and permission to raise mercenaries from their Italian lands. He gave command of these troops to Count Johan Tserclaes Tilly (1559–1632), who marched into Bohemia in 1620 at the head of the army of the Catholic League (mainly Bavarians) and routed the Bohemians' ragtag mercenary army at the battle of White Mountain (*Bílá Hora*), not far from the Hradčany castle and the modern airport. For the most part, it was a confused combat between the untrained and the untrainable,

---

* Among the Protestants evicted was Johannes Keppler.
† Maland remarks on the Protestant combination of jubilation and ambition, fuelled partly by Rosicrucian pamphlets predicting the downfall of the Antichrist in 1620. This should remind us not to think of anyone in this period as holding modern secular values. As for contemporaries' abilities to forecast elections, even Frederick's representative somehow voted for Ferdinand, who won unanimously. The elector of Saxony was rewarded by an imperial grant of lands in neighbouring Silesia – an important step toward closer involvement in Poland.

between the frightened and the panicked, but it meant the complete downfall of the Protestant cause in Bohemia. Frederick fled, retaining only the derisive title of 'Winter King', a reference to his short reign.

Thus began what David Maland called 'the seven fat years of the Habsburgs'. So complete was Tilly's victory that Ferdinand saw an opportunity, not merely to restore the power and prestige of the house of Habsburg, but to reverse the entire Protestant Reformation, perhaps to eliminate its every vestige. He began with a purge of Protestant nobles in Bohemia, executing twenty-seven and confiscating the estates of all those who fled into exile; most of these were minor nobles, the high nobility having prudently or devoutly converted back to Catholicism before the crisis began.*

Tilly's Army

Tilly had been born to noble parents in the Spanish Netherlands, educated in a Jesuit school in Cologne, and trained in the wars against Holland, the most terrible of all the wars of religion. In 1600 he went to Hungary to serve in the imperial army, earning universal respect and ever greater responsibilities. In 1610 he entered the employ of Maximilian of Bavaria (1597–1651), commanding the armies of the new League of Catholic States. His Bavarian army, though small, was the first to be paid from state revenues rather than subsisting from plunder.

Inflation, however, soon undermined this plan – disrupting trade and reducing agricultural production. As prices shot up, rulers reduced the silver content in coins – driving good coins out of circulation. Peasants and citizens, suspecting the worst, refused to accept the new money, as did the tax collectors. Since credit became unobtainable, businesses went bankrupt. Military supplies became more expensive, and Tilly, like everyone else, had to accept contributions in kind instead of hard cash.†

Communities that produced weapons of war – like Cologne (near the iron and coal fields of the Ruhr), Aachen and, most of all, Solingen (still a well-known name for fine knives and razor blades) – prospered, selling to all sides with great profits.

The musket replaced the arquebus; it became quickly lighter, so that a support fork was no long necessary, and paper cartridges were

---

* Ingrao suggests that perhaps 150,000 Bohemians emigrated, together with 40,000 Austrians. Protestant ministers and teachers were fired, their buildings destroyed, their books burned, and their places taken by members of Catholic religious orders, most notably Jesuits. German was made equal to Czech, and the peasant subjected to a 'second serfdom'.
† Parker, *The Military Revolution*, describes the intense economic pressure that each ruler was under, with military expenses taking up to 90 per cent of income. Thus, the 'military revolution' led directly to major changes in state management.

introduced. Efforts were made to standardise calibres of artillery and to control the quality of powder, but since each gun had to cool before the next shot was fired, continual fire was impossible. Also, artillery required an immense wagon train.*

Tilly's army was the best there was, but that was because the standard was still very low and because Tilly was a competent and experienced commander.

The Palatinate War

Frederick fled from place to place, seeking aid in Brandenburg, Denmark and Holland, but not finding anybody foolish enough to challenge the emperor; those rulers saw Frederick as incompetent, but also holding dangerously radical religious views – Lutherans considered Calvinists lacking in respect for rank and tradition. Meanwhile Ferdinand consolidated power in Bohemia, then invaded the Palatinate – sending Tilly at the closest of the elector's scattered lands, the Upper Palatinate, arranging for another army in the Spanish Netherlands to invade the Lower Palatinate on the Rhine.†

Frederick's best hope had been a coalition led by his father-in-law, James I of England, but James could offer only a few troops. Frederick, who could have made peace by renouncing his claims to Bohemia, re-fused to do so, and was consequently declared an outlaw by the emperor; not long afterwards the Protestant Union, which had promised to defend the Palatinate, bowed to imperial pressure and dissolved itself. The most that Frederick's general, Mansfeldt, could do was delay – he parlayed with Tilly, seeming to suggest that he might put his army under his command – until he finally retreated into Alsace, then a Habsburg territory, where his men could pass the winter eating food that would otherwise support the enemy. By spring, having created an unemployment crisis there by ravaging the countryside, he was able to enlist enough men to bring his force up to 22,000.‡

---

* Roberts, *Gustavus Adolphus*, notes that rust was such a problem for iron guns that large ones could only be made of bronze; see Guthrie, *Battles of the Thirty Years War*, for the many types of firearms. Parker, *The Military Revolution*, has a long chapter on supplying war.

† Parker, *The Thirty Years War*, emphasises the unpredictability of the times by describing the near involvement of a new crusading order organised by the duke of Nevers and Austrian field marshal Michael Adolf von Altheim, which would first restore Catholicism in Sweden, then attack the Turks. Instead of an army, however, the order donated substantial sums to the emperor's cause. France was strongly supporting the emperor at this time, and was ready to attack the new Spanish possessions in Alsace – which had been exchanged for the use of Spanish troops.

‡ Ernst, count of Mansfeldt (Mansfield, 1580–1626) was Frederick's military adviser – a good choice, since, as one contemporary commented, Frederick had never seen a battle or a

A second Protestant army was raised by Georg von Baden-Durlach (1573–1638), a Calvinist prince on the Upper Rhine who read Ferdinand's pronouncements as condemnations of every kind of Protestant beliefs; moreover, he saw that Catholics were filing lawsuits in the imperial courts for the return of properties secularised by the Peace of Augsburg (1555), a process that would threaten his own lands. He named his son regent, then raised 11,000 men and marched off to war.

A third army was led by the Winter King's son-in-law, Duke Christian of Braunschweig-Wolfenbüttel (1596–1626). His land, later known as Hanover (Hannover in German, or Lower Saxony) contained more moor and woods than good farms, but it was large and comparatively prosperous. He raised 10,000 mercenaries from the Low-German language states, then marched into Westphalia, where he looted Catholic churches and extorted money from prosperous cities. He was considered unstable, if not insane, a curious mixture of idealist and criminal.

The Protestants had made a brave start, but they failed to unite into a single army, whereas Tilly managed to join the Spanish forces in May 1622, then routed Georg's troops in the Palatinate. In June he caught Christian trying to cross the Main river, and although the victory was not total, Frederick told his armies to disband and go home.

The Protestant mercenaries, however, were not about to give up their jobs or put their necks in a Catholic halter. Led by Christian and Mansfeldt, they made their way to Holland, arriving just in time to break the Spanish siege of Bergen-Op-Zoom. The Dutch immediately offered them work.

The Catholic forces, meanwhile, took Heidelberg and Mannheim, cleaning up all but the last pockets of Protestant resistance in the south. English volunteers were too few to save Heidelberg, and the Protestant party would perhaps have collapsed altogether if Ferdinand had not decided in 1623 to award the Palatinate to another Catholic prince, Maximilian of Bavaria. This upset even the Catholic lords, who saw it as a precedent that could be used against them.

Christian returned to Lower Saxony to raise another army, planning to join Mansfeldt in Holland, but Tilly got in between the two forces and routed Christian's half-trained army. At that Mansfeld lost hope – without money he had no hope of beating Tilly; he disbanded his army, advising his men to go to Holland.

---

corpse – and Spanish troops were on their way from the Low Countries. Parker says that Mansfeldt was among the first of the 1,500 military enterprisers who raised troops during this war, all with commissions from a landed lord or city, or as subcontractors for recognised warlords. He also served as a model for upward striving men, having risen from an obscure status as the illegitimate son of an obscure Habsburg governor of Luxemburg, having served in the imperial army in Hungary only to fall out of favour, then to find employment with the duke of Savoy, who sent him with 2,000 troops to assist Frederick in hopes that the Habsburg ambitions might be blunted. A Roman Catholic, he usually fought for Protestant princes.

This brought the Catholic army right to the frontiers of Denmark, an act that persuaded the Scandinavian monarchs that they, too, were in danger. More importantly, Cardinal Richelieu, the dominant personality in French policy, came to see that the balance of power in all Europe was being tipped – unless righted soon, he would see Habsburg armies invading France.

Denmark Enters the War

King Christian IV (1577–1648) had been profiting from the confusion in the Holy Roman Empire to expand his control over more of northern Germany. He ruled Schleswig-Holstein by hereditary right (his ancestors had been dukes there before they became kings of Denmark); in 1621 he had brought the Hanseatic city of Hamburg into his empire and arranged for his second son to be elected archbishop of Hamburg-Bremen. He was rich, thanks to the tolls levied on ships travelling between the North and Baltic Seas. All this would be lost if Ferdinand managed to consolidate his control of the region and re-impose the Catholic faith.

Cardinal Richelieu, believing that Christian was the only monarch with any chance of standing up to Tilly's army, secretly promised to provide funds for hiring troops; more cash came from England and Holland.* Once Christian made the decision to go to war, in 1624, it did not take long for him to raise an army of 20,000 men.† That was about the maximum size of an effective force at that time – greater numbers would be as much a distraction as an addition. 20,000 men should certainly be sufficient for dealing with Tilly, whose troops were now dispersed as garrisons of occupied towns, especially if he could join with Mansfeld. There was also Brandenburg, whose elector had just acquired title to East Prussia and Cleves, widely separated states, but which promised to make him into one of the most important German lords.

Ferdinand, however, had a surprise waiting – he had authorised an experienced officer, Albrecht von Wallenstein (1583–1634), to raise a second army. Wallenstein had promised the emperor that he could field the

---

* Richelieu (Armand Jean du Plessis, 1585–1643) had to deal with Catholic fanatics (the Dévot) who wanted to enter the war in support of Ferdinand. There had been negotiations with Sweden, but Gustavus Adolphus wanted too much money; instead, the Swedish king attacked Poland in 1626, first in Livonia, then in Royal Prussia (West Prussia). The Spanish countered by promising ships to Poland. King Charles of England authorised his favourite, the duke of Buckingham, to make a raid on Spain in 1625. This venture, like so many of this king's projects, was a failure.

† Kirby notes that the Danish national militia, composed of peasants from crown lands, had only three days of drill each year and no access to weapons for training. Guthrie, *Battles of the Thirty Years War*, rates the army higher. He calls Christian a talented amateur up against Europe's foremost professionals.

largest army yet seen in Germany and do so without using any imperial funds; all he needed was permission to plunder the Protestant lands without imperial interference. Ferdinand happily agreed to the conditions.*

Tilly dealt with Christian's army in 1626, while Wallenstein routed Mansfeld, then devastated Brandenburg and Pomerania. The elector of Brandenburg, a very untalented person, was now persuaded by his advisor Adam zu Schwarzenberg (1583–1641) that he could better defend Pomerania from Sweden by joining the imperial coalition. As Nelson wrote about him, the elector tried to straddle the fence, but 'it turned into a rail and he was ridden out on it'.

The main drawback to Wallenstein's method of warfare was that he could not take strongly held towns and fortresses – his troops were reluctant to serve as garrison troops, long months in which they would not be paid, and the work involved in sieges was arduous, unpleasant and dangerous. Thus it was that he bypassed fortresses such as Magdeburg, which was later besieged by Tilly's more disciplined army.

All Europe watched the progress of Habsburg arms. In England Protestants urged King Charles I to join the fight. Even Venice, an un-doubtedly Catholic country, obtained permission from the Ottoman sultan to raise mercenaries from Bosnia, Albania and the Peloponnese to protect their trade routes over the Alps from Ferdinand's interference.

Wallenstein

Albrecht Wenzel von Wallenstein (1583–1634) was born in Bohemia to wealthy parents who belonged to the Bohemian Brotherhood, an early Protestant sect. He had studied at a Lutheran university, but after transferring to the Jesuit university at Olmütz (Olomouc), he became a Roman Catholic. He served in Ferdinand's forces in suppressing Protestantism in Styria, then in wars against Venice and Bohemia, contributing so much to the imperial victories that Ferdinand awarded him vast estates in northern Bohemia.†

---

* Roberts, *The Swedish Imperial Experience 1560–1718*, quotes Gustavus Adolphus in 1623: *bellum se ipsum alit* – war must pay for itself. Tilly calls the practice of exacting money from communities under the threat of turning mercenaries loose a 'protection racket'. Parker, *The Military Revolution*, describes the practice of *Brandschatzung*, a variation of demanding 'contributions' by which a commander would give citizens a choice of paying a ransom or having their town burned. This was ultimately a self-defeating practice, since armies needed supplies year after year, and destroyed communities could not provide them.
† Asch attributes Wallenstein's ability to raise an army to his experience in the Bohemian coinage syndicate and his connection to a prominent banker; he was an entrepreneur who used his own money in anticipation of great profits later on. By 1629 he had revenues of three million thalers.

Wallenstein's campaigns in Silesia, Transylvania, Mecklenburg, Holstein and Jutland were all successful, but his brutality horrified contemporaries. He increased the size of his mercenary army to 150,000 men, so that he could fight on several fronts at once and intimidate all opposition, but he slowly fell from favour by arguing against imperial involvement in the Spanish war against Holland and opposing more help to the Poles after 1629, when a favourable truce made Sweden abandon many of its recent gains – what were such great armies for, Catholic enthusiasts asked, if not to crush Protestantism everywhere? His inability in 1627 to build a navy strong enough to threaten an invasion of the Danish islands and Sweden worked against him; as did his subordinates' botched siege of Stralsund in 1628, and his own setback there by Danish forces reinforced with Scottish troops led by Colonel Munro.* But even more important, many considered him overly ambitious – especially in his plan to make a princedom for himself in Mecklenburg, a strategic territory that guarded Germany against Denmark and Sweden. Rumours circulated that in private conversations Wallenstein had disparaged Ferdinand's talents and judgment. Thus it happened that, although Wallenstein drove Denmark out of the war in 1629, soon afterwards the emperor asked for his resignation. After all, it seemed as though the war was over. Why keep Wallenstein in power, why allow his army to continue to plunder what would soon be *Catholic* subjects? Moreover, Tilly had taken many of his men to Italy, to crush the few duchies which were still independent. Why could Wallenstein not do the same?

Furthermore, why had Wallenstein sent what remained of Tilly's army back to its bases in the Catholic League, so that his army alone occupied the Protestant states? It was all highly suspicious. Wallenstein, realising that everyone in the Catholic camp was now against him, delivered his resignation without complaining.

There was a hurried reordering of priorities – in October 1630 French representatives to the Reichstag in Regensburg (Ratisbon) proposed a peace settlement that gave the emperor a dominant position in Germany and French allies in Italy a new lease on life. Ferdinand, seeing no point in maintaining an expensive army, reduced its size; and after some arguments about the exercise of command, named Tilly to the post again. The emperor sought desperately to have the electors name his son as successor, a ploy that had worked well for him, but the electors – even the Catholic ones – were determined to regain some of their lost authority. The Holy Roman emperor had overreached.

Wallenstein's victories had been followed by an 'Edict of Restitution',

---

* Parker, *Thirty Years War*, gives Scot casualties as 500 dead and 300 wounded, out of one body of 900 men. But the Scots still considered themselves lucky – after six weeks of combat, they would all have been killed if their position had been taken by assault.

which reclaimed for the Catholic Church all the lands it possessed in 1552; this was a dramatic blow aimed at the Protestant princes and their nobles, one which would cripple all future opposition to the Holy Roman emperor. So sweeping were the implications of the edict that the Swedish King, Gustavus Adolphus, entered the war before the Reichstag adjourned. Perhaps more important, he could not allow a Habsburg fleet on the Baltic; and he took the anagram of his name – Augustus – seriously. He was destined for greatness.*

Tilly moved slowly to counter this threat, partly because of the continuing discussions at Regensburg, partly because the Swedes were operating in Pomerania, far to the northeast and where it was believed that sufficient imperial forces existed to contain him, and partly from overconfidence. Tilly gave command to Heinrich, count zu Pappenheim (1594–1632), his cavalry commander.

Pappenheim was a Bavarian who had fought at the White Mountain, had raised a famous cavalry unit in 1623 (the Pappenheimers, sometimes called the Black Cuirassiers), then took another mercenary force to Italy to assist the Spanish army against the French; he demonstrated his ruthlessness in Austria by suppressing a rebellion, then fought successfully against the Danes. His ambition was to become an important lord in Lower Saxony. He would prove that he deserved such a reward by capturing Magdeburg, the most important city on the middle Elbe.

The Heyday of the Mercenaries

Given that we know that most armies of this period were composed of mercenaries, it is striking how little we know about them. Researchers currently buried in dusty stacks – to use a perhaps outdated metaphor – will soon provide us with more information, but the most important question – motivation – will probably remain an educated guess forever.

Money was one inducement for enlisting in an army, though the pay was rarely much above farm wages. Unemployment was significant, especially once farm jobs were no longer available. Religious motivation was significant at the beginning of the war, but would lose its attraction later; similarly, national identification was important early on, but since all armies replaced losses by recruiting locally, wherever they happened to be, all armies became more international and more alike. The desire for adventure, or to get away from the dullness of life at home, has to be

---

* Roberts, his biographer, emphasises the king's love of life and activity, of simple pleasures and strong religious convictions. Whether joking with his men, dancing with the women of occupied cities, or leading cavalry charges, he was a personality who inspired his men not only to respect, but also to love him. As for the anagram, consider u and v interchangeable.

taken into account. And then there is that XY-chromosome desire to join groups, to participate in 'male' activities such as drinking, smoking and random acts of violence.*

Loot became a problem. Not only were entire districts left so devastated that they could not supply food, but the soldiers became so overburdened by their plunder that marching was difficult; and none wanted to entrust their gains to the doubtful care of their employers or the guards at the camps. The most effective way to make the soldiers mobile again was to encourage them to change bulky items into money. Wagon trains were the next best expedient.

Old soldiers earned double the pay of new recruits and were spared such ignoble duties as digging trenches, but they were always placed in the front rank, often as pikemen, where steadiness was most needed. Their contracts were short – often only six months – and they did not hesitate to change sides; such conditions made training difficult – there was insufficient time to perfect tactics, and the troops resisted the long hours and the discipline.† Lounging about, drinking and smoking, especially during the winter, was the favourite occupation. Sometimes they had to accept their pay in kind – food, most often – but Germans were particularly keen to get cash.

Pay came irregularly once the mustering-in money and the first month's wages were received. Of necessity, the mercenaries usually fought on the promise of future wages, but quite often they simply refused to perform any duties until paid. Since all soldiers wore armour that looked alike and soldiers changed armies without changing their clothes, uniforms were a questionable expense. For soldiers to discern friend from foe, commanders chose some distinctive emblem, such as an armband or a plume in the hat.‡

We know much more about the commanders, many of whom were mercenaries, too. And, therefore, our story must centre upon them and the deeds and misdeeds of their armies.

---

* Parker, *The Thirty Years War*, notes how easily men transferred from one army to another, apparently without criticism, and with few accusations of treason. Lutherans were especially noted for a willingness to serve in Catholic ranks. It became difficult to describe any unit as representing one state; one Bavarian unit in 1644, though containing a majority of Germans, had men from fifteen other nations in its ranks.

† Roberts, *Gustavus Adolphus*, compares the companies to guilds (unions), not only for their hard-nosed negotiations on pay and conditions of service, but for the ceremonies and their touchy sense of honour. New recruits in the Swedish army received two weeks of basic training, then exercised in some field manoeuvres; and his Articles of War were orders, not a negotiated agreement.

‡ Roberts, *op.cit.*, says that uniforms became commoner in order for units to look smart on parade. But the practice of giving regiments uniforms of different colour meant that battlefield confusion would persist long into the future.

The Sack of Magdeburg

All Germany was shocked by the destruction of Magdeburg on 20 May 1631. It may have been foolish for 2,000 men to resist 24,000 besiegers, but the walls had seemed exceptionally strong and one condition for surrender was that everyone, garrison and citizens alike, convert to Catholicism. The defenders had thrown back attacks by the army of the Catholic League in November and April, then resolutely withstood the besiegers until they ran out of gunpowder. Tilly rounded up all the surrounding peasants and forced them to carry brush and dirt to the moat; after cannon fire created a breach in the wall, a series of assaults almost broke into town; two days later Pappenheim's cavalrymen, apparently attacking without orders, rode directly into the city and went on the rampage.

The attackers, after raping the women, young and old, murdered them, then set their homes ablaze. Tilly and Pappenheim gave orders to put out the fires, but were soon concerned only with getting their men out of the town. Only the cathedral and four or five houses escaped the conflagration. There was no discrimination in the massacre – several hundred Catholics who hurried into the streets to greet their liberators were mowed down with the Protestants. Of the 30,000 inhabitants only 5,000 were believed to have survived. Few of those chose to stay in the burned-out city.

Croats and Walloons (French-speaking Belgians) were said to be the worst offenders, but no one made a serious effort to stop the plundering and destruction until it was too late. Tilly was greatly upset, because he had wanted to use Magdeburg as a base for future operations; even if the supplies had been largely consumed, he could have kept his army in the houses and stables. The city was useless for anything now.

The citizens had contributed to their own downfall, having refused to pay or even feed the garrison, but instead charged high prices for every kind of supply. Their over-confidence had extended to an assurance that they had laid in sufficient stores of gunpowder.

Protestant resolve was great stiffened by the atrocity, and for years thereafter, when Catholic soldiers attempted to surrender, they would be offered 'Magdeburg quarter' – i.e., no mercy.

At that same moment the minor contributors to the Catholic League began to demand a share in the spoils of war – it was not right that everything went to the emperor, especially not when Bavarians provided the core of Tilly's army. The elector of Bavaria wanted churches given to his brother, the archbishop of Cologne; and the emperor's Protestant allies began to worry about what lay in store for them.

Gustavus Adolphus

The Swedish king was a military genius, but his talents would have been useless if he had not been able to pay his troops. This money was raised by his chancellor, Axel Oxenstierna (1583–1654), who reformed the administration in Sweden and made a semi-secret alliance with France.* His principal interest had been the war with Poland, but he understood that once Catholicism triumphed in Germany, it would soon give aid to his Polish adversary. In 1620 he had toured Germany in disguise and seen for himself the disarray in the Protestant ranks.

France was governed by Cardinal Richelieu – the king, Louis XIII, was a nonentity, but smart enough to stay out of his minister's way. The minister, in turn, was intelligent enough not to interfere with the royal pleasures. The cardinal may have been Catholic, but he was no prude. Neither was he reluctant to spend Catholic money on Protestant princes – he understood that his first duty was to France, and at this moment France was endangered by Habsburgs, not Protestants.† The Habsburg lands in Spain, Italy, Germany and the Low Countries pinned France against the Atlantic coast, and every informed Frenchman believed that the natural boundaries of the state should be on the Rhine or even further north and east. Nevertheless, Richelieu made it clear to the Swedish king that a Catholic cardinal could not risk his career and perhaps his life by supporting him before the Swedish army demonstrated a capacity to stop the Habsburg war machine.

In addition, the king's announcement that his would be a godly army, Protestant saints without the brutal habits of the imperialists, caused his enemies to smile; they were equally doubtful of the dour piety of his Scottish officers. As for his lightly armed horsemen, especially his Finnish cavalry, military experts disdained their emphasising the sabre more than pistols. While northern Protestant rulers slowly and without enthusiasm chose to support Gustavus Adolphus, southern Protestants bowed to the superior might of the imperial forces.

---

* Roberts, *The Swedish Imperial Experience*, emphasises the importance of subsidies, and of requiring occupied lands to pay the army's expenses. Together they made the army less expensive in war, when it was large, than in peace, when it was smaller. Moreover, since Sweden had the only significant copper supplies in Europe, it received a good income from its export. That, however, brought another problem – Swedes believed that economic security could be assured only by complete control of the Baltic Sea. Later iron became important, both for export and for the armament industry. Parker, *Thirty Years War*, gives the annual French subsidy as 400,000 silver thalers; this was not a large amount, but it was timely.

† Richelieu had just crushed the French Protestants at La Rochelle, then made peace with Charles of England, who had ineptly attempted to interfere. He saw a peace party forming among the German princes, a peace that would leave France fighting alone against Habsburgs on all fronts. Parker, *The Army of Flanders*, describes Spanish efforts to bring troops from Italy to resist French attacks.

Few contemporaries expected the Swedish king to last long against the battle-tested Habsburg army. Tilly had the financial backing of the Spanish king, who freely spent the silver of the New World to support the plans of the imperial family and its Church in the Old World; in addition he could borrow extensively from wealthy bankers.

Moreover, Tilly was a very competent commander, with good officers, especially the energetic and courageous Pappenheim. As soon as he heard that the elector of Saxony had joined Gustavus Adolphus, Tilly marched north to Leipzig, where he met the allied army on a plain appropriately called Breitenfeld. He was outnumbered, 33,000 to 40,000, and had much less artillery, but he was confident that his more experienced soldiers could handle the enemy alliance.

Tilly's units were organised in squares of almost 3,000 men. The mass of pikemen was expected to push against similarly organised enemy formations, the musketeers firing into the masses of men from the side, with the cannon blasting away at a distance. Tilly had seventeen such squares, drawn up in three formations, with the cavalry guarding the flanks.*

The Swedish king, in contrast, arranged his men in two long lines, pikemen in front, musketeers in the rear, each line five men deep. This allowed him to bring more firepower to bear; with cannon interspersed between the units, he could pour grapeshot into the enemy from close quarters. However, if the front line collapsed under the pressure of the larger imperial squares, the battle was irretrievably lost. Awareness of this had prevented other commanders from experimenting with linear tactics; although everyone understood the value of firepower, only the king had sufficient confidence in the ability of his men to reload and fire fast enough to prevent the enemy formations from closing with deadly effect, and to stiffen the ranks of pikes against charging horsemen, he had them drive additional stakes into the ground, so as to create a mass of overlapping pikes. He planned to unleash his cavalry at the proper moment, catching shaken musketeers reloading. Mobility and speed, and the individual initiative of the officers, were paramount.†

The elector of Saxony was not ready to experiment – his forces were in the traditional squares, commanded by Georg von Arnim (1581–1641). At Breitenfeld they stood to the left, on a rise, where their immobility would be less of a problem.

The battle opened at noon with the customary artillery exchanges;

---

* Black, *European Warfare, 1494–1660*, minimises the importance of new formations. More experienced and more motivated troops, and larger armies tended to win victories. Guthrie, *Battles of the Thirty Years War*, calls Tilly conservative, but defends the use of proven tactics.
† Roberts, *Gustavus Adolphus*, notes that the new Swedish field piece, a copper three-pounder (a 'regiment piece') was central to the army's success. On a new gun carriage, it could be moved quickly and fired rapidly. Even his twenty-four-pounder could be drawn by horses and was not dependent on water transport.

after two hours or so, the shelling having produced no significant effect on either army, Tilly sent his infantry towards the centre of the Swedish line. More significant was the imperial cavalry charge on the flank. Passing behind the Swedish position in what would normally have been a decisive manoeuvre, Tilly found his way blocked by swiftly realigned infantry, then outflanked by Swedish cavalry. Gustavus Adolphus had been drilling his men to prepare for such an eventuality, and the more open formation allowed them to move swiftly to face their attackers. Pappenheim's men were shaken by a terrible Swedish volley, but they made six more caracoles, hoping to flank the Swedes, but always finding new cavalrymen in the way.

Late in the afternoon the imperial cavalry charged the Saxons, driving their cavalry off the field. While the red-cloaked Croatians pursued their enemy, Tilly ordered his infantry forward against the inexperienced and now shaken Saxon foot. Soon the Saxons were in wild flight all along the line, abandoning their cannon and slowing only to sack the Swedish camp on their way north. The Saxon elector, in fleeing the battlefield, ceased to be a figure of any political importance. (An English volunteer, hearing him threaten to hang everyone who had run away, commented that he had better start with himself.)

The Swedes under Gustav Horn (1592–1632) calmly realigned their forces to face this new imperial attack – a manoeuvre that no army of the era had ever made successfully. Then, once the Swedish cavalry had driven Pappenheim's horsemen from the battlefield, the king moved against the centre of Tilly's line before the units could reorganise. His men were hungry and exhausted, but a dust storm blew up in the face of imperial troops, blinding them; this as Swedish cannon, supplemented by fire from captured guns, poured into Tilly's men until they broke and ran.

The Swedish king had lost 3,500 men, his Saxon ally 2,000, but his army was actually stronger after the battle than before, because he recruited 6,000 prisoners into his forces! Tilly, in contrast, had lost 7,600 men, and so many of the survivors had scattered that he could only round up 6,000 of them later.

As the king moved towards the Rhine, money began to pour in, mostly from his new (and often unwilling) Protestant allies. Gustavus Adolphus was able to reduce the tax burden on his subjects while more than tripling the size of his forces. His army was called Swedish, but it was far from being universally composed of Scandinavians; most soldiers were Germans; a few were English and Scot.*

---

* Roberts, *The Swedish Imperial Experience 1560–1718*, says that only 20 per cent of the Swedish army at Breitenfeld were Swedes. However, this core was essential – it provided the steady centre around which the mercenary forces could be organised. And the commanders took great care to prevent these units from being worn down – often assigning them to garrison duty or the strategic reserve, to be inserted into battle at the critical moment. In

Eventually the allied Swedish–Saxon forces pushed south, occupying Bavaria and proclaiming the liberation of Bohemia; other forces operated in Lower Saxony and on the Rhine. Meanwhile, the frontiers of France were extended over large parts of Alsace, promising protection from all the armies if the people would recognise Louis XIII as their future sovereign. German lords were now joining the Protestant alliance. The Habsburgs' 'fat years' were at an end. But it would not be the dynasty alone which would suffer lean years, years in which the labours of decades would be consumed, but all of Germany.

Only mercenaries had reasons to rejoice, and of them only the most callous.

Tilly's Death

The Swedish advance south was hampered by Pappenheim's cavalry raids on his supply lines, until Gustavus Adolphus finally cut loose from all ties to the north and unleashed his men on Bavaria. Supplying his men off the countryside, he left a wide trail of burned villages and farms behind him.

Tilly reorganised his forces and began striking at Swedish garrisons, routing General Horn at Bamberg, then trying to prevent the king from crossing the Lech river. However, unlike the earlier, more famous battle of the Lech, where an imperial army had wiped out Hungarian invaders in 955, his imperial army was able to do no more than inflict heavy casualties on the enemy. When the Swedes closed in, Tilly's men fled. Tilly was wounded and died shortly afterward. Swedish depredations then extended over all of southern Germany.*

Moreover, the emperor's plans for Italy were being undermined by the vain and quarrelsome pope, Urban VIII (1623–44), who feared that a

---

1632 Sweden had 175,000 men in arms; obviously, in a nation of 1,200,000 people, such an army could not be filled by national levies. Parker, *The Military Revolution*, explains the reasons for hiring foreigners—the quick wasting away of all armies, the need to have veterans in the ranks, and avoid draft resistance. Recruiters earned a bonus for each recruit, no matter how they got them.

One new unit was composed mainly of English and Scottish volunteers, led by the duke of Hamilton. 6,000 strong at the beginning, it was soon down to 4,000, then to a few hundred. Joining it at the end of 1633 was seventeen-year-old Frederick Herman von Schomberg. His father was a prominent Calvinist noble from Baden who had died in the battle of White Mountain, his mother a lady-in-waiting to the Winter King's wife. Thus, he had close connections to the Stuarts in England that would help to make him one of the most outstanding international warriors of the era.

* This prompted one of the author's friends trying in vain to do genealogical research in Bavaria to say that he was ready to go and burn down some Swedish church in revenge. German, Czech and Polish librarians feel much the same way, but they would be satisfied if their books were returned – many ended up in the Swedish Royal Library.

strong emperor would dominate the Church.* He contributed some money to the emperor, but far less than he could have.

Under the circumstances Ferdinand had no choice but to recall Wallenstein. Given almost dictatorial powers, Wallenstein quickly invaded Bohemia at the head of a new mercenary army, causing Gustavus Adolphus to come north to meet him. The two armies met at Nuremberg, where Wallenstein surprised the Swedes by not fighting, but digging a gigantic earthen defensive wall that cut them off from supplies; Gustavus Adolphus, realising that his army was suffering from a shortage of fodder and a surplus of flies, tried to storm the fortifications, but failed. The Swedish king moved south, looking for winter quarters, but when he heard that Wallenstein was invading Saxony; he turned north. Near Leipzig the two armies confronted one another, each too cautious to offer battle, each living off the countryside.†

The Battle of Lützen

In November 1632, the king's army was not far from Wallenstein's. The imperial commander had been dispersing his men in winter quarters – looking forward to a spring campaign with an army so enlarged by recruits that he would be unbeatable – when Gustavus Adolphus made a surprise march on his last known position. The king had learned from Croatian captives taken in a skirmish that the imperial forces been divided – Pappenheim having been sent with the best cavalry thirty-five miles distant – so that the Swedes now greatly outnumbered Wallenstein. The imperial commander, alerted by the skirmish, sent word to Pappenheim to join him in all haste – an order the cavalryman instantly obeyed – and set his outnumbered forces in battle formation behind a series of water obstacles and trenches, with his artillery on a low hill.

Gustavus Adolphus, arriving at the imperial position late in the day, made camp. In the morning he sent his men forward as soon as the mist lifted, around 9 a.m., and attacked with the Swedish and Finnish cavalry at 11 a.m. The forward units were rolling up the imperial left when

---

* He concentrated on acquiring lands and offices for his family the Barberini, and on building projects, for which many ancient monuments were torn down. Italians joked bitterly about the motto he put on one building, *Quod non fecerunt barbari, fecerunt Barbarini*, whatever the barbarians did not do, the Barberini did. He put the bee from his family crest everywhere, and was a great patron of the arts; he also warned Galileo to give up his foolish idea that the earth rotated around the sun – it was simply contrary to scripture.

† Roberts, *Gustavus Adolphus*, notes that Swedish discipline, so excellent early in the war, was breaking down. Where the king could not supervise his army personally, his generals – excessively cautious and prone to mutual jealousies – held endless councils of war; meanwhile, the troops began looting. Soon the victims of the atrocities would depict them as bogeymen, the stuff of folk-legend.

Pappenheim's cavalry arrived and swept the attackers away with an unexpected and utterly courageous charge. However, just as Wallenstein was rejoicing, Pappenheim was hit by cannon fire; loaded onto a coach for evacuation to the rear, he died soon afterwards.*

Gustavus Adolphus had been shot down as well, though such was the smoke, fog and confusion that his men did not realise this for a long while; he had fallen during a cavalry attack – shot, then dragged by his horse; Piccolomini's cavalry finished him off and stripped the corpse. Eventually command was assumed by Bernhard (1604–39), the younger brother of the Saxon duke, known commonly as the duke of Saxe-Weimar.†

Bernhard's career had prepared him well for this situation. He had served in the armies of Mansfeld and Baden, in his brother's army, in the Danish army, in the Dutch forces, and as a colonel in the Swedish cavalry. He had often been entrusted with independent command during plundering expeditions, once reaching the Rhine, a region filled with rich Catholics. Now he took command of the rattled Swedish army. When one cavalry commander refused his order to charge, he killed him on the spot, rallied the men and eventually drove Wallenstein's forces from the field. The Finnish cavalry distinguished itself in what was one of the bloodiest battles of the war. The Swedes lost 6,000 men, almost twice the number of fallen imperial troops, but it was widely conceded to be a Swedish victory. Wallenstein could have resumed the fighting after Pappenheim's infantry arrived, but, having lost his artillery and seen how exhausted the infantry was, he prudently withdrew.

Wallenstein had done all any commander could: one spur was blown off by a cannon shot, and several musket balls had lodged in his heavy coat; every member of his staff had been slain, wounded or dispersed. He had fought for eleven hours. Daylight was fading and he was exhausted. Moreover, he expected that the Saxon army would arrive at any moment. He gave the order to retreat.

What was the effect of the battle on the future? That depends on one's point of view. The Protestants hailed it as their salvation, Catholics its mixed results (military defeat balanced by the death of their greatest enemy), and the historian Roberts, with the advantage of hindsight, gloomily saw the sixteen years of horror to come – and worse, that a century and a half would pass before idealism and faith were significant again in warfare.

The Swedish army remained unbeatable, but there was no inspiring purpose. The king had been a practical man who understood the difference

---

* Roberts, *The Thirty Years War*, notes that an imperial colonel, von Hofkirchen, who had a brother in the Swedish army, refused to continue the attack, but led his men to the rear, precipitating a panicked flight.

† Asch considered him the only military entrepreneur in Wallenstein's class. He managed to get a clause in his contract with the French for payment of a ransom, in case of his capture, equal to that of a French marshal.

between security and an empire; those who governed afterwards could not – they could neither maintain national unity nor extricate themselves from the Continental war. A six-year-old girl was now queen, and precocious though Christina was, she could not be a leader of armies.*

Wallenstein's Fall

Wallenstein rebuilt his army, recovered Bohemia and Silesia, and took steps to detach Saxony and Brandenburg from the Swedish alliance; but he refused to abandon his base and advance further rapidly, as Ferdinand wanted – wars should be fought by generals on horseback, not courtiers in armchairs. It would be foolish to destroy Germany and lose Bohemia, he reckoned, when those goals could be reached by diplomacy. Unfortunately, relaxing imperial religious expectations was essential to successful diplomacy.

Frustrated in what he saw as logical steps towards a peace that satisfied all parties, Wallenstein came to see the emperor as a small man surrounded by fawning midgets; if God had not chosen to remove him, perhaps the army should. No one knows exactly what Wallenstein's exact plans were – not even the Saxon general, von Arnim, with whom he was corresponding.† Essential to any successful conspiracy is keeping the dissatisfactions and plots secret, but also involving enough men to seize power everywhere at once. This is difficult because anyone powerful enough to head a conspiracy is likely to have many enemies. Such circumstances practically guarantee failure. Not surprisingly, Wallenstein's conspiracy was broken in the shell before it could hatch. According to Schiller, whose plays are important for the popular understanding of the episode, Wallenstein wanted to remove Ferdinand and make himself king of Bohemia, then unify Germany (*von der Etsch bis an den Belt,* from the Adige to the Belt – as the words of a future national anthem put it), and lastly end the war and its terrible destruction of the German people.

An ambition to become king of Bohemia was perfectly plausible: George of Podebrady ruled Bohemia from 1458 to 1471, and Czech

---

* Kirby praises the regency of the phlegmatic chancellor, Axel Oxenstierna, who was regent.His greatest concern was Poland, not Germany; Roberts stresses the conflict with Denmark over control of the Baltic and Holstein.

† Hans Georg von Armin-Boitzenburg (1581–1641). This fascinating officer had served Sweden before the war, then Poland, Wallenstein, and finally Saxony – where his Protestant sympathies helped bring Gustavus Adolphus and the Saxon elector together on the battlefield of Breitenfeld against Wallenstein; later he refused a commission in the French army and retired to the family home, only to be arrested by the Swedes in 1637 on suspicion of treason; he escaped from his prison in Stockholm after being held for a year. His unexpected death disrupted efforts to raise a German army to expel all foreigners from the Holy Roman Empire.

fears of ultra-rigid Catholic rule had been central to the outbreak of the conflict. But to succeed, Wallenstein had to bring key officers into the conspiracy and also obtain the cooperation of the Swedes (and eventually the French). This could not be done without surrendering territory – some to France, some to Spain, some to Sweden. Not even the Protestants were willing to give up German lands to any foreigner, not even one they had invited in to save them; and the emperor counted every inch sacred. Certainly Wallenstein was talking about a revolt – Schiller had him reflect on the average person's blind, stupid obedience to those who hold 'ancient, holy possession' of their lands. But talking, as Schiller has Wallenstein say, can be bold because it is not a deed (*Kühn war das Wort, weil es die Tat nicht war*).

Wallenstein's astrologers, among them Johannes Keppler, had warned him that February 1634 was a dangerous month, but Wallenstein preferred to follow his own star, not those of the experts.

Whatever the truth might be, the fact is that Ferdinand struck first – offering a reward for the general, dead or alive. Clearly, he preferred him dead. As Wallenstein realised that he was surrounded by potential murderers, he entrusted his life to Walter Butler, an Irish nobleman who had distinguished himself in the defense of Frankfurt and was now his cavalry commander. On his way to Eger, a stronghold commanded by John Gordon, a Scottish Calvinist, he was said to have explained to Walter Leslie his plans to join his army to that of the Swedes, then force peace on everyone else; he felt certain that he could trust both Leslie and Butler because they had been captured by Gustavus Adolphus in 1632 and then been released without ransom!

Wallenstein was, however, mistaken. The plot against him had already gone too far. Butler explained the plans for the assassination to his lieutenants Alexander Macdonald, Edmund Borcke und Thomas Browne; he counted on his troops obeying any orders instantly, no matter what their personal feelings about Wallenstein were. He had them bring a half-dozen trusted Scots into the castle, while Butler gave similar instructions to Walter Devereux and Robert Geraldin, to bring an equal number of Irish mercenaries. He then had Leslie invite Wallenstein and his three most trusted subordinates to a banquet.

At Leslie's signal, Devereux burst into the room, his men shouting, '*Viva la Casa d'Austria*', and cut Wallenstein down. Of the other guests only Trczka managed to arm himself – he killed two Irishmen and a Spanish nobleman, then forced his way past Devereux and down into the courtyard. There, however, not knowing the new password, he was recognised and killed.

Walter Butler received 225,000 guilders and a rich Bohemian estate; also a title of nobility and an important command in the imperial army. Late in 1634, however, he took sick, worsened and died.

John Gordon received 178,000 guilders, title to lands in the north yet to be conquered and an estate in Bohemia. He then disappeared! Various sources say that he was murdered in Prague by another Scot, that he continued in command of his regiment or that he was arrested by the Swedes.

Devereux received 12,000 guilders in cash and a small estate; he was given a small command in the imperial army, but mentioned only twice – once for putting down peasant resistance to forced recruiting and quartering of troops. He disappeared from all records after 1637.

Leslie carried the news of the murder to Pilsen, personally informing the man immediately behind the intrigue, Francesco Caretto de Grano, an officer Wallenstein had removed from command for stealing ransom money. Leslie received 20,000 guilders, a noble title, and a command; he became field marshal in 1650, leading a successful campaign against the Turks, then in 1665 vice-president of the imperial war council; he married very well, to Anna Francisca de Montecuccoli, and when he died at the age of sixty-one in 1667, he was buried in the Schottenkirke in Vienna. His brother, Jacob Leslie, married Maria Theresa von Lichtenstein and thus became incredibly wealthy. Caretto had to wait five years for his reward, but ultimately settled down on an estate in Bohemia.

Octavio Piccolomini (1599–1656), whose family belonged to the highest Italian aristocracy and even boasted a famous pope among its numbers, did well, too. Though he had once commanded Wallenstein's bodyguard and had distinguished himself in combat at Lützen, he was unhappy that he had been passed over for advancement in rank. Dismissed by Wallenstein for extortion, he joined the Habsburg court, where he had recognised early the change in the wind and had made himself prominent among those denouncing Wallenstein's ambitions. He was rewarded with the Order of the Golden Fleece and high command, alternating between Spanish and Austrian service; after successfully concluding important diplomatic missions, he was awarded the duchy of Amalfi in 1639 and Hagenau in 1650. Interestingly, he was not entrusted with command of Wallenstein's army.

Nördlingen

While the Catholic forces were distracted by the Wallenstein conspiracy, the duke of Saxony, Wilhelm, the supreme commander of the Swedish-Saxon army, led his army back into Bavaria, where the troops could live off Catholic farmers and workmen; after all, they had not been paid since 1631. He sent Bernhard south with General Horn in order to spread as much destruction as possible, hoping thereby to force Ferdinand and Maximilian to conclude that the war was lost.

The imperial forces were entrusted to Johann von Aldringer, a Bavarian intriguer without peer, who had managed to take no position during the recent crisis, but still escaped blame. Cruel to those who helped the Protestants, he was nevertheless unable to prevent Catholic cities from paying heavy ransoms to escape attack; Protestant cities like Ulm, of course, regarded the Swedes as saviours – though there were many times that they would have preferred to have been rescued more cheaply, the Swedish garrison being extremely expensive. Aldringer was under suspicion of treason when he died in July, perhaps murdered by his own Croatian troops to avoid his sending them to what seemed certain death, perhaps trampled to death by retreating troops.

Bernhard did well for himself, temporarily, making himself ruler of the bishoprics of Würzburg and Bamberg. In September 1634, however, the imperial armies met his army and Horn's at Nördlingen, a small city in the centre of an ancient meteorite crater, and utterly routed them. It appeared that the emperor had won, as well he might have, had he offered generous terms of peace; instead, as is often the case, Ferdinand believed that he was in a position to crush his enemies utterly.

Ferdinand's judgment seemed confirmed in the summer of 1635, when the Swedish mercenaries mutinied, threatening to invade Sweden if not paid promptly. Paying the troops and keeping them busy thus became a major policy goal of the Swedish crown. When money came from France, the Swedish mercenaries began their years-long rampage through Germany, Bohemia and Poland. As Protestants had already begun to wonder if the Swedish army not a greater danger than Catholicism – Saxony went over to the imperial cause; the seriousness of the elector's commitment was shown by his increasing the monthly salary of General von Armin from 2,000 to 3,000 thalers a month. But it was too late to do anything more than change the composition of the alliances.

Bernhard of Saxe-Weimar rallied from the disaster at Nördlingen, taking refuge in France. French armies were now attacking the Spanish king in the Low Countries, drawing imperial troops out of central Germany and making it possible for the German Protestants to re-organise. Richelieu gave Bernhard four million *livres* a year to raise 18,000 mercenaries; meanwhile, the Protestant German princes named the Saxon warlord commander of their newly raised army. Bernard's double loyalty was difficult to maintain, but he performed well enough to be promised lands at Breisgau on the Upper Rhine, perhaps even all of Alsace; naturally, his brief reign over bishoprics in Franconia was over.

One of Bernhard's new commanders was Frederick von Schomberg, who had purchased a German infantry unit, then had raised French cavalry. He was able to smooth over difficulties between the troops because he spoke both languages so fluently; this was not surprising, since his upbringing in France, England, Holland and Germany had taught him not only languages, but also opportunities to see how prominent men exercised leadership.

In 1638 Bernhard led his armies to victories in Baden, capturing some of the strongest fortresses in Germany, but he unexpectedly fell victim to one of the great killers of this war – disease. While many Germans were murdered, and some starved, most deaths probably came from disease, the epidemics made worse by hunger, exhaustion, stress, bad water and the breakdown of most normal commercial, religious and governmental services. It was impossible to provide food and clothing, or shelter, to the refugees, or hospital services or even to enforce quarantines.*

It is difficult to assess the death toll. There were numerous depopulated villages, but had the people died or simply gone elsewhere and stayed? But without question, vast areas were left without houses or barns, people or animals, to the mercy of roving bandits and soldiers in search of food and fodder.†

Such was the stress on finances that even silver-rich Spain could not pay its troops. First, there were the widespread rebellions in 1640, then a steady lessening of the flow of silver from the Americas, more local resistance to colonial governors, and no incentives for entrepeneurs to do what the state no longer could. Privateers and pirates began to appear, and the English fleet took control of the Caribbean. Spain was to remain a great power, but the road henceforth led steadily downward.

The French War

Richelieu, whose portrait is deservedly displayed in many royal palaces and museums now visited by tourists, died in 1642; his successor,

---

* The supplies for even a single regiment could easily exhaust any community. According to the website *Wer war wer – im Dreißigjährigen Krieg*, a regiment contained 3,000 infantry (1,500 musketeers, 300 cannoneers, 1,200 men with pikes and 300 with halberds), with up to 1,600 horses cared for by teamsters and youths – a supply train that grew larger as the war dragged on – more wagons being needed to carry the supplies collected from the farmers and the personal booty of the men and officers; eventually the camp followers outnumbered the troops by a factor of three, sometimes five. The officers lived especially well, with quarters and banquets that would do honour to any court; they were served by a small army of servants, courtiers and prostitutes. The staff alone required 1,000 guilders a month, 10 per cent of the total needed to pay the soldiers; of course, much of the 10,000 guilders allotted to the soldiers each month was stolen by the junior officers. For subsidies, see Guthrie, *Battles of the Thirty Years War*.

† Roberts, *The Thirty Years War*, says that since the countryside could no longer support infantry, the generals were reduced to using small cavalry forces that achieved little beyond destruction. In contrast, Parker, *Thirty Years War*, is struck by how few travellers make note of devastation, and how quickly the economy and population rebounded. Asch finds that all governments broke through a psychological threshold of taxation, making it possible to

Cardinal Jules Mazarin, was the chief minister of France to his death, after which young Louis XIV took the reins of power into his own capable hands.*

Louis had no role to play in this war, being born in 1638 to a father who hated sex and a mother who loved it. Two years later his father died, destabilising a state which had not yet recovered from its own religious wars. The Edict of Nantes had brought a tenuous end to the religious wars in 1598, but French Protestants were anxious about their rights being guaranteed. Every time the motto 'one king, one law, one God' was uttered, they became nervous. It helped only little that the two Roman Catholic cardinals who dominated the affairs of state had thrown their support to the Protestants in Germany, not the Catholic emperor; that was only practical statecraft and could quickly change. They disliked the Italian swordsmen that Mazarin imported from his homeland, but fortunately for the cardinal, this public outrage did not come into the open until 1648–53. The two uprisings known as the *Fronde* were partly tax revolts, partly dislike of foreigners (especially Mazarin's greed and his policy of marrying nieces to prominent men), partly discomfort with the prominent role Louis's mother (Anne of Austria) took in the government, and partly the ambitions of nobles and semi-legitimate descendants of former kings. The civil war was fought with foreign troops – Spanish, German, even Czechs and Poles. Louis XIV never forgot the sight of Spanish troops in Paris.

The events in France promised to a frightening degree to follow those in England, where in 1649 Parliament put King Charles I on trial and then beheaded him. Also, it became apparent that national armies were less subject to discipline than mercenary ones; natives were not only more prone to looting and desertion than foreigners, they tended to be revolutionaries as well. Once again the example was England, but the lesson was confirmed in France.

Fortunately for Louis XIV, the Thirty Years War no longer required great attention. For Germany it came to an end in 1648–50 with the Peace of Westphalia, a peace of exhaustion, with no hope of victory by

---

collect ever larger sums without setting off protests. Guthrie, *The Later Thirty Years War*, notes an increasing need for supplies rather than plunder.

* Jules Cardinal Mazarin (Giulio Raimando Mazzarino, 1602–61) whose military and diplomatic talents were recognised by Richelieu, who entrusted him with responsibilities so significant that Pope Urban VIII, suspecting that he gave priority to French interests, removed him from papal diplomatic service. After Richelieu's death 1643, Mazarin became the dominant figure in France. Asch estimates the French subsidy at 300,000 thalers annually between 1631 and 1633; between 1638 and 1648 it totally 3.5 million thalers. Customs duties and excise taxes covered (inadequately at times) the expenses of many participants in the war; most borrowed money, and some sold government monopolies; no one was eager to collect direct taxes, but the French collected much from the *taille*.

either Protestants or Catholics, certainly none by the imperial army. It was not until 1659 that French arms triumphed in the Spanish Netherlands – providing a foothold there that Louis XIV would spend his life attempting to enlarge. The French king was able to concentrate on that war and to suppressing internal enemies. Louis XIV's army, according to Wolf, remained a mercenary force of Italians, Germans, Scots, English, Irish and Swiss, the principal difference being that the king eventually managed to make himself its head. This was not an easy task, because the officers objected to 'civilian' control. (It is misleading to separate the king's civil and military roles.) Louis relied on a father-son team, Michel Le Tellier and Louvois, to create a well-functioning ministry of war; he assigned his chief military engineer, Vauban, the task of fortifying the 'gates' of France, and he ordered Marshal Turenne and the diplomatic corps to make those gates part of France. The army was trained by Inspector General Martinet, whose name came to symbolise rigorous discipline. At first Louis saw his wars of aggression as essentially defensive, but success in expanding into the Holy Roman Empire made him, and his advisors, eager for more.

Austrian arms began to recover under Raimondo, count of Montecuccoli (1609–80), duke of Melfi, etc. Wounded and captured at Breitenfeld, wounded at Lützen, engaged at Nördlingen, and captured again in 1639, he wrote an important treatise entitled *Memorie della guerra* which was published in Venice in 1703 and served as a manual of arms for many years. In 1643 he fought in Italy, then in 1645 fought the Hungarians, the French and the Swedes! After the war he served on the council of war, became field marshal, and later, in 1673, outfought Turenne on the Rhine.

Scottish Mercenaries

In *A Legend of Montrose* Walter Scott referred to a book he consulted often, a book bearing the noble baroque title: *MONRO his Expedition with the worthy Scots Regiment, called MacKeye's Regiment, levied in August 1626, by Sir Donald MacKeye Lord Rees Colonel, for his Majestie's service of Denmark, and reduced after the battle of Nerling, in September 1634, at Wormes, in the Palz: Discharged in several duties and observations of service, first, under the magnanimous King of Denmark, during his wars against the Empire; afterwards under the invincible King of Sweden, during his Majestie's lifetime; and since under the Director-General, the Rex-Chancellor Oxensterne, and his Generals: collected and gathered together, at spare hours, by Colonel Robert Monro, as First Lieutenant under the said Regiment, to the noble and worthy Captain Thomas MacKenzie of Kildon, brother to the noble Lord, the*

Lord Earl of Seaforth, for the use of all noble Cavaliers favouring the laudable profession of arms.

Indeed, this was a golden age for Scots. Most served the Protestant cause, some the Catholic monarchs. Many were drawn home after 1640, when Charles I foolishly (in retrospect) attempted to make his northern subjects join the Anglican Church, provoking a war with Scotland that he could not win.

Croatian Mercenaries

The Croatians were experienced fighters from the southern frontier of Austria, skilled at countering the irregular tactics of Turkish and Tatar cavalry. They were first recruited by the Habsburg generals, but by 1633 were also fighting for the French – the not-so-secret enemy of the Habsburg emperor. At least, they could have reasoned, they were fighting for another Catholic, a Catholic nation governed by a cardinal. They arrived in Paris under the leadership of their *ban* (governor) and ultimately their regiment was incorporated into the royal army. (However, the oft-cited *avenue des croates* in France was named to honour a Croatian army unit's rebellion against the Nazis in 1944, not the hussars.)

Their uniform, such as it was, was distinguished by a large piece of cloth worn around the neck. This led to the German definition of a necktie as a *Krawatte* (*Hravt* = *Kroat* = Croatian); in France the word is *cravate*. This kerchief was popular partly because it was more colourful than a lace collar, more durable and more affordable, but also because it was much easier to keep clean.

Benecke cites a Bavarian monk at Andechs who wrote about an effort by the people of Augsburg in September 1633 to ambush Croatian marauders who had just sacked Landsberg. The Croats had been sustaining themselves by plunder, so that they were more hated than even the Swedes! The monk's information was confused by the simultaneous passage of Spanish soldiers which had caused peasants to seek hiding places and shelter. A rumour spread that Swedes were raiding a local inn, another that it was an imperial force. Then it was heard that imperial troops had routed the raiders, only to retreat ahead of 3,000 Swedes. From that point on the monk's story became even more confusing – by December thirty Croats and Poles controlled the area, once demanding of a local priest that he give them his horses, and, when he refused, shot him dead.

Had the abbey at Andechs been as famous for its fine beers then as today, it is doubtful that the monk would have survived to write his tale, no matter how secluded his lair, high in the rugged hills outside Munich. As much as the marauding soldiers wanted food, they were even more eager to get beer, wine and brandy.

If the local peasants were hungry and ill-clad, the soldiers were worse off. In their small numbers they could not capture cities where food and clothing were stored, and where many peasants took refuge. Having eaten all the dogs and cats they could find, all the root plants they could dig up, they sought in vain to buy food – but no merchant dared transport anything across such lawless county. Many died of cold and starvation. Their officers, however, lived well.*

Brandenburg-Prussia

Brandenburg-Prussia became the most powerful of the northern German states, but that was because the other states were so weak. It was often referred to as the 'sandbox' of Europe, partly in jest because so much of its sandy soil was suitable only for potatoes and asparagus, but it also serves as a metaphor for its treatment at the hands of neighbouring rulers.

When Frederick William (Friedrich Wilhelm, 1620–88) became elector in 1640, his state was in chaos. Swedish armies had crossed it repeatedly, always supplying itself from the locals' food and fodder; the petty nobility – the Junkers – ignored the central government; and the population had fallen below 600,000.

Worse, power was in the hands of Adam von Schwarzenberg, an ardent Catholic and adherent of the emperor. After sending Frederick William to Holland, on the dubious pretext that he would be safe there learning the art of war, Schwarzenberg was able to gain the complete confidence of the mercenaries. He later 'exiled' the young elector to Königsberg, again for his safety, and governed Prussia himself from Berlin.

When Schwarzenberg keeled over in the middle of a banquet in early 1641, the Great Elector – as Frederick William was later called – set to work. He first demanded that his officers give an accounting of expenditures, and, when they refused, he put their mini-insurrection down ruthlessly. Making peace with Sweden in 1643 and a marriage with the royal house of Holland in 1646, he was rewarded with lands in central Germany when the Peace of Westphalia was signed. This was possible because of the military reforms that he had begun, despite limited resources, as soon as he came to power.

Until this moment the Brandenburg army had been composed of undisciplined mercenaries who were more of a danger to the local

---

* Roberts, *The Swedish Imperial Experience*, ascribes the sparing the Swedish army from this kind of suffering to the College of War and good administration. Every gun, every spade, every cannonball was accounted for. The Swedish model was copied by many other states, most notably Russia. Asch suggests that lowering the pay of mercenary soldiers – possible when such men became a glut on the market – contributed to the problem.

populace than to any enemy. Releasing many of them, he concentrated on a core of 2,500 men, then, using the income from his Westphalian territories, added draftees and mercenaries until he had 8,000 good troops by 1648. The Great Elector was considered slightly unbalanced in his insistence on working hard and working well – when he was not going down to the marketplace in Potsdam to see that the women selling apples were also knitting, he was drilling his troops. He next converted the Junkers into a 'service nobility'. There would be no petty nobles sitting at home, idly, on their estates – such estates as had managed to survive the plundering of the war were small and poor. He offered these nobles attractive positions in the state bureaucracy and the army, and he saw to it that both operated efficiently – there were heavy fines for officials who failed in even the most minor duties; those who refused to cooperate eventually regretted it – Frederick William was not afraid to conscript anyone into the army, even in peacetime.

Frugality and hard work made the sandy, watery land of Brandenburg bloom; that and the promise of religious liberty which had attracted hardworking Protestants from Holland, the Palatinate and other lands to Brandenburg and Prussia; after 1685 Huguenots expelled from France by Louis XIV made a permanent imprint on Potsdam, just outside Berlin, where the future kings would reside as much of the year as possible.

This provided the Great Elector with the money to hire more mercenaries, so that ultimately he had 40,000 men in his army – this in addition to the tens of thousands of subjects in militias from Prussia in the east to the Rhineland in the west. Unlike his contemporaries, he did not sell commissions, but awarded them on the basis of merit. It was an honour to be in the Prussian army, and every Prussian knew that his was the best fighting force in Europe.

This was not yet the army of Frederick the Great, but it was a good start.

The Peace of Westphalia and Demobilisation

Cardinal Mazarin was in no hurry for peace in Germany – he would have liked both present and potential future enemies to exhaust themselves further. A Germany at peace would undoubtedly resist French expansionism, and France had not yet gotten all he wanted from this war. Moreover, the terms proposed in the settlement left the emperor stronger than he had been earlier, and a strong emperor would surely be another obstacle for French policy to overcome.

No one was under the illusion that the masses of mercenaries in Germany could simply be dismissed; only the most self-deluded would believe that a soldiery which had lived for years off an impoverished and terrified peasantry and from extortions from beleaguered cities would go home quietly – if they had homes to go home to.

Instead, the various armies were billeted around the country and supported from a special 'peace tax'. This lessened the likelihood of mutinies or organised rampages. The pay was sufficient to satisfy the average mercenary (Benecke cites a report from Ulm that each Swedish horseman received twenty-four kreuzer a day) and long enough (more than a year from the signing of the treaty to the demobilisation conference in Nuremberg in June 1650) to give some thought to the future. In total, the German Circles (the ten regional groupings of states for organising defence) paid the Swedes three instalments of 1,800,000 thalers to leave the country.

Since relatively few Swedes were in the Swedish army, demobilisation usually meant little more than discharging the soldiers. But it meant a great increase in the Swedish military budget, which had been paid almost entirely by the occupied regions in Germany and Poland. Perhaps for this reason, Swedish forces remained in Poland for years, occupying the kingdom from 1655–60 – that terrible period Poles call 'the Deluge'.

City after city poured treasure into deep moats and thick walls to shield themselves from a renewed war. Experts like Johann von Valckenberg had fortified cities in the Low Countries early in the century, but German cities like Ulm and Bremen had merely looked at his plans and then decided that the projects were too expensive. After the war they took up the plans again. Bremen, a prominent commercial centre of 20,000 citizens, finished its work in 1664 after the erosion associated with the construction created sandbars that made it necessary to build a new harbour. The city counted itself lucky – it had accepted bribes from both sides to remain neutral and was afterwards named an imperial free city. Swedes and Danes had crossed and re-crossed its territories and often demanded its surrender, but it was not until 1653 that Bremen was forced to capitulate to the Swedes. Fortunately for the city, the council had hired several thousand mercenaries, thus buying sufficient time for the elector of Hanover to arrange favourable terms.

In 1688 the Swedes agreed to leave Bremen, if paid 100,000 thalers; once having that sum in their hands, they demanded 150,000 more! Then they stayed. It was not until 1712 that the Danes drove the Swedes away, and then sold the city to the elector of Hanover, who had just become King George I of England.

Hamburg had been better prepared, completing its fortifications in 1625. It had sent contingents to fight with various Protestant armies only to suffer from the depredations of Danish and Swedish forces. Both Scandinavian kings wanted to tax Hamburg's rich trade, while the Catholic Union wanted to restore the old religion; in between peasants rebelled and robbers attacked any and all merchants. Thieves set fires in hopes of robbing houses during the confusion; there were floods, famine and hunger. But the citizens rejoiced that they had not suffered the hardships of their fellow countrymen to the south. In 1643 the citizens capitulated to Christian IV of Denmark, paying a ransom of 300,000 thalers; after the conclusion of peace in 1648–50, the city became independent again.

Denmark had tried to rebuild after the disasters of the 1624–8 war, maintaining a strict neutrality, but the libertine monarch found new ways to throw away money on girlfriends, illegitimate children and marriages. His fortifications were impressive, as was his new navy, but his effort to create a national army failed – too few Danes were willing to enlist, and mercenaries were too expensive. The king quarrelled repeatedly with his subjects and royal council over taxation.

Still, Christian was not about to assist the national enemy, Sweden, in its war for Protestantism and empire; in fact, he conspired (ineptly) with the emperor to undermine his rival, Gustavus Adolphus. When war with Sweden finally came in 1643, the inexperienced Danish forces managed to keep the enemy from the heart of the country, but nothing else. The humiliating peace signed in 1645 was followed by a total collapse of law and order. Christian, who died in 1648, was remembered proudly as a doughty warrior, but his reputation as a good ruler is owed largely to comparison with his incompetent successors.

The Impact of the War

With little question, those who benefited the most from the Thirty Years War were those who participated in it the least – Spain, France and Britain. That is, their towns and villages suffered the least damage, their national cultures the least disruption. But there were also relative winners in the east – Sweden, which emerged with a much enlarged empire and a greater awareness of national sovereignty and self-worth; Lithuania, a minor (if large) state that had been in danger of becoming a rural outpost of the vibrant and attractive Polish culture (hence the phrase, *gente lituanus, sed natione polonus*, by birth Lithuanian, by nationality Polish) produced Kazimieras Semenavičius (1600–51), who wrote *Artis Magnae Artilleriae, pars prima* (The Art of Artillery, first part) in 1650. Semenavičius went from Vilnius (Wilno) University into the army, fighting in Russia and Holland, then in 1648 to become second in command of the new Polish Artillery Corps, then retired in Amsterdam to work on his never-finished *magnum opus*. However, translated into French, German and English, his book remained a basic manual for artillerymen and manufacturers of rockets and pyrotechnics for the next two centuries. In such little ways we see a nation which had once tottered between the Russian/Orthodox world and the Western/Catholic world making its decision for the latter. Poland, which became the prey of Swedish armies, suffered long after Germans were too exhausted to kill one another.

Even more influential was the book by the Dutch scholar, Hugo Grotius *De jure belli et pacis* (On the law of war and peace), which still today is cited to describe the proper behaviour of civilised rulers and armies. No longer could rampaging armies simply be accepted as the way of the world.

The lustre once attached to military service was gone. Knights were now common horsemen, ordinary soldiers were, in Glozier's words, the 'scum of society' – felons, vagrants and social deviants. In 1671 the duke of Tuscany gave Louis XIV permission to send recruiters into his lands, but only on condition that they took no married men, no peasants and no artisans. Who was left?

No wonder that recruiters took anyone was available, no matter his background or religion. No wonder, either, that so many collected their enlistment bonus, then deserted.* Geoffrey Parker, in *The Thirty Years War*, is not eager to criticise the soldiers. Instead, he emphasises how little we know about them – we do not even know for certain how they dressed (apparently they often only had a sash or emblem in common) or how they were armed. Almost all were volunteers – that is, mercenaries. But money alone was not the incentive, since the pay was no higher than that of farm hands, and sometimes there was no pay at all. But it was safer to be in an army than its victim, and many enjoyed the excitement. He warns us against overlooking the lure of adventure and change.†

Black, in *European Warfare, 1660–1815*, suggests that some mercenaries were merely following their fathers' trade. This is an attractive thesis – what else did these young men know how to do, what community could they call home except that of the regiment? Some were mere criminals.

One conclusion reached by political leaders was that mercenary armies could never again be allowed to get out of control. Never again allow the dogs of war to slip the leash. From now on, monarchs would seek to manage their troops more carefully. If only experienced officers could rein in mercenary soldiers, it mattered little what the nationality of the officer was, only his competence.

---

* Parker, *The Thirty Years War*, calls desertion rates high, usually in response to not being paid, or not being paid much, but finds only a few units with reliable statistics.

† Parker cites a wartime proverb that each soldier needed three peasants – one to give up his home, one to provide his wife, and one to take his place in hell. The worst looters were musketeers. Commanders punished looters severely, sometimes to death, so that the peasants would not turn to guerrilla warfare against them.

Chapter 6

Europe Under Attack

The Siege of Vienna

The Turk – as Europeans somewhat inaccurately called the multi-ethnic Ottoman Empire – had been on the march since the eleventh century. With each victory the sultans and their grand viziers smiled at European panic and despair – it was proof that God was on their side and that the infidels were doomed; their armies had taken fortress after fortress, city after city: Constantinople in 1453, Belgrade in 1456, Budapest in 1512. Then came the setback at Vienna in 1529. But surely that was temporary.

The European nightmare never materialised, however, as the Ottoman armies were drawn east and south. Although the Ottomans occupied most of Hungary in 1541, they never mobilised fully for another attack on the Habsburg capital. That was partly because they first needed to take the fortresses south of Vienna, and Croatian and Slovenian resistance proved difficult to overcome. Almost annually some Ottoman force, large or small – mostly Turks, with their local allies, Serbs, Bulgarians, Hungarians and, occasionally, Tatars – ravaged the Christian border-lands.* This kept their men in fighting trim, but it made their Croatian victims into excellent warriors. As Turkish attacks slackened, the Croatians could sell their talents to European employers; they became the most sought-after mercenaries in Central Europe.

The Habsburg Army

Habsburg military responsibilities ran from the Rhineland to Italy to Hungary; while facing down the excellent French army required armies

---

* Ingrao notes that many Austrian and Royal Hungarian towns built tall church towers called *Türkenglocken*, from which watchmen could ring warnings of Turkish raiders. Barker calls the Ottoman decline a misleading cliché – contemporaries had not noticed it. McNeill describes the process by which all borderlands south of Russia, Poland and Austria became desolated by raiding parties and armies.

with artillery and engineers, fighting Hungarian Protestants and Muslim Turks was best done by cavalry.

This diversely equipped army was the first line of defence for western Christendom.* A mixture of conscripts and mercenaries, with militias assisting in defending cities, it was neither large nor well trained, but was expanded in moments of need. The commanders were often foreigners, often from the emperor's Italian domains, but Austrian nobles were able to offset their influence by continual presence at court and in the war council. Powerful princes in Germany insisted on participating in all discussions of imperial defence. There was also the Pope, then important clerics and members of religious orders, most importantly the Jesuits. All considered themselves experts on military affairs. Imperial relatives, of course, assumed that they would be given important commands – and the relationship did not have to be close to be claimed.

The basic assumption was that the standing army could be kept small in peacetime, then rapidly expanded in time of war. As long as there was bullion in the treasury, the state was safe – mercenaries came running quickly at the jingling sound of coins. Saving money, of course, was not easy; there was almost some worthy reason for spending every pfennig, groschen and thaler that the financial officers could raise.

Nor was recruiting soldiers always easy. Neighbours discouraged their subjects from enrolling in foreign armies; they allowed recruiters to speak to their subjects only after the payment of fees. Internally, recruiting often resembled a draft, but this was done reluctantly – the public disliked it, and officers preferred country boys over worldly-wise conscripts from cities. The responsibility for raising, training and equipping units was that of commanding officers whose commissions were often accompanied by grants of money for expenses – grants calculated according to a paper count, which encouraged officers to keep the number of actual soldiers low, then pocket the rest of the money. How else could they afford to buy their commissions? Or maintain their status at court, where noble families competed fiercely for prestigious posts? To become a general was to become rich.

The commissioned officers often hired foreign professionals to take care of boring details during the long years of training and to take responsibility during the frightening hours of actual battle. Thus it was that the foreign officers, more so than the largely anonymous enlisted men, were the true mercenaries of the coming era.†

---

* Barker says that the troops were equipped with matchlocks, but a few had the new plug bayonet that could be inserted quickly into the muzzle; a handful had rifles – which during the siege of Vienna proved themselves deadly within one hundred yards. Paper cartridges were standard. Uniforms were not yet uniform, except within regiments; red was preferred, but it was too expensive for general use. Artillery was becoming surprisingly sophisticated.

† Territorial rulers supervised personally – but not always closely – the building and supply

As for the common soldiers, there would be sweet words before enlistment, whippings, imprisonment, even execution for failure to obey orders afterward. Poor food or none at all, poor housing, and inadequate clothing drove many a man to desert. Proud ceremonies, religious fervour, eloquent exhortations and martial music, and hatred of the enemy kept many in the ranks.

The Defences of Vienna

The Ottoman Empire had not been a threat for many decades. After 1600 it suffered from inept leadership, palace coups, mutinies among the elite Janissary and cavalry corps, and mobs demanding (and getting) the heads of prominent administrators. Its under-funded and outmoded army still won battles, but it was largely due to the divisions among its Christian enemies that there was no war. After 1650 the Turkish army became stronger – making another advance northwards possible, though not inevitable; by 1680 nobody dismissed the idea that there would soon be a significant clash between Christian Europe and Islam. The surprise was that the great encounter would come at Vienna, not some obscure fortress in Ukraine or Moldavia.

Perhaps the plague epidemic of 1679 encouraged the sultan and grand vizier. It struck all of eastern Europe, but was especially terrible in Vienna – the populace could not bury the dead as swiftly as they appeared in the streets. As death appeared certain, some prayed, some settled their affairs, and other drank themselves into a stupor.* Surely such people could not stand up to the magnificent Ottoman army.

Vienna had been strongly fortified according to the latest concepts in military design – the forty-foot-high wall was relatively unimportant compared to the twenty-foot-deep dry moat and the thick bastions; the glacis – the outward slope from the top of the moat's outer wall – protected the wall from direct cannon fire; ravelins – triangular outworks – hindered an enemy from digging trenches to the glacis and filling the

---

of fortresses, since these took time to build, were necessary to discourage neighbours from attacking, served as residences, and offered opportunities for their friends to skim some money off the top. Military units were nice to have for parades, but were not nearly as impressive as a mountain-top fortress. Moreover, well-designed fortresses, such as several on the southern frontier of Austria, could easily hold out against attack until a relief army could come to the rescue.

* Barker uses *Schlamperei*, sloppiness, as the old definition of Habsburg inefficiency. One presumed victim was a minstrel who awoke atop a pile of bodies – pulling out a little bagpipe, he summoned rescuers with a tune (perhaps the one identified with him, '*Ach, du lieber Augustin* – My dear Augustine!'); the prince of Schwarzenberg, later a hero of the siege, saved many stricken citizens and maintained public order.

moat. The intent of the defensive system was to keep attackers at a distance until a relief army could arrive – no army could safely storm a strongly defended position if there was the likelihood of an attack in the rear; moreover, no commander dared to order his troops over the glacis until the bastions were destroyed, because indirect fire from those strong points would slaughter anyone in the killing zone; moreover, few troops could clamber back over the counterscarp to escape the inevitable, deadly counter-attack. Cannon in the bastions could fire across the cleared ground beyond the glacis, delaying besiegers' efforts to establish gun positions and dig trenches where infantry could gather before attempting to storm the wall.

To the east were the Danube river and canals, but the canals were shallow and the water there and elsewhere had weakened the mortar in the brick walls and bastions. Meanwhile, Vienna's expanding population had pressed beyond the walls, building houses that an invader could use as cover. There was no effective city guard after the plague of 1679, and many citizens did not take their military training seriously.

The Holy Roman emperor, Leopold (1658–1705) never seemed to have enough money, or to make himself master of regional politics. Though in hindsight we can see the essential stability of the political situation, at the time everything seemed to be in flux. The emperor felt frustrated at every turn. Nowhere was this truer than in his inability to discourage Ottoman attacks on his southern borderlands; he was distracted by German politics, where Protestants allied with the Catholic king of France rejected his proposals for increasing national unity and protecting the national frontiers.*

Louis XIV of France (1638–1715) had recently expanded eastward, even crossing the Rhine at Freiburg; his influence over Bavaria was growing, and Bavaria bordered on Austria. It was an open secret that Louis XIV wanted to be elected Holy Roman emperor when Leopold died.

The emperor was not old, being only forty-two when the French threat became obvious in 1682, but few lived long in those days. Under the circumstances Leopold could not dismiss his mercenary troops. This financial burden became even greater after he joined German rulers along the Rhine in 1682 to resist an expected French land grab – Louis's promise to remain neutral during what seemed to be an impending Ottoman invasion of Austrian lands may have been sincere, but every German was sceptical.

---

* Barker calls Leopold 'somewhat slow but basically sound'. He was very conscious of his overdeveloped lower lip and worried that people would laugh at it. His only strength was in selecting competent generals and administrators. That is a rare and valuable trait.

The German States

The best German army was that of Protestant Brandenburg, but the Great Elector put local political feuds over national interests – and he favoured the French. To be more precise, he favoured acknowledging recent French gains and holding Louis off by diplomacy, then playing on Ottoman weakness to recover Hungary. He made his assistance to defending Austria conditional on the emperor accepting his entire package of proposals. Leopold, however, did not believe he could not do that without sacrificing his claims to national leadership.

Catholic Bavaria was sliding into the French orbit. Other than impeding the movement of Habsburg troops to the Rhine, the new elector, Maximilian Emanuel (1662–1726), seemed to have few interests except in the pleasures of his court. However, his army was large and it was easy for him to send supplies down the Danube to Vienna; however, though hereditary president of the imperial war council and Leopold's brother-in-law, he made it clear that he would not assist unless made supreme commander of the armies.

Protestant Saxony was accepting French subsidies, and the new elector, Johann Georg III (1647–91), was unwilling to switch sides without a subsidy at least equal to the French one; in addition, he was loath to see the emperor become stronger. However, he was comparatively rich and had a well-trained army. He had just copied the French use of grenadiers – elite troops armed with muskets, but also given, along with the twelve cartridges for their matchlocks, four grenades; to mark them distinctively from regular infantry, they were dressed in blue coats, hats and stockings.

Brunswick had been so divided among various lines of the Welf family that none was of significant importance. However, after Ernest Augustus (1629–89), a fourth son of the Calenberg line, had married Sophia of the Palatinate, the ties to England became significant. In general, the concerns of these northern states were more with Denmark and the Hanseatic League than distant Turkey.* The hot-tempered Louis of Baden (1655–1707) had become an important figure at the age of twenty-three, when his uncle Hermann turned over the governance of Baden to him; he had expected to spend his career opposing French ambitions in Alsace, but hurried to Austria to offer his services to Leopold.†

---

* Brunswick (Braunschweig-Lüneburg) became Hanover in 1692. Since Sophia was the granddaughter of James I of England, this was the link that would bring George I (1660–1727) to the English throne in 1714. He had been nominated to be the 'secular bishop' of Osnabrück (according to the terms of the Treaty of Westphalia the bishop was to be alternately Protestant and Catholic), but his three brothers died. Having finally reunited Brunswick, he had to fight his own children to establish the principle of primogeniture.

† Louis (Ludwig) of Baden had been essentially on his own at the age of fourteen, after his father died in a hunting accident; his mother, a princess of Savoy, had expected he would

Attitudes among these princes and the others represented in the Reichstag began to change as it became apparent that the sultan was arming for an attack on the Habsburg capital – it was difficult to ignore the Ottoman declaration of war!

Ottoman Intentions

The sultan, Mohammed IV (1641–91) was psychotic, but all the more dangerous for that.* Not having the talent for or interest in foreign affairs, he probably declared war on the advice of his grand vizier, no doubt only in hopes of lessening Habsburg pressure on his allies in Transylvania, Calvinists led by Thököly; but it had not worked – the border conflicts had intensified, not lessened, and the Austrian emperor had increased his efforts to impose the Counter-Reformation on his Protestant subjects. Only a direct attack on the Habsburg lands would be effective, the grand vizier had reasoned, but this would be all the easier, perhaps, if the Protestants refused to aid the emperor and if Louis XIV would continue to tie down Habsburg forces on the Rhine.

This plan did not work as expected. Louis XIV announced that, in order to facilitate a common defence, he would suspend military operations in Germany – but he made no sincere offer of troops or money to his fellow Catholics, and he undermined efforts to present an image of Christian unanimity by informing the sultan that he would not assist the emperor. Louis's hope was, it seemed, to come to Europe's rescue once the Habsburgs were defeated, with the imperial crown upon his own head. He was, in John Wolf's phrase, playing on his royal title, the 'Most Christian Turk at Versailles'.†

Roman Catholics and Protestants in Germany more or less put aside their deadly feuds – if Vienna fell, everyone was in danger. Everyone

---

live in Paris, where he was born, and refused to come to Baden after Louis was essentially kidnapped so that he would grow up among his future subjects. He would become leader of the imperial army after the siege of Vienna. Known as Türkenlouis, he would become immensely popular. Hermann had been destined for a career in the church; his Jesuit education reinforced his natural inclinations, enabling him to live a celibate life.

* Barker says that Mehmed IV, who had reigned since the age of seven, was addicted to sex and hunting; he entrusted his mother and grand vizier with the details of governance, but struck out ruthlessly at everyone who appeared to be a threat. Keeping the army busy was a means of keeping himself safe; moreover, he believed that war against Christians was a religious duty.

† See Wolf's biography of Louis XIV. Fortunately for Leopold, the French king honoured his pledge to not be a major distraction; after all, they were cousins. Rather, from time to time, it appeared that he would support the alliance, or even go to war with sultan over separate issues; this never happened, but neither did Louis XIV make a formal alliance with the sultan. What Louis XIV provided was uncertainty.

included Poland, which had been sheltered behind the Carpathian Mountains; if Vienna fell, Poles could expect Ottoman armies to sweep into Moravia, then through the passes into Silesia and Little Poland. Already, fighting on the eastern frontier had been intense; Cracow, the capital, could be in mortal danger. However, to fight in Austria, the Polish king, Jan Sobieski (1629–96), had to come to an accommodation with Russia; unless he could obtain a promise from Moscow that there would be no attack on Lithuania, he could not take his army south. Sobieski would rather have attacked the Tatars in the Crimea, thus tying down those valuable Ottoman alliances, than bringing Cossacks to Vienna – but the papal advisor, no friend to Orthodoxy, warned that there would be no money available for war on the steppe.

Louis XIV and the Swedish king, Charles XI (1655–97), did not drive into Germany as the grand vizier hoped, and local rivalries did not spin out of control – Brandenburg and Denmark remained at peace. This allowed some German princes to send replacements for Habsburg troops to the French frontier, thus contributing to the war effort even though not a single one of their soldiers saw a turban; also the inexperienced new Habsburg regiments could be stationed there, allowing the best troops to be transferred to Austria. Thus went awry the plans of the grand vizier of Turkey, Kara Mustafa Pasha, the latest member of the powerful Köprülü family to hold power, to use the emperor's many distractions to strike at Vienna almost by surprise with an overwhelming force.

Though the grand vizier was well aware of the diplomatic negotiations that were pulling together a European coalition to oppose him, he did not believe that it made much difference. The Ottoman army may not have been what it had been earlier, but it was still strong. Moreover, nobody could be certain how accurate estimates of military strength were – experienced men could easily remember miscalculations, and they doubted the emperor's ability to put a significant force into the field. The Germans remained divided, were still fearful of Louis XIV, and promises to help the emperor might be no better now than in the past. Determination and leadership would play a role, too, and nobody would consider Leopold a match for the grand vizier in either of those characteristics.*

The grand vizier had not come up with the plan to march on Vienna at the last moment. He had actually been constructing bridges and improving roads for years – it was a long way from Andrianople (the centre of government for military affairs) to Vienna, and no march could be commenced until the grass was up in March, and time had to be

---

* Barker calls the Grand Vizier arrogant, cocksure, proud, probably bisexual and certainly prone to violent outbursts. His hatred of Christians suggests mental illness, and he was both corrupt and greedy. Faroqhi emphasises the commonalities of Ottoman and Europeans, but admits that because sources are lacking, understanding the pasha's strategy is pure guesswork.

allowed for the army to return home before the first freeze; moreover, Hungary had many rivers which flooded each spring, making roads almost impassable. Providing supplies for 170,000 men – about half of whom were non-combatants – required careful planning. Taking Vienna by siege would not be easy – so time was of the essence. But if time was his enemy, it was Leopold's foe, too.

Gathering a Christian Host

The emperor had added 20,000 men to his armies in 1680–1, giving him 50,000 soldiers under arms. To pay these men he had raised new taxes, and he even hinted that it might be necessary to tax the nobility. He issued warrants to officers and nobles, giving them permission to recruit troops; in many cases he broke up existing formations so that experienced men could assist in training new units. He appointed Rüdiger von Starhemberg, an experienced officer, commander of the Vienna garrison and Charles V Leopold, the exiled duke of Lorraine, commander of the field army; both were in the prime of life and were experienced and competent officers.*

Habsburg diplomats reached a general agreement with the king of Poland in late 1682, offering him 200,000 thalers; with the duke of Brunswick to provide 20,000 soldiers for 50,000 thalers a month; and Max Emanuel of Bavaria to provide 10,000 for 400,000 guilders a year, with a promise to discuss marriage to an imperial daughter. The pope supported all these payments liberally (a million Gulden to the emperor, a half-million to the king of Poland), and persuading Italians and Spaniards to contribute vast sums to what he portrayed as the culmination of the long struggle of Christendom against Islam. 1683 would be a decisive year.

Hopes to stop the sultan's forces en route proved vain. Hermann of Baden, who had just inspected the Hungarian border defences, reported that the garrisons were too small to be effective.† The gathering troops might be assigned either to the fortresses or to the field army, but there were too few to do both. The field army was more important.

Efforts to recruit the Calvinist Hungarian leader, Imry Thököly, failed – there were no concessions that Leopold was willing to make which were more attractive than his current relationship with the sultan. This was

---

* Ernst Rüdiger von Starhemberg (1638–1701) and a cousin, Guildobaldo (1657–1737) were members of a very prominent Austrian family. The duke of Lorraine and Bar (1643–90) had been in the Austrian army since 1664; he was also Leopold's brother-in-law.
† Hermann von Baden (1628–91), the president of the imperial war council, was responsible for the artillery and engineers. He devoted his life to the task of defending the empire, surrendering his duties in Baden to his nephew, Louis.

doubly awkward, since the Hungarian rebel was capturing fortresses that could otherwise have slowed the Ottoman advance on Austria. But it made clear to the emperor that he could not maintain his earlier positions vis-à-vis the German princes – he either had to compromise, or promise to compromise, or do without their help; this applied also to Poland, which wanted to recover lands along the Black Sea and which needed financial aid to raise the 40,000 men – this force could tie down Ottoman troops in the east as well as provide assistance to the relief of Vienna. But it was the promise to the Polish king, Jan Sobieski, that he would be in command of the allied army, that won him over. Sobieski, like many great men, was susceptible to appeals to his vanity and the prospect of immortal fame.

As a young man Sobieski had fought against the Swedes during the lowest period in Polish national history – he had bitter memories of those years. He also had the close ties to the uncooperative Lithuanian half of his realm, which was continually on the verge of secession from the union with Poland (it seemed almost that the more thoroughly Lithuanian nobles were steeped in Polish culture, the less they cooperated; they had great pride in their long and glorious history as an independent people; recently the king had introduced Polish as the language of command throughout the army and increased taxes – neither popular measures). Sobieski had been born in the east, in Lwów, reputedly during a thunderstorm while Tatar raiders were attacking – an omen of his future prowess. His rich and powerful family had many contacts to the rich local nobles known as magnates and to the Cossacks. He had fought repeatedly against Tatars and Turks, almost always with success. He had even learned Turkish in 1653–4, when he was a hostage in Istanbul. When he returned to Poland, he created a sensation by dressing in what became known as the 'oriental' style – soon everyone had to have Persian carpets and Turkish silks. His army was filled with Tatars and Romanians, Cossacks and Germans, and the occasional Frenchman.

Sobieski knew the West well. He had visited Paris and London, studied in Cracow, and spoke Latin, French, Italian and German. Tall, rather too fat, wearing a full beard, dressed in exotic clothing (plenty of furs and jewellery) that blended northern and Turkish costumes – he exuded all the qualities necessary for a great prince and trusted commander. Even his beautiful wife, Marysienksa, was a personality to be reckoned with – when the king was not present, she was fully capable of taking command. She was not popular; her pride, her excessive ambition and changing moods offended many; but she knew how to lead.*

---

* Barker notes that the king had been dedicated to Mars and Eros, but once he had seduced his future wife (she was married to a prominent magnate), he changed his ways. Contemporary opinion of her was mixed, but generally low. Sobieski himself was a paradox, sometimes hyperactive, sometimes slothful.

The king's most famous military innovation was to emphasise heavy cavalry; his army had as its centre a force of hussars whose gleaming armour and helmets were framed by enormous wings which fluttered in the wind of their thundering charge. The psychological impact on enemy forces was substantial!

But so too was the financial cost of raising and supporting these warriors. Sobieski could sometimes persuade national and local diets to pass tax laws and requirements for the people to feed and house regiments over the winter, but it was more difficult to collect the money and to coerce communities into bearing what was of necessity an unequal burden. For this reason Sobieski also cultivated light cavalry (often of Tatar origin), which were much cheaper and also more effective on the eastern plains; and he could count on young nobles, who could not attain any office until they had performed voluntary military service; and his magnates had private armies – if they would send them.*

As much as his finances allowed, Sobieski reorganised the infantry around musketeers rather than pikemen. He had few engineers and little artillery, which perhaps also reflected the fact that most of his troops were raised not by the crown, but by the magnates. He faced a crisis at the end of every war when the soldiers, released from service and no longer paid, turned into bands of brigands that set upon the local peasantry and burghers. He faced a crisis also at the beginning of every war, because a single noble could cry 'veto' and prevent the signing of treaties or the collection of taxes. The king needed friends willing to prevent this, even to threaten obstreperous nobles – a practice that made a mockery of Polish democratic processes.

Financing Sobieski's wars was never easy, and as time passed, his appeals to patriotism received ever weaker responses – Poland was simply becoming exhausted. Under such circumstances Sobieski sought foreign subsidies, which eventually made him subservient to Louis XIV of France; this had the effect of lessening French help to its traditional ally – Sweden. As a result, Sobieski had opposed Habsburg policies until Central Europe was threatened by the greatest Ottoman invasion in memory. Only now would he choose to throw in with his Catholic neighbour and rival against the common Ottoman foe – that is, he first agreed to rent out part of his army (2,800 men led by Count Jerome Lubomirski for 150,000 florins), then later to bring a larger force to the rescue of Vienna.

The emperor made extraordinary efforts to pay Polish expenses: he agreed to forego repayment of earlier loans, he committed the revenues from salt mines to the subsidy, he raised new taxes in Silesia, and he

---

* Barker lists among the foreign forces he commanded almost every nation and ethnic group in the vicinity, but most importantly the Cossacks and Tatars. On the whole the Polish army looked nothing like any western force, and it relied more on loot than pay; discipline was its greatest weakness.

persuaded the pope, Innocent XI, to sell lands belonging to the archbishop of Prague. The 360,000 Florins allowed Sobieski to raise a force of 40,000 men.

Innocent XI (1611–89) was then in his sixth year in office. He had reduced expenses significantly, increased his personal control of the curia, demanded higher personal and professional standards among the clergy, and challenged the claims of Louis XIV to control the French church. Seeing the Ottoman advances as a challenge to the Roman Catholic Church, he was ready to pour immense sums into efforts to stop the sultan, but neither he nor most other astute observers were quickly aware of the magnitude of the threat.

Once the Pope grasped the seriousness of the situation, he ceased to object to Sobieski's arrangement with Peter of Russia, which effectively gave the young autocrat whatever lands south of Kiev that he could take from the Turks. Earlier popes had worked to keep those lands in Catholic hands; or, if not Catholic, in the weakening grasp of the Ottoman Turks until the kings of Poland could quell the Cossack uprisings and re-establish Polish–Lithuanian authority there. However, great crises require great risks; and abandoning the east temporarily was a risk that both the pope and Sobieski were ready to take – if Peter could tie down Tatar and Ottoman forces, Sobieski could bring more troops with him to Vienna.

Transferring Habsburg troops east from the Rhineland took longer than anticipated, so that many units were not in place in time to strike the Hungarian supply centres for the Ottoman forces before the grand vizier's first units arrived. Leopold insisted on keeping Charles of Lorraine as commander-in-chief over Max Emanuel's objections and suggestions that Louis of Baden would be more competent. There was a grand review of 32,000 men near the frontier on 6 May 1683, but Charles soon succumbed to the stresses of command – mostly over his inability to prevent crippling criticisms at court, but also fear of the growing number of irregular Turkish and Tatar forces facing him. Then the main Ottoman force crossed the frontier.

As Charles beat a poorly organised retreat, bells began to peal across Austria, summoning believers to special masses, to pray for protection from the Turk. Messengers were dispatched into Germany, Poland and Italy, requesting the urgent dispatch of men and money. And prayers, of course. Armies began to march. Slowly.

Leopold ordered the crown and crown jewels brought from Pressburg (Bratislava) to Vienna, then dispatched them further west for safe-keeping. The emperor delayed departing himself, concerned about the empress's advanced pregnancy, but at last discouraging letters from the front to wives at court changed his mind. Panic broke out as the emperor fled. He was followed out of Vienna by 60,000 people, many of them undoubtedly refugees from other endangered places; their empty homes were quickly occupied by yet more refugees. The roads were filled with wagons, the Danube with boats. Government authority collapsed over wide areas, so that robbers competed with raiders to strip the countryside and refugees of moveable property.

Morale was collapsing. If the emperor was a coward, who would lead the army? Charles of Lorraine was relatively unknown, the king of Poland still far away, and Max Emanuel too young. Would the garrison and city militia – 11,000 soldiers, with the citizens hardly to be counted on – be able to defend the city?

The sheer numbers of the Islamic army stunned observers – the camp stretched as far as the eye could see. Those who came close enough to see well were struck by the magnificent costumes, the incredible splendour of tents, headdresses, robes and weapons. And the growing thousands of chained captives, some bound for the slave markets of the east, others destined to dig trenches during the siege. Raiders swept into Hungary, Moravia and Austria. One Austrian province may have lost 100,000 people.

140,000 Ottoman troops and allied forces reached Vienna in mid July 1683. The sultan was not with the army, but had remained in Belgrade, where he could pursue his favourite hobby – hunting. Command was exercised solely by the grand vizier.

When the emperor reached Linz, he ordered all relief armies to gather there, promising that they would march east together to drive the Ottomans away.

Starhemberg faced a difficult situation in Vienna. Tatar bands cut off communication with the emperor except for the occasional flares shot into the sky from the Vienna Woods (the *Wienerwald*); he was badly outnumbered, outgunned and short of supplies. He was courageous and resourceful, but he was not well. In preparing for the siege he had been capably assisted by Count Caplirs, the vice-president of the war council, and the Vienna city council – they had calmed fears and offered high wages to anyone who would work on getting the fortifications ready. Starhemberg had promised to use force if volunteers failed to appear. Work had proceeded quickly, strengthening collapsing walls and burning the buildings in the suburbs (over the protests of owners who stubbornly doubted that an invasion would actually happen). Powder was removed from the arsenal to more secure cellars.

Money was in short supply, but Prince Schwarzenberg, upon discovering that he could not take away the 50,000 florins he had kept in Vienna, nor the 1,000 containers of wine, patriotically 'lent' them to the imperial forces. Similarly, sufficient foodstuffs were collected to last into the fall. Church treasures were melted down to mint coins. Supplies and reinforcements continued to arrive by water.

Austrian regional forces were tied down to ward off raiders and to suppress peasant protests against the additional taxes and confiscations.

The pope sent troops and money, and the Saxons, though fiercely Protestant, sent a strong force – this was, after all, perceived as a struggle involving all Christians, and the wars of religion were already beginning to recede into memory. The Lithuanians, long-time allies of the Austrians, declared their readiness to help the Polish king.

Sobieski had already begun to assemble his army. Ignoring French efforts to hamper the rescue effort, the king ordered the army to gather in Cracow. It helped that the imperial ambassador had given him 1,200,000 ducats in April. By midsummer he had 26,000 infantry and 29,000 horse ready to move – twenty-five regiments of hussars, seventy-seven of Cossacks, but no Lithuanians yet. He sent one force towards the Black Sea to draw off Ottoman forces, and sent word to the Lithuanians to follow him as quickly as possible. He waited in Cracow until 10 August, then divided his forces in two to cross the mountain passes with minimum crowding, then united them in Olomouc; they waited for the Lithuanians in Brno, but in vain – they were always just a day's march away. Consequently, it was only on 30 August that Sobieski moved down to the Danube to join the German forces under Charles of Lorraine.

The Siege

Ottoman engineers had already determined that the weakest part of Vienna's defensive works was right in the centre, at the Hofburg, the royal palace; this was an error, caused perhaps by faulty intelligence, but the slightly elevated ground there was dry, perfect for trenches and tunnels. Although they put men to work with shovels, serious entrenchments were delayed by the lack of lumber to reinforce the sides of the trenches. Awkwardly, Tatar raiders had burned a large supply of wood that the defenders had not been able to bring into the walls in time.

Vienna was not a large town. Squeezed inside an arc of fortifications consisting of a series of strong bastions linked by a wall and protected by a deep moat, its buildings were overshadowed by the impressive height of St Stephan's cathedral. The location can be easily imagined today: the eastern approach was protected by the Danube river, the western wall was thrown into the moat to make the present Ring Strasse; an excellent exhibit in the museum of the city of Vienna (the *Historisches Museum der Stadt Wien*) can be seen at small cost near Karlsplatz, and more in the military museum (*Heeresgeschichtliches Museum*) a few blocks from the Südbahnhof, neither of which is on the main tourist itinerary. One can stand at the Hofburg, look across the Ring, and imagine the Ottoman troops staring down into the city – small in comparison to Istanbul, but still a prize worth taking and looting.

Meanwhile, Tatar and Hungarian raiding parties spread panic as far away as Linz, sacking and burning villages, monasteries and towns. Local communities were on their own, organised forces being reserved almost totally for the relief army that slowly made its way down the north bank of the Danube almost to a position opposite Vienna.

The grand vizier, having encountered no serious opposition on his march, had established a large camp on the plain west of Vienna; his gigantic tent stood in the centre of the camp, the flags and pennants fluttering gaily in the breeze, but his command post was closer to the city – actually within cannon-range, but protected by the walls of a suburban villa. He had no siege cannon, because the Danube was not safe for navigation and they were too heavy to drag along the primitive Hungarian roads, but he did not worry – his men were famous for their ability to dig mines under fortifications, and light artillery was considered sufficient to prepare the way for assaults – no one ever underestimated the willingness of Ottoman troops to go forward against well-prepared defences. As his trenches came within artillery range, he placed batteries where the cannon and mortars could shell both the city and the bastions. While some engineers drove the trenches to the edge of the moat, so that dirt could be thrown into the ditch and soldiers held ready to launch an attack, others supervised the digging of mines under the bastions, preparing to blow one defensive position after another into rubble. Early in the siege Starhemberg was injured by brick fragments sent flying by a well-aimed cannonball, but he quickly returned to his post and reassigned artillery to the Hofburg wall.

The grand vizier soon had trenches around the entire city, and was making feigned attacks to determine the strength of the troops facing him; bridges brought attackers against the defences on the east. But there was no question of where the main attack would come – against the Hofburg.

Fortunately for Starhemberg, the Ottoman cannon were too small to level his fortifications completely. However, he had very little room on his chief bastion, the Burg ravelin, to place many guns there, while the Ottomans could concentrate their fire on it from a very wide arc. Moreover, he knew that Ottoman engineers were digging tunnels under his bastions, ready to fill them with powder and blow them, literally, sky-high. He sent miners underground to locate the tunnels, then kill the workers or use Greek fire to asphyxiate everyone in the Turkish shafts.

On 23 July the Turks exploded two mines under the Christian bastions, but without inflicting significant damage. The ensuing assaults failed with heavy loses. Two days later they exploded another large mine at the Burg ravelin; this time the attack nearly succeeded. This prompted the garrison to intensify the subterranean war against the Muslim engineers and their workers.

Not surprisingly, Starhemberg was becoming more nervous with each passing day. His flares indicated an increasing desperate situation –

soldiers and citizens alike believing that food and ammunition were running out, that losses could not be replaced, and the Ottoman lines crawling ever closer. He knew that Charles of Lorraine had brought his army closer to Vienna, but it was still out of sight – actually still on the north bank of the Danube, hoping that the grand vizier would abandon the siege to protect his supply lines. He could not be certain that any German could see his signals, nor would be for weeks to come; nor did he know that the grand vizier was worrying little about the road from Buda – he had brought almost everything he needed, his raiders were bringing in cattle, and he had sufficient forces entrenched around Pressburg to protect convoys as they brought up powder and other essential supplies.

By August the Turks were at the edge of the moat, able to both tear down the brick walls and make assaults easier as well as to build up vantage points from which they could look down on the defenders. One of these strong points was elevated even higher for a few moments by a Christian mine that blew Muslim officers and soldiers into pieces and paradise. But day by day the Ottomans filled the moat higher and higher, while lowering the profile of the Burg ravelin and the walls. On 12 August a mine almost levelled the ravelin – in hand-to-hand fighting the Turks occupied part of this key element in the Christian defences.

Disease spread through the garrison, prostrating even Starhemberg. Messages could not be sent out until mid August, when two adventurers of obscure ancestry (Serbian or Polish, dressed up as Turks) passed through the enemy lines. The pay was appropriate to the danger. On 18 August Colonel Dupigne led his dismounted cavalrymen in a sortie and was slain together with many of his men; fortunately for Starhemberg, the besiegers were unable to follow the retreating men back to their sally-ports. On 2 September another great explosion shattered the Burg ravelin, followed by an assault involving for the first time elite units. No more sending forth the weakest and most expendable troops! The Christian defenders drove the attackers back once more, but everyone could see that an inevitable defeat lay ahead. And not far off.

On 8 September two mines exploded under another bastion, but the Christians once again drove the attackers back. Then came reports that digging could be heard from five different locations! The defenders – now down to 4,000 effectives – were bracing themselves for a general storm along the entire line when they saw the first rockets sent up by the relief army.

The Christian Host Approaches

As the Polish army had approached the border, Charles of Lorraine had driven the Ottoman forces and their Hungarian allies away from the Morava river crossings. He had sent Ogilvie's Baden troops to Pressburg, but despite the unhappy results of that first effort, he was encouraged sufficiently (or alarmed) to continue the advance, leading his own men and the Poles under Lubomirski south while Ogilvie slipped into Pressburg to reinforce the garrison. The attack succeeded largely because Thököly had quarrelled with the Ottoman commander, then simply rode away, leaving the Turks heavily outnumbered and the defensive positions incompletely manned. This victory made possible more harassment of the Ottoman supply line from Buda – it was obvious that the grand vizier was consuming powder, food and other supplies at an immense rate.

On 2 September Charles had led his army west up the Danube to two bridges that had been thrown across the swift stream. Bavarian infantry was meanwhile arriving by boat, cavalry overland – a total of 11,000 men. From central and western Germany (Franconia) and Holland came an additional 8,000 led by the count of Waldeck. 1,000 men from Lorraine, then the regiment of Leslie, then another unit from Habsburg lands in the west. He could not wait for Jan Sobieski, he wrote to the emperor, but advised crossing the Danube, then moving to the relief of the city. The emperor ordered him to wait: more troops were on the way. He was right – the Saxons (at first 1,250 men, hurrying despite the lack of promised supplies, then another 8,000) and Poles (rumoured at 50,000 – an exaggeration, probably closer to 28,000) arrived soon.

The best of the Christian forces were perhaps the Saxons – heirs of a proud military tradition and more numerous than Johann Georg's taxpayers liked. The infantry was especially welcome, because the Poles alone provided all the cavalry that the allied force required. A tiny force from Hanover had come, but not the main army, and nobody from the best army of the time – Brandenburg. The Bavarians, Rhinelanders, the Habsburg forces and the Poles would be barely sufficient to challenge the huge Ottoman army to a general engagement – and then only if they arrived before the city fell. And time was running out.

Charles of Lorraine, with his 21,000 men, had long waited on the north bank of the Danube, guarding Moravia from any attacks that might disrupt the progress of the Polish forces. This had left the Austrian villages on the right bank of the river essentially unprotected, but he did not dare divide his army. The peasants could only take refuge in their stout churches or flee into the hills and forests below the Alpine chain.

When the Christian host was assembled – about 36,000 infantry and 43,000 cavalry – and it was agreed that command should be shared, Charles of Lorraine and Jan Sobieski crossed the Danube. This required almost three days, from 5 to 7 September, after which they made plans for an order of battle: originally the Saxons, Bavarians and other Germans were on the left, near the river, the Habsburg forces in the centre, and the Poles on the right, but quickly some German infantry was moved to the right wing, and Polish cavalry to the left. This created a more balanced force, with the artillery distributed more or less equally along the line. Some troops being left to protect the rear, they had about 65,000 men in their army.*

The two commanders understood the need for haste. The Turks had captured a strategic point on the 10th – they were now able to dig mines under the remaining Christian strongpoints. The Christians had to hurry.

There was one obstacle to an immediate advance south – the Kahlenberg. This only highway led right across this high hill. If the grand vizier had fortified that strong point, the Christians would certainly have been delayed for days, while the fate of Vienna would be determined in hours. However, he only stationed observers there. Before dawn on 11 September Italian volunteers – among them perhaps a recent addition, Prince Eugene of Savoy – seized the hill.

At dawn the entire Christian army was in motion, marching in columns led by red flags with white crosses. Heavy rain slowed the march, and equipment had to be abandoned, but at last, after fourteen or fifteen hours of scrambling up and down inclines and along narrow paths, the van of the army could look down on the Danube plain and see clearly in the distance the desperate battle being fought at Vienna. There they rested; or at least some did. Most of the army had to march through the night.

The grand vizier was not worried. Given the recent heavy rains, it seemed likely that the Christians, who could not come at him in a single narrow column, would have to advance along narrow forest tracks. They would stagger down from the forested heights of the Vienna Woods too disorganised to form a line of battle. Also, how could they haul their cannon over such terrain?

The grand vizier was waiting confidently, a blocking force manning several strong forts. He knew that the Christians could not deploy easily – and, indeed, when Sobieski looked down from the Kahlenberg, he was shocked by the rough country in what he had been told was a 'plain'. The grand vizier, after 'interrogating' two captives, moved north troops not involved in siege activities and kept them awake all night in anticipation of a Christian advance into his trap. However, when the morning came, there were no enemies in sight.

The grand vizier listened to scouts' reports of activities in the rough hills of the Vienna Woods, then decided against trying to block the byways there. In any case, recent intelligence had not been reliable. As far as he knew, the main Christian army was still on the left bank of the Danube, ready to advance on his supply lines. As for the forces which were on the

---

* Austrian and Polish historians disagree about which commander was most responsible for the important decisions to come. The question of what became of captives – all captives is answered as much as possible by Faroqhi: that there is relatively little information. Some were ransomed, some became household slaves (there was a fad for wealthy families to have exotic servants), and other divided among the victors and sold as labourers.

Kahlenberg, what supplies would they have? What shelter? Nothing. Surely they could do little beyond being silent witnesses to the greatest triumph of Ottoman armies in recent history. If they stumbled haphazardly down the rolling hills of the Vienna Woods, he would use his cavalry to destroy them.*

The Battle of Vienna

Not able to see the Christian army himself, and having only intermittent scouting reports, the grand vizier must have envisioned his fate if he abandoned the siege to face what might be, after all, only a small relief army, and perhaps one that refused to fight – he would be handed a slim silken cord, then formally strangled to death. No prudent commander would trust scouts for completely accurate reports.

The Ottoman commander drove his men harder – he had to capture the city, then rebuild its defences, with time left to march south before the arrival of winter. He had stationed the Crimean khan on the Danube, with 30,000 men. Now he learned that the khan had retreated, abandoning the bridges across the river without destroying them completely, and that it might be the entire Christian army – not just a strong force – that was making its way through the hills towards him. But he did not interrupt the engineers' work – he was not going to allow the Christians to disrupt the siege, then pull back into a safe defensive position. Instead of collecting his entire army to face the Christians, he left many men to supervise the captives who were digging the trenches and mines. Maybe if the Christians witnessed the fall of Vienna themselves, they would understand better the full extent of his power and retreat. The grand vizier could present the city to the sultan as one of the greatest triumphs of Ottoman arms.

It was not an idle thought – the Ottoman army had long been superior, man for man, unit for unit, to any Christian force. The Janissaries, a professional infantry composed of fanatic Muslims, were well trained and excellently armed. Their colourful costumes (red fezzes with gold trim, white pantaloons and blouses, and, for parades, magnificent scimitars) made them stand out on any battlefield, and when their band struck up the attack march, enemy knees tended to quiver. But not all of them were present at Vienna, and their tactics relied too heavily on sword and spear, but many thousands of them stood across

---

* Barker quotes a Turkish historian to the effect that the Ottoman army was weakened by drunkenness, whoring and sodomy, by diarrhoea brought on by eating horsemeat and the incredible stench of their camps. More seriously, morale was low, and the Tatars cared more about protecting their booty than in acquiring more; the horses had been without fodder for several days.

the Christians' line of march.* There were excellent light cavalrymen, good for fighting in broken country. Still, many Ottoman forces were useful only for carrying supplies and digging trenches. It would have been difficult in any case to get uniformity out of the empire's diverse forces, but many were equipped with totally outmoded weapons and poorly trained for facing a formidable enemy in the open field.

At this critical moment the grand vizier underestimated his opponents – an understandable error. Turks were accustomed to defeating larger enemy armies. He moved some cannon to face the new enemy, and he posted infantry on hills to the north. These forces, hurriedly but effectively entrenched, gave good account of themselves later, and cavalry were ready to contest every step of the Christian advance. They were too few, but anyone who would later have suggested to veterans of the battle that the Turks were not ready to fight would have had gotten a sharp rebuke.

At dawn the Christian host could see the Danube on the left and the city in the distance. Making its way down through the roughest country, the regiments forming a line of battle before moving through the trees and vineyards towards Vienna, doing their best to prevent leaving their flanks uncovered – which would have invited a devastating cavalry attack. Terrain caused the left flank to be closer to the Turks by almost five miles than the columns to the centre and right. Thus, the imperial infantry closest to the river ran into prepared defences first.

The Turks were about to surround those Austrians when the Saxons came up, flanked them, then made a quarter turn to deliver a murderous fire from the right. As the Saxons were then about to be flanked, Franconian troops came to the rescue. Charles of Lorraine quickly saw that a small hill called the Nußberg was the key to the battlefield – he ordered it taken. Four hours later it was in Christian hands, and German artillery sprayed over the Turkish lines.

The Polish forces had farther to come, proceeding by different routes through the Vienna Woods, and were consequently exhausted by the time they reached the enemy lines, then they were slowed by a courageous Ottoman cavalry attack, but after desperate fighting the Poles took strategic heights facing them.

The fighting could hardly be called coherent – it was more a series of running fights, troops struggling through vineyards and across gullies, ambushes, rescues, confusion. Groves prevented commanders from observing anything but the ground in front of them; Sobieski was too old and fat to move quickly himself, much less give direction to a chaotic

---

* That 50,000 men force was now less raised by a tax on Christian families than by natural reproduction; this practice, as Finkel notes, was probably less onerous and much less resented than the Christian practice of conscripting adult men. The Janissaries lived well on their estates and had a tendency to mutiny when not paid (which was fairly often) or paid in devalued coins.

battle. The heat prostrated many, and nobody had eaten or drunk anything since the previous day.

Late in the afternoon, when everyone – including the grand vizier – was assuming that the Christians would halt to rest until morning, Charles of Lorraine and Sobieski, without consulting each other, ordered their men forward.* Seven formations advanced – three Polish, one Austrian, one Bavarian, one Saxon and one Italian. When Starhemberg saw the relief army moving, he ordered the garrison to sally out and create as much confusion as possible.

The grand vizier did not lack for courage – once he saw his first line broken, he ordered a red tent planted in the centre of the next defensive line, so that everyone could see that he was fighting there personally. Sobieski, seeing that, offered his gunners fifty crowns for each cannon-shot that hit the tent, then ordered his hussars to charge directly for it. The lancers, their armour gleaming and their wings singing in the wind, tore into the Turkish lines. Charles of Lorraine, having broken through the formations opposite him, swung to the right and came at the Ottomans from the rear.

Three hours later the remnants of the Ottoman army was running for their lives. The grand vizier delayed his flight only long enough to save the Standard of the Prophet from immediate capture (and to slay a rare ostrich, so that it would not be displayed in a Christian menagerie); he had lost a least one horse in combat, all of his officers, innumerable gold objects decorated with jewels, and immense piles of military stores. Numerous captives rounded up in Austria for the Istanbul slave market celebrated their liberation.†

John Stoye quotes an Irish officer that the victory would have been even greater if the enemy had not run away so cowardly.

The Aftermath

The Lithuanians arrived the next day. The pursuit of the defeated army could have begun then, but for Sobieski and the other Christian lords, celebrations came first – banquets, parades, writing letters home to impress subjects and enemies. Sobieski took the bulk of the booty suitable for display.* Thus, the grand vizier's tent is to be seen today in Wawel Castle in Poland, while the Vienna City Museum can display only a smaller one.

---

* Barker credits a Saxon general with the decision – asked his opinion, he said that he was an old man and wanted to sleep in a bed in Vienna that night. The duke of Lorraine, pleased, said, '*Allons marchons!*' – Come on, let's march!

† Barker reports the rescue of 450 children whose enslaved parents had been murdered by the retreating Turks. He also says that the citizens of Vienna were of very little use during the siege, except as labourers, but now they swarmed out of the city to steal what they could.

Long term, the greatest prize may have fallen to the Viennese – coffee.†

The Saxons, whose discipline kept them under arms while others plundered, took home relatively little – a pile of Korans, five tents, eleven cannon, an elephant (which died soon) and camels for a planned breeding herd.

No doubt, the Christian army was played out. The march from the Danube over the Vienna Woods had been exhausting, and the troops had not paused for food or water before going into combat. Also, Sobieski, grossly overweight, had good reason to feel sympathy for men younger and in better shape than he was – he must have been desperately in need of rest, too.

The Saxons went home first, unhappy with the treatment meted out by their Catholic hosts, with their meagre share of the glory and the spoils, ignoring their concerns about Hungarian Protestants, and without receiving the promised pay. But what should Lutherans expect? The imperial general, Waldeck, took the Rhenish troops next, to fight against Louis XIV, who had not even waited for the outcome of the battle to attack. Then, while the princes who remained quarrelled over the command, as many as half the troops fell ill of dysentery.

The departing units were replaced by Brandenburgers. The Great Elector, hitherto a staunch French ally, was so disgusted by Louis XIV's apparent support of the Ottoman cause that he dispatched 3,000 men under Wolfgang Truschseß zu Waldburg.

The advance of the Christian army eastwards and south was hindered by the lack of supplies – western Hungary had been so depopulated that it was described as a desert; fodder was not to be had.‡ The decisive battle, at Párkány on 6 and 7 October, began as a Ottoman success (ambushing Sobieski's proud hussars, who were caught with their matchlocks unlit, then overwhelmed and driven into wild flight), allowing the Turkish commander to send a thousand heads to the sultan; he almost had the king's as his prize, too. However, the Germans came up the next day and

---

* Sobieski neglected to spread the word that he had captured the grand vizier's treasury. He tried to take a nap amidst the drunken revelry of his troops, the celebrations of the Viennese (who were making up for the short rations of past weeks), capped off by the accidental explosion of one of the Turkish powder magazines.

† Legend has it that the Viennese were originally puzzled by the bags of coffee beans they captured, but that once they learned the art of preparing it, coffee houses rapidly spread throughout Europe. There is some truth to this, but it is exaggerated. Still, Viennese coffee is widely held to be the best in the world (certainly by the Viennese), though the present form of preparation did not evolve until much later. Throughout much of southern Europe one still makes a distinction between Kaffee (boiled and filtered), Espresso (made with steam), and Turskaya (Turkish or Greek coffee, made from unfiltered coffee).

‡ The retreating Ottoman army had almost disintegrated along this stretch. The grand vizier, however, drove his men hard, while simultaneously executing every officer he could imagine having some blame for the disaster; he named his most successful officer, Kara

the pasha risked everything for a decisive victory. It was a victory, but for the Christians. It became, in fact, thanks to the pasha's determination to make his troops understand that retreat was impossible, the greatest massacre of the war – 9,000 Ottoman dead, 1,200 captured, and only 4,000 escaping in intact units. The victors, enraged at the sight of heads impaled by the hundreds, slaughtered many prisoners, but most Turks died in the river, either trying to swim or falling from the collapsing bridge; only the wounded pasha and a few hundred of his bodyguards safely crossed the river – thanks to an early start. Sobieski, reinforced now by more German troops, moved on to the fortress at Esztergom (Gran), situated on a high, rocky crag, and persuaded the strongly reinforced garrison to surrender – the Bavarians had dug two mines under the walls and were ready to explode them. When winter came, the Poles and Germans went north and west, the Turks and Tatars south and east.*

The grand vizier, now in Buda, ordered the execution of the officers in command at Esztergom. The condition of his army was now deplorable, with many troops deserting, some plundering defenceless communities for supplies, and others merely collecting booty while the authorities were distracted. His Hungarian subjects were desperate, some hoping for rescue by the Christians, others wanted nothing more than a restoration of law and order. The grand vizier, however, could do nothing. He was ordered to Belgrade, where the sultan had him stripped of his symbols of office, then ritually strangled to death. He died with resigned dignity.

There seemed to be no obstacle now to the emperor conquering Hungary. No obstacle, that is, except that Louis XIV had invaded Germany, that his allies had their own interests to consider, and that money was short. The Sun King, though piously expressing his pleasure at the Christian victory, did all that he could to prevent the Habsburg emperor from profiting from it.†

Thus ended a military crisis of the first order for western Christendom. The crisis had been managed not by the emperor alone, certainly not by the pope, but by a loose coalition of princes who had a maximum freedom of action – they raised their own mercenary armies, demanded taxes from their intimidated and propagandised populaces, negotiated alliances with minimum restrictions, and 'played' the high-stakes game of grand politics

---

Mehmed Pasha, to command of the field army. The sultan, far away, went into a rage, then confiscated the possessions of fallen officers.

* Barker reports that Lithuanian depredations during their march across northern Hungary ended Sobieski's chances of winning the people there over to him. As he reached winter quarters, some of his troops ran amok and many units dissolved. He had almost no army left for next spring's campaign.

† McNeill notes that the French had sent military experts, even special units, to provide advice and examples, but that French armies tying down Habsburg troops were more important; after Louis XIV made peace in 1697, French trainers were no longer welcomed.

with all the flair and self-assurance of gifted amateurs. The professionals operated at a lower level – that of army commanders and troops – but without the professionals, the hereditary amateurs could have done little.

A Turning Point in European Affairs

The military arts changed rapidly in the next few years. One had to look no farther than the smartly dressed ranks of the Austrian army, where a new unit – grenadiers – paraded proudly in their tall bearskin hats and white overcoats (which were sufficiently thick as to protect the wearer against spent bullets and splinters) and specialised in storming fortifications, throwing grenades ahead of their bayonet charges. Dragoons, originally a form of mounted infantry, were armed with carbines (short muskets) and pistols, and, of course, a sabre. Artillery, engineers, supply services, pontoon boats – all became more important. Officers were required to wear wigs and lesser officers pigtails; all began to wear the uniforms of their units, distinguished only by symbols which could hardly been seen at a distance and by their carrying batons, often with a silver or gold knob, as the symbol of authority and command.

These efforts at uniformity and modernisation are reflections of what historians have long called the Age of Reason – the effort to subject everything in life and mind to logical order. And who was to direct this process? Enlightened despots – properly educated rulers who, with the advice of the best men in the state or from abroad, could move past the accumulated barriers of tradition and outmoded experience. Society and religion being conservative, the enlightened monarchs had more success in military reforms than in areas which were either more resistant or about which they understood less than they believed they did.

Austria, alas, had to wait for its enlightened despot. Leopold was a brilliant man in many ways, but success seemed to confirm the rightness of traditional policy, not a need for basic reforms.*

If Habsburg Austria seemed about to revive as a great power, the same could be said about Russia and Poland–Lithuania. However, while Russia was successful in pushing south, Poland–Lithuania – surprisingly – was not.

Norman Davies, a lively authority on all things Polish, disagreed with

---

* Ingrao attributes the acclaim of nobles, clergy and subjects for Leopold's inability to see his empire's basic weaknesses in population and resources. While Protestant Europe grew stronger, thanks to economic and intellectual freedom, Habsburg Europe basked in the glory of the baroque arts. He further notes that diversity, which became a fatal affliction later, was not a problem at this time – the various peoples of the empire (now more numerous) protested against feudal dues, religious persecution and lost traditional rights, but had no animosity against one another.

those historians who criticised Sobieski for wasting Polish resources in a war that would eventually help only Germans and Russians. There was more than vanity in his proud announcement to the Pope that accompanied the green banner of the prophet – '*Veni, vidi, deus vicit*', I came, I saw, God conquered – a pious boast that devout Poles take pride in to this day. If the Turks had taken Vienna, Poland would have been in danger. But Sobieski's subsequent wars brought few advantages to his state. He was unable to resolve his Lithuanian problems and eventually his unpaid soldiers went on rampages comparable only to those of the free companies in the Hundred Years War. This anarchy, Davies says, was 'a foretaste of things to come'.

For Western Europe, however, the future would be more orderly. Whereas the typical mercenary had once been an individual soldier wanting money and adventure, now he was an officer of foreign extraction or a prince ready to rent out his army for the right price. Such men disliked disorder and unpredictability. Soldiers who worked for them would have to follow rules and commands, and earn 'the King's Shilling'.

Chapter 7

Europe on the Offensive
The Turkish Wars

The lifting of the siege of Vienna was followed by efforts to drive the Turks back from the frontiers of Christendom – to expel them from the Balkans, the Ukraine and the northern shores of the Black Sea. This loosely coordinated Christian endeavour is associated with the names of its leaders: Peter the Great in Russia, Jan Sobieski in Poland, and Eugene of Savoy and Louis of Baden in the Balkans.

The Christian advantage lay in better weapons and more flexible formations. After 1684 most Christian soldiers were equipped with flintlocks and field artillery and their muskets were equipped with a new bayonet that they did not have to remove in order to fire. The Ottoman Turks relied on traditional weapons – the sword, spear and matchlocks; the matchlock was a simpler weapon than a musket, but it had the disadvantage of having to light the matchcord; the spear had length, but a spearman on the defensive was helpless against firearms; and a swordsman had to charge into concentrated volleys of musket fire.

Military engineering was progressing quickly, with the Christians having a slight edge in devising fortifications that enticed an enemy into a killing ground where cannon and muskets could first slaughter attacking troops, then prevent their escape. The model was Vauban's fortresses on the frontiers of France, widely considered to be virtually impregnable. Field fortifications were more difficult, since the sites were often awkward, but they could be thrown up in a few days by any army with shovels and an experienced engineer. There was no way that the methods could be kept secret – anyone could see the general principles, and engineers were attracted by high salaries abroad. Arranging for supplies in the right quantities, in the right places, at the right time was more complicated.* The

---

* Tilly says that an army of 60,000, with 40,000 horses consumed almost 1,000,000 pounds of food each day (some eaten, some put in storage). That was the equivalent of the daily wages of 90,000 workers. Only the great states could manage this.

Christians, who had more wars to provide experience, were better trained than the Ottomans – who had to rely on French experts sent by Louis XIV (who wanted to maintain the balance of power – that is, to remain on the offensive along the Rhine – by weakening his Habsburg opponent).

The Ottomans were superior in cavalry, both in the Sipahi formations of free Turkish farmers and in the employment of Tatars, whose speed and archery were unmatched by Christian horsemen. In the course of time specialised Christian cavalry forces would become superior to traditional Ottoman units. Heavy cavalry, with large horses and more armour, could smash through cavalry and foot formations alike, while 'light' hussars armed with a curved sword and firearms could drive away even the most determined Tatar attackers; Christian lancers with pistols had a significant advantage over Muslim cavalry employing swords alone.

But it was in artillery that the difference could be seen most easily. Western technology was advancing faster than the Ottoman equivalent, and the existence of numerous Christian states provided the incentive of competitiveness – whichever state had the best artillery would prevail, and all the others would have to copy its innovations or go under. The Ottomans, secure in their world empire, had been slower to adapt.

Eugene of Savoy

The most prominent Austrian general during the wars against Turkey and France was the expatriate French noble, Eugene of Savoy. Born in Paris in 1663, the son of the count of Soissons, his talents as a military commander became apparent during the 1683 campaign that drove the Turks from Vienna.

Being a close relation of the dukes of Savoy guaranteed good military training and a command at a very young age, but it did not hurt that his mother was the niece of Cardinal Mazarin, who had effectively governed France during the minority of Louis XIV; she was also Louis's first mistress.*

Eugene applied for a commission in the French army, but was turned down. This was surely no accident, since Louis XIV supervised the appointment of every officer and official personally; moreover, the king's decision coincided with Eugene's mother being banished from France on suspicion of attempting to poison him! She was mostly likely trying to slip the king a love potion – being his first mistress, she was also the first to

---

* McKay notes gossip that Eugene participated in homosexual practices as a boy, which is not surprising considering his mother's dissolute household, but that such rumours never circulated after he left Paris. That was the same moment that he turned away from a career in the Church – his family's ambition for him, since an elder brother was already destined for the military; later he took minor orders that qualified him to become the titular abbot of wealthy church properties in Savoy.

grow old on him. There was no doubt that she was fascinated by magic and chemical potions.* Her judgement was poor – in 1682, according to Nancy Mitford's lively biography, a poison scandal reached right into the court and led to thirty-six persons being burned at the stake, four sent to the galleries, thirty-six banishments and eighty-six persons sentenced (without trial) to life-long confinement in convents.

Court intrigues and Eugene's apparent lack of physical strength and stamina may have been significant, too.† Eugene made no comment about the rebuff, but left the court to join his mother in Brussels.

When Eugene heard that his brother had died in the fighting the Turks, he slipped away with his close friends, the princes of Conti (Bourbons, hence royal blood, by a junior line), and approached Leopold of Austria, hoping to take over his brother's command. He was too late, a replacement having already been named, but he joined the army and fought so bravely that his cousin, Louis of Baden, later found a command for him. He quickly adopted Louis's practice of wearing highly visible clothing – Louis's bright coat caused Turks to call him 'the red king' and to concentrate their fire on him, but it also earned him the admiration of his troops, whose confidence soared whenever they saw him leading new formations into battle.

Leopold came to see advantages in employing the young prince, short, thin and ugly though he might be; seeking to keep Louis XIV from expanding into Germany and Italy, he understood that Savoy was a critical battleground in this generations-long struggle. However, the duke of Savoy was in exile, and the mountain passes firmly under French control; more importantly, Leopold wanted to put off a conflict with France as long as possible. For the first time in a century and a half there were plausible reasons for believing that he could recover Hungary and much of the Balkans from the Ottomans; perhaps even capture Constantinople. Intelligence arrived regularly that the sultan's forces were in disarray, that the Christian peoples of the Balkans were ready to revolt, and that enemy fortresses could be taken easily. If he could acquire a power base there, he might later be able to organise not only that loose federation called the Holy Roman Empire, but also the independent-minded Habsburg lands along the Danube and Rhine rivers.‡

---

* Barzun describes a bizarre ceremony to win the king's heart. It must have worked. Madame de Montespan remained Louis XIV's mistress for fourteen years. In short, the belief in magic, magic potions, numerology, alchemy and horoscopes was a characteristic of the age.

† The king knew everyone in court, and had an opinion about each one. If homosexuality had been a consideration, he would have probably have taken legal action against many Eugene's friends (half of whom went around in women's clothing), but he didn't. Perhaps he knew that he could not keep his own brother's name out of the affair – Philippe of Orleans was certainly bisexual, extremely fat, wore excessive make-up, and had very effeminate manners.

‡ Barker emphasises Leopold's excitement at the prospect of a broadly supported crusade, led by the pope's Holy League. However, Louis XIV threatened to make it a two-front war.

Nevertheless, Leopold did nothing more in 1684 than give Eugene command of a regiment of dragoons that he had to outfit from private funds. Though Eugene had little money to start with, he persuaded relatives to support him temporarily; and he had to deal with regular financial crises until 1688, when funds from his abbeys in Savoy began to come in. Remarkably, Eugene never followed the usual practice of appropriating for his own use the funds designated for his men and their equipment. Perhaps that is one reason his troops served him so loyally.

His reputation rose swiftly in the war against the Turks. Serving under Louis of Baden, he participated in the capture of Buda and Belgrade; in 1689 he was transferred to the Rhine, to help defend Baden and the Palatinate against Louis XIV. In 1697 he was back in the Balkans, this time in command. Within two years he forced the Turks to accept the humiliating terms of the Peace of Karlowitz.

Augustus the Strong of Saxony

Augustus the Strong acquired his name from his immense personal strength. Unfortunately, this gave him the exaggerated self-assuredness of the bully. He was, it must be admitted, a bully with an eye for art, and for women – he was rumoured to have sired over 300 illegitimate children by the end of his long life.*

As a general, he was mediocre at best, but these defects were hidden by the excellent organisation of his army. Because Saxony was a rich province, he could afford to equip his regiments of foot with bayonets in 1682, and create one of the first grenadier regiments in 1692. Three years later, at age twenty-five, he led 12,000 soldiers into the Balkans, a sufficiently impressive contribution to the coalition as to qualify him for a high command. Though his dilatory marches contributed significantly to the failure of the 1695 campaign, everyone had been impressed by the performance of his troops.

The Saxons had been in each Balkan campaign, had distinguished themselves at Belgrade in 1688, at Mainz in 1689, and had established a cadet school in 1692 for future officers – with studies in mathematics, manners and French, with riding, religion and morals added soon afterward. In 1698, Augustus would order the Saxon army out of Hungary and into Poland. The Great Northern War would take Poland and Saxony out of the Balkan war except for Augustus renting a few regiments to the emperor.†

---

* Augustus (1670–1733) had incomes from silver mines and the beginning of the manufacture of 'white silver' (that is, porcelain, which hitherto could only be obtained from China); Leipzig and Dresden were becoming centres of art and learning.

† Pay in the Saxon army in 1699 was considered good: generals of cavalry received 200 thalers a month, infantry 150; colonels 100 thalers, lieutenant-colonels of cavalry 50,

Peter of Russia

It would be premature to call this extremely tall young man Peter the Great (1672–1725), and the name would have been surprising those who knew him in 1682, when he became the titular ruler of Moscow at the age of ten; it was not likely that this fourteenth child of the quiet Tsar Alexei would ever amount to much – even survival was rare in the imperial family, and he had two elder brothers, Fedor and Ivan. So much authority had been usurped by the great nobles and the guard regiment (the *Streltsy**) and so vast and impoverished was his land-locked empire that there seemed little room for him to operate.

Such authority as existed was exercised by his elder sister, Sophia (Sofia, 1657–1704), who assumed the management of the state at age twenty-five. She was not without gifts, for her mind was as quick as her body was (according to a foreign visitor) fat and deformed. But in a country which needed personal leadership, she had travelled little and had no military experience; she was naturally reluctant to marry, since everyone would automatically look to her husband for orders.

There had been an interlude, 1676–82, when their frail elder brother, Fedor, had governed. At that time Peter and his mother were state prisoners, expecting to be murdered any day, but Peter's education had begun anyway. He was only a mediocre scholar, but he mastered the essentials of reading and writing, which was more than many of his boyars achieved. Fortunately for Peter, Fedor made one great reform – choosing his administrators partly on the basis of competence rather than according to the strict rules of the complicated genealogical tables maintained by the great families. This had little immediate impact, but it meant that Peter was later able to avoid one more unpopular 'innovation'. Change was hated in Russia. Once innovations were allowed, it was said, one might even end up discussing union with the hated Roman Catholic Church. Russians were piously Orthodox, and experience had shown that most change was bad. Boyars and clergy had a deep suspicion of everything foreign and strange; and everything western was strange.†

---

infantry 40; majors 30 thalers; non-commissioned officers (*Feldwebel*) 6, cavalrymen 2, and infantry 1. Each was allowed generous expenses for baggage: generals 22 servants with four wagons and 40 horses; colonels 7–8 servants, 2 wagons and 14-16 horses; majors 3 servants, one wagon and nine horses; captains two servants, one wagon and six horses; and common soldiers only whomever they could persuade to follow along at no cost. Camp followers were discouraged, but in practice they were difficult to eliminate. Only a forced march and the prospect of immediate battle would cause them to drop behind.

* This body of 22,000 elite troops (*streltsy* means shooters, which once meant archers but now indicated musketeers) was organised into twenty-two regiments, with most of the men living near the Kremlin with their families; often they pursued private occupations, and in general they tried to avoid actually taking the field.

† McNeill suggests that Peter was able to overcome Orthodox resistance partly because the

To western observers this was a cause of wonderment, because no state they knew had contact with as many exotic cultures as did Moscow. Most important among these was the long, close and usually hostile relationship with the Tatars and the Tatars' protector, the Ottoman sultan.

Sophia governed a state where women had few rights and fathers and husbands few limitations. Women were kept in seclusion, uneducated, encouraged to concentrate their energies on religious devotion, and, perhaps wisely, kept away from the all-male parties and feasts. Entertainment resembled a drunken orgy more than the etiquette-ridden western banquets.* That meant that Sophia, though well educated and having witnessed many sessions of the imperial council, had less practical experience than would have been desired.

It was a revolt of the Streltsy in 1682 that brought Sophia to the regency. The original complaint of the mutineers seems to have been against their officers (who were quickly beaten and dismissed), then against the current government ministers. The regents were caught by surprise when the Streltsy began marching through the streets, demanding to see Ivan, who was rumoured to be dead. The rioters stormed into the Kremlin, into the imperial palace, then lynched imperial councillors and relatives. After three days Sophia managed to take charge, but only after surrendering her uncle to the mob and promising to distribute the troops' backpay. This had been a dangerous moment, one that Peter never forgot. He determined at that time that he would bring discipline to the army. That meant, among other reforms, that he would hire western mercenaries – men he could fire. That would free him from the tyranny of the Streltsy.

Peter even associated this memory of rioting troops with the Kremlin and Moscow itself. He would spend as little time there as possible.

Ivan lived in Moscow during Sophia's regency, frail but still able to produce children, while Peter was sent off to the countryside, to live with Preobrazhensky regiment, a small unit that was more western in arms, equipment and uniforms than the Streltsy; its officers and advisors were foreigners, mostly from Germany and Holland. There Peter learned much about artillery, shipbuilding and sailing. This would be important for Peter's first military adventure – to conquer the northern shores of the Black Sea from the sultan and his Tatar allies in the Crimea.

Sophia had authorised war in 1685, after an impressive Polish delegation 1,000 strong had come to Moscow to discuss an alliance. Jan

---

Old Believers' expectation of an end to the world; they might denounce the tsar as the Anti-Christ, but they put their energy into religious ecstasy, not revolt. The same phenomenon was seen among Jews and Dervish sects. It all helps to explain why main-stream Orthodoxy came to see every new idea and innovation as a threat.

* In the frustrating way that reality deals with all generalisations, in private families the opposite of every stereotype could be true. Moreover, while each Europe state had its contradictions and contrasts, Russia had more of them.

Sobieksi, the victor of the battle of Vienna two years before, had just lost Kiev to the Tatars and was hard pressed to hold the gains he had made west of the Black Sea. It was mainly his desperate situation that made the king willing to offer the southern steppe to the tsar, but also he now had almost no control over the Lithuanians, who had never liked Polish rule. Since Lithuanians feared the loss of their eastern lands to Russia, Sobieski indicated that if they would not be good subjects, he might just abandon them to their ancestral Russian enemy, too.

For the Russians this was the first large-scale alliance with the west in many years, and therefore it was not popular. But it was an opportunity to curb the Tatar raiders who were carrying away people and cattle for sale in the Ottoman empire.

Everyone understood the risks – the Tatars were unsurpassed horsemen, and Russian infantry could fight them only when and where the Tatars allowed. Indeed, the campaign of the summer of 1687 stopped short of the Crimea – the Tatars burned the tall grass, denying the Russian cavalry and baggage animals fodder. It was estimated that 45,000 Russians died without ever sighting the Tatar army.

In the spring of 1688 the Tatars struck into Russia and the Ukraine, retreating only after burning towns and cities right into Poland, and leading 60,000 captives into slavery. The Russian response came in December, when snow made burning the grass more difficult. This time the army reached the Crimea, but it was neither able to engage the enemy horsemen fully nor capture the Tatar capital. One Swiss officer in Russian service, François Lefort (1656–99), wrote home that the Russians had lost 20,000 dead and 15,000 prisoners.

The military failures undermined Sophia's position. In August of 1689 the Streltsy rebelled again, this time to give Peter authority. Those soldiers could not have made a worse choice. Worse for them. For Russia it was a decisive moment in its history, a major step toward becoming the dominant power in Eastern Europe.

From 1689 to 1695 Peter prepared for war. He was in no hurry. First of all, he was very young himself, and consequently very inexperienced; but also, he had no army or navy worth speaking of.

Living among his foreign advisors, he slowly built up model regiments on western models; on his visits to Archangel he learned what western warships could do. He was impressed, and he became ever more determined to master all the skills of modern warfare himself. In the summer of 1694 he was able to stage a massive military review and a mock battle between the Streltsy and his new regiments. His intent, it seems, was to demonstrate to the Streltsy and their boyar supporters the need for reform. However, everyone was too drunk to play the game properly – the attack on the Streltsy fort came too quickly to demonstrate the siege crafts that had been so laboriously learned, and the defenders fled too quickly for anyone to appreciate the western tactics.

Peter, frustrated in his hopes of persuading his courtiers and boyars to embrace western practices, decided to use his yet-unused autocratic powers to force Russia into the modern world. He was then still only twenty-two years of age.

The 1695 campaign to the Black Sea, which centred on the siege of the Ottoman fortress at Azov, was less than a total success. One of Peter's most trusted artillery commanders, a Dutchman named Jacob Jensen, slipped into the Ottoman lines and informed the enemy commander of critical weaknesses in the siege lines; a subsequent Ottoman sally almost destroyed Peter's forces. Even more troublesome, the Russian officers were unable to surround Azov properly; this was due more to incompetence and inexperience than lack of men and materials. Peter's Streltsy commanders were simply not up to the job. Austrian experts arrived, nodded approvingly at the works, but suggested improvements that might have been decisive if the engineers had come earlier.

We know the details of the siege, thanks to a journal kept by Patrick Gordon, the most experienced officer present. Gordon wanted to draw the siege lines closer; but Peter was persuaded by other advisors to attack from the existing trenches. The result was a disaster.

Peter persisted in the siege for another two months, only reluctantly ordering his army to return north before winter set in. He lost more men and material in this retreat than in the siege. To make his mood worse, one of his generals, Sheremetev, with a larger, old-fashioned army, succeeded in sweeping the Tatars out of the lower Dniepr region.

Peter's response was, first, more foreign help; he contacted the Austrian emperor, Leopold, and the elector of Brandenburg, to solicit officers willing to work in Russia; and second, to build a fleet that could seal Azov off from reinforcements and supplies. In May 1696, thanks to German and Venetian shipbuilders, he was able to launch twenty-five galleys on the Don river to protect the 1,300 troop barges that had all been constructed during the winter under impossible conditions. Impossible for anyone but Peter. Being an autocrat with an unlimited power of life and death had its advantages.

Peter gave his richest boyars orders as to how many labourers to provide, and assigned them the responsibility for constructing the vessels; he made similar requirements of the Church. Peter must have smiled when these magnates, not know where to start on such a project, sent money – he had followed tradition in not imposing taxes on rich subjects, and had increased his authority over them.

The production of this first naval force was rough mass production, with the workmen as new to the job as the wood from the loggers, but it was sufficient to the task. Skilled foreign workmen came to supervise, and Peter was present personally to put his back into the work and see that everyone else did so, too. It would be harder to train crews for real warships, which was Peter's ultimate goal – once he captured Azov. He named Lefort admiral, despite the officer's total lack of naval experience, because he trusted him to drive his men hard.

Boatmen from all the Russian rivers made their way south, followed by regiments of infantry, Cossack cavalry, an immense train of artillery, and huge stores of ammunition, food, fodder, tents and personal supplies. What could be put onto the barges was floated down toward Azov; what could not be, was marched or hauled.

Peter's army was smaller than the year before, but he had more Cossacks this time, and some steppe nomads as well. Moreover, he was fortunate in his enemy's lack of energy and courage – the Ottoman fleet, surprised in the midst of delivering supplies, sailed away. Though the Turks returned twice, it was too late – Peter's forces had invested the city so completely that relief was now impossible. Also, the commander at Azov had not filled in the trenches from the previous year, so that Peter could resume the siege rather than start it anew.

As reinforcements arrived, the Russian lines drew ever closer to the fortifications; soon there was a huge mound from which cannon could fire down into the city. At this point, at the end of June, the Cossacks became disgusted with the constant shovelling of dirt and, without orders, charged the Ottoman defences. The tsar's officers were appalled – they had been calling for digging mines and more artillery bombardment. The officers were right, in a sense, in that the attack was repulsed with heavy casualties. But psychologically the Cossacks were right – the Ottoman commander asked for surrender terms.

The Turks were allowed to march out with all their possessions and their families. Only Jensen was left behind, fettered hand and foot, screaming not to leave him.* Afterwards, there was a ceremonial parade into the town, then a wild rampage by the Cossacks who seized the little that had not been destroyed or carried away.

Peter was ecstatic at his victory. He gave orders to build a new port, a deeper one than Azov; he required the Moscow merchants, the Orthodox Church and the boyars to build ships; he sent fifty sons of prominent men to western Europe to study seamanship (at their own expense); and he announced that he himself would make a tour of Germany, France and England so that he could better understand how a modern state and modern military services operated.

In short, Peter (who at six foot seven was anything but short) was doing what many modernising nations do: he was using the army and navy to bring his nation into the modern world. An indispensable part of

---

* Peter saved Jensen for a bizarre execution in Moscow, first displaying him to the public in the victory parade, then torturing him for seven days. He then put Jensen's head on a stake.

this was to hire foreign experts – mercenaries.

In 1698, after his grand tour of Europe, Peter ordered sweeping reforms – cutting beards and wearing western dress being the most famous. He then executed almost 800 Streltsy who had languished in jail since the failure of a poorly planned revolt; after torturing their leaders for information, he had them hanged, beheaded or broken on the wheel. Autocratic power, exercised ruthlessly – sometimes logically, sometimes unpredictably – warned potential traitors and complainers against resisting his will. Executions also provided entertainment to a public eager to see haughty oppressors suffer.

War of the Spanish Succession

The Holy Roman emperor broke off his war in the Balkans to send Eugene to Italy, then to the Rhine, where he worked closely with the commander who would soon be known as the greatest English general ever – the duke of Marlborough. Rumours began to circulate that Eugene was the illegitimate son of Louis XIV. The king had been an enthusiastic womaniser in his youth and Eugene's mother had indeed been his mistress, second because of the widespread belief that talent corresponded to birth – thus, the greater the talent, the more likelihood that the possessor of the talent was descended from high nobility, and one did not get higher than Louis XIV – and, third, because the thought that a rejected son was taking revenge on his father was just too scandalous not to gossip about.

With Austria out of the war with the sultan, Peter the Great fought on – and such rewards as came from the contest went to Russia. But victories were few and hard-earned. The new war gave the Ottomans a respite to gather their strength, to secure their hold on the Balkans, and to organise new military forces that could offset the Christians' now superior armies. Europe might dream of a war of liberation later, but when that day came, 200 years later, it was more like a nightmare.

Evolution in the military arts was more rapid now. Officers began to wear corsets – these not only improved the posture (standing straight always impressed the troops, and even well-conditioned men became tired) but provided a bit more protection. And all military men began to wear the tricorne, a hat with the brim turned up on three sides which shed rain effectively and was not affected by wind; often they could sew an iron rim inside the brim for discreet protection against sword strokes.

Above: Charles V, Duke of Burgundy, King of Spain, King of Naples and Sicily, Archduke of Austria, was poised to become master of Europe in 1519, when he was elected Holy Roman Emperor. However, he could never quite deal with one opponent before the next came on, and his subjects began to object to the heavy taxes needed to pay his mercenaries. When he abdicated in 1558, his Habsburg successors were no longer able to dominate their realms as he had done. Portrait by Bartel Beham, 1531.

Right: A *Landsknecht*, the professional infantryman of the era. From a drawing by Hans Holbein the elder.

Above: Saint Anthony and the City, by Albrecht Dürer (1519) captures the mood of Germany in the years when Protestantism was just appearing. The aged monk presents the solidity of simple German piety, rejecting the neo-paganism of the Italian Renaissance.

Right: Albrecht Dürer's *Four Horsemen of the Apocalypse*, though dating from 1498, came to represent the troubles of the sixteenth century, when Death, Famine, War and Pestilence rampaged across Germany and many other regions of Europe. Dürer's influence on printmaking will be seen in the pictures of soldiers, fortifications and landscapes of subsequent generations – right up to the invention of photography.

Above: View of Reval in the nineteenth century. This port city, today Tallinn, the capital of Estonia, is among the most important tourism attractions of the Baltic. The Lower City retains its ancient charms and the impressive walls and towers of the Upper City (the Domberg or Toompea) allows one to imagine vividly the drama of mercenaries seizing it in 1570, or Ivan the Terrible's long siege in 1577.

Below: Coins from Livonia. Upper left: Half-mark jointly issued by Archbishop Wilhelm von Brandenburg and Master Heinrich von Galen in 1554. Centre: Ferding from Riga (lion in the city gate) from 1566. Right: Schilling of Duke Gotthard Kettler of Courland, 1576. Lower left: three groschen from Riga, with a portrait of Stephen Batory, 1585. Lower right: Schilling from Riga, S signifying Sigismund Augustus, 1569. In 1562, when the currency was devalued, inflation resulted. The poor were to suffer the most, but the mercenaries were not happy, either.

Right: Gustavus Adolphus, the 'Lion of the North', was successful as King of Sweden and as a warrior – the two achievements working powerfully on one another. He found the income necessary to build an army, then financed his wars by 'contributions' from the occupied territories. His mobile artillery and linear tactics were combined with an increased rate of fire and an aggressive spirit that made Swedish armies nigh unto invincible. Putting himself at considerable risk, he inspired his men, but was wounded several times.

Below: At the battle of Lützen in 1632, charging at the head of his cavalry, the king became separated from his men and lost in the mist and smoke. He was cut down, but his army continued to fight until Wallenstein was forced to retreat. Most of the Swedish army was composed of mercenaries, many recruited locally in Germany.

Left: Polish Nobleman by Rembrandt von Rijn was painted in 1637. Although it would be decades before the colourful national costume of the nobility (Sarmatian dress) would reach its full magnificence (with aspects of Russian and Turkish exotic culture) the richness of Polish–Lithuania is visible already.

This dress reinforced the nobles' belief that they were descended not from Slavs, but from ancient Sarmatians – proud horse-men, superior to those who ploughed the soil and toiled for a living.

This was the era of 'Golden Freedom', when nobles ruled and kings obeyed – unless Poland was being invaded by foreign mercenaries.

Below: View from the heights of the Vienna Woods, showing the Christian forces advancing on the Ottoman army besieging Vienna. Illustrations include both sides of a medallion celebrating the victory of 12 September 1683, a Turkish soldier and possibly the banner of the Prophet captured by forces under the command of King Jan Sobieski of Poland.

Above: Banquet of the Amsterdam Civic Guard in Celebration of the Peace of Münster, that is, the Peace of Westphalia in 1648, ending the Thirty Years War. Such guard units – uniforms, weapons and camaraderie – were typical of the era. Typical also was the celebration of the end of the long war.

Left: Louis XIV, the Sun King, ruled France from 1661 to 1715. During the Thirty Years War he used a great army of mercenaries, led by talented marshals, in his efforts to conquer the borderlands – a process that would take him to the Rhine and beyond. The magnificence of his palaces and the creativity of his artists, musicians and playwrights made him the personification of an era.

Right: The Duke of Schomberg was born in Germany, but after his family lands were annexed by France, he entered the service of Louis XIV. However, in 1685, when Louis IV revoked the Edict of Nantes and expelled Protestants from his army, Schomberg went to Brandenberg – together with thousands of other Huguenot exiles. He was hired by William of Orange to command Dutch troops in the invasion of England that sent James II into exile.

Left: The walls of Ypres, destroyed in the First World War, show how fortifications continued to improve, resulting in major changes in strategy and tactics. First, strongholds contained barracks and store-houses, so that mercenary troops did not have to be housed in the countryside or allowed to forage for food (conditions that allowed easy desertion) and they could be kept from harassing the local population. Second, they required larger armies, since many troops would be tied down as garrisons; some of these troops were mercenaries, some were militiamen. Third, they required more taxes and labour services. Last, they served to stimulate local economies, and the economies of towns which produced cannons, muskets and other implements of war.

Right: John Churchill, later Duke of Marlborough, was sent by King Charles II to assist Louis XIV in his war against the Germans. Offered a permanent command by the French king, he declined. Later, as commander of the British forces on the Continent, he led his coalition army to the Danube, where he joined with Prince Eugene to defeat the French and Bavarians at the Battle of Blenheim.

This achievement was all the more remarkable because he had to rebuild the royal army after all the Stuart loyalists had been released.

DRAGONS
DE MONSEIGNEUR LE DUC
DE PENTHIEVRE,

En Garnifon à Quimper, en Bretagne.

DE PAR LE ROI.

COURAGEUSE Jeuneffe, qui brûlez du defir de feivir votre Roi, accourez dans PENTHIEVRE, dont la gloire eft auffi ancienne que l'origine; c'eft dans ce beau Corps que vous apprendrez à vaincre; adreffez-vous avec confiance à M. DU HOULLEY, Officier audit Régiment de Penthievre; il les prend de la taille de cinq pieds deux pouces, & d'efperance. Ceux qui lui procureront de beaux Hommes, feront bien récompenfés.

Le Sieur DU HOULLEY, Officier, eft logé rue du Bouteillier, à LISIEUX.

Above: Recruiting poster for the duke of Penthievre's dragoons, to be garrisoned in Quimper in Brittany. This unit was first commanded by Louis Joseph de Bourbon, duc de Vendôme (1654–1712); his successor was Louis-Alexandre de Bourbon, Comte de Toulouse (1678–1737), the third son of Louis XIV by his mistress, Madame Montespan. The poster promises good pay for promising young men above the height of 5'2".

Right: Troops on the march to Spain in a French calendar for 1720. Pictured are the Duke of Berwick and the Prince of Conti during the War of the Spanish succession. Berwick was the natural son of James II and Marlborough's sister; Conti (Louis-Armand II du Bourbon, 1695–1727) was not a good commander, but his appointment reflected his relationship to Louis XIV, not his talents.

Above: French recruiters paying the enlistment bonus. Use of the drum as a desk was common, as in the term 'drumhead court marshal'. The young man at the left is rather too well dressed to be a common soldier. Is the man with the walking stick just seeing that everything is done properly? What is the sergeant with the halberd whispering to the clerk holding what appears to be a list of names?

Left: Eugene of Savoy had been refused a commission by Louis XIV and encouraged to enter the church. Instead, he became the most important Austrian general of his era. Here, in 1714, he meets with his old enemy, Marshal Villars, to negotiate peace at Rystatt. This brought an end to the War of the Spanish Succession.

Villars had bled the British and Dutch at Malplaquet and beaten Eugene at Denain. He was a colourful boaster, but no one could deny his courage and competence.

Above: Peter the Great made his famous 'incognito' trip to Europe in 1697, visiting the important courts, cities and ports. Of course, it was impossible for a gigantic and gregarious figure such as him not to be quickly recognised, as this picture of Peter at the court of Louis XIV illustrates.

Peter quickly observed the superiority of western weapons and military organisation. He returned home determined to transform Russia, not merely to arm it properly, but to transform the economy and national habits – that is, to draw Russians willy-nilly into the modern era.

A key aspect to building a modern army and navy was hiring foreign experts. Traditionalists criticised Peter for employing mercenary officers. Not only were those men not Russian nobles, but they were also Roman Catholics or Protestants.

Above: Foreign visitors considered Moscow a strange, exotic city. Mercenary soldiers appreciated the high pay and opportunities for advancement, but were nevertheless ambivalent about working in such unpredictable circumstances and fighting against such dangerous enemies as Swedes, Turks, Tatars and sometimes Cossacks.

Below: East Central Europe had numerous fortresses that were seldom visited by westerners. This stronghold at Kaminets in Podolia (modern Ukraine) was at various times held by Lithuanians, Poles, Turks and Russians. Garrisons of such isolated frontier posts were often composed of mercenaries, who were considered more trustworthy than locals. Kaminets is a UNESCO site today.

Above: The Battle of Poltava (1709) by Denis Martens the Younger, painted in 1726. Peter the Great of Russia annihilates the undefeated army of Charles XII. The Swedish king was outnumbered, almost out of powder and many of his men were suffering from illness and the summer heat, but his attack on the Russian fortifications almost succeeded. Of his 20,000 men less than 10 per cent escaped death or captivity.

Below: When Peter the Great captured Riga from the Swedes, he completed the conquest of Livonia. However, the city and region remained long dominated by German-speaking nobles, merchants and artisans. 'Baltic barons' with German names filled the ranks of the tsarist armies.

This nineteenth-century view of Riga shows it as a wealthy commercial and cultural centre, one of the major cities of tsarist Russia. Today it is the capital of Latvia.

Above: Moriamur pro rege nostro! Let us die for our King! With those words the Hungarian nobles pledged their loyalty to Maria Theresa in a dramatic session of their Diet (parliament) on 11 September 1741, after the young ruler appealed to the delegates' chivalry, her heir in her arms.

Above: A cartoon from 1739, when Britain was about to go to war with Spain (The War of Jenkin's Ear, so called because Captain Jenkins, who had lost an ear to Spanish officials trying to stop smuggling, whipped up parliamentary outrage by displaying his pickled ear). The Dutch declared their neutrality. Britons, who had paid an annual subsidy in the expectation of being able to hire Dutch soldiers, were outraged.

Above: Cartoon from 1749, after the Peace of Aix-la-Chapelle ended the War of the Austrian Succession. Britain was bankrupt, while the Dutch had profited greatly.

Above: Madame de Pompadour caught the eye of King Louis XV in 1745. A woman of intelligence and taste, she was highly influential in matters of culture and art. As France became ever more the centre of European culture, rulers across Europe found themselves in a dilemma: should they continue to support their mercenary armies or could they build palaces similar to Versailles and have mistresses like Pompadour? As usual, *amor vincit omnia.* Except in Prussia.

Below: Coins from Austria and Prussia: Two Maria Theresa Thalers, 1765 and 1780. Thaler of Frederick the Great from 1785; Leopold of Austria, six kreutzers, 1685, and the Archbishop of Salzburg, three kreutzers, 1681.

Above: Poverty of one century resembled the poverty of another. This *Winter Scene* by Isaac van Ostade, painted in 1645, catches the poverty and boredom of small communities – conditions often aggravated by war, famine and pestilence – that drove many men to become mercenary soldiers, and women to become camp followers.

Right: Marshal Maurice de Saxe was the first of Augustus the Strong's 350+ illegitimate children. His mother was one of the most beautiful women of her era (in 1702 Augustus sent her to Charles XII, with instructions to seduce him and arrange a peace settlement; the mission failed). His greatest triumph was at Fontenoy in 1745, for which Louis XV awarded him the great chateau at Chambord.

Left: 'Old Fritz' (Frederick the Great, der *Alte Fritz*) was idolized by his men and his countrymen. This was partly because Germans had not been seen as particularly good soldiers, certainly not the equals of Frenchmen and Swedes; he changed this reputation forever.

Above left: The boy is willing, even if he does not quite 'measure up'. Soon enough he will work off his baby fat. Cartoons from 1756–7.

Above right: According to Wright, in *Caricature History,* the cartoon on the right mocked the Earl of Sandwich, a noted cricket player who was remarkably slim. The joke was that efforts to persuade him to enter the cabinet were as unsuccessful as efforts to recruit men for an unpopular war.

Chapter 8

The First Parallel Universe
The Great Northern War

The Great Northern War began in 1700, when Peter the Great, tsar of Russia, and Augustus the Strong, elector of Saxony, king of Poland and grand duke of Lithuania, invaded Sweden's seemingly unprotected province of Livonia. A year earlier the tsar had joined in a secret alliance with Augustus and Fredrick IV of Denmark (1671–1730), to divide between them the lands of the new Swedish monarch, Charles XII (1682–1718). Initially, Augustus had not been eager to involve the tsar – his Lithuanian subjects were very suspicious (and properly so) of Russian desires to seize their lands; but thanks to careful management by Johann Reinhold Patkul (1660–1707), an exiled Livonian nobleman, the two great lords had agreed that Poland would get Livonia, Russia the lands around the mouth of the Neva.*

Augustus enlarged his army significantly, new regiments under new commanders. This required the appointment of an inspector general to assure that high standards were maintained, a new council of war (*Kriegsrathskollegium*) for planning, and a new Articles of War. There was inexperience at all levels, but few doubted that the Saxons could beat anyone they faced.

Augustus had close ties to Denmark through his mother; this made it easy to arrange an attack on widely separated fronts – the Danes to cross into Scania, the Saxons to invade Livonia from Courland, and the Russians to attack Dorpat and Narva. Augustus's attack certainly came by surprise, but the Swedish commander at Riga, Erik Dahlberg, was the most experienced, capable and versatile general in Charles's army. Though seventy-five years old, Dahlberg was twice able to prevent the

---

* Roberts, *The Swedish Imperial Experience*, notes the Livonian nobles' resistance to the *Reduktion* (reclaiming lands that had ever belonged to the crown, many of which had been given out by previous kings) and efforts to better the lot of the serfs. Patkul managed to 'throw a specious cloak of 'patriotism' over crass class-interest'.

Saxons from crossing the Daugava, in February and May 1700. In July, however, he had to retreat to the stronghold at Riga (he was a noted specialist at designing and building fortifications), where he held off Augustus and Patkul for six weeks.

We are fortunate to have good contemporary accounts of the ensuing wars, especially Voltaire's biography of Charles XII, which appeared in 1728, only a decade after the king's death. His interviews with eye-witnesses, especially the French officers who served in the armies of the various monarchs, are extremely valuable. In addition to his fine style and a sly sense of humour, Voltaire also had a sound grasp of politics and strategy. His description of Sweden at the moment of Charles's accession is vivid – royal lands parcelled out to the nobles, who were now pressing for rights that would give them control of foreign policy; the peasantry crying out under the already excessive burdens imposed by nobles who were responsible for raising armies and paying for them; and the king's youth and inexperience. Charles XI had ruled strongly, but he had been in poor health for years before his death in 1697; and he failed to provide his young heir with a proper education in anything but military matters. Charles XII, though immediately invested with full authority by the Senate, was, after all, still a boy.

It was a situation that Sweden's many enemies thought could be exploited, most of all the king of Denmark, Christian V (1670–99), who lusted after Holstein, possessed at that time by Charles's cousin, the duke of Gottorp.

Charles, a Military Genius

The young Swedish king, to almost universal surprise, understood how to recruit and train armies, then employ them successfully in lighting campaigns into hostile territories. He was six feet tall, but unusually slim, and dreadfully shy around women (which probably reflected his strict Lutheran upbringing, not his sexual orientation); his tutor was Carl Magnus Stuart (1650–1705), a fortification expert, the son of a Scot who had left the army of Charles II for the adventuresome life of a mercenary. Until the war began Charles XII had behaved immaturely; now, concluding that drinking excessively not only made him appear foolish, but also weak, he gave up all alcohol.

Charles struck first at Denmark, countering the Danes' superior navy with an alliance with Holland and England (whose monarchs wanted to profit from a share of the Baltic trade); it helped that Christian V had just died in a hunting accident, leaving the military crisis in ineffective hands. Fredrick may have been the most intelligent man to ever rule Denmark, but he had more interest in women (he was twice a bigamist and kidnapped one wife) and architecture than in war. By insisting on keeping power in his own hands, Frederik guaranteed that the Danish army would be poorly led; he failed to strike while the Swedish army was still crossing the Sound; after that, it was too late – crushed on the battlefield, he had to accept the humiliating peace offered by Charles XII.

The Swedish king then hurried to Livonia. He intimidated the Saxon–Polish army into retreating across the Daugava, then turned on the Russian forces, annihilating Peter's army at Narva in November 1700. Although the night before the battle his men had been forced to stand in mud and water too deep to lie down, he correctly believed that their fighting spirit had not diminished. In a few hours of desperate combat he captured Peter's entire artillery park (135–45 pieces) and took many prisoners.

This was to have profound results for both Sweden and Russia. It meant, first of all, that Charles would have little trouble recruiting troops for his campaigns. There would have been few young men in Sweden who had not been reared on the stories of wealth and honour gained during the Thirty Years War. This generation surely saw the forthcoming war not as a national calamity, but as an opportunity. Charles, now famous and cocksure, despised his Russian foe – this proved to a long-term mistake, though he was reinforced in it by the superiority of his Swedish troops to the much large Russian forces. Charles also trusted completely to his luck. After all, he had two horses shot from under him in this one battle, but came away without a scratch.

Mercenaries in Russia

Peter vastly increased his efforts to westernise his army, now with less resistance from the conservative elements in his realm – it was especially important that in 1698 he had effectively eliminated the Streltsy, who would have vetoed his plans to make war simultaneously against Turkey, Sweden and Poland. They had even opposed his taking power from Sophia in 1689, but Peter had prevailed, thanks to the mercenary officers coming to his side – especially Patrick Gordon (1635–99) – the most prominent of the 3,000 foreigners living in the German Quarter (foreigners were not welcome in the capital itself, and the Patriarch of the Orthodox Church stormed against their heretical religious views).* Scots were especially prominent among the officer corps – Gordon, Drummond, Crawford, Graham, Leslie – and these were Peter's friends

---

* The very name of this colony informs us that the Orthodox Church and Russian law did not rule there. It had been established in 1652 to prevent the foreigners from contaminating Muscovites, with rules against wearing Russian clothing or engaging in commerce with

during his youth, when, neglected by Sophia, he gravitated to their colony, learned German and a smattering of other tongues and threw himself wholeheartedly into the project of westernising his country.*

Patrick Gordon (1635–99) grew up in a family of Stuart loyalists, but when Cromwell won the English Civil War, then invaded Scotland, there was no future for him in the British Isles. He left for the Continent, studied in a Jesuit school, and – despite his Catholic beliefs – became a Swedish officer. Captured in Poland, he changed sides instantly. Taken prisoner by the Swedes, he reverted to his original employer, only to be captured again and converted back into a Polish officer. In 1660, just as he was about to return home, a Russian diplomat offered him a command at a salary too great for a Scot to refuse. Life had not been easy in Russia, but he had married, begun a family, and become rich. He might as well have – the empress refused to allow him to leave.

A Protestant close to Peter was François Lefort (1656–99), who had abandoned his family's mercantile business in Geneva to fight for Holland. In 1675 he had gone to Russia, taken employ in the tsarist army, married one of Gordon's cousins and befriended the future tsar. He was gregarious, humorous, generous, attractive to women, and, more than anyone, he introduced Peter to western ways – not all of which were ones westerners would have wished. One of his former mistresses, the very beautiful and very blonde Anna Mons, was Peter's constant companion for the next twelve years.

The revels of 'the jolly club' were thoroughly drunken affairs – a combination of the worst Russian and western habits. Peter loved buffoonery and encouraged his fellow revellers to mock the superstitions and habits of Orthodox believers. Not surprisingly, the Church disapproved. Equally, the Streltsy, who were not only ultra-Orthodox, but disliked the western drills being forced upon them, concluded that Peter would be an unsuitable ruler.

Peter's torturing, then executing, the Streltsy was an object lesson to all who hesitated about bowing unconditionally to his will. Peter created factories for making cannon and mortars, so that by 1703 he would have 400 at his disposal; he conscripted peasants for twenty-five years service – effectively their life-time – and equipped them with muskets and bayonets. He founded the Russian navy, personally working in the naval yards; since almost every shipwright, captain and sailor was a foreigner (in 1698 alone he had hired seven hundred English and Dutch maritime

---

ordinary Russians. Huddling all the experts together made it easier to turn the suburb into a highly efficient centre of industry and information about the West. The name correctly suggests a German domination, but there were also Poles, Italians and Frenchmen.

* Grey notes that the Scots were the only Catholics Peter hired, and that was because their persecutors had executed Charles I.

experts), it was not easy to teach their skills to the peasants who would eventually take over their duties; nor was it particularly effective. Reforming the army was easier, partly because the innovations were fewer, but also because he named his most competent commander, Boris Petrovich Sheremetev (1652–1719), field marshal. Peter's new army was western in most respects, mainly because he did not hesitate to hire western specialists. He also generally stayed out of the line of fire. Almost seven feet tall, he would have made an excellent target!*

Gordon and Lefort dying within months of one another in 1699, Peter came to rely on a second-generation Scottish expatriate, George Benedict Ogilvie, who had been born near Brno in Moravia and entered Russian service in the 1660s. His father, probably the George Ogilvie who was the captain of Cunnottar Castle in Perthshire, had been a mercenary general in the Thirty Years War, but unlike the majority of Scots who fought in the Swedish forces, he had remained in the Czech lands as commander of the fortress at Spielberg; that is probably because – family historians surmise – he had gone into exile after protecting the 'honours of Scotland' from Cromwell's men in 1651.†

It was not easy to command Russian soldiers – at one moment they were courageous beyond measure, at another succumbing to panic, at others dead drunk, but they were always able to endure extreme hardship and brutal treatment. Officers were always frustrated by the stolid simplicity of their men, who seemed to respond only to beatings and intimidation, and by their addition to vodka and other alcoholic beverages. Trained to obey orders without thinking, the Russian soldier was formidable when well led, but at a loss when there was no one to give orders. It was a vicious circle: the training killed initiative, lack of initiative led to slow responses in critical moments, slow responses led to defeats. This was hardly a manpower pool suitable from which to draw officers. Since Peter did not feel he could trust Russian noblemen, and he lacked a military school to train officers, he found it necessary to recruit foreign officers.

Ogilvie's long experience with unpredictable Russian troops made him very confident of his ability to command them in battle, even against the best soldiers in Europe, the Swedes; he was equally confident that he could assess the limits of their abilities better than the confident and ambitious young tsar, and, therefore, he was willing to ignore direct orders if he thought them wrong.

---

* Black, *European Warfare, 1660–1815*, says that Peter created twenty-nine 'new' (western) regiments in 1699; these were not ready for combat in 1700 and so failed in their first engagement, but Peter pressed on, creating ever more such units. The cavalry, in contrast, remained the preserve of the boyars.

† The story, still very mysterious and confusing, is told by Magnusson in *Scotland*.

Mercenaries in Sweden

Charles had no such problems with his officers or troops. He originally relied on an allotment system (*indelningsverket*) to raise his armies. Begun about 1640 as a means of rewarding officers with lands, so that they would be available in time of war, it was extended to common soldiers. In principle, these small farmers would have to serve when summoned. In practice, only one in ten would be selected by lot or by means which assured that the best workers were kept at home, with the least suitable draftee sent to royal service. Charles XI had reformed the system in 1682, so that counties would be required to supply regiments (roughly 1,000–1,200 men), fully equipped and trained. Most soldiers were volunteers, and their land would be worked by those who were not required to perform military service. As a result, the core of Charles's army was composed of Swedes or Swedish subjects; and he did not shy away from promoting men out of the ranks.

Foreign mercenaries, though reduced in number during peacetime, remained important. This was especially true for Charles's generals. Competent commanders were difficult to train at home – the opportunities to acquire combat experience simply did not exist, especially not in a thinly populated land such as Sweden. For this reason many Swedish professional soldiers went to Holland, where William of Orange was perceived to be defending the Protestant cause against Roman Catholic aggression – against Louis XIV, who by the 1690s was waging war against the Holy Roman Empire and England.

The Saxon Invasion of Livonia

Augustus the Strong had served in the Balkans before becoming elector of Saxony in 1694, then had converted to Roman Catholicism in order to qualify for election as king of Poland–Lithuania in 1697. Poland and Saxony had been close since the Turkish wars, and his promise to use his highly regarded army on the Lithuanian frontier was very important in his election. It was somewhat awkward that he had promised not to station Saxon troops in the kingdom, as that would complicate both this short operation in the east and his many subsequent campaigns against Swedish armies.*

He swore to defend the Roman Catholic Church, which ran against the wishes of his Protestant subjects in Saxony. His decision to allow his

---

* Augustus faced two problems as the successor of Jan Sobieski. First to demonstrate that he was a great military leader, second to reclaim lost Polish lands on the Baltic. Livonia, having once been a Polish possession, was a logical place to start.

Saxons to remain Protestant was equally unpopular in Poland, but it won him some supporters in Livonia because it gave them hope that he would protect their religious beliefs.

His guide in the Livonian enterprise was Patkul, who had been exiled from the Swedish empire by Charles XI for standing up for the ancient rights of the Baltic barons in Livonia. His was a kind of hereditary rebelliousness – his father, Friedrich Wilhelm Patkul, had been a Swedish major and royal councillor, but in 1657 he had been taken to Stockholm to answer charges of treason. Johann had been born during this long process and lived his first six years in the Swedish capital, returning to Livonia only after his father died. Trained as an officer, he was a captain in the Swedish army in 1689, when he joined a delegation of Livonian nobles who attempted to persuade the king to modify his efforts to reclaim crown lands; he impressed the king with his eloquence, but also offended him by speaking too forcefully. Five years later he repeated this error. Hearing that he was to be sentenced to death, he fled Stockholm and went to the Swiss Confederation – a land where the king had no influence. Learning that his estates had been confiscated and all his writings burned, he went from court to court, ending up in Dresden, the magnificent residence of Augustus the Strong. He followed the elector's court into Poland.

Poland was an attractive model for those who resented royal efforts to curb aristocratic pretensions – Poland was a nobleman's paradise, where taxes were low, royal authority very limited, and those who aspired to be king passed out bribes lavishly. Culturally, it was distinctive for its 'Sarmatian' dress and customs – an exotic combination of baroque and Turkish influences, shaved heads, excessively complex manners, lavish feasts, extreme emotions, and elaborate religiosity. Poles, proud of their superiority, looked down on more plainly dressed and restrained foreigners; they boasted of their colorful Catholicism and exalted the new Counter-Reformation religious orders (especially the Jesuits), thereby offending both their Protestant and Orthodox subjects.

Polish nobles each possessed a veto on legislation, which could be used arbitrarily as long as a significant minority of the Diet was willing to protect obstructive noblemen from those peers who backed the proposed law or policy. It was, therefore, in Norman Davies's words, the 'most wretched and the most humiliating' period in all of Polish history.*

Augustus was ambitious. He understood that Livonia had once belonged to Poland–Lithuania, but the religious issue had persuaded many Livonian burghers and nobles to help the Swedes drive the Poles

---

* Others might suggest 1655, during 'the Deluge', when Swedish armies flooded over Poland, inflicting as much psychological damage as physical destruction. The Black Madonna of Czestochowa was widely credited with saving Poland.

out; moreover, Livonia, unlike Poland – an elective kingdom – could become his personal, hereditary possession. Still, challenging Sweden was risky, and Augustus was too cautious to take on even an inexperienced and seemingly inconsequential kinglet by himself. This is where Patkul came in, to pull a grand alliance together – Russia, Saxony, Denmark, Norway, Courland and perhaps Prussia, too – which could fall on Sweden simultaneously and tear its empire apart. Poland would be neutral, but Augustus could draw on supplies there.

The new Polish king was impressed both with the idea and his own abilities to pull it off. His self-confidence may have grown out of his immense personal strength.* His wealth was enormous, based as it was on silver mines, commerce and luxury industries such as, after 1710, fine china (Dresden and Meissen are still among the world's best). With taxes pouring in, he could hire the best soldiery in Germany, and seek out competent and experienced officers. Saxon officers were unhappy with his policy of replacing them with men from other German states, but they could no more object than the Saxon assembly could prevent his raising additional taxes to support his standing army of 30,000 men.

Augustus, aware of his subjects' unhappiness and Polish reluctance to have Saxon troops stationed on their soil, saw leading his army into Livonia as a form of tax relief. Understandably, the Livonians were not happy at the prospect of having the burden transferred to their shoulders. Burning, looting, raping, murder – those were not pleasant prospects either, but in modern warfare surely such incidents would be few and swiftly forgotten.

When Augustus invaded Livonia in 1700, he expected an easy victory. He did not even envision a Swedish army being able to come to the relief of Riga, and once Riga fell, the rest of the country would inevitably surrender quickly. Moreover, He was confident that Sweden would be bogged down in the Danish war indefinitely. However, Charles knocked the Danes out of the war in one battle, then quickly loaded his soldiers on to ships and sailed to Livonia.

Augustus now sent messages offering peace – on terms highly advantageous to the young Swedish king – but when he learned that Charles was determined to exact revenge, he withdrew discreetly south across the Daugava, hoping that Peter would bleed the Swedish army sufficiently that he could lead his troops back to Riga. However, in November Charles won the great battle at Narva. Six months later, in July

---

* It was said (suspiciously, by nineteenth-century historians rather than by contemporaries) that Augustus could bend coins between his fingers and break horseshoes with his hands. Unfortunately for him, his promiscuity offended the puritanical Poles, whose Samartian culture emphasised chastity over every other virtue; this provided one more excuse to add to his unfortunate German birth. Few Poles gave him more than lukewarm support.

of 1701, Charles led 15,000 men across the Daugava against Augustus's 10,000 firmly entrenched Saxons and 19,000 Russians. Many Russians fled almost without fighting, Patkul was wounded in the last desperate attack before the Saxon army hurriedly retired, abandoning its camp and all its supplies. Augustus led his army home via East Prussia. The rulers of Courland and Brandenburg took note of the changed situation.

Charles XII Goes on the Offensive

The Swedish soldier seemed invincible. Equipped with the new socket bayonet that could be kept on the musket while firing, they could loose a devastating close-range volley, then follow it immediately with a deadly bayonet charge. Russians unable to flee tried at first to feign death, only to be bayoneted ruthlessly; later they would throw themselves into raging streams and drown rather than face the wrath of their adversaries from the north.*

Fortunately for the tsar, Charles XII moved south, believing that subordinates could hold Livonia with only a small number of capable troops and the local levies of German-speaking horsemen and native militiamen. Charles left Stuart as governor of Livonia and marched into Lithuania in support of the Hetman (military commander) and governor of Vilnius, Jan Casimir Sapiehas, who had been gathering power into his own hands at the expense of the gentry and the king. Because Charles was less an invader than an ally in a civil war, he moved quickly through Lithuania, then, ignoring all Polish claims of neutrality, captured Warsaw almost without fighting.

Augustus hurriedly issued mobilisation orders and rushed to meet him with half-prepared troops. Although he sent orders to his units in the imperial army to join him as quickly as possible, they were far away; moreover, few Poles showed up at the assembly point, and few of them ready to fight. Nevertheless, he believed that field fortifications would offset these shortcomings.

On 9 July 1702, Charles found Augustus entrenched at Kliszów, about sixty miles north of Cracow. After scouting the enemy positions, he

---

* Native Swedes and Finns made up only the core of the army. Roberts, *The Swedish Imperial Experience 1560-1718*, notes that Charles had 100,000 men in arms, later 110,000, which would have been 5 per cent of the population of his kingdom. Nor could Charles have paid his troops from Swedish revenues – he may have felt compelled to move into Poland so that he could draw supplies and money from the people there, much as had been done during 'the Deluge'. It was exactly the dilemma that had urged Augustus II to invade Livonia in the first place. Kirby, *Northern Europe*, agrees, but adds that diplomatic considerations – most of all the interests of England and Holland – were more important than is commonly realised.

marched his troops under fire right past the Saxons until he could align them obliquely to the Polish entrenchments, then sent his men surging forward while Augustus awkwardly tried to shift his formations to meet the attack. The Polish cavalry, outdated and dressed in costumes more suited to a folklore parade than war, came up bravely only to be shot down in large numbers, after which the survivors prudently fled (understandably, it was the heavily-armed hussars' last appearance in battle); the Swedes were then able to storm the fortifications and roll up the Polish and Saxon positions, inflicting horrendous casualties. Charles was driving the Germans before them when Augustus's cavalry commander, Jacob Heinrich von Flemming (1667–1728), counter-attacked, but he ran into swampy ground; the Swedes swept his troops away before reinforcements could come from the other wing. Flemming, wounded twice, left the field, followed by what remained of the Saxon army, followed by exuberant Swedish cavalry.

Charles proceeded on to Cracow, then decided against pursing Augustus east into Sandomir; instead, he turned north to besiege Baltic ports so that he could receive supplies and reinforcements directly from Sweden. His 25,000 soldiers were unbeatable in the field, but the fortresses were well designed; moreover, they were defended by experienced Saxons summoned from the imperial army. This slowed and limited Swedish progress.

Peter Invades Livonia 1701–1704

When Charles marched south, he left few troops in Livonia, but the government was in the hands of an experienced campaigner, Axel Julius de la Gardie (1637–1710), and Colonel Anton von Schlippenbach (1658–1739). Schlippenbach, having no more than a handful of regular army units, had raised a force of Estonian peasants under the command of local German-speaking nobles. This force, including a cavalry regiment he had raised at his own expense, was no more than 6,000 strong. The two most important units were led by Lieutenant Colonels Karl Adam von Stackelberg (1669–1749) and Hans Heinrich Lieven (1664–1733, with experience in the Dutch wars); most effective was a cavalry unit from Finland that managed to drive away Russian raiders until the onset of winter, at which time they assumed military operations would be suspended.

The Russian attack came wholly by surprise, both in its choice of late December 1701 as the moment to cross the border and in consisting of 50,000 men and twenty-six cannon. Nevertheless, Schlippenbach's first encounter with Russian forces, not far from Dorpat, went in his favour, even the second, just outside his winter camp at Erestfer, went well at first

– but masses of attackers kept coming on and there were no more than 3,500 in the Swedish ranks, against 18,000 in the Russian. The Swedes were retreating in good order, slaughtering those who came wildly against them, until suddenly they were surrounded by Russian cavalry. The battle became a mêlée, and Russian numbers prevailed.

Peter exulted over the fact that he had beaten Swedes, the best soldiers in all Europe! His officers conceded that Russian troops were now, indeed, the equal of any in Europe, and there was no need now to recruit common soldiers from abroad. However, they hastened to say, Russian troops would still need foreign officers, since commanders cannot be trained quickly; moreover, they could have added, Peter's boyars were resistant to discipline and his soldiers were completely unsuitable for great responsibilities.

The Swedes had to agree that they were now up against a worthy opponent. Although Stackelberg and Lieven had managed to extract their units, many Swedes and Estonians died or were taken prisoner – to be marched through the streets of Moscow as part of the victory celebration.

In the summer of 1702 Sheremetev again faced Shippenbach. The odds were in his favour, almost 24,000 men versus fewer than 6,000, but that was nothing to Swedes. They estimated the Russian force at twice that number, and they had always prevailed before. However, the tsar's army was better now, and the names of some of his officers illustrate how willing he was to employ foreign experts: Nicholas Balk, von Delvden, Wilhelm von Sweden, Fedor Balk, Denis Ridder, Rodion Bauer, Nicholas von Verdin. Sheremetev surrounded and annihilated the Swedish infantry, and destroyed much of the Swedish cavalry. He then marched on the border fortresses, easily persuading the garrisons that their situation was hopeless.

Only Riga, Reval, Pernau and Dorpat remained in Swedish hands. With Charles XII still in Poland, fighting against an allied army of Poles, Saxons and Russians, there was no hope of rescue.

Peter then set out to fulfil an ancient Russian hope of securing the main trade route to Europe. Until then all merchants had to pass through Swedish customs houses at the mouth of the Neva River, paying tolls and demonstrating that they were not carrying war matériel. Now Danish, Dutch and English merchants could pass through the Baltic Sea to the Gulf of Finland, then, protected by Peter's new naval base at Kronstadt,* sail a short distance to Peter's future capital, a city built on artificial islands – St Petersburg.

In the summer 1704 Peter captured Dorpat, the key to south-eastern

---

* Peter was a Germanophile – an admirer of all things German – and gave not only his fortress a German name, but also his sumptuous summer estate on the opposite bank – Peterhof.

Estonia. Once a powerful fortress, now one of its walls was awaiting only – in Peter's joking assessment – an order to fall down. The defenders were more formidable, however: Although Sheremetev had been able to make three breaches in the walls, he had been ready to abandon the attack before Peter looked over the situation and ordered an assault on the river wall; that location had seemed too difficult even to approach, but the Russian troops made such quick progress that the courageous Swedish commander accepted the tsar's generous offer to allow his men to march out honourably, with weapons and flags, leaving behind only their cannons. Peter even provided the garrison with a month's provisions.

Peter then ordered his favourite general, Alexander Menshikov, to move against Narva, now a much stronger fortress than the antiquated castle which had fallen almost accidentally into the hands of Ivan the Terrible in 1558.* Narva had proved too strong for General Ogilvie to capture in 1700, though the siege had undoubtedly worn the defenders down; Peter's chief engineer, a Saxon named Hallart, had been making progress despite a lack of heavy artillery when Charles XII had interrupted his operations. Ogilvie was effectively employing cannon which had been transported by sea from Saint Petersburg, slipping past the watching Swedish fleet, but his opponent was the competent and courageous Rudolf Henning Horn (1651–1730), a sharp-tongued man, who, when asked to surrender, replied that the Russians could give him their cannon, after which he would allow them to withdraw in peace.

Horn expected relief from an army then being raised by Schippenbach, so he was not surprised to see a force in the blue uniforms of the Swedish army approach from the west, bearing the white and yellow royal banner. When Russian troops cut them off from the city, there was apparently a tremendous battle brewing. Gunshots and cannonfire could be heard in Narva, smoke from the guns could be seen, men were observed falling.

It took Horn only moments to order 1,100 troops to sally out, about a third of the garrison, to strike the Russians in their rear and bring Schippenbach's force into safety. However, the blue-clad soldiers were Russians in disguise – the whole plan was a clever trap devised by Peter personally. Once the Swedes were outside the fortress, they were ambushed. Although a thousand managed to fight their way back into the fortress, the garrison's morale was badly shaken. Two months later Ogilvie's men stormed the walls, taking the fortress in less than an hour of

* Alexander Danilovich Menshikov (1673–1729) was an old and close friend of obscure ancestry but great ability, determination and ruthlessness, who was introduced to the tsar by François Lefort. Corrupt and arrogant, he was nevertheless one of the few native Russians who understood the tsar's program of reform. In the end he overreached himself, was stripped of all his possessions and banished to Siberia. There was, however, no one to take his place. Afterwards the pace of reform slowed greatly.

furious fighting. The slaughter, however, lasted considerably longer. Peter even slew personally one soldier who ignored his order to stop the killing – he wanted to use the prisoners as skilled labour.*

Soon afterward the Swedish fortress at Ivangorod, on the opposite bank, surrendered. Peter then paraded the dejected captives through the gaily decorated streets of Moscow.

It was at this time that Peter met his future wife, Catherine. She had been born in an obscure Livonian village. Probably illegitimate, she was orphaned at the age of three and adopted by a Lutheran minister; two years later she was passed out of that overly large family to a heavily burdened minister living in Marienburg, for whose wife she was a domestic servant until age seventeen. Understandably, Catherine never learned to read or write. At seventeen a Swedish dragoon saw her in church, courted her and asked permission to marry her. Less than a week after the ceremony, her husband went off to face Sheremetev's army. She never heard from him again.

When the Swedish commander of Marienburg decided to blow up the fortress rather than surrender it, he warned the pastor, Catherine's protector, of his intentions. The pastor went to Sheremetev's camp, offering his services as a translator. The family was sent to Moscow, but Catherine remained behind, to become part of the general's household. Told that she was married, Sheremetev said that that was not important to him. A half year later Menshikov was attracted to her – he was a great joker, vivacious, outgoing, inventive, unconventional and, therefore, appealing to women. She was in his household when Peter saw her. She was soon his mistress, too. (Menshikov was the sharing kind, particularly with the tsar.) By late 1705 Catherine had presented him two children, both boys.

Peter was not much of a womaniser (he chided Augustus the Strong for his many affairs), but he enjoyed Catherine's earthy habits. Peter was unconventional – often working alongside his men, wearing western clothes, wearing work clothes, drinking, swearing, talking. Catherine could keep up with him in all that – and was always in a good humour. She was not the type to complain about muddy boots on the table.

Peter's Mercenary Generals

The other Livonian German who became a part of the tsar's family was Patkul. Peter was instantly impressed with his genial combination of

---

* The Estonian ambassador to the United Kingdom, Margus Laidre, well known as a historian himself, confirmed the accuracy of this account, which has been surprisingly ignored by Peter's biographers.

pleasant personality, wise counsel and practical knowledge. He invited him to Moscow in the spring of 1702, then persuaded him to leave Augustus and enter his own service – after all, only Peter could restore to him the family estates in Livonia. This caused the Poles to become sceptical about the alliance, so that although cooperation was promised, it was not fully implemented.

When entrusted with the job of recruiting mercenaries, Patkul issued a proclamation offering good wages, travel and moving expenses from the border, freedom of worship and important responsibilities. There would be a council of war composed solely of foreign commanders, who would be responsible for pay and provision of their forces!

Patkul named Ogilvie supreme commander, then hired Carl Evald Ronne and Heinrich von Huyssen for other high commands; he also employed Peter Lacy, the Irish exile from Limerick.*

But other potential officers, though interested, demurred after investigating the situation – Russia was just too backward, too super-stitious, and Peter too unpredictable. The tsar tried to counter these impressions by redoubling his efforts to westernise his state. But although Peter could make immediate changes at court, and have some impact on cities such as St Petersburg, his orders went unread in the countryside, even by those who could read.

Another discouragement to serving in the Russian army was the likelihood of having to fight Charles XII. No European army was able to stand up to Swedish armies – and Charles seemed to be an improved reincarnation of Gustavus Adolphus. At the head of his forces, he should have been shot down long before, but he seemed invulnerable as well as invincible.

War in Poland

The Poles, dissatisfied with Augustus's inability to defend them, deposed him in 1704 and elected Stanislas Leszczyński (1677–1766), the youthful, rather indolent son of the count palatine of Poznań. The new king-elect, whose primary qualifications seemed to be that he was not somebody else and did not seem intelligent enough to be dangerous, promised to make peace with Charles, but many Poles were furious about his cowardly readiness to abandon lands which their ancestors had earned by the expenditure of blood and treasure; many nobles and clerics

---

* Pipes in Cracraft estimates that Peter drafted three times the proportion of men as any other European power, and that by 1705 96 per cent of all government expenses went to the army. New taxes tripled the imperial income, so that by his death Peter had a standing army of 210,000 troops and 110,000 auxiliaries such as Cossacks.

would have preferred one of the great Sobieski's sons, Jakub or Alexander, but they were prisoners in the impregnable Königstein castle in Saxony. While Stanislas was quickly dismissed as an ineffective Swedish puppet, Augustus was agreeing to a new alliance with Peter, who had hitherto been considered too eager to seize Lithuanian lands – the fear (well-founded) was that the Russian army would soon become an occupation force.

The key figure in these negotiations was Patkul. Complicating the situation, Augustus the Strong did not abandon his claims on the throne, but remained in the field. He, at least, unlike Stanislas, had a good army and was an imposing personality.

Meanwhile, one of Peter's colonels, von Ronne, had defeated a Swedish army near Vyborg in July of 1703, slaying a thousand soldiers at the cost of thirty-two men. Peter, who had been present to witness the battle and close enough to the flying shells to worry his officers, rewarded his commander with additional responsibilities and promises of future riches. Saint Petersburg was now safe from attack.*

Peter continued to build his city in the northern swamps, ignoring every difficulty and obstacle. If the Dutch could build great towns below sea level, he could overcome storms, floods, lack of food, disease. It was simply a matter of hiring the best foreign experts, then providing them with everything they needed – including a limitless supply of labourers, who were replaced as quickly as they died. By 1706 his city was well on its way to becoming an impressive capital, one that would astonish westerners as much as Moscow depressed them.

Charles XII ignored these developments – other than to strengthen his garrison at Vyborg, whence it would be easy to capture St Petersburg once the Polish campaign was concluded. Or so he believed, ignoring the pleas of his subjects and even his mother, who begged him to hurry to the rescue of Livonia. He refused, saying that Poland-Lithuania was the more important foe; and his army was winning victories in almost every corner of that vast state. In 1702, with only 300 cavalry, he had captured the Polish capital, Cracow, his bravado intimidating the garrison's commander. In 1703 he began a long siege of the Vistula fortress at Thorn defended by 5,000 Saxon troops. As his troops gathered in the wealth of the Polish countryside, many Polish nobles entered his service – in this era Polish allegiance was for sale, and the price was low.

Charles also benefited from the War of the Spanish Succession, which tied down the rulers of Austria and France for years to come, making it

---

* Karl Ewald von Rönne (1663–1726) was a German-speaking noble from Courland who commanded the tsar's army in the Ukraine from 1711 to 1716. In 1728, Ronne's widow, Anna Lucia de Preen, would buy a large estate in Courland which by then was part of the Russian empire.

impossible for either to intervene in what came to be known as the Great Northern War; the emperor, Leopold, could have given significant support to Augustus the Strong; instead, he relied on him to provide sizeable forces for the struggle against France. Augustus did send troops west – as long as he received money, he could recruit armies.

The fighting along the Lower Vistula wore the Saxons down and cost them most of the fortresses; after Thorn surrendered, 1,600 men were taken to Danzig and put on ships for transport to Sweden, but most drowned in a storm.

Poland Up For Grabs

In 1704, Peter sent General Repnin to reinforce Augustus the Strong for a strike against Warsaw, and ordered Sheremetev to gather troops in Polotsk for a future invasion of Courland.* That province, relatively rich, was technically an independent duchy and relatively unplundered; however, it was defended by the capable general Adam Ludvig Lewenhaupt (1659–1719).

Repnin's army reached Augustus at Warsaw, which the king had just taken. The allies then marched on Poznań, where the king left 12,000 men, about a quarter of his army, with Patkul, and entered Silesia in hope of preventing Charles from invading Saxony. The ensuing battle was another spectacular Swedish success – the allies were then unable to prevent the dynamic king from dashing from one province to the other, barely slowed by his soldiers' enthusiastic burning and plundering. His generals quickly captured numerous cities, including Warsaw.

Patkul meanwhile was at Grodno, the fortress that had long guarded the western gate of Lithuania – swamps to the north and south and the Nemunas (Niemen) River forced invaders to pass through the city. Patkul gave Ogilvie tactical command, while Shermentov and Menshivok collected forces farther east.

When Menshikov reached Grodno, the plan was to spend the winter there, so that in the spring they could either move up the Bug into the Ukraine or go west into the Vistula river valley. Those plans changed in December 1704 when word came that Stanislas was to be crowned in Warsaw – that had to be prevented. Patkul marched on that city with 10,000 Russian and Saxon troops, only to be routed by 2,000 Swedes.

The tsar's concentration of forces in Polotsk – 40,000 infantry and 20,000 cavalry, all equipped by the tsar's new munitions plants south and

---

* Anikita Ivanovich Repnin (1668–1726) came from one of Russia's most prominent families. He earned the tsar's trust by saving his life from rioters in 1682. His military fortunes were mixed, but he ended his life, loaded with honours and riches, as war minister.

east of Moscow – was designed to allow the army to move down the Daugava River into Livonia and Courland in the summer of 1705. While nothing went quite right, nothing went completely wrong, either. Shermetov fought a desperate battle against Lewenhaupt, but lost many men and all his cannons; but Lewenhaupt was so weakened that he was unwilling to risk another engagement – he fell back on Riga. Peter was then able to advance from Vilnius and occupy Courland.

Meanwhile, Charles had attended Stanislas's delayed coronation in Warsaw, then begun refitting his army and preparing it for a winter campaign. Somehow, the alliance's spies were unable to confirm his intentions – though it should have been obvious that a winter campaign would be directed toward Russia.

It was now apparent that Patkul was a better diplomat than a general. Accordingly, Peter sent him to Berlin to persuade the elector of Brandenburg to enter the war – Frederick's troops were the best in all of Germany.* The elector's titles had recently been expanded by the emperor into include 'king *in* Prussia' in order to woo him into his own anti-French coalition; thus, Prussian troops were now fighting in Germany and Italy. The elector, moreover, was wary of exposing himself to Swedish attack while Charles was on a rampage – and it would have been difficult in any case for him to defend East Prussia, a lightly populated district not even directly connected to Brandenburg. Patkul, disappointed, went on to Dresden in hopes of persuading the royal council to enlarge the alliance to include the Holy Roman emperor. However, the Protestant Saxons were reluctant – the emperor was Catholic, and it seemed very likely that he would become the dominant figure in the coalition if he could ever extract himself from the War of the Spanish Succession. The newly elected Holy Roman emperor, Joseph I, was himself hesitant to take on a second war without some indication that would have the resources to be effective. Patkul suggested that the Russian troops under Saxon command be transferred to the emperor for one year. The Saxons delayed making a commitment until December 1705, when they suddenly arrested Patkul and imprisoned him in the fortress of Sonnenstein, holding him there until September 1706, when they transferred him to Königstein.

Charles, who was thought to have been immobilised by the weather, suddenly appeared at Grodno in mid January 1706. What was winter to a Swede? Charles knew that this was an excellent month for moving troops, as long as they had tents, fodder and food – the roads were frozen, ambushes were unlikely. He had crossed Poland in two weeks – faster than couriers could make the journey. Menshikov immediately hurried to

---

* Friedrich I of Hohenzollern (1657–1713) had succeeded his father, the Great Elector ,in Brandenburg in 1688; he became king in Prussia in 1701.

Peter, not even bothering to inform Ogilvie of his intentions. He told the tsar of a council of war, in which King Augustus had agreed that the best plan was to retreat eastward, but that Ogilvie refused to budge – he preferred to risk siege inside the fortress; then Augustus had left, taking a roundabout route to Warsaw, to join the Saxon-Polish army that was following slowly behind the Swedish forces.

Life inside a fortress is unpleasant at the best of times. Under siege far too many men are crowded together, with meagre rations, no exercise, poor sanitary facilities. Ogilvie's men began to sicken and die in large numbers.

Peter sent repeated orders to Ogilvie to retreat eastward, but with Charles waiting to ambush him, the Scot general delayed in hope of Augustus's relief army arriving. The exchanges between the tsar and his general are almost humorous, but they demonstrate the superior ability of the mercenary over the employer. When Peter ordered Ogilvie to retreat at once, even if it meant throwing his cannon in the river, Ogilvie asked for reinforcements – a large herd of camels and 20,000 courtiers. But Peter was more correct in assessing the Swedes' ability to handle the Saxons – the 30,000 Saxons marching to relieve the siege were routed by 8,000 Swedes under one of the royal lieutenants. Only after that did Ogilvie agree to break out of the trap and escape toward Kiev.

Even so, Ogilvie waited until the March ice floes carried away the Swedish bridge across the Nemunas river before he ordered his men across his own secure bridge and hurried east to join with Menshikov's army in Pinsk. Charles almost caught him, but gave up when the short cut he had chosen across thawing marshes threatened to engulf both man and beast.

Not surprisingly, Peter now accepted Ogilvie's offer to resign – poor health was a convenient excuse. Menshikov took over command, while Ogilvie went west to accept a position in Augustus's army. Charles, meanwhile, turned on the Saxons.

The change in command did not save the Saxon army from the rapid advance of Charles's forces. It had appeared that Augustus had recovered from the earlier setbacks. In 1704 he had recruited a new army, but his troops were demoralised, his subjects in panic, and many units were stationed in Poland to keep open communications with Russia or to assist the emperor in Germany. Augustus authorised his ministers to enter into negotiations, carefully keeping the details secret from his allies, then went himself went to eastern Poland to greet the newly arrived Russian forces led by Menshikov. This reinforcement allowed Augustus to pull together forces for an offensive and gave his troops the confidence to fight; he even won an engagement in November. The fighting in 1705 had mixed results, but it was sufficiently distracting that Charles XII decided to knock Saxony out of the war.

Charles hit the combined enemy force in February 1706, inflicting 8,000 casualties and taking 7,000 captives in an hour and a half, losing only 400 men killed and 1,000 wounded. Charles pushed on into Saxony. Augustus, meanwhile, hurried to Poland, where he raised a new army and marched against the Swedish supply lines. The Saxon-Polish-Russian force won a victory over the Swedes at Kalisz in northern Poland – the numerical advantage was only two to one – and Menshikov reluctantly delivered the prisoners to Augustus.

Saxony was lost, however. When the Russians fled at rumours that the young Swedish king was heading their way and the Polish-Saxon troops were routed, Augustus admitted defeat – he obtained peace at the cost of paying Charles 500,000 thalers a month in cash and sending 125,000 thalers' worth of supplies. He made some of this money by renting regiments to the emperor for use against France.

The Peace of Altranstadt ended the war between Sweden and Saxony. One term of the treaty required Augustus to deliver all prisoners, deserters and exiles to the Swedish king; Patkul was specifically mentioned. There was a general uproar, the delivery of a diplomat into hostile hands being inconsistent with all accepted practices – but that did not save Patkul from being broken on the wheel in October 1707 (his shattered limbs being laced between the spokes, his broken ribs filling his lungs with blood), then being quartered, his body parts put on public display as a warning that treason would be neither tolerated nor evaded.

With Augustus now renouncing his claims on the Polish throne, with Stanislas receiving unenthusiastic recognition by the foreign powers, Charles was ready to turn to Russia with undivided attention.

Mazeppa

Charles was ready to move toward Moscow in the spring of 1708. Peter, uncertain as to which route he would take, ordered total destruction of towns and fields along all potential roads – from Dorpat to Smolensk a band of 120 miles of burning villages and fields denied the Swedes food, fodder and shelter. But Charles, reckless as ever, dismissed appeals from friends, foes and neutrals alike to accept favourable offers for peace. Instead, he planned a two-pronged assault on Russia – one from Riga led by Lewenhaupt to take Pskov and St Petersburg, his own directly from Grodno toward Moscow.

Charles successfully manoeuvred past the Berezina river defences, then sought out the main tsarist army. He found it heavily dug in at Golovchin, behind the swamps of the Babich river. His attack violated most principles of war, but he nevertheless drove the Russians from their trenches. It had not been the easy victory he had anticipated, nor had the

Russians been routed, but he attributed the change to the foreign officers in the tsarist army, saying that if the Russian soldiers had been half as courageous as their leaders, the Swedish attack would have failed completely.

Perhaps this was the king's typical disparagement of his opponents, but it was an acknowledgement that the Russian campaign would not be easy. He would need reinforcements. He summoned Lewenhaupt from Riga, and he made contact with a Cossack Hetman, Ivan Mazeppa,* who had offered to bring 30,000 Cossacks to Charles's side, and there was some potential for bringing the Ottoman Turks and Tatars into the war. It was a well timed offer. Charles had previous disdained help from others, but now he was in dire need.

Mazeppa had once been Peter's favourite, and the great magnates liked him as well. However, there were strains in his loyalty – Cossacks hated boyars, Menshikov repeatedly insulted and humiliated him, and Peter's western practices offended his conservative religious principles. More important, perhaps, was Mazeppa's desire to be on the winning side – and in 1708 that seemed to be Charles XII. If Mazeppa was skilful enough, he might become the ruler of an independent Ukraine. But the ultimate reason for Mazeppa's 'treason' was a woman – the father had gone to the tsar, who wrote to Mazeppa that he did not believe the accusations. But since he could not expect the tsar not to be furious when he learned that the accusations of seduction and abduction were true, Mazeppa captured and beheaded the father. After that, there was no turning back.

Charles gave up the march through the burned borderlands that led to Moscow, turning southeast to join up with Mazeppa. He moved away from Lewenhaupt, but he had confidence that his general could reach him with a huge column of supplies.

Mazeppa was dismayed when Charles entered the Ukraine – his plan had been to benefit from the Swedish capture of Moscow, not to have Charles bring armies and civil war into the Cossack lands. Certainly not to have Menshikov following with an even larger army. Nor to have his

---

* Mazeppa (c. 1645–1709) was not a Cossack by birth or education. He had been born in southern Volhynia, a part of the Lithuanian state inhabited by Orthodox and Uniate Russians. When he was a page at the court of King Casimir, he was often taunted by Catholic boys for his Orthodox beliefs; once he drew his sword in defiance, causing him to be exiled. Later he was humiliated by a Volhynian nobleman whose wife he had seduced. After that he sought refuge with Ukrainian Cossacks – rough frontiersmen who judged a man on the basis of his qualities, not his birth. This was an unexpected fate for a man trained in Jesuit schools and well-travelled in western Europe. Mazeppa's knowledge of the world, his fluency in Russian, Polish, German and Latin, his courage and leadership abilities led to his becoming the local Hetman's secretary and diplomatic representative. In 1687 Mazeppa became his successor.

alliance denounced as selling out Orthodoxy to the Roman Catholics (Charles was a Lutheran, but Cossacks paid little attention to such differences). As a result, though Mazeppa joined Charles, most Cossacks remained loyal to the tsar or were intimidated by his armies. Mazeppa's rebellion was crushed before it really began, drowned in a series of massacres by the Russian army and loyalist Cossack leaders. Mazeppa, excommunicated by the Orthodox Church, barely managed to bring 1,500 horsemen to the Swedish camp.

Although later thousands of local peasants came to volunteer, Charles had no weapons to equip them, no time for training.

The Battle of Poltava

Lewenhaupt, meanwhile, was conveying reinforcements from Riga across Lithuania – almost 13,000 men. He was not pleased with the plan to meet somewhere in south-western Russia, but he obeyed orders – setting out in May and persisting even after learning that Charles was moving south, away from him. His army would be a sufficient reinforcement to tip the balance. Therefore, he kept marching. In late September Peter's scouts managed to locate Lewenhaupt's army; soon afterward cavalry attacks disrupted the long column of soldiers and supply wagons.

Lewenhaupt decided to take a stand at Lesnaya, to delay the Russian pursuit long enough for the supply train to reach the king. Among his officers were de la Gardie and Schlippenbach. The odds were slightly in Peter's favour (11,600 men versus 8,500), but the contest was evenly matched until the end of the day when Russian reinforcements arrived. The Swedes retreated to the cover of a circle of wagons until dark, then, when the Russian attacks ended, attempted to slip away unobserved. The swift Russian pursuit, however, made escape impossible. Lewenhaupt lost 2,000 wagons of supplies (burning some to prevent their being used to feed Peter's troops) and arrived at Charles's camp with only half his original force, no cannons, no food, no tents or winter clothing.

It was the hardest winter in memory. The Baltic Sea froze, swift rivers were covered with thick ice, even the canals in Venice were iced over. The Swedes plodded south in search of a winter quarters, suffering terribly – on one night 3–4,000 soldiers froze to death, and others suffered frostbite.

Peter offered soldiers bounties for every Swede captured or killed, and he promised food and good pay to every Swedish soldier who would desert. Few of Charles's men, however, abandoned their monarch. For better or worse, they followed him to the end.

In January 1709 Charles took advantage of a brief warm spell to march eight miles to a Russian fort garrisoned by more than a thousand Russians under the command of an English officer. At dusk he forced the officer to surrender his position, but the losses were severe – 400 dead and 800 wounded. He then began to move into the Ukraine, toward Peter's distant base at Azov, leaving behind a wide belt of devastation incapable, he thought, of sustaining his Russian pursuers. But the Russians persisted, too, coming on no matter what the cost in men to weather and skirmishes. Finally, in February, when heavy rains brought flooding, Charles could go no farther in that direction. He turned toward the Vorskla, a river famous in Russian military history for the many combats fought at its handful of good crossings, and headed for the ford at Poltava. Though that fort was defended by stalwart Russians, no enemy fortress had yet been able to withstand Charles's men. If he could capture supplies there, he would be able to fight or continue his march. His generals urged him to bypass the fort and hurry on to Turkey, but Charles would not hear of anything that smacked of retreat. He commenced a siege of Poltava in May.

Charles was placing great hopes on Turkey. He believed his diplomats could persuade the sultan to provide the additional troops needed to capture Moscow and put an end to Peter's ambitions. He had good reason to believe that the sultan would listen sympathetically – the tsar's new navy threatened to make the Black Sea into a Russian lake, and Constantinople itself was just over the horizon; also, there was a war faction in the imperial council. Logic suggested that the sultan would at least send Tatars to the king's rescue. However, it was not to be – the sultan dithered, failing to act in time to be effective and even ordering the Tatar khan to stay out of the fight. It was a missed opportunity that would not come again. As for Charles, his faith that reinforcements would arrive caused him to miss the opportunities to escape.

Poltava was a good place to await reinforcements from Poland, from the Tatars, the Turks or other Cossack brotherhoods, but none were coming. Not that knowing this would have made a difference to the stubborn king. Although Charles now had almost no artillery, no powder, no bullets, and only a quarter of the numbers of the Russian army, he led the attacks on Poltava personally until mid June, when he was shot through the foot, length-wise, the limb being so mangled that the royal physicians wanted to amputate it. He refused, of course, but the wound required him had to be carried around on a litter. Heat, hunger and despair began to wear the remaining Swedes down.

Peter, hearing of the king's injury, closed in, establishing trenches around the Swedish camp. In late June Charles decided to drive him away, his 13,000 men against Peter's 80,000 – swords and spears against the best modern weapons. Against all odds, Lewenhaupt captured the positions assigned to him. But at the critical moment he received an order to halt. He did so, and precious time was lost before it was determined that the king had given no such instructions. His next wave of attackers was shot down by the Russians, then scattered by Cossack cavalry.

Credit for the victory belonged, of course, to the tsar, but some observers say that Peter Lacy's advice to order the musketeers not to fire until almost in contact with the Swedes was decisive – the traditional uncoordinated shots at a distance were replaced by deadly volleys.

Charles was carried away, and, when most of his bearers were shot down, he was placed on a horse and led away to Turkey. Many Swedish cavalry and infantry units escaped briefly, but 3,000 had fallen and 2,000 had been taken prisoner.* Charles's reputation would never recover.

Peter Occupies the Baltic States

Peter followed up his victory by posting Menshikov to watch the southern border, to prevent Charles XII from crossing into Poland and making his way back to Sweden; the tsar then hurried to Riga, which Sheremetov's army had just reached. Peter personally opened the bombardment in November, but soon agreed that it would be foolish to leave the army exposed to the rigours of a northern winter.†

He sent more troops to Poland, where they joined with Augustus to pound at the Swedish fortresses along the coast. This tied down Swedish troops so that he could make a strike against Vyborg, which succeeded in June 1710. Riga surrendered in July, the remaining Livonian cities in September.

Peter graciously confirmed the extensive privileges of the German nobles and burghers in Livonia, thus guaranteeing their loyalty for the next 200 years. The Baltic barons provided future tsars many generals and bureaucrats, so much so that a Russian noble was once said to have responded to a tsarist request to name a favour with, 'Make me a German'.

Indeed, it was henceforth not necessary for Peter and his successors to make extraordinary efforts to seek out foreigners for their fighting abilities – they had annexed enough noblemen for all imperial needs. If these Germans became loyal to the Russian state, the Estonian and Latvian peasantry did not. For them national liberation would mean not only overthrowing the Baltic barons, but the tsar as well.

---

* Black, *European Warfare, 1660–1815*, says that one unit had only fourteen survivors out of its original 700, another forty of 500. He estimates Swedish losses at 10,000, with the surrender of the rest of the army adding to that total.

Disease was another concern. Plague had begun to spread across east central Europe. John Alexander, in Cracraft (ed.), *Peter the Great Transforms Russia*, estimates 100,000 would die in Sweden within four years, 200,000 in Courland, 100,000 in Poland and 500,000 in Hungary; over 20-60,000 perished in Riga during the siege, and almost 10,000 in the Russian army.

The mercenary heroes of the early days of the war began to pass away. George Benedict Ogilvie died in 1710, a field marshal in Saxon service. Carl Hermann Ogilvie (?–1740), his son, was first a general, then governor of Prague. Arvid Horn, who held Sweden's shrinking empire together through the king's absence, was curtly dismissed by Charles when he returned home.

Turkey's Missed Opportunity

Charles was to remain in Turkey five years. With his best Swedish troops dead or prisoner, he could not start a new campaign; he had no means to raise another army, and it was unsafe to travel through enemy lands – Russia, Poland, Saxony, Prussia, Hanover, England – back to Sweden. In any case, much of his empire had been lost. His principal general in Sweden, Steinbock, had performed miracles with raw recruits, but had at last been overwhelmed – Holstein and Scania went to Denmark, Livonia to Russia, the Baltic coast to Poland and Prussia, and parcels to Hanover.

He rejected Louis XIV's offers of a French vessel to bring him home. No doubt there would be a price to pay for that – perhaps involvement in the War of the Spanish Succession. But more important, probably, was his hope that he could persuade Turkey to declare war, with himself as the commander of a new Turkish-Swedish-mercenary army.

As it happened, when that war did come about in early 1711, the Turks invited Charles only to accompany the army as an observer. Charles held out for command, which the Turks refused. This turned out to be a colossal mistake on everyone's part, because once the Turkish army had Peter surrounded at Pruth, Charles would have finished him off, or persuaded the Turks to do so. The grand vizier – a man of peace who understood little of war except that it was bad – allowed the tsar to escape at only the cost of promising to abandon his recent gains around Azov; the grand vizier also obtained a modest but still substantial bribe. When the sultan learned more about the missed opportunity, he dismissed the grand vizier, but did not honour him with the customary strangulation.

It was a decisive moment in Russian history – the tsar turned away from an advance southward, choosing instead to increase Russian holdings in the west.

Last Days of the War

Charles's overly long stay in Turkey, described in great detail by Voltaire, was based on the hope that an anti-Russian party would come to power and give him command of a Turkish army reinforced by the surviving handful of his veteran troops and by mercenaries from Germany and France; however, nothing came of this interlude except to disturb Ottoman politics and Charles's running up a debt to the sultan that was repaid only in 1738. Had Charles returned home, he might have been able to revive his fortunes. French monetary help was being provided, though Louis XIV, having been defeated by Prince Eugene and Marlborough, was unable to guarantee a military diversion. His governors in Sweden were raising another 50,000 men, though the agricultural base of the economy could ill afford to lose them. His enemies were quarrelling among themselves; and even Stanislaus was considering making an arrangement with Augustus to divide Poland between them; and there was the proposal by the king of Prussia that Augustus abandon his alliance with Peter of Russia to join Charles in a grand alliance to recover Livonia!

Robert Massie writes eloquently about the fear inspired in Swedes by news that the war would be continued – how men took to the woods to avoid conscription, university students blew off fingers or toes, officers raided churches and entered mines to drag men away, and of the terrible lashings inflicted on draft dodgers. Men of military age disappeared from entire communities, along with imported goods and even necessities; in their place were more taxes and more taxes. The money went both to the regular army and to hiring mercenaries.

There were mercenaries available, too, often in the most unexpected quarters – a regiment of French soldiers captured at the battle of Blenheim in 1704 by Marlborough had agreed to serve Augustus of Saxony, then had surrendered to Charles and agreed to serve him; in November 1715, having been at the fortress of Rügen on the Baltic coast when it was captured, they agreed to serve the duke of Anhalt, the commander of the besieging forces. There were many more such units available, men who now knew no other occupation than that of war. There was a fleet of pirates at Madagascar, resting from their depredations of the Spanish Main, with sixty ships ready to fight the Danish and Russian flotillas, and the English navy, too, now under the command of the elector of Hanover – George I of England. But this wild idea was soon diverted into a plan to put the Stuarts back on the English throne – with French soldiers, Irish and Scottish exiles, mercenaries from everywhere, and Russian money.

All these possible means of escaping disaster were rejected by the wilful king. Charles doggedly held on to his original plans, even after Turkish troops stormed his refuge and brought him prisoner to the sultan. By the time he reached Sweden in November 1714, all he had in his favour was national enthusiasm and his own determination. Yet, out of that he almost snatched victory out of the mouths of his hungry but divided enemies. If Sweden was ready to collapse, his foes were financially exhausted, too, and they saw no profit in sending their armies into distant Sweden, a land that promised little booty and no hope of holding permanently.

Charles lost battles, even campaigns, but he always came back. Even on the eve of his death, it seemed that he could turn his fortunes around. But to what end? Even his most loyal subjects saw no end to his wars. Victory would bring only another war. Then the king was suddenly dead.

On 27 November 1718, Charles XII was reconnoitring the Danish positions at the fortress of Fredriksten in Norway. He was accompanied by a French engineer, Maigret, who was in charge of the siege, and by his aide-de-camp, Siquier, a Frenchman who had joined his staff in Turkey; his Swedish officers stayed at a distance, partly to avoid attracting the attention of Danish musketeers who were keeping up a hot fire at the Swedish lines, partly to avoid encouraging their king to demonstrate his courage by exposing himself even more. Then he slumped. He had been shot in the temple by a round of grapeshot (or, Roberts suggests, a patriot's bullet) and was instantly dead.

Conspiracy theories soon abounded.

The Russian Naval Campaign to Sweden

Peter and his allies wanted to eliminate any potential for Sweden becoming a major power again. While the Danes and Prussians gobbled up the last Swedish holdings on the mainland, Peter occupied Finland and sent his armies onto the Åland Islands, which could serve as a base for a projected invasion of Sweden itself.

Peter's fleet of galleys had been built by foreign experts – mostly Dutch and English – who captained the ships in the Finland campaign, though command belonged to Fedor Apraxin (1661–1728). The fleet took position after position, rowing on whenever encountering significant resistance. In 1714 Peter doubled the number of vessels, giving command of many galleys to Venetians and Greeks; he also built one ship of the line himself and ordered three more from England. The large Swedish warships, unable to pursue the galleys into shallow waters, did less damage to them than did the weather – a third of Peter's fleet was lost during a raid on Umeå, a strategic port in northern Sweden. Documents and archeological studies of the wrecks indicate that crews were a mixture of foreign and Russian origin, as were the weapons. In August Peter's admiral ordered the galleys to row straight at the Swedish ships; his men suffered terrible casualties from the gunfire, but successfully boarded the larger vessels – one Swedish warship capsized from the weight of the men climbing its side.

Although British squadrons were entering the Baltic Sea, coming to

Sweden's rescue, George I wanted peace. He had been a competent and brave soldier, but now he wanted was quiet and the company of his two ugly mistresses who were jokingly referred to as 'the elephant and the castle', the witticism based on existing London public houses and coins dating from Charles II.

In 1719 Russian forces struck all along the Swedish coast. Arpaxin sent Peter Lacy up the northern coast to burn towns, factories and military bases; Cossacks struck inland, spreading terror through the villages. Lacy was back again in 1721, burning 506 villages. The Swedes finally agreed to the Russian terms for peace – the surrender of Livonia. The peace of Nystadt, 1721, ended the Great Northern War.

Summary

The Great Northern War had been a disaster for all concerned – except perhaps Russia, in the sense that Peter was able to expand his borders in every direction. Saxony, which had become a cultural centre rivalling Florence – attracting artists and musicians (J. S. Bach for one) and educators – was too small to live up to its king's political ambitions. Sweden was bankrupt. Poland was in disarray – Davies notes that the term 'Polish anarchy' first appears at this time; Poland had been ravaged from end to end, resulting in a population decline in the neighbourhood of 25 per cent. Nor was there any end to the anarchy in sight: Polish nobles and gentry looked abroad for leadership or rescue; and Augustus II could rule only by disregarding all traditional restraints on his authority, by the use of first Saxon troops, then Russians, to cow opposition and by winking at those magnates who ran their regions as virtually independent states. Augustus eventually introduced significant reforms, one of which trained young Polish officers in Saxony for future service in an expanded and modernized army. Unfortunately, upon his death the ruinous War of the Polish Succession (1733–6) increased the steepness of the kingdom's long slide into impotence.

Russia had partially westernised, but was exhausted, too. However, because the tsar retained authority, and the state remained intact, there was the potential for recovery and future growth. The Russian army, moreover, could now rely on the services of Livonian nobles; it was not necessary to go abroad for 'foreign' generals?*

---

* M. S. Anderson in Cracraft warns against believing that Russia was 'languishing in medieval obscurantism and hopeless stagnation'. The forces of change existed before Peter ruled; he strengthened those forces, but he did not create them. Black, *European Warfare, 1660-1815*, says that the new emphasis on uniforms symbolised the change in the orientation of the state.

Augustus retired to Dresden, where he soon put on considerable heft. His rival, Leszczyński, married a daughter to Louis XV and was briefly king again during the War of the Polish Succession; however, a Russian-Austrian army placed Augustus's immensely fat son on the throne – and Poland collapsed under the weight of his disinterest.*

And what is history's judgment of Charles XII? Voltaire noted that he carried all the virtues of a hero to an excess, and that, under such conditions, these virtues became as dangerous as their opposites: resolution became obstinacy, liberality became wastefulness, courage became rashness. By the end of his reign, Charles had become a tyrant, but an unusual one – instead of enlarging his realm, he gave kingdoms away; he sacrificed his political advantage in a search for glory and a desire for revenge. He also misjudged the long road to Moscow – that it is a path best not taken. His fate stands as a warning: a peaceful and prosperous government has much to recommend it, but when war is unavoidable, do not let it become a consuming passion.

---

* Augustus's best general, Jacob Heinrich von Flemming, served with distinction through the war, piling up honours and estates, serving in the cabinet, writing widely about philosophy and military music, and building the 'Japanese palace' in Dresden and a magnificent palace at Übigau. In 1725 he married the daughter of Lithuanian chancellor Karol Stanislaw Radziwil.

Chapter 9

The Second Parallel Universe
The War of the Spanish Succession

This conflict can be seen either as a continuation of Louis XIV's wars of expansion or as an effort to restore the balance of power upset when the physical monstrosity, Charles II of Spain, finally died, naming Philip of Bourbon, Louis's grandson, his heir.* Philip was barely seventeen at the time, spoke no Spanish, and had never been in Spain. This was a crisis because the allied powers (Spain, Austria, the German states and England), fighting on France's three frontiers, had barely been able to contain Louis XIV; if Spain joined France, the Sun King would be almost invincible. Preventive war was discussed at every court, by all who imagined themselves expert in grand politics.

Poor Charles was, as cruel contemporaries said in an age before political correctness, a mental defective. All the most odious physical characteristics of the Habsburgs were exaggerated in Charles's person. Perhaps this was caused by spells cast by witches (hence his soubriquet *El Hechizado*) or from hereditary insanity, but he may have suffered from a rare bone disorder that made it impossible for him to chew, difficult to walk and unable to have sexual intercourse; alternatively, he may have suffered from congenital syphilis. His first wife chose to eat herself to death, dying at the age of twenty-seven, bloated beyond recognition. Charles, though almost blind and deaf, often visited her crypt to view her corpse. Logic, tradition and statecraft had suggested that he should name an Austrian Habsburg as his heir; the compromise had been a young Bavarian prince, the emperor's young grandson, the son of Max Emanuel of Bavaria and nephew of Charles's imperious second wife; but the young

---

* Charles II 1661–1700; his supporters were known as Carlists from the Spanish form Charles. Philip of Bourbon (1683–1746). In the cruel way that history repeats itself, the inbreeding that perhaps contributed to Charles's physical debilitation would be continued by the new dynasty. The policy of marrying cousins would eventually result in a Hapsburg king who was as unhappily endowed as Charles.

Bavarian died in early 1699 – suddenly, mysteriously and suspiciously – setting off an intense competition for the nomination.

It was not completely surprising that Charles II chose Philip, a great-nephew of his first wife, who had been the niece of Louis XIV and his Spanish queen, and a granddaughter of Anne of Austria; also, it was a way to spite his second wife. The tangled genealogies of the leading houses are almost impossible for modern readers to follow, but contemporaries were as familiar with them as today's young people are with the multiple entanglements of stars of stage and screen. This meant, as John Wolf reminds us, that the Bourbon boy had more Habsburg blood in his veins than did Archduke Charles of Austria (1685–1740), who was the alternative candidate in case Philip declined the crown. There was little chance of Philip doing that, since even the Pope had endorsed him. Louis had been bullying Charles mercilessly, demanding at the least territorial compensations somewhere – perhaps Milan, thereby separating the two Habsburg domains and opening the way to Naples, perhaps the Spanish Netherlands; and the Spanish were loath to relinquish anything. To back up his threats, Louis massed his army on the Spanish frontiers. Charles gave way. He may even have thought he was avoiding war. The reality was otherwise.

Philip, choosing the name Felipe V, was accepted enthusiastically by the Spanish people, who wanted at all costs to avoid a terrible war over the succession and to prevent their empire from being divided. However, almost anyone with eyes could see that the English and Austrian dynasties could not allow Louis to add the Spanish domains to his empire, any more than Louis could allow an Austrian to acquire Spain; Portugal shared their fear, and even the Protestant German states of Brandenburg and Hanover (traditional French allies) believed that France had become a greater threat to the Holy Roman Empire than ever. In theory, of course, the Spanish empire was supposed to remain Spanish, but the diplomats of that time were too practical to imagine that this would remain the case; instead, there was every likelihood that the French and Spanish crowns would eventually be united.

The only uncertain aspect of this appraisal was how far off *eventually* was – Louis had already ruled for sixty years, but he seemed fit enough for another decade (as proved to be the case). The short-term outlook was almost as dour. Spain would relinquish the forts in the Spanish Netherlands to France, thus opening Holland to invasion, and it was expected that parts of Italy would be handed over as well. This relieved Spain of paying for another expensive war in the Low Countries, but at the cost of a naval war with Holland and Britain; on the good side, although the French fleet had been crippled in the last war, it might now be sufficiently strong to help Spain recover its long-lost domination of Caribbean waters. Of course, all these plans were nothing if the new king could not persuade the French to represent Spanish interests sufficiently. And Philip, among the laziest teenagers ever to have a crown fall into his lap, refused to wear it effectively – he turned policy over to his advisors and his much more intelligent and ambitious wife, who was all of fourteen at the time. In effect, he was ready to defer to Louis XIV's every wish except that he take an active role in the government himself.

Everything depended on William of Orange, the dominant personality in Holland and king of England. William was still mulling over the situation, considering how to bring the Tories and Whigs to agree on any policy, when Louis made a mistake.

According to Voltaire, when Louis heard of the death of the exiled James II of England, he had said he could not recognise James's son as the legitimate king, because that would bring on a war. During a personal interview with James's widow, however, he was so moved by her appeal, and that of his own wife – a religious fanatic who wanted to restore Catholicism to England – that he changed his mind. That made war with Holland and England inevitable.

The Habsburgs now protested, advancing Charles of Austria for the Spanish crown, claiming he had the best hereditary claim. Within months military operations began in the Spanish Netherlands and Italy. The Pope, like other minor Italian lords, entered the war on the French side, then, threatened by the emperor, switched sides.* Later, Catalans – always desirous of breaking Castilian domination – summoned Charles of Austria to Barcelona in 1705. He took the name Carlos III.

The Irish Brigade: Dillon, Burke and Galmoy

The opening salvos of the War of the Spanish Succession were fired in Italy in 1701 by troops under Prince Eugene of Savoy and Marshal François de Neufville, duc de Villeroy (1644–1730, often spelled Villeroi). Eugene had come west from his successful campaigns against the Turks, while the marshal owed his command to his popularity at Versailles – the king had known him since childhood, and he was the queen's favourite; he had even survived the 1683 scandal, when his grandson, who was serving at Vienna alongside Eugene, wrote homosexual love letters to friends at court. Villeroy had demonstrated in the Low Countries that he lacked ability, and he had repeatedly insulted the duke of Savoy, whose friendship was necessary to assure easy passage through the Alps, but he

---

* Voltaire, *Age of Louis XIV*, quoted a common witticism that the pope resembled the Apostle Peter in the garden of Gethsemane – *L'empereur força alors le pape Clément XI à reconnaître l'archiduc pour roi d'Espagne. Ce pape, dont on disait qu'il ressemblait à saint Pierre, parce qu'il affirmait, niait, se repentait et pleurait* (agreeing, denying, repenting and weeping).

was absolutely loyal to the king. Louis XIV valued loyalty.

Eugene had been frustrated in earlier operations in Italy by his superiors' fear to commit troops to combat. Perhaps that was the wisest choice, given the allies' tendencies to change sides abruptly or give away winnings in peace treaties that hardly lasted long enough to dismiss the troops, then rehire them. Now Eugene was in sole command, able even to pick his subordinates. His first task was to find a new route across the mountains, every pass being occupied by troops from France, Spain and Savoy. Eugene chose a path from the Tyrol into Venetian territory, employing local peasants to dig paths through the mountain snow for his men and artillery. The commanders opposing him cautiously refused battle, allowing him to manoeuvre them back towards Mantua.

This prompted the boastful Villeroy to say – despite specific orders to avoid any risk – that he had not come to Italy to observe the enemy through a telescope. He summoned back into service the Irish regiments disbanded in 1698, then in alliance with the duke of Savoy marched on the Habsburg army at Chiari. It was a trap – what had seemed to be a poorly garrisoned city was filled with hidden troops and many cannon. The French and Italians stormed the walls for two hours before retreating – 2,000 died, while Eugene lost only 117. Although Irish losses were relatively few (Irish sources say many), several Irish soldiers were later admitted into Louis XIV's hospital and retirement home at Les Invalides (today the French military museum) in Paris.

The two armies went into winter quarters, the French in Cremona, the Austrians in nearby Mantua; the French collected supplies by force, prompting uprisings that were put down brutally, while Eugene allowed his soldiers to come near starvation, only paying them one month of the five that winter so that he could buy food from Venice; McKay reports that he even executed four dozen men for looting. This concern for the natives would pay off handsomely in late January 1702, when spies informed him that the French headquarters could be taken by a surprise attack. Prince Eugene, with his customary optimism and enthusiasm, persuaded his troops to act on this information. Cremona was widely considered impregnable, but a priest told him that there was a dry sewer from his church under the walls; a picked squad led by Francis MacDonnell (1656–1702), an Irish officer, made their way into the city after most of the French had passed out from a drunken revel. In pouring rain the Austrians attacked the gates from within and without, trying to open them for the main army. Marshal Villeroy, awakened by the gunfire, hurried out in his nightshirt, but was captured by MacDonnell's men. MacDonnell turned down handsome offers of money and promotion to free him, and the unfortunate marshal was later ridiculed with a poem for his famous misadventure. Wolf quotes this version:

Français rendez grace à Bellone,	Frenchmen, give thanks to Bellona,
Votre bonheur est sans égal,	Your luck is unequalled,
Vous avez conservé Crémone	You saved Cremona,
Et perdu votre Général.	But lost your general.

Eugene entered the city, expecting to capture easily the disorganised pockets of troops hurrying to the city square from their quarters in private homes, when his plans were disrupted by the Irish regiments, which, for reasons unknown, were cold stone sober and thus able to form up and attack. (It may be that they had already spent their wine allowance or that the beer was not up to Irish standards.) Eugene tried to bribe them into coming over to his side, but they refused even to listen to MacDonnell; instead, they took him prisoner. After ten hours Eugene, believing that a French relief force had to be on the way, broke off the street fighting and retreated with his 500 prisoners. He had lost 500 men, while inflicting twice that many casualties on the French. Of the 600 Irish, about a third were killed and wounded.

In 1898 Sir Arthur Conan Doyle (author of the Sherlock Holmes stories) wrote this poem about his countrymen's achievements in *Songs of Combat*:

The Grenadiers of Austria are proper men and tall;
The Grenadiers of Austria have scaled the city wall;
They have marched from far away
Ere the dawning of the day,
And the morning saw them masters of Cremona.
There's not a man to whisper, there's not a horse to neigh;
Of the footmen of Lorraine and the riders of Dupres,
They have crept up every street,
In the market-place they meet,
They are holding every vantage in Cremona.
The Marshal Villeroy he has started from his bed;
The Marshal Villeroy has no wig upon his head;
'I have lost my men!' quoth he,
'And my men they have lost me,
And I sorely fear we both have lost Cremona.'
Prince Eugene of Austria is in the market-place;
Prince Eugene of Austria has smiles upon his face;
Says he, 'Our work is done,
For the Citadel is won,
And the black and yellow flag flies o'er Cremona.'
Major Dan O'Mahony is in the barrack square,
And just six hundred Irish lads are waiting for him there;
Says he, 'Come in your shirt,

And you won't take any hurt,
For the morning air is pleasant in Cremona.'
Major Dan O'Mahony is at the barrack gate,
And just six hundred Irish lads will neither stay nor wait;
There's Dillon and there's Burke,
And there'll be some bloody work
Ere the Kaiserlics shall boast they hold Cremona.

The next French commander, Louis Joseph Vendôme (1654–1712), did not have to court Bellona, the Roman goddess of war – he was a warrior who took what he wanted.*

Villeroy was soon released, as was MacDonnell. Eugene praised the Irish troops, saying that they were the best in the French army. Unhappily for him, he would have many more encounters with them before the war ended in 1714.

Military Reforms

The French army was widely considered the best in Europe. With a peacetime strength of 150,000, it could be quickly expanded to 400,000. The great commanders of the past – especially Turenne (1611–85) and Condé (1621–86) – were acknowledged geniuses. But only Vendôme now stood out among the king's eight marshals, and he was employed in Italy, occupying Savoy and integrating the duke's troops into his own forces; he was Eugene's first-cousin and, like him, was no courtier – he did not even dress well, and often slept well past lunchtime, but he knew how to fight. He must have made Prince Eugene regret having captured the less capable Villeroy.

Rapid expansion of the French army, however, could be achieved only by hiring entire units of foreigners. The favourite recruiting grounds were in the Swiss Confederation, Ireland and Scotland – the latter two regions producing devout, even passionate Catholics, eager to fight the Protestant enemies of their homelands. Even the Swiss took the view that it was patriotic to fight the Habsburgs, who time out of mind had lusted after control of their passes.†

The Austrian army was larger, too, but also much improved. Prince Eugene's insistence on instant obedience led to a greater uniformity of

---

* Saint-Simon (Claude Henri de Vouvroy, 1760–1825) has little good to say about his pride, vulgarity, insolence, lack of self-control, corruption, confidence and idleness. As for his homosexuality, young officers having to satisfy the marshal's tastes to earn promotion deeply offended the courtier-philosopher.
† Black, *European Warfare, 1660–1815*, notes the importance of fortresses, where supplies could be stored that would permit swift offensive strikes by Louis's enlarged armies.

regimental discipline, and a corresponding decline in the number of independently organised mercenary units. Seeing that the hereditary officers knew little of artillery and siegecraft, he introduced systems for training cadets and for instruction in engineering.* He punished severely officers who were caught stealing funds intended for pay, food, clothing and housing; and he sought to provide invalid homes for soldiers who were permanently injured, so they would not have support themselves by begging. He attempted to recruit only Germans – believing that Frenchmen, Poles, Italians, Swiss, Hungarians and Croats were nothing but cowards and braggarts who flitted from one army to the next, contributing nothing toward the creation of an effective military force; he favoured hiring these nationalities for service in their own lands, where the knowledge of the language and customs was important, but not for service in the Empire.

Nevertheless, Eugene recruited large numbers of Croats as light hussars, reinforcing Hungarian and Austrian cavalrymen long associated with the royal army. Unexpectedly, their colourful flowing neck cloths became the rage of fashionable society, leading ultimately to the invention of the necktie. As horsemen they were unsurpassed, and their relatively unsympathetic relationship with Germans meant that they were also unsurpassed as scavengers and raiders.

Eugene was supported in these efforts by Gundaker and Guido Starhemberg, one the president of the war council, the other an accomplished general who suffered constant pains from a spearhead lodged in his shoulder from the capture of Buda; they worked valiantly (if often ineffectively) against the emperor's ultra-cautious and jealous advisors, who expected generals to accomplish much with minimum resources. If troops were not paid, well, what should they expect? As long as the officers maintained rigorous discipline, who cared what the troops thought?

Eugene did. It was occasionally asked why he did not marry. It was because, if he did, he would lose the revenues from the abbeys in Savoy, and he needed the money to augment the imperial allotments. No matter who occupied Savoy – France, Austria or the feckless duke – his lands belonged to the Church, and the revenues came in regularly, to be used as Eugene wished. They were especially secure after the duke of Savoy came over to the imperial alliance in 1703.

Still, the revenues of a few abbeys would not sustain armies, and there was little Eugene could do when the emperor could not provide him funds, no more than he could restore his lungs to full health. He had

---

* McKay says that the new army was the creation of Montecuccoli, not Prince Eugene, whose main contribution was the standardisation of weapons and the introduction of the light grey uniform (which was eventually replaced by one that was almost white) – his own red coat stood out brilliantly against this drab colour on the battlefield.

experienced bronchial troubles in his first Balkan campaign – no surprise to anyone who looks at his portraits, which indicate that he was not only extremely slim, but also had a weak chest – and his habit of sniffing snuff made the condition worse.

Political Alliances

Although the interests of the Empire were in Italy, the 'maritime states' (Holland and Great Britain) supported that enterprise only to the extent necessary to keep the emperor in the war. Their interests centred on Flanders. The Dutch Republic, which contributed the largest contingent of troops in this war, hired soldiers from Brandenburg and Denmark, states which were staunchly Protestant. Having lost the traditional support from the Spanish, whose fortresses had protected Holland previously, the Dutch desperately needed English aid. Although King William governed in both Holland and Britain, the Tory Parliament refused to vote funds for the army – Stuart loyalists favoured peace with France as the essential preliminary to bringing James II back to the throne; moreover, King William was both a French prince and a stolid Dutch burgher – he resembled his grandfather, William the Silent, in being taciturn and in speaking no English at all. He was short, somewhat hunchbacked, and dressed plainly.

Meanwhile, Louis went from triumph to triumph – Portugal joined his alliance, as had Savoy (briefly), Luxembourg and Cologne, opening the way into Italy and Germany; if Denmark joined his enemies, he could count on Sweden to take the other side (his), and Augustus of Saxony had embarked on a Polish adventure that removed his fine army from the imperial ranks. But the greatest triumph was in making Max Emanuel of Bavaria into an ally – he promised the imperial crown to the elector, whose fat, ugly sister was married to the inconsequential but happy Dauphin of France, and made him governor-general of the Spanish Netherlands. Max's brother was archbishop of Cologne, one of the most powerful men in Germany and one of the nine electors. Also, he was a highly regarded warrior, having once shared the command of the allied army in the Low Countries with William the Silent.

Max Emanuel, like many other observers, had concluded that the Habsburg monarchy was finished. The emperor, Leopold, was not a dynamic personality, and his closest advisors were more concerned with their position in court than supporting their generals in the field. The Hungarian revolt required more troops and money than any other campaign, and no policy (short of political liberty and religious tolerance) seemed likely to work. Until now the 'court Jew', Samuel Oppenheimer, had worked magic in raising money, but his death in 1703 revealed the sad state of his financial empire – he had loaned far too much to Leopold, who now refused to pay a groschen, much less a thaler, and the creditors now closed in. It was the traditional policy toward Jews – encourage them to make money, then squeeze them dry, and finally toss them to their enemies. Prince Eugene's campaign in Italy slowed, then stalled; he could not pay his troops, nor recruit more. Yes, there were some successes – as in any war, each side had gains here, losses there, but on the whole, the balance of power seemed to have shifted irreversibly to France.

An advance French force under Villars joined the Bavarians and drove down the Danube as far as Passau;* the offensive ended only when Max Emanuel turned into the Tyrol, a move intended to deprive the imperial army in Italy of supplies, thus forcing it to retreat. Villars, who had once been the elector's boon companion, was now frustrated by his erratic policies – rumours of panic in Vienna, sure knowledge of a serious revolt in Hungary, made him believe that the Austrians could be driven from the war if only the Bavarians would advance on Vienna; in truth, the imperial court would have fled if there had been anyplace to go. Villars asked to be replaced, and, as he predicted, the misbehaviour of the Bavarians quickly provoked a peasant uprising that drove them out of the mountains; moreover, Vendôme had to break off his Italian campaign to come to the elector's rescue. A second French army under Tallard waited at Strasbourg, its easiest route east blocked by a strong line of fortifications held by Louis of Baden;† however, its participation in the campaign was not deemed essential – between the Hungarians and the Bavarians, with its position in Italy deteriorating and the war in Spain stalemated, Austria was surely finished.

It would not be the last time such a miscalculation was made.

The Holy Roman Empire

For the first time since the wars of the Reformation the Holy Roman Empire was widely seen as a necessary and desirable institution that represented German interests. The Empire had never completely lost its theoretical role, but until the wars against the Turks, Protestants had never trusted the Habsburgs and the smaller states had feared domination by Austria. Now, with French aggression becoming obvious to everyone,

---

* Claude-Hector (1653–1734), duc de Villars, was not born to the nobility, but rose through the ranks of the pages to demonstrate his military talents. His courage and ability were rewarded by his being named marshal in 1702 and general marshal in 1733 – a rare honour.

† Camille duc de Tallard (1652–1728) was trained by Condé and Turenne; he was famed for having plundered Protestant territories in Germany, mostly importantly the Palatinate.

there was not only a national centre, but also a national enemy.*

Still, it was difficult for Leopold to provide leadership. Some of this was his fault, because he was not an inspirational leader, not even when acting as the titular leader of the crusade against the Turks. Also, the Habsburg lands were poor, having an economic base only a fifth as large as France's. The emperor had to rely on the German princes for help, a dependence which highlighted constitutional restrictions that prevented him from taking swift and decisive action even when he could be moved to do so.† Though the imperial organs – legislative, administrative, military and judicial – moved slowly, they did work. The Reichstag had been in permanent session in Regensburg since 1663, so members could be summoned there on short notice for deliberations, but it was not so easy to make the deliberations short.

The ambitions and jealousies of the princes hindered every proposal. Augustus the Strong, who should have been a major player, had become king of Poland in 1697; that consumed his time, interest and money. Frederick I of Brandenburg was persuaded to abandon his pro-French leanings in 1701 by being given the title of King *in* Prussia. George of Hanover, who became elector in 1698, was eager to fight the French, principally because he was in line to become king of England, should Queen Anne die without heirs.‡

For the purposes of organising territorial defence the Empire had long been organised into Circles (*Reichskreise*), each circle's military preparations assigned to a local prince. The imperial army – actually little more than the Austrian forces – was supported by contributions from the states. While the size of the army was fixed in 1681 – a moment when the Empire was threatened by both the French king and the Ottoman sultan – at 4,000 cavalry and 20,000 infantry, that number could not be maintained in peacetime because the princes simply failed to deliver their allotted contributions.

---

* What difference did it really make? That reasonable question was answered by John Wolf in a description of a decadent party at Versailles that 'helped to hide from his majesty the fact that the French image in Europe was grotesque, distasteful, and fearsome'. The criticisms were not 'the croaking of frogs hostile to the sun'. Nice touch there about the frogs, but it was Dutch and Germans croaking, not just Louis's internal enemies.

† Gagliardo notes how modern students struggle with frustratingly complex political and constitutional nature of the Holy Roman Empire, but he also remarks that it was these very qualities that gave princes and people alike assurances of stability and predictability; if swift response to French attacks was impossible, so, too, was it impossible for any one prince or combination of prices to threaten anyone else

‡ Georg Ludwig of Hanover (1660–1727) became George I of the United Kingdom of England, Scotland and Ireland in 1714. In the coming war he would earn universal respect for his competence and courage. However, his connivance at the murder of his wife's lover in 1694 bothered contemporaries almost as much as his doting on his mistress and her three children.

The princes assigned to maintain the military forces of each Circle often just pocketed the money (which, it might be noted as an excuse, was their own money). Although a few had small standing armies of their own, usually they maintained a ragtag collection of mercenaries who lacked standard uniforms, standard weapons and standard discipline. Their titles sounded impressive (for example, *Generalfeldmarschalleutnante*), as did their costumes, but their mercenary armies were not. Still, in an era when sieges were more common than battles, speed in mobilisation and marching was not as important as assuring that every state felt that its contributions and obligations were fair.

Once German armies began to move, they were sufficient for anticipated needs. Germans saw their wars as defensive, and mercenaries were quite up to the job of holding fortresses.

Building fortresses was another matter, but at least every fortress was obviously defensive – no money put into a fortress would threaten life and liberty elsewhere.

The Battle of Blenheim: Prelude

The English commander in the greatest engagement of the war, John Churchill, is best known by his later title, the duke of Marlborough; therefore, most scholars call him simply Marlborough, though, strictly speaking, that is an anachronism.

In his youth John Churchill had served in Marshal Turenne's army against the Dutch – where he became known as the *bel Anglais* – and even been introduced to Louis XIV as a man of valour and great promise. Only falling in love prevented him from making a career in the Sun King's army. That and the death of Charles II in 1685 – Churchill's access to the king had come through his courtship of one of the royal mistresses, and his sister had been the mistress of the duke of York (who became James II);* and Charles had rented 5,000–6,000 English troops to Louis in return for a secret subsidy.

The Churchill family's rise to power is a fascinating one, and his descendant, Winston Churchill, tells it very well in his biography of the great commander. Turenne (1611–75) had been a good model – calm, orderly, courageous and competent – for an ambitious young man like Churchill. Turenne was also determined, and daring. After viewing the

---

* Trevelyan in his *The England of Queen Anne* wrote that Churchill was no great public servant, nor did he feel shame at his sister's situation – he 'had no higher standards than the world he found himself in . . .' More importantly, 'The secret of Marlborough's character is that there is no secret'. He loved his wife, he loved his country, he loved money, he loved to use his talents; he was 'abnormal only in his genius'.

Dutch fortifications at Maestricht in 1673, he formed an elite storm battalion from the best men of each unit; Churchill was among them, together with his patron, the duke of Monmouth (Charles's illegitimate son) and Frederick von Schomberg, who had been with the English army in Portugal – an excellent warrior, but possessed by what Glozier calls 'overweening arrogance'. After Churchill had planted the French flag atop the Dutch walls, he turned the captured works over to French troops. When the Dutch counter-attacked, Churchill went back into the fray, accompanied by French musketeers led by a real but already legendary commander named D'Artagnan; throwing away their guns, they charged with swords in hand and retook the fortifications. In 1674, Turenne, though outnumbered at Enzheim 38,000 to 22,000, threw all his mercenary forces into a desperate effort to capture a wooded redoubt held by superior forces. First the Irish were shot to pieces, then an English regiment, and finally Churchill's unit. Churchill lost half his men and officers, but took the position, thus 'winning' the engagement. Among the lessons of this battle was that victory was not determined by losses, but by the impact upon the enemy's confidence and morale – and intimidating the commander was even more important than cowing the troops. In the next year Turenne made a stunning forced march against a much larger German force in Alsace, catching its commanders by surprise and driving them back across the Rhine.

Turenne was well pleased with Churchill's contributions, arranging with the king to offer him a permanent position in the French army. Churchill, however, turned the colonelcy down – these wars seemed to be irrelevant to English interests (and six English and Scottish regiments were now serving in the army of William of Orange). Moreover, he wanted to marry Sarah Jennings. She brought neither wealth nor high social contacts, and her Whig sympathies made her suspect, but she was to be a full partner in his career. Churchill accepted the colonelcy of King Charles's Life Guards and spent much time in that sensuous monarch's corrupt and brilliant court; Sarah resumed her close friendship with Princess Anne, a connection that would be important in years to come, when Churchill's Tory sympathies would be held against him.

King Charles's death in 1685 precipitated a crisis. Earlier his brother, and heir, James II, had possessed praiseworthy skills in military organisation and some understanding of politics. These almost totally vanished. He now dismissed Protestants from high positions and replaced them with Catholics. This was self-destructive behaviour perhaps inspired by approaching old age and fear, certainly by his Jesuits advisors, that he would miss his chance to save the souls of his benighted subjects; or, as Voltaire suggests, his desire to become an absolute monarch. Fortescue probably had it right: 'James was a narrow-minded, a vindictive, and, like all the Stuarts, essentially a wrong-headed man'.

The duke of Monmouth led a Protestant rebellion, but the king's French general, despite his giving commands in broken English, outmanoeuvred him, and Churchill was able to rally the royal troops when Monmouth's night attack almost overran their camp. Churchill, however, took no part in the retaliations known as the 'Bloody Assizes' – the hanging and exiling of rebels and suspected enemies of the crown. James called the army back from Holland and Tangiers (Britain's first African colony), and began removing Protestant officers. The army henceforth was more Irish and Catholic – and James pushed hard to remake similarly the universities, the church and parliament. The king also wanted to reverse the present alliance with Holland and return to that of France, a policy that Churchill worked against as best he could.

When the Whigs finally rose against these catholicising schemes, Churchill took their side, not that of his royal patron; the issue was not so much the king's bigoted religious policies as the fear of royal tyranny: would James II become another Louis XIV, and would England's Protestants suffer the fate of France's Huguenots – death or exile?*

Under the circumstances, a monarchy headed by the king's daughter, Mary, and her Dutch husband, William, appeared even more attractive than it did in the last conspiracy-filled years of Charles II.†

At the invitation of English notables, William loaded a Dutch army upon a Dutch fleet and sailed for England – hiring troops from Prussia and other German states – perhaps as many as 25,000 – to help ward off the expected French attack on Holland. Everyone asked, what would Louis XIV do? But James, apparently fearful of the public's reaction, declined both the offer of French troops and a French alliance. That might have been his only chance. His many follies had cost him the support of all parties except the most resolute Catholics – and even they doubted his competence. No sooner did James make a decision than he reversed it.‡

The royal army of 25,000 men was under the command of two French brothers, but several of the most loyal Scottish and Irish regiments were still far away. Even so, James's host vastly outnumbered the Dutch army, even after English volunteers hastened to join William. However, the

---

* About a quarter of France's Protestants left the country after 1685. Among them was the duke of Schomberg, who resigned his position as marshal and went to Portugal; he shortly accepted a position in Brandenburg that allowed him to keep his French and Portuguese pensions, but was soon recruited for service under William of Orange – France's foremost enemy! In a further slap at the French king, Schomberg's son went to Austria. Schomberg was a mercenary, but his biographer reminds us that most mercenaries had motives beyond just earning money. Schomberg, though born in Germany, considered himself first a Calvinist, then an Englishman.

† Ashley reminds us that William was also the grandson of Charles I.

‡ Turner notes the opposite counsels of the king's Protestant loyalists and his arrogant Jesuit confidants (whose advice was seconded by the queen). The king was also ill, paranoid and vindictive. His clumsy efforts to meet Whig complaints only increased public suspicion.

officers, including Churchill, were against fighting – and the king was aware of that. While the king dithered, making personal addresses to the enlisted men in a vain effort to win their allegiance, the officers went over to William. When reports of new desertions reached him, a thoroughly dispirited James followed his wife and son to France. Churchill, now the effective commander-in-chief of William's army, was rewarded for his services with the title of duke of Marlborough.*

Though war broke out immediately with France and 8,000 English soldiers were soon on the continent, Marlborough found himself in England – out of favour! When Princess Anne quarrelled with her sister, Queen Mary, over money, Sarah Churchill had sided with the princess. It was a distraction that King William did not need, and he blamed Marlborough for allowing it to get out of control. When James made his way to Ireland – thanks to the French fleet's temporary control of the seas – with 5,000 French troops and French officers to whip the Irish into shape, William hurried there himself, but left Marlborough at court.†

When William returned to the Continent, he sent Marlborough to continue the campaign in Ireland. However, he assigned a Dutch general, Godert de Ginkel (1630–1703), to back up the English troops with 5,000 Dutch, Danish and Huguenot mercenaries. It is understandable that William placed little trust in the new regiments of Protestants, but he seems to have believed that Englishmen were of little value in war even when well drilled. To universal surprise, Marlborough ended the war in twenty-three days.

It was less surprising that William gave him but grudging praise. William mistrusted the quarrelling Englishmen, their partisan feuds, their ancient rivalries, and their inability to remember that the great enemy was France. As Winston Churchill wrote, the Dutch were William's children,

---

* William, it should be noted, was born and reared in southern France, usually spoke French, and shared many French habits. (Nancy Mitford suggests, or more than suggests, that he was rather too close to young English courtiers who, like Louis XIV's brother, were open sodomites – as they were called in those days, implying a certain social sophistication and approval – and appointed one ambassador to France.) Perhaps because the French king had confiscated his ancestral land, William hated Louis, and Louis hated him; also Louis had once offered him as wife one of his mistress's babies, but William had refused, saying that his family was accustomed to marrying the daughters of kings, not their bastards. In any case, the breach was unbridgeable. Louis attempted to entangle William's ambassador in the embarrassing complexities of court etiquette, but soon came to like him immensely – any time either mentioned the duke of Savoy, a notorious turncoat, both broke into peals of laughter. In return, Louis sent Marshal Tallard to the English court, where he became immensely popular.
† Baxter remarks on the need to rebuild 'James II's toy army'. The Catholic officers and many Irish troops had gone into exile. The officers who remained had little experience and that was fighting for France, not against French troops; and they were more prone to intrigues than combat. There was no administration, few weapons, no medical service, and no system of supply. William would provide all this, based on Dutch models.

the English his stepchildren. Queen Mary's death from smallpox in 1694 changed attitudes in Parliament, which now regarded him as a temporary (and foreign) ruler; ever more attention was given to Princess Anne. Moreover, Marlborough's Tory sympathies were well known, causing royalists in exile to speculate as to where he would put his loyalty should the French fleet manage to land James on the English coast – if the Tories came to the support of the exiles and the French regiments, James just might drive the Whigs and their Dutch king out of the country. With Marlborough and his wife continuing their correspondence with Tory friends in France, it was easy for a professional informer to accuse him of treason – and Marlborough spent uncomfortable days in the Tower before the informer was proven false (and beheaded).

These were perilous days, with 10,000 Irish waiting in France to be transported across the Channel; and William had taken most of the army to the Continent, or sent it to Scotland and Ireland. In a day when officers purchased their commissions, Marlborough was a poor man, without lands equal to his title. Still, King William did not appoint Ginkel to negotiate the treaty of Limerick because of money, but for the expert manner in which he had put down the Scottish regiments that had mutinied and declared for James. Ginkel remained William's most trusted lieutenant and later contended with Marlborough for command of the allied armies.*

Marlborough received his first command in 1701, on the Continent, when Parliament finally realised that the alliance of France and Spain meant disaster for English and Dutch commerce. King William's death in 1702 at age fifty-two of complications following a riding accident – his horse stepped into a mole-hole, and the broken collarbone was not allowed to heal before the king resumed his busy schedule – brought the Whigs to power. The policy was now to prepare for war, to prevent France from extending its military sway, economic interests and religious fanaticism over the Low Countries.

Queen Anne appointed Marlborough commander of Britain's Continental forces. Holland was independent from Great Britain, with a fourteen-year-old monarch, but thanks to the experienced statesmen who governed the Republic, the alliance remained strong. Moreover, since Anne was married to George of Denmark, Danish troops now joined the allied army.†

---

* Black, *European Warfare, 1660–1815*, credits the victory in Scotland partly to luck – the Jacobite commander, John Graham, falling at Killiecrankie, with no successor skilful enough to follow up that victory.

† George was a handsome and attentive husband, courageous in battle, but without any spark of genius. Fortunately, he also lacked ambition or any desire for fame; therefore, he did not interfere in political or military matters. His sole duty was to get Anne pregnant, which he did regularly, though she often miscarried or lost the child soon after birth (this has sometimes been attributed to his having contracted syphilis and passed it on to his wife)

Sarah Churchill, being Anne's closest friend and a Whig sympathiser, was able to protect her Tory husband from his many enemies. Marlborough did not go out of his way to make enemies – even his foes admitted that he looked like a great general, that he was cool and courageous, and that his speech rarely contained phrases or intonations that offended – but this was a vicious period in British politics, and the very institution of the monarchy was threatened. Partisan controversies arose over among every matter, and almost every matter involved money. Wars were expensive, and many nobles and parliamentarians thought that the money should be spent on them, and on their friends, rather than go up in smoke on some foreign battlefield.

The Battle of Blenheim: The Gathering of Armies

Marlborough sent his recruiters throughout the British Isles, to cajole those they could, to offer bonuses to others, and to empty the jails and poorhouses where the discharged veterans of past armies were to be found. He began to select his officers, taking this person because of his money, hoping to find a place for another because of his bravery and competence. Money almost always won the regimental commands, but, fortunately – as Marlborough knew – the colonels often looked to their subordinates for advice and expertise. To the extent he could, Marlborough always sought to reward competence and courage.*

He next encouraged his sovereign to assure that the treasurer and prime minister would support him; he could not maintain an effective army if he had to fear that suddenly, for frivolous or partisan reasons, money was no longer available for pay and supplies. A relative by marriage got the job. Fortunately, he was very good at it.

The war had already begun in Italy, where Prince Eugene's victories had given reasons to imagine that the French juggernaut could be stopped. Once the northern princes agreed upon the goals of the war, they declared war. The first action was by the elector of Hanover, the future George I, who struck at the mercenary army collected (with French money) by the duke of Brunswick-Wolfenbüttel – those troops promptly surrendered, then agreed to serve in the imperial army.

---

or the child succumbed to smallpox before reaching adulthood. George was more a retiring gigolo than a prince consort, and everyone was satisfied with that.

* Trevelyan called the army 'a polyglot epitome of Europe'. Of the 40,000 recruited in 1701–2, only 18,000 were British. The Recruiting Acts of 1703–4 put restrictions on the practice of 'impressing' (essentially kidnapping) men into service, but local magistrates still used it as a means of ridding their localities of undesirables. Desertion was common, and understandable. The wagondrivers of the artillery, in contrast, remained civilians earning civilian pay – i.e., more than soldiers.

Officers similarly moved from paymaster to paymaster. This explains why they could be so courteous to one another, so accommodating in issuing passes to cross the lines for visits home or to recover from illness or wounds, so willing to exchange compliments at conferences and during those awkward moments when surrender had to be discussed. At our distance of three centuries, we have little patience with the distinctions between 'the honours of war' (marching out with drums beating and flags flying') and 'honourable terms' (without weapons), but soldiers were expensive and intact fortresses were more valuable than destroyed ones; it was better to allow an enemy to leave quietly than to lose trained men in storming a ruin.

The officers were professional – most were well born, or with pretensions to noble status; all were aware that their appointments were not guaranteed forever – just as they understood that their prince could at any time withdraw from the conflict, or even change sides. This meant that their foes might become their companions in arms, or even their commanders.

This mirrored the practices of their paymasters – kings almost always married outside the kingdom, usually to cement alliances, but occasionally in hope of redrawing those lines or to draw a hesitant dynasty to their side. Sometimes the rulers were themselves foreigners – for example, Catherine the Great and George I.* While consorts might have attachments to dimly remembered homelands, their true allegiance was to their spouse and children, to their new kingdom. Anne's husband, George of Denmark, is the example we should keep in mind. If some royal women were brood-mares, others were active in politics; and some prince-consorts, like George, were kept as studs – in his case, a very docile stud.

The soldiers were ruder and more practical. They disliked service abroad, partly because they were surrounded by people they could not understand, food they did not like, and religious practices they thought heretical. But more because the farther they were from home, the more difficult it would be to slip away for a visit to family, friends and girlfriends; or simply to local taverns and tarts.

In these habits the common soldiers exhibited a closer connection to the future than did the officers. The day of the national army was a century away – soldiers were not eager to volunteer yet, to serve with minimum pay and food, but they felt a more a part of their nation than did their betters. No wonder that in 1789 French soldiers stayed loyal to the nation, while the officers went abroad or to the scaffold.

---

* Certainly, few kings could justify their right to govern if their ancestry were examined outside the strict limits of male descent. Bonnie Prince Charlie, the romantic favourite of many Scots, had more Polish ancestors than Celtic ones, and he was more at home in Italy than in the Highlands. But he was nevertheless considered a Scot.

The Battle of Blenheim: Frustrating Caution

Marlborough faced formidable challenges in late 1702. The Spanish Netherlands and the archbishopric of Cologne were technically neutral, but their fortresses were held by French troops; together they held Holland in a vice-like grip, with the potential of falling on the Dutch at any moment. More importantly, Marlborough's plans had to meet Dutch approval, and they feared to risk battle; as far as the Dutch leaders were concerned, victory would bring limited benefits, while defeat would mean incalculable harm.

But luck was with Marlborough, nevertheless. In November, while sailing to a meeting, his vessel was captured by a French unit. Coolly, he handed the enemy officer an outdated pass made out to his brother. The officer recognised his Dutch companions and was certain their passes were genuine, but he was not sure about the Englishman. At length, the customs of war prevailed – he allowed the entire party to proceed on its way. As roads turned to mud, then deep mud, Marlborough sent his men into winter quarters.

1703 began sadly. The duke's only son, who was of an age to join his father in the field but had been left at Cambridge to avoid the smallpox, died of that dreaded disease. Thousands of soldiers succumbed annually to this pestilence, which spread rapidly whenever troops were brought together, then spread again among the people living along each army's march. Every commander was familiar with smallpox, and properly feared it. Bleeding, the cure-all for every disease and every condition, was administered widely to smallpox victims – with predictable results that contemporaries failed to see.

The duke, however, had no time for mourning – spring meant campaigning season. His principal objective was to open the Rhine. Hitherto French garrisons in fortifications made communication difficult between the allies in the Low Countries and the Habsburg forces commanded by Louis of Baden on the Upper Rhine. Marlborough succeeded in clearing the French away from the juncture of the Mosel and the Rhine, but subsequent efforts to break the French lines around Antwerp achieved the capture of only three of the many great fortresses threatening Holland. Once again, Dutch caution prevailed, and while the alliance barely held together on the continent, in Parliament Tories denounced the costs of the war and Whigs complained that nothing was being done to win it. Meanwhile, a French army under Marsin* had joined Max Emanuel in Bavaria, threatening the very heart of the Habsburg lands. Prince Eugene, though arguing forcefully the need for

---

* Ferdinand, comte de Marsin (1657–1706) was known for his combination of courage and diplomacy. Both were necessary to work with Max Emanuel.

immediate action, found his hands bound by his cautious Viennese superiors as securely as Marlborough's by the Dutch. The English duke warned everyone that the time had come to take risks: should Austria be lost, everything would be lost!

The Battle of Blenheim: Britain's Rise to Greatness

Tallard was among Louis's most experienced marshals. He had demonstrated his talents in the contests along the Upper Rhine and in 1690 had daringly taken his men across the frozen river. He was the logical commander to lead the French forces into Germany and even into Austria; his enemies would be distracted by seven other armies, each led by a talented and experienced field marshal. Unhappily, he had two weaknesses, one his being so nearsighted that he could not see more than twenty paces, second, that he was so eager to take part in the fighting that he lost all overview of the action.

Tallard's army had been tying down Louis of Baden near Strasbourg while Max Emanuel and Marsin once again prepared to move on Vienna, to deliver a decisive blow against the Habsburg emperor. Blocking them, ineffectively, were vastly outnumbered Austrian and German forces. It was at that moment that the grandest of grand politics came into play. Although the German princes displayed, in Winston Churchill's words, 'a strange embroidery of half-friendships and hungry ambitions,' Marlborough slowly brought them around to accept a bold strategy that he would not explain fully, lest word reach the French. Prince Eugene would bring his army from Italy, while Marlborough would hurry south with his Dutch and British forces. The duke would be joined by units from Hanover, Brandenburg-Prussia, Hesse and Denmark – a total of 40,000 men; he sent recruiters to scour the jails and taverns of England, raising several new units.

Marlborough made a 'swift' march to Bavaria – 250 miles in five weeks. His infantry (marching, in Winston Churchill's words, like a red caterpillar) could have moved faster, even the cavalry, which could go only where fodder was to be found, but the artillery had to be dragged rather than pulled along the dirt (i.e., muddy) roads. Also, for security's sake, he made a fortified camp every night. This both prevented surprise attacks and hindered his soldiers from slipping away for an evening of rape and robbery that might stretch into a permanent absence; it also avoided earning a reputation equal to the French, whose rapaciousness was now a by-word among the peasantry of all Germany. 'Corporal John', as Marlborough's troops called him, was a stickler for discipline; he wouldn't even tolerate cursing and drunkenness. But he usually paid promptly, he was utterly calm when bullets whizzed past him, and, even when his daring appalled every officer and soldier, he had the knack of winning. British troops responded to that.*

As the red columns moved south, the French generals wondered what the duke was doing. It appeared that he might be merely shifting his armies to the Mosel, to strike through Luxemburg into France – that is what he told the hesitant Dutch. The French commander, Villeroy, hesitated to shift more than a few regiments to oppose him. First of all, France was protected there by a series of excellent fortresses. Second, Marlborough could return north quickly by simply putting his redcoats and cannon onto barges and riding the swift current of the Rhine back to Holland; thence he could strike into French-controlled territory before the French army could come back overland.

Marlborough had anticipated Villeroy's half-hearted response – once he had achieved his purpose of pulling some French forces away from Holland, he moved quickly south towards Heidelberg, then east towards the Danube, knowing that Villeroy lacked the strength to capture quickly the fortresses protecting the Rhineland; he conferred with Prince Eugene for several days, long enough to discuss strategy and become firm friends, before joining Louis of Baden near Ulm.

Once word spread that Marlborough had passed the Main river, it was clear to everyone where he was heading. Tallard was ready to abandon Bavaria until a reinforced army was ready, but Louis XIV sent a direct order to support Max Emanuel – he would not give up this chance to knock Austria out of the war. Moreover, he had worked too hard to bring Bavaria over to his side to abandon his new ally so easily. Tallard obediently hurried east.

This was fine for both Eugene and Marlborough. Each of them believed in achieving victory through decisive battles. French officers, however, doubted that the allies would take the risk of confronting France's finest troops; they knew that strong Bavarian fortifications blocked their line of supply; and they while they dismissed Marlborough's men as low quality, they were even more contemptuous of the newly appointed English officers. However, they would happily have had Villeroy's reinforcements, which had belatedly begun a hurried march to the Upper Rhine, then across the Black Forest toward Bavaria.

Column after column of troops covered the roads of southern Germany, miles and miles of marching troops in variously coloured uniforms – some were German, others English, followed by Danes, Prussians and Dutch, others belonged to the multinational Austrian forces hurrying in a great half-circle from the Upper Rhine through

---

* Trevelyan notes that on the march the British soldiers found the Fräuleins prettier and the beer and wine good. In addition, the population cheered them as liberators and protectors. It was 'a soldier's paradise'.

imperial lands toward the Danube at Donauwörth, and then there were the French, with their Swiss and Celtic units, making the shorter march toward the great river. An army could make ten miles a day through hilly, wooded country toward the Bavarian plain, the cavalry proceeding first, the artillery dragging after. The elector and Marshal Marsin, moving on interior lines, hoped to keep the British and imperial forces in check until Tallard arrived.

Marlborough's daring, however, upset his plans. The elector had hoped that his advanced forts would block the English and Austrian forces – and, indeed, Louis of Baden had argued for a slower approach, argued so intensely, in fact, that some wondered if his loyalties lay with the emperor or his old comrade-in-arms, the elector. But Marlborough believed that his men had the stamina necessary for extraordinary efforts, and once Louis of Baden was wounded in a desperately fought engagement at the Schellenberg fortress outside Donauwörth, there was no more resistance to his orders among the allied commanders. Louis was hurt only in one foot, but that injury was sufficiently serious that he returned to his army then besieging Ingolstadt. In fact, he never fully recuperated, but died three years later from complications of that injury and the accumulated troubles from past campaigns. Louis's victory was very important, however, in that it opened a supply line from central Germany.

The political situation was very unclear. Everyone, including Louis XIV, expected the Bavarian elector to go over to the emperor – sufficient inducements seemed to have been offered and his situation was precarious. If he had followed Marshal Villars's advice the previous year, to strengthen the fortress near Donauwörth, all this could have been avoided, but Max Emanuel was surrounded, as the marshal had reported, by fools. Apparently, he still was – despite losing a major part of his army, he determined to stick by the French king.

The allies would have been satisfied with Max Emanuel changing sides, and assist in destroying the French forces then entering his lands; when he refused, they began burning his villages and hamlets as far as the eye could see – at least 400 were destroyed. This caused the Bavarian elector to disperse his troops to guard as much of his lands as he could. As a result, his army was scattered south of the Danube when the French arrived in Augsburg. Tallard joined as many Bavarian troops as he could to his force, then crossed to the north bank, where he could threaten the allies' lines of communication. He made camp on an island-like rise above the marshes and woods north of the Danube at the villages of Blenheim (Blindheim) and Höchstädt; each army made camp in battle formation – infantry in the centre, cavalry on the wings – which meant that the centre of the Bavarian-French line was held by cavalry.

Marlborough and Eugene recognised the scent. Tallard's position, though seemingly well protected, smelled like an error – he had the cavalry in the centre, not on the wings. Moreover, Eugene knew Max Emanuel well – he had served under him in the Turkish wars – and his opinion of him was not high. The French general and Bavarian elector, of course, had not sensed anything amiss. Only a fool, they thought – or in this case, two fools – would attack them. They had marshes and brooks covering almost their entire front, they had more men, and they had twice as many guns. There was no reason for the French field marshals and Bavarian elector to worry. Quite, the contrary, their main concern was how to cut off their enemies' retreat.

Marlborough divided the allied troops into nine columns for greater speed, then set off in the middle of the night. The risks were great, but when they approached the French positions at dawn, they could see that they had achieved complete surprise. Marlborough took the left and centre of the line himself, Eugene the right (with its more difficult terrain), and various forces were assigned to the more level ground on the left that ended only at the banks of the roiling brown Danube. They had about 52,000 men; the French and Bavarians had perhaps 60,000.

Tallard had assigned numerous regiments quarters in the two villages, turning them into small fortresses. Blenheim was close to the Danube, with other French units camping to the northwest along a four-mile long ridge; there was the swift river to the south and thick woods to the north. Tallard had proposed fortifying the crossing of the small stream in front of their position, the appropriately named Nebel (meaning mist, which covered the valley each morning), but his officers laughed at the idea that anyone would dare to attack them in such a strong position.

When the alarm was sounded, that enemy troops were approaching through the lifting fog, the French and Bavarian regiments fell into line where they were, not in a proper order. The cavalry was equally disorganised, the French and Bavarian camps being at a distance from one another to prevent a spread of disease that had appeared among the horses longest in Bavaria. They should have charged at the first units they saw. Instead, they stood on the defensive, along the ridge, waiting for orders.

Tallard, Marsin and Max Emanuel climbed the church tower in Blenheim for an overview; the elector proposed to prevent the allies from crossing the Nebel, but Tallard overruled him. In effect, let them come closer, then bag them all. Moreover, with the enemy cannons on the other side of the Nebel, why move closer? Let them come to ours.

Marlborough lost 2,000 men to artillery before his engineers could prepare ways to bring the rest of his army over the marshes; and he had been obliged to wait for Eugene to get in position, so their attacks would be in unison. He had prayers read to the units, which must have been effective, because he and his horse were covered by dust from a cannonball fired at a great distance, but neither was hurt; his men, respecting the skilful French artillery, chose to pass the time prone on the ground, but they formed their ranks readily enough when summoned to the attack.

The French and Bavarians heard mass, the allies Protestant services. Bands played, trumpets sounded, and cannons thundered, everyone waiting for the allies to get into position . . . or into a trap – there was no good line for retiring in case of defeat. Shortly after noon Marlborough heard that Eugene was in position. He then sent his first units over the Nebel.

Since troops in the villages of Blenheim and Oberglau could fire into the flank of any force on the ridge line, Marlborough made their capture his highest priority. Though the French in Blenheim vastly outnumbered the attacking British and Hessian troops, they were too crowded to generate more firepower than their attackers – firing through the palisades, they failed to form into line and mount the counter-attack necessary to prevent infantry and cavalry from crossing the marshes and lining up on the dry ground; and allied volleys could hardly fail to cut down many defenders. Still, the attackers had to fall back. Tallard, seeing this, ordered the finest horsemen in France – the Household cavalry (the *Gens d'Armes*) – downhill into their flank. They were intercepted by Hessian infantry, then confronted by English cavalry and driven back. Tallard could not believe it. His best horsemen were driven into flight by a smaller force.

The combat quickly became too confused for observers to remember the sequence of events. Gunsmoke obscured everyone's view.

Bringing the rear units up was slow work, each regiment having to file over narrow bridges or wade, then form up again; this meant that the brunt of the fighting was borne by the few regiments in the van. By mid-afternoon those men were so exhausted that they, and the French, too, stopped fighting altogether; they stood sixty yards apart and stared at one another, panting to recover their breath. Marlborough and Eugene rode among their men, urging them forward, but without results until the soldiers voluntarily took up their weapons and advanced.

The decisive action came in the centre, where Marlborough's nerves held better than Tallard's. Though worried about the likelihood his left wing would collapse, the duke resisted the temptation to send more than a few units there, while French troops from the centre were sent into Blenheim, where they were useless. When the duke of Holstein on Marlborough's right led Dutch troops toward Obergau, he was routed by Irish troops charging out of the village. It appeared that the British lines would be broken.

That was the moment Tallard was waiting for – he sent 10,000 cavalry forward, expecting to drive the allies back into the marshes. That would win the day unconditionally. Marlborough, however, had been rounding up cavalry units, and he had requested more from Prince Eugene. The Austrian commander, though hard pressed himself, complied instantly, sending a unit that hit the Irish in the flank, driving them back. The

French cavalry, instead of charging home, pulled up short to fire their pistols, then were cut down by concentrated musket fire.

Marlborough knew that the near-sighted Tallard could do little now other than 'watch' helplessly as he gathered 8,000 cavalry into a long line, then matched the French placements of infantry with footmen of his own, and cannon against cannon. Marlborough had more men, and fresher men and horses, against exhausted French units. He ordered his cavalry forward and pushed Tallard's back.

The French infantry had moved downhill to drive away the cavalry, but now had to retreat. Fighting completely on the defensive, they lost what Voltaire said was their greatest virtue – their enthusiasm and willingness to attack, virtues that declined the longer a contest lasted. It also deprived them of using the bayonet, a weapon more menacing than murderous, to intimidate their foes.* Seeking to protect themselves from cavalry attack, they formed into squares, whereupon Marlborough brought forward artillery and Prussian infantry, who then proceeded to annihilate the defiant but defenceless Frenchmen.† Tallard's pleas for help from Marsin received only an answer that he, too, had all he could handle.

Advancing at a trot the English horsemen now drove some regiments pell-mell into Blenheim, where they were surrounded, others into wild flight. Tallard, courageously trying to rally his men, was surrounded, wounded and then captured – he mistook approaching Hessian troops for his own. Marlborough turned to the left, driving 3,000 French cavalry over a twenty-foot bank into the river, where many drowned.

Eugene's primary duty had been to tie down the Bavarian-French army, so that no help could be sent to Tallard. This explains his sending forward his outnumbered Prussians and Danes repeatedly into heavy fire. Leopold of Dessau kept his men from breaking as they fell back from the overwhelming numbers, then Dutch troops from Marlborough's wing came to the rescue.‡

The Bavarians fought more than well until late in the day, till they realised that Tallard's army was in full flight – only the inability of the victors to recognise one another in the dying light provided sufficient delay for them to escape via Höchstädt.

Marlborough chose not to pursue the retreating army into the gathering darkness, but to finish off the units trapped along the line of battle. When his men closed in on the 10,000 French trapped in

---

* *Les Français, par leur impétuosité, avaient un grand avantage en se servant de cette arme. Elle est devenue depuis plus menaçante que meurtrière.*
† Trevelyan praised the young French recruits, 'The poor lads never moved, but were mowed down in their ranks and lay in straight lines of white-coated corpses'.
‡ According to McKay, Eugene shot two troopers who, after being repulsed in three charges, refused to go forward again. 'I wish to fight among brave men,' he said, 'and not among cowards.

Blenheim, the surrounded troops yelled loudly about preferring death to surrender, crying to themselves *'Que dira le Roi?'* (What will the King say?) But they really had no choice – continued resistance would have been a massacre. And anyone could see the long piles of bodies where the forces had stood facing one another, firing until shot down; and anyone could have heard the cries of the wounded men and horses.

Marlborough and Eugene had won more than a battle, more than capturing 250 guns, more than taking 5,400 wagons of food and ammunition, more than seizing Tallard's chests of money. They had destroyed the myth of French invincibility, they had reversed the momentum of the French conquests, and they had brought unity back into an unsteady alliance; the grand alliance could see, after years of defeat, the prospect of victory over the French armies. Creasy wrote: 'Throughout the rest of the war Louis fought only in defence. Blenheim had dissipated forever his once proud visions of almost universal conquest.'

Tallart had lost more than a battle – his son died from wounds and he would spend the next seven years in prison in Nottingham. His quoted congratulations to Marlborough about having defeated the finest troops in Europe were overshadowed by the duke's quiet correction that the French were the finest except for those who had beaten them.

It had been an extremely bloody conflict, Marlborough and Eugene losing 12,000 men (6,000 dead), the French and Bavarians more than 30,000 (or perhaps only 12,000 – nobody liked to admit excessive losses in those days any more than now). 3,000 Bavarians and 13,000 Frenchmen had managed to escape the battlefield, but most surrendered later at Ulm; afterward desertion and attacks by peasants in the Black Forest brought about the near total destruction of the fleeing force, so that only only 900 French soldiers actually recrossed the Rhine.* Whatever the actual number of casualties, the momentum of the war had changed: the remnants of the French and Bavarian armies retreated back into Alsace; Marlborough and Eugene marched to the Rhine, then joined their forces with the Dutch and prepared to invade France over the gently rolling hills of Flanders.

Politics then intervened, sending Eugene to Italy and making it impossible for the allies to seek an immediate victory on the northern battlefield.

The tens of thousands of wounded must have been very pleased – once they got home, in front of an audience in a local inn. Given the low velocity of musket balls, many must have displayed missing limbs – they did not call surgeons 'sawbones' for nothing. The officers received medals, promotions and occasionally rich rewards; but whatever they got,

---

* Trevelyan says that 3000 German mercenaries in the French army enlisted in the victorious forces.

they had earned – at the front of their troops, exposed to the aimed fire of the enemy, they suffered proportionately more wounds and deaths than did the common soldiers. Many a manor house had portraits of family members who died in royal service.

The mercenary officers were generally not so lucky. Unless they had married and started a dynasty – as often happened – the best they could hope for was to be praised by some future family historian.

Charles XII

With Eugene absent with his best troops, Marlborough's army had to remain on the defensive, which meant unengaged, because there was almost no potential for a French offensive. Marlborough, however, had delicate political matters to deal with. At the end of 1704 he went to Prussia to hire 8,000 soldiers to be used by Prince Eugene in his Italian campaign – where the fighting was now the heaviest. Austria could spare no more troops, having more than 20,000 tied down in Hungary, which was in a rebellion that threatened to undermine the whole Austrian position in the Balkans. Then the Bavarians rose in November of 1705 – too many taxes, too much destruction from the 1704 campaign, no food, and recruiters forcing unemployed men into service. An epidemic among the horses dismounted most of the allied cavalry. All the gains made at Blenheim seemed to be melting away.

Charles XII was wintering his army in Saxony. What would happen if the seemingly invincible Swedish king acted on his complaints about the persecution of Protestants in Hungary and Silesia? An invasion of Bohemia, then perhaps Austria, was a prospect that no one in the English–Austrian coalition wanted to contemplate. Charles was unpredictable, and the allies naturally feared that he would seek to humble the new Holy Roman emperor, Joseph I, since his predecessor had favoured the Saxons and Poles.*

To make his task even more difficult, Marlborough's sovereign, Queen Anne, was married to a Danish prince. Although George was capable of little beyond getting Anne pregnant seventeen or eighteen times, Denmark was Sweden's most persistent foe. Since George was the nominal commander of the Danish fleet, which was a standing danger to Swedish supply lines, Marlborough had to persuade Charles that he was

---

* Joseph I (1678–1711) had ascended the throne in 1705 after Leopold had died in agony from some intestinal malady. He was a courageous man who had seen action in 1702 with Louis of Baden – when his courtiers said that the situation was dangerous, he told them that they could retire themselves if they wished. He would die young of smallpox (or, more likely, of his doctors' efforts to treat him by wrapping him in stifling sheets). His successor was his less gifted younger brother, Charles VI (1685–1740).

nothing more than a colourful nonentity. Still, the trade interests of England, Holland and Denmark were intertwined, and Charles knew it.

The greatest danger – unlikely but impossible to dismiss – lay in Sweden entering the war on the side of Louis XIV. Once Charles laid the English allies in Germany low, the war would be lost.*

Marlborough met the king in April 1707. After delivering a personal letter from Queen Anne, he said, with outrageous flattery, that he wished he could study the art of war under a gifted leader like the Swedish king. Marlborough was then fifty-seven, Charles twenty-five. Charles returned the compliment, then assured him of his friendship if Marlborough could persuade the Habsburgs to remain neutral in his wars. Tensions remained high for another year, until Charles marched off into Russia, but Marlborough came away from the conversations convinced that the Swedish ruler's aversion to all things French made it unlikely that he would give assistance to Louis XIV. He even said that the subsidy given to Sweden for remaining neutral was no longer necessary.

The War Ends

Bloody combat in the Low Countries resulted in slow but significant gains for the allied coalition. Marlborough had broken through the line of French fortresses, but the public had also tired of the bloodshed and expenses. As a result, Louis XIV was able to wait until he was offered favourable terms for peace. Still, it required much courage for him to withstand the multiple crises of the next years: his overweight, shy son, recovering from smallpox, succumbed to multiple bleedings at age fifty; soon afterwards, his second son and his wife died of measles, then their eldest son. Years ago Louis had lost most of his teeth; he had since felt poorly. Gout and general weakness limited him to hunting from a carriage. Moreover, he had feared that God was punishing him, a state of mind that his confessor played on (together with his wife's nagging) to persuade him to abandon his mistresses; this made it difficult for him to

---

* Earlier the Dutch had tried to hire Swedish regiments for service against France, but were refused, and they wanted Danzig to remain independent and to open trade with Russia. This unhappiness with Charles was reflected in disagreements with Marlborough, who was ready to accept political realities by recognising Stanislas as Polish king – almost anything, in effect, that would get Charles out of Saxony. He was also concerned about the situation enabling the Stuart claimant to the English throne (Great Britain since the act of Union in 1706 and that of May 1707), James Francis Edward Stuart, to return to Scotland. Had Marlborough been able to see ahead to 1719, when the Stuart pretender married Maria Clementina Sobieska, the granddaughter of John III Sobieski of Poland, he would have worried less, since that would have been seen as a direct challenge to Charles's arrangements in Poland. But at this time all was uncertainty, danger was everywhere.

get the daily sex, sometimes twice a day, that he was accustomed to. But the coalition opposed to him was coming apart – most importantly, Queen Anne, governing by whim and desire for revenge upon her Whig critics, tormented by grief at the deaths of her husband and children and suffering from premature age and illness, helped bring in a Tory government. Marlborough continued his drive into France for another year, but Louis XIV saw that the Tories had driven the duke's supporters from office and were impeding his actions, that the allies were dropping away, and that Austria was no longer an effective party in the war.

The emperor, Joseph, died of smallpox in 1711, followed by the unpredictable duke of Savoy. As the principals vanished from the scene, their successors began to look for ways out of the endless conflict. English parliamentary leaders, referring to the leaders of the Bourbon and Habsburg parties in Spain, exclaimed that it was foolish to get killed for 'two such boobies'!

Charles reluctantly chose the secure Austrian crown over the contested Spanish one. It was clear that his allies were not enthusiastic about a potential union of Austria and Spain, any more than they had been about the potential union of France with Spain; the British government had signalled its unwillingness to maintain the corps that was the heart of Charles's army. Moreover, the Spanish had come to associate him with Protestants. Indeed, his army had been led by a French Huguenot, the earl of Galway, who managed to advance from Portugal to Madrid; but the victorious Bourbon army was commanded by an illegitimate son of James II of England and Marlborough's sister!*

Charles's troops may not have behaved worse than any others, nobody having sufficient supplies to forbid foraging (which easily became looting), but once the great coalition of 1710 – 14,000 Germans, 4,000 English, 1,400 Dutch, 1,400 Portuguese, and 3,000 Spanish Carlists, all commanded by Guido Starhemberg – took Madrid, it had to retreat under the pressure of a national uprising; Vendôme's newly arrived army made short work of Charles's remaining forces outside Catalonia.† Still, because Charles had come to see himself as Spanish king, he required territorial concessions in Italy before he signed the treaty (his refusal to abandon his claims to the throne would soon bring about a new war, one concluded by

---

* James Fitz-James, the earl of Berwick (1670–1734), had fought in the Balkans under Prince Eugene, in Ireland at the battle of the Boyne, and shortly before the decisive encounter in 1707 had been made a French marshal; in 1718 he led French troops into Spain, and died in 1734 fighting against Prince Eugene, struck by a cannon ball.
† Nancy Mitford notes that Vendôme's nose had not only been eaten away by syphilis, but that he otherwise looked like 'an old, fat, dirty, diseased woman'. He openly practised almost all the deadly sins – 'gluttony, sloth, sodomy' being foremost – but was nevertheless a fine general. Voltaire agreed, except to condemn his clothing and praise his valour more. How typically British, how typically French!

peace treaties that swapped territories around like so many counters in a game); Charles brought so many Spanish advisors with him to Vienna that the language of the new royal council was Spanish, and the intricate rules surrounding his daily routine known as Spanish court etiquette were strongly reinforced. Charles was a quiet, very private man, whose principal activities seemed to have been making Vienna into the musical capital of Europe, playing billiards, collecting books and preparing for his own death, which came in his mid-fifties; it was just as well – he did not look like an emperor, was uncomfortable around commoners, and was surrounded by idiots, the same men who had helped him lose Spain.

Marlborough was recalled from the Continent and relieved of his command, then charged by hostile Tories with misappropriation of funds. The complaint was his failure to bring the war to a conclusion, though the real problem was the stubbornness of Louis XIV, who could ignore public complaints about the collapse of the economy and general war-weariness. Marlborough escaped prosecution by going abroad until Anne's death in 1714; he was brought back to England by the new monarch, George I. In any case, he was too ill to take any significant part in politics. He retired to the Woodstock estate given to him by a grateful nation and renamed Blenheim. When he died in 1722, his title passed to the family of his daughter.

Eugene attempted to retire to his estates in Austria, but with less success: Austria was surrounded by unstable neighbours and ambitious princes. He had much to do as president of the war council, but he still found time to supervise the construction of the Belvedere (which required the labour 1,300 men) and the Winter Palace, play cards with his purported mistress, the handsome and wealthy widow, Countess Elenora Batthyány, hunt and fish, collect books and art, and avoid the musical events that were the pride and joy of Emperor Charles VI.*

The death of Louis XIV brought a definitive end to combat. If the light of the Sun King had set, that of the international officer was now at its zenith. Every day would lead toward its setting. Still, there was a long afternoon ahead.

Training the Next Generation

The long war was a training ground for many outstanding officers of

---

* McKay cites an anecdote that Eugene's beautiful cream-coloured horses knew the way from his palace on Himmelpfortgasse to the countess's home so well that when the prince, his coachman, footman and guard (whose ages totalled 310 years) would fall asleep *en route*, they would pull up right at her door and wait until her servants awakened the passengers. Ingrao says that when Eugene did go to work, he spent more time fighting court intrigues than supervising the army

future conflicts. Maurice, the comte de Saxe (1696–1750) was sent to Eugene to observe war first hand. It was unlikely that his father, Augustus II of Saxony, wanted this most promising of his many illegitimate sons exposed unnecessarily to danger, but there was no way that de Saxe could be dissuaded from proving himself courageous and competent. Eugene is said to have warned him about confusing rashness with valour, a warning all the more serious in light of Eugene's own tendency to court danger and ignore wounds until the battle was won. De Saxe's first command was with his father's ally, Peter the Great, in the 1711–12 campaign in Pomerania. He would attain fame in French service during the War of the Austrian Succession and through his widely read memoirs.

Kurt Christoph (1684–1757) count of Schwerin, a lieutenant colonial in a Mecklenburg-Schwerin regiment, fought at Malplaquet. Known popularly simply as 'Schwerin', he would fight alongside Charles XII, then in 1720 accept employment in the Prussian army. There he swiftly rose to the rank of general field marshal.

Leopold of Anhalt-Dessau (1676–1747), later famed as 'the Old Dessauer, commanded the Prussian forces on the Lower Rhine in 1700. His conduct at Blenheim, where he fought under the command of Prince Eugene, was highly praised for telling his generals that they would be transferred from Marlborough's command to the imperial army, because the duke lacked sufficient supplies for all his troops. The choice, Dessau explained curtly, was between obedience and starvation; the generals opted for food. No one wondered when Eugene took Dessau and his corps to Italy the following year. Distinguishing himself in two great battles there, he followed Eugene back to the Netherlands to serve under Marlborough at the battle of Malplaquet. There he so impressed the crown prince – the future soldier-king, Frederick William – that he was later given command of the forces in the war with Sweden. He shared with the king the credit for eventually making the Prussian army into the most fearsome fighting force in Europe. His strict discipline was legendary.

Louis XIV's efforts to make his nearest relatives into generals was, on the whole, a failure. They became competent enough to criticise the field marshals, and, in an earlier time, they would have been considered good. In this era, however, they faced Prince Eugene and Marlborough. Thus, they had to be more than good. But they were not.

The Peace of Utrecht

Great Britain, the Dutch, Savoy, Portugal and Brandenburg signed the peace treaty with France at Utrecht in 1713. France surrendered the Spanish Netherlands to Austria, various territories in the Americas to Great Britain; Spain surrendered all claims to Gibraltar to Britain and

Sicily to Savoy. This treaty was augmented in 1714 by the Peace of Rastatt, by which France ceded to the Holy Roman Empire the Rhineland, and to Austria the Spanish Netherlands, Milan and Naples. With lands passed around as casually as royal brides, with monarchs trading one crown for another, changing names from Charles to Carlos to Karl, thinking men had to wonder (in French) if somehow there was not a more enlightened means of managing international politics

Louis XIV had kept his nation in the struggle by sheer personal will. Simon Schama reports that that 1714 'saw simultaneously the spectre of bankruptcy, the virtual disintegration of the French army in the field, tax revolts and mass famine'. The debt, if parcelled out among the citizenry, amounted to two-thirds the income of a master carpenter or tailor. The French nation would never crawl out from under it.

Universal exhaustion was one reason that almost another generation passed before there was another general European war, and the peace might have been longer than that if Charles VI had been able to produce a son. Just as the expiration of the house of Habsburg in Spain produced the War of the Spanish Succession, the expiration of the male line in Austria would bring about the next great conflict.

Chapter 10

European Power Reshapes Itself
The War of the Austrian Succession

It seemed that there was a war every time some king died. It was enough to make even the most unhappy taxpayer shout '*Vive le roi!*' They may not have liked the king, but it was wise to wish him a long and happy life.

In this case, it was a most silly war, with meagre results for the winners and widespread destruction and impoverishment for the losers. The only winners were those who earned good wages as soldiers, and even then the losses in battle were so staggering that being a mercenary was a poor career choice.

The Pragmatic Sanction

Long ago the electors of the Holy Roman Empire had decided to simplify the decision-process for choosing the next German king, whose name would be sent to the pope as the only candidate to be crowned Holy Roman emperor. Choosing to consider only male candidates was partly common sense – it eliminated the many powerful men connected to the imperial family through a female ancestor – and partly policy to keep the crown inside the Habsburg family. However, when it became clear that Charles VI would have no legitimate male heir, there was a widespread concern that a succession crisis was coming.

Charles knew all about civil war and disputed inheritances. He had been the Habsburg candidate in the War of the Spanish Succession; and he had abandoned that claim only when his brother, the emperor Joseph, died without heirs. Charles had hurried back to Vienna, where he reinforced the elaborate Spanish court etiquette and established the Spanish Riding School. He also asked all neighbouring rulers to sign the Pragmatic Sanction of 1713, which stated, first, that the realm would never be divided, and, second, that females could inherit.

The anticipated heir was his daughter, Maria Theresa (1717–80), who married Francis I, the duke of Lorraine, in 1736. Francis was a nonentity in all respects but one: he was, according to all patriotic Germans, the rightful ruler of Lorraine, a border territory that had been occupied by Louis XIV. Given a totally meaningless duchy in Florence to govern, he was little more than an Austrian puppet. Maria Theresa's proposal in 1740 that Francis be elected Holy Roman emperor, shortly after the unexpected death of Charles VI while still in his mid fifties, was a slap in the face of France; it was almost a declaration of war.

The war, however, came from Prussia, not France. Frederick II (1740–86) recognised the widespread dissatisfaction with Maria Theresa. Who would lead the army, the generals asked; who would govern when she was pregnant, the nobles complained (and she was already on the third of her sixteen pregnancies). Frederick offered his support, but only on the condition that she cede him several territories in Silesia to which he had vague but valid claims. When she refused, he decided to take them by force.

The Bavarian Challenger

Not many expected Maria Theresa to hold on to much, if any of her lands – her husband lacked talent as much as she lacked experience. But the Austrian privy council, preferring to work with a known entity rather than a foreigner, had recognised her as queen and summoned her from Florence.

An opposition was organising, too. Charles Albert of Bavaria (1726–45) had never recognised the Pragmatic Sanction – indeed, he had thought it had been intended to disqualify him specifically, since he had an excellent claim through his mother; and his father, Max Emanuel, had only narrowly failed to seize the imperial crown earlier. Now he called attention to the wording of the will of his ancestor, Ferdinand I, which mentioned only the failure of 'legitimate' children. Louis XV (1710–74, king in 1715) of France, who wanted to revive the old alliance with Bavaria and weaken the Holy Roman Empire, offered his support.

Had the Austrian army performed well in recent conflicts with France and Turkey, the vultures might have circled, but probably only at a distance. Reforms of recent decades should have made for a better fighting force – more emphasis on discipline, less tolerance of officers embezzling funds given for equipment, clothing and food, pensions for invalids and aged soldiers, and an engineering school to train officers in siege techniques – and no one doubted that the German peasants recruited into the ranks and the petty nobles appointed to command them would happily die when ordered to put their lives at risk; their courage and loyal was never doubted. But it just had not all come together. Lack of money is the usual reason given for this failure, which had made it impossible to maintain a large peacetime army; this meant few drills, almost no musket practice, and many units kept at half-pay in garrisons. But the lack of an inspired leader might have been equally responsible. Not every generation produced a Eugene of Savoy, and even he had been subject to the ailments of advancing age – forgetfulness and lethargy. But even when inspired to action, as in the War of the Polish Succession in 1733, Eugene's hurriedly expanded forces had not done well against the French army, which had come into combat fully mustered and well drilled. In 1736 Eugene had died of pneumonia; his successors mismanaged the 1737 war with Turkey.*

In June 1741 an alliance of Prussia, Bavaria, Saxony, Spain and France was announced. It seemed, once again, that Austria was doomed.

Frederick the Great

Frederick was born in Berlin in 1712, son of Frederick William of Prussia, who was popularly called the 'soldier king' for his eccentric passion for making his army the best in all Europe. 'Fritz' grew up in a military atmosphere, commanding a miniature regiment of children at age six, surrounded at Potsdam by his father's elite unit of 1,200 gigantic blue-clad soldiers, and generally being treated as a commoner who was expected to give his life and his love to the state. Frederick, however, took after his mother (whose father was King George I of England) in her love of poetry and music (and therefore was all the more discouraged in these pursuits by his father, who detested all Englishmen and King George II in particular); he was removed from such idleness completely in his teenage years after he tried to run away – his best friend was beheaded for having encouraged him; another managed to escape to Holland, then England, thanks to a hastily scribbled note, '*Sauvez-vous, tout est découvert*' (Save yourself, everthing's revealed) and Lord Chesterfield's assistance, then served in the Portuguese cavalry;† another was confined in Spandau prison for a year, after which he entered Dutch service. The crown prince himself could hardly be shot for treason (Prussia was not Turkey), but he was put under the most brutal discipline imaginable. 'Fritz' learned to never ask anything of anyone that he would not do himself; this was a characteristic that endeared him to his troops – that is, to those lucky

---

* McKay suggests that some of the blame must be given to Eugene, who had opposed having a general staff or councils of war, where young officers could experience the give and take of discussions, and his insistence on strict obedience and lines of command stifling initiative and imagination.

† Peter Karl Christoph von Keith (1711–56), one of two sons of Peter Keith, a general in Prussian service; his brother, a page at the time, confessed, threw himself on the king's mercy and was sent to the ranks in a grenadier company.

enough to survive his two terrible wars, the War of the Austrian Succession and the Seven Years War.

Frederick's unhappy childhood has to be balanced against his father having hammered into him the military skills and self-denying habits that made him into one of the most famous commanders of world history. It was an arduous education that many have admired from a distance, but chose not to impose upon themselves or their children. And probably rightly – who can guarantee that such mistreatment will produce anything more than an emotionally stunted and crabbed personality.

Then there was the incomparable Prussian army. Though Frederick William had carefully refrained from getting it into a war, he had trained it with the same brutality and thoroughness that he had used on his son – and with great success. Frederick's troops would be able to fire faster (Voltaire says six times a minute, thanks to a new iron ramrod and intensive practice), march more swiftly, manoeuvre with dazzling precision under even the most impossible conditions – no rain or snow, no enemy fire was feared as much as a Prussian sergeant, or the king's withering criticism. His cavalry would strike harder and his cannon fire more accurately than anyone's.

Frederick William also bequeathed Fritz an officer corps without parallel at that time. Formerly, every ruler had entrusted command to officers with experience, which in practice meant foreigners or, at a minimum, sons of prominent nobles with foreign battle experience; or sons of neighbours he wanted as allies – for example, August Wilhelm of Braunschweig–Lüneburg (1715–81), known to contemporaries as Bevern, who entered his service in 1731. Frederick William forbade his own subjects to enlist in foreign armies, then he coerced his Junker nobles into accepting low-paying commissions – those who resisted were often drafted into military service; and, finally, he provided professional training. As recompense, he guaranteed the Junkers a near-monopoly on commissions, treated the officers as a privileged class, and made certain that citizens and soldiers understood that the officers were to be respected and honoured; insults, or even implied insults, and disobedience were severely punished.

The high standards were maintained by Leopold von Anhalt-Dessau. Leopold's first independent command had been at the siege of Stralsund, a fortress defended by Charles XII of Sweden. The Prussian contribution to the victory was rewarded with the possession of Pomerania, an expansion which increased significantly the number of nobles of the Junker class. Leopold himself had learned his craft in the Dutch army, and he had fought under Prince Eugene and Marlborough at their greatest triumphs – and he was praised by Prince Eugene for his bravery and coolness under fire. Working closely with the king, Leopold standardised uniforms, weapons, and tactical movements – and introduced the iron ramrod; he applied the regulations drawn up by the king, making certain that their contexts were kept strictly secret – allowing a foreigner to see them or describing their contexts was punished by life imprisonment.

To some the life of a recruit was much like prison, since military service was for the best years of a man's life. But Frederick William shrank from universal military service – he understood that this would disturb the economic foundations of the nation, thus reducing the revenues that allowed him to pay the troops' wages and other expenses. Exemptions were granted generously to skilled labourers, professionals, immigrants and sons of prosperous farmers, but little mercy was given to students, lawbreakers and the unemployed.

He required districts to present volunteers, and should a district fail to supply its quota, recruiters would draw up a list of eligible men and select the ones they wanted; each draftee was to serve for twenty years, though he was only on active service for three months of each year. There were also numbers of foreigners who chose to enlist – mercenaries who wanted to serve in the best army around (and an army which rarely went to war – even the force sent to assist Prince Eugene in the War of the Polish Succession was not sent into battle). Veterans and invalids were given preference in government jobs, often as schoolteachers.

The king was also willing to buy entire units. In 1717 he had sold his porcelain collection to Augustus the Strong of Saxony for a regiment of dragoons; one would have thought that Augustus, with the factories in Dresden and Meissen, had all the fine porcelain he would want – but one would have to wonder if Frederick William would ever have as many soldiers as he wanted.

The Regiment of Giants

Frederick William had a mania for enormous men, all of whom he put into his blue-clad household regiment at Potsdam. Each was over six-foot four, extraordinary in an age of short men, and when wearing their mitred hats, they seemed tall indeed. The tallest was an Irishman, James Kirkland, for whom the king paid almost 9,000 thalers! Kirkland did not go voluntarily to Prussia, but as valet to the Prussian ambassador. Only after arriving did he discover what his fate was to be.

This was not unusual. Prussian agents often used strong drink and even kidnapping to bring home large men. Trickery was preferred, of course, since communities were known to pursue and punish Prussian recruiters; and it was well known that, though it was easy to enter Prussian service, it was almost impossible to get out. Opera lovers have to accept such recruiting practices as necessary to the plot of *The Elixir of*

Love.* Frederick William had between 800 and 1,000 agents across Europe, and a few went so far as to kidnap a tall monk from a Roman monastery.†

International incidents were common, and at one point the elector of Hanover almost declared war over the excesses of Prussian agents – there was bad blood between the future George II and Frederick William anyway, because George had married the woman the king wanted. Several agents were sentenced to prison at hard labour and a few were executed.

Peter the Great sent several groups of tall Russians, first 75, then 150, then more on an annual basis. There was an eight-foot-tall Swede he purchased from Augustus the Strong, but he was too dim-witted to learn the drills; after being thrown out of Potsdam, he walked to Berlin, where he starved to death; when one of Frederick William's recruiters was spotted in Saxony, he was chased down, put on trial and hanged. The guards' drills were merciless, nothing less than perfection permitted; not surprisingly, the desertion rate was about 250 per year.

To make the giants happy, the king sought to find them wives (especially tall ones) and provided them cottages. One humourous incident came after the king encountered a tall Saxon girl near Potsdam. Asking her if she would deliver a message to the commander of the Berlin garrison for a thaler (a nice piece of money!), he gave her a note ordering the commander to marry the bearer of the note to his largest grenadier, an Irishman named Macdol; however, the girl gave the message to an old woman, who dutifully delivered it. The puzzled officer dared not disobey the strange command, and he intimidated the Irish giant into complying; when the king heard of the confusion, he issued an immediate annulment of the marriage. The girl was never located.

The king's other means for keeping the giants from running away consisted of terrible floggings and other harsh punishments. Women who assisted runaways by giving them clothing were hanged – though one has to wonder how such gigantic men could hope to pass themselves off as women. In practice such assistance was rendered only to men of average size, but it fits with the habit of mothers telling their sons 'don't grow too tall or the king will get you'.

---

* Donizetti's weak plot required the tenor, Nemorino, to be so desperate for money to buy a love potion for the rich and beautiful Adina that he was willing to enlist in the army for the bonus offered by Sergeant Belcore, who would be marrying Adina in fifteen minutes.

† Robert Ergang cites instances when the king bartered for tall recruits. When a Saxon field marshal needed a bassoon player, the king swapped one for a tall Saxon, despite (or perhaps because) the musician was the star of the queen's orchestra – and the king hated music, education and other activities that wasted time which could be spent drilling troops. The king even refused to turn over an accused murderer to the king of Denmark until he sent twelve recruits.

Ultimately the regiment grew to 3,000 men. Most were barely over six feet tall, and few were as handsome as the king wanted. But they were suitable for opening the royal balls on the few occasions when the king was willing to spend money on entertainment. Foreign representatives were often startled at being asked to dance by a huge guardsman, but none dared decline. Presumably the guardsmen led.

In practice, the regiment of giants was useless. Not only were they magnificent targets, but they were too heavy to ride ordinary horses; and large horses were more expensive and less hardy than regular cavalry horses.

Fritz Becomes King

Frederick's first task was to persuade his officers and advisors that he was indeed king. Nelson reports an anecdote about one of his friends making a joke of the kind that young Fritz had once enjoyed greatly. The response was a frosty, '*Monsieur, à présent je suis roj*!' (Sir, I am now king!) He quickly distanced himself from his juvenile friends and associated with men of intelligence and ambition.

But Frederick was not all business: he set about building an opera house in Berlin, he abolished torture (the first monarch in Europe to do so) and eliminated many of the most bizarre means of execution; he encouraged trade and commerce; and he entered into correspondence with important *philosophes* (intellectuals, mostly from France). He spoke French habitually, once supposedly saying that he spoke German only to his horse.

He rewarded those friends who had risked their lives for him. Peter Karl Christoph von Keith was brought back from Britain and eventually made a member of the Academy of Sciences. Other Keiths, distantly related, made their way to Berlin – when the Empress Anne's Russification policy cost James Keith his positions in 1747, he went to Berlin. Frederick immediately named him field marshal and entrusted him with the most important military responsibilities. In short, Frederick valued talent, and he sought out the best for his army.

Frederick was not imposing in stature but a good musician, a passable poet and architect, and a great conversationalist. He sent his wife to exile in Berlin, then, as Nelson put it, 'Frederick enjoyed being king enormously.'

He changed his title instantly from King *in* Prussia to King *of* Prussia. There was no one to object – Charles VI having just lost a war with Turkey and then, by dying, thrown all Europe into diplomatic turmoil. Frederick, for his part, was determined to get his share of Austria's lands, just as he would later take a generous share of Poland when that monarchy collapsed.

The Great Battles

Frederick invaded Silesia in April of 1741. There he won a total victory at Mollwitz. Or so the short version of the event goes. Actually, it was a close-run battle. The Austrians, commanded by George von Browne, had the early advantage, driving off the Prussian cavalry, then coming in on the flank so strongly that Frederick left the field, believing the day lost. However, Frederick's experienced field marshal, Schwerin, understood that no battle is lost as long as troops continue to obey their commander. His men, with their superior rate of fire, decimated the attacking Austrians and drove them from Silesia.*

That seemed to be the end of Austria, but Maria Theresa appealed to the chivalry of the Hungarian nobility at Pressburg (Bratislava), a dramatic occasion because the Hungarians had been leaning toward independence, especially the Protestant areas which had been so often in revolt. When she appeared with her infant son in her arms and appealed to their sense of honour and justice, then promised to treat Hungary as a more equal part of her empire, with Pressburg as a principal residence, she won them over. Once Maria Theresa was recognised as queen by the Hungarians, she was able to attract an increasing number of supporters.

Carlyle described the moment:

> Sunday, 25th June, 1741, that is the day of putting on your Crown, – Iron Crown of St. Stephen, as readers know. The Chivalry of Hungary, from Palfy and Esterhazy downward, and all the world are there; shining in loyalty and barbaric gold and pearl. A truly beautiful Young Woman, beautiful to soul and eye, devout too and noble, though ill-informed in Political or other Science, is in the middle of it, and makes the scene still more noticeable to us. See, as the finish of the ceremonies, she has mounted a high swift horse, sword girt to her side, – a great rider always, this young Queen; – and gallops, Hungary following like a comet-tail, to the Konigsberg [KING'S-HILL so called; no great things of a Hill, O reader; made by barrow, you can see], to the top of the Konigsberg; there draws sword; and cuts, grandly flourishing, to the Four Quarters of the Heavens: 'Let any mortal, from whatever quarter coming, meddle with Hungary if he dare!' Chivalrous Hungary bursts into passionate acclaim; old Palfy, I could fancy, into tears; and all the world murmurs to itself, with moist-gleaming eyes, 'REX NOSTER!' This is, in fact, the beautifulest King or Queen that now is, this radiant young woman; beautiful things have been, and are to be, reported of her; and she has a terrible voyage just ahead, – little dreaming of it at this grand moment.

---

* Black, *European Warfare, 1660-1815*, asks why Frederick's efforts to seek a decisive battle usually failed. Partly because Frederick had too many enemies to follow up any victory, and partly because the army was still too clumsy to take advantage of tactical opportunities.

In 1742 she made peace with Frederick, ceding him Silesia, in order to concentrate on her Bavarian-French opponents. When England entered the war against France, the balance was tipped in her favour so quickly that Frederick realised that unless he acted soon, he would be fighting Maria Theresa alone. He declared war again, before she could expand her coalition.*

As Frederick advanced swiftly on Prague, panic and excitement reigned in Vienna. As Carlyle tells the tale:

> Of Maria Theresa in Hungary, – for she ran to Presburg again with her woes (August 16th, Diet just assembling there), – let us say only that Hungary was again chivalrous; that old Palfy and the general Hungarian Nation answered in the old tone, – VIVAT MARIA; AD ARMA, AD ARMA! with Tolpatches, Pandours, Warasdins; – and, in short, that great and small, in infinite 'Insurrection,' have still a stroke of battle in them PRO REGE NOSTRO. Scarcely above a District or two (as the JASZERS and KAUERS, in their over-cautious way) making the least difficulty. Much enthusiasm and unanimity in all the others; here and there a Hungarian gentleman complaining scornfully that their troops, known as among the best fighters in Nature, are called irregular troops, – irregular, forsooth! In one public consultation . . . a gentleman suggests that 'Winter is near; should not there be some slight provision of tents, of shelter in the frozen sleety Mountains, to our gallant fellows bound thither?' Upon which another starts up, 'When our Ancestors came out of Asia Minor, over the Palus Maeotis bound in winter ice; and, sabre in hand, cut their way into this fine Country which is still ours, what shelter had they? No talk of tents, of barracks or accommodation there; each, wrapt in his sheepskin, found it shelter sufficient. Tents!' And the thing was carried by acclamation.

Maria Theresa quickly obtained Russian support, but Frederick countered with a Swedish alliance, promising to assist the king restoring his state to great power status. How Frederick was supposed to be able to do this was less than clear, but high politics was no more logical then than it was in the twentieth century. It was in that war with Sweden that the Russian field marshal, James Keith, came to Frederick's attention.

The Battle of Fontenoy 1745

The war was fought as much in the Austrian Netherlands as in Bohemia.

---

* While the British were concentrating principally on grand strategy, it was also important that George II was the elector of Hanover, and that this territory stood right in the way of the advancing French army.

The French, led by the talented Marshal de Saxe, had advanced on the fortress of Fontenoy with 49,000 men. The English and Austrians raised a force equally large known as 'the Pragmatic Army' to be led by the twenty-four-year-old Duke of Cumberland (1721–65), King George II's second son, and hurried south.

The Dutch and Austrians look the left wing of the battle line, the English and Hanoverians on the right. The French position was described by Carlyle in his usual overwrought style: 'Marechal de Saxe, whose habit is much that of vigilance, forethought, sagacious precaution, singular in so dissolute a man, has neglected nothing on this occasion.' The result was an almost impregnable French position, against which the Dutch bled themselves. The duke of Cumberland had meanwhile attacked uphill, at the head of the Black Watch regiment, ignoring withering fire from the woods on the right and the village of Fontenoy on the left. When the English attack faltered, Carlyle comments, 'His Royal Highness blazes into resplendent PLATT-DEUTSCH rage, what we may call spiritual white-heat, a man SANS PEUR at any rate, and pretty much SANS AVIS'. (That is, he was swearing in Low German, without fear, but also without good judgement.)

The innovative tactics of the Black Watch in this, their first engagement – throwing themselves on the ground when the French were about to deliver a volley, then rising up and firing – could not be copied by less disciplined troops.* On the other hand, there is the anecdote about Sir Charles Hay, who upon leading his men onto the plain, to find himself confronted by the best of the enemy force, said, '*Messieurs les Gardes Françaises, s'il vous plait tirez le premier*' (Gentlemen of the French Guard, you may fire first'). If true, this was not a pointless invitation: whoever fired second had a tremendous psychological advantage in making a bayonet charge upon troops still disorganised by the impact of the volley.†

The British tactics worked to perfection. Marshal de Saxe, seeing his units breaking up and fleeing, ordered the Irish brigade of 5,000 men forward. The brigade commander, Thomas Lally, was able to bring up artillery and train it on the enemy ranks; otherwise, no matter how enthusiastically his men shouted, 'Remember Limerick', they would have been shot down in rows. Telling his men not to fire until they practically had their bayonets in the bellies of their ancestral enemies, the Irish made possible the subsequent French counter-attacks that drove the British

---

* It was, in fact, a tactic that Szechi calls typical for Highland Scots. The principal difference was that the Black Watch did not throw away their muskets and charge with swords.

† An alternative version of the story, given by Voltaire, is that a French officer made that retort after Hay promised to drive his men into the Scheldt river as they had previously done into the Main; such a reference to the collapse of a bridge under the weight of retreating troops at the 1743 battle of Dettingen would have been a grave insult – if, indeed, such remarks could have been heard at all under the circumstances.

back before they could roll the wavering French lines up.

Cumberland had taken the central redoubt, but gave the order to retreat after his allies had decided that the contest was becoming a second Malplaquet. 7,300 French fell, 7,500 British and allied troops. Louis XV, a witness to the intense fighting, gave his personal congratulations to de Saxe and his troops.

One of the survivors of the battle was Richard Hennessey, who settled in France, and founded the Hennessey distillery in Cognac. Others accompanied Bonnie Prince Charlie to Scotland in 1746, to die in their ranks at Culloden. The battle was Cumberland's revenge for Fontenoy. Alas, for Scotland, it was the beginning of an oppressive rule that would almost equal in harshness that imposed on Ireland.

Lally himself remained in France, but in 1757 he was sent with a French army to India. The war is known in America as the French and Indian War, but relatively few Americans are aware that the principal theatre of conflict was in Europe (the Seven Years War) and that there was another 'Indian War' in Asia; the North American theatre was less important than the other two, as Americans facing French invasion and Indian attacks learned, but in the end the British were victorious every-where. Lally, who had surrendered in 1761, was warned that it would be dangerous for him to return to France. With Irish stubbornness, he ignored the advice, only to be immediately thrown into the Bastille, then tried on charges of treason and, in 1766, beheaded.

Jacobite Rising of 1745–46

The French victory at Fontenoy gave hope to Louis XV and the Stuart pretender that George II might be toppled; he had been king since 1727, always quarrelling with his family and speaking French. All that was needed, Stuart loyalists in Scotland assured them, was a Stuart leader and a few of the Irish and Scottish loyalists in exile, perhaps backed by a handful of French troops. Scotland had been rent by clan feuds, Ireland was in permanent rebellion, and the English – though admiring George II's military abilities – had no enthusiasm for him personally. George's English subjects were offended by his preferring Hanover to London, and his unwillingness to learn their language; in addition, governmental corruption was at its usual worst of all time.

The rebel hopes rested on Charles Stuart.* His father, the 'Old Pretender', was considered too aged for the enterprise; moreover,

---

* Edward Louis John Casimir Silvester Maria Stuart (1720–88, born and died in Rome) is better known as 'Bonnie Prince Charlie'. His full name was not only impossibly wieldy, but betrayed his Polish and Italian ancestry – his mother was the granddaughter of Jan Sobieski.

memories of his failed leadership in the 1715 rebellion lingered, none of them good. Charles was a much more personable figure, and his lack of military experience would be offset by the presence of capable advisors. In July of 1745 he landed in Scotland, to be greeted by many Protestant and Catholic clans, both Highland and Lowland. However, his welcome was not universal; after all, this was Scotland, and whatever one clan wanted, its traditional rivals opposed.

The preferred leader of the army was James Keith, but the Russian empress ordered all correspondence from the Jacobites intercepted, so he was unaware of the opportunity until too late. Command, therefore, was given to Lord George Murray (1694–1760), whose military experience went back to the days of Marlborough, but who had forfeited his future in the British army by joining the 1715 uprising. After fleeing to France, he may have fought in Sardinia and assisted a Spanish intervention in Scotland before asking for amnesty in 1725. This history made Charles mistrust him, and even more so when Murray advocated a defensive war, with no invasion of England. Charles insisted on recovering all his lands, not just Scotland, and while he admired the quick and efficient manner that Murray made an army out of disparate and untrained units, he interfered with his plans at every critical moment.

The clan army was enthusiastic, but poorly equipped – its main asset was that Celtic love of attack which modern scholars have condemned so roundly and its admirers love so dearly. The march south went quickly, with Edinburgh surrendering without resistance, and the British army performing so poorly in the initial engagements that it appeared the Scots would reach London. However, the anticipated Jacobite uprising did not occur, and the promised French help had not appeared. Charles wanted to push on, no matter the risks, but his advisors voted to retreat. After that, there was no place to stop.

The British army was now led by the duke of Cumberland, who had brought some of his best regiments from Flanders. As he marched north, unable to catch the Highland army, he attracted so many Lowlanders to his force that eventually he had more Scots in his army than did Charles Stuart. Cumberland capably arranged for supplies to be brought by sea, thus upsetting the prince's hopes that a lack of food and fodder would limit the forces employed against him to a size that could be defeated on the battlefield. Cumberland then tarried in Aberdeen for six weeks to train his men before advancing – he needed steady men, men who would not run when attacked by howling clansmen or panic when bagpipes were heard through the fog.

Charles withdrew into the Highlands, but by mid-April there was not much of Scotland left to retreat into. Murray and others advocated dispersing into guerrilla bands, but Charles insisted on fighting. Unfortunately, he ended up on a flat, marshy field more suitable for the

English cavalry and artillery than for a charge by sword-wielding clansmen. An effort to surprise the English with a night attack failed when day rose before the Scots reached Cumberland's camp, and, with the supplies having gone astray, the clansmen had to fight without food, drink, shelter or rest. Charles ignored Murray's advice to retreat from Culloden Moor while there was still time. Soon overwhelming numbers took their places on the opposite side of the field and devastating artillery fire began. Charles allowed his men to stand under this bombardment for half an hour, perhaps hoping against hope that the English would come forward, so his charging men would not have to run through many volleys; when he did order his men forward, some refused to move, having been shot to pieces, others angry at not having been given the place of honour in the line. Those who did go forward were caught by deadly fire from the British infantry from the front and flank, then charged on the other flank by the cavalry.*

As the Scots attempted to escape – Prince Charles being led forcibly from the battlefield by faithful retainers – Cumberland gave orders to murder all the wounded ('no quarter'), later justifying this on the basis of a forged order by Murray to do the same.

The battle was a massacre – its murderous course detailed in a powerful, low-budget 1964 movie, *Culloden*, by anti-war director, Peter Watkins. The aftermath was as bad – the Highlands were scoured for rebels, families being rounded up for exile in the Americas, the kilt (the make-do uniform of the rebels) being banned, and the hostile clans being broken up. Although most rebels were Episcopalians, Roman Catholics suffered most; and the Gaelic language ceased to be widely spoken.

'Charlie' was hunted through the Highlands, but Flora MacDonald and others refused to deliver him to his enemies; eventually, he took ship for France, together with all his money and treasure, leaving his supporters with nothing but memories.

Murray escaped to the Continent, received a pension from the Old Pretender, was snubbed by the Young Pretender, and died in Holland, awaiting another opportunity to drive the Hanoverians from the throne.

Charles Stuart went into a legend that life could not emulate. In exile he acquired the attributes of heroism and chivalry that his actual deeds did not justify. The praise belongs to his followers, who laid down the lives and lost their lands in his cause, and who kept the memory of the event as bright in Scotland as it was forgotten in England.

The lesson for the English was that professional soldiers can beat any army, no matter how motivated by patriotism and religion.

---

* Black, *European Warfare, 1660–1815*, sees the Highlanders' wild charge less as a manifestation of Celtic habits than a characteristic of warfare as practiced by every non-modern state at that time.

Frederick's Art of War

In 1748 Frederick wrote his *Essai sur la grande guerre* (in French, of course), instructions for his officers, most of which were observations that any intelligent person could have worked out on his own. In this era, however, and perhaps in almost any time, this type of insight is not to be expected in the average officer (most Prussian officers could at least speak French, though it is doubtful that many of them had anything to say). Frederick, however, was not the type of man to trust to anything – if his officers were blockheads, his men were the meatheads destined to be put upon the block and hacked to pieces. Since his army was composed equally of draftees and mercenaries, he was especially concerned that the mercenaries would take the first opportunity to run away.

His advice on avoiding desertion, greatly summarised:

a) Do not allow soldiers to see any movement toward the rear; that may cause them to believe you are retreating. If you are retreating, call it something else.

b) Provide the troops with regular rations and drink. Otherwise, they will seek it themselves.

c) If desertion becomes a problem, inquire as to why. Have the troops been paid their bounties? Have they been allowed to go out alone to get water and fodder?

d) Have patrols around the camp. Never camp near a wood. Never march at night. Call the role frequently.

e) Never relax discipline. Since the ranks are filled with idlers, find them tasks to do. Remind them that the officers are always watching them.

More importantly, he reflected on the philosophy of command. This came naturally to him, a talent honed by long conversations with the most learned men of his era, *philosophes* like Voltaire. Frederick said that the most important task of a commander is to determine the aim of a war – a political goal – then to determine the military strategy necessary to achieve that goal, and finally to select appropriate tactics for making the strategy successful. All this must be done with economy, with the forces on hand.

Reconnaissance was necessary to locate the enemy, then speedy marching so as to attack with superior numbers at the decisive point. This meant taking the offensive, striking by surprise. Then, since nothing ever worked as expected, a commander had to be flexible and daring enough to correct mistakes and take advantage of enemy errors. The morale of the armies was extremely important – troops who expected to win usually did.

His customary practice was to concentrate his forces on one wing, then attacking 'in echelon' or obliquely (*schiefe Schlachtordnung*), thus achieving numerical superiority over the enemy at a strategic point while 'refusing' his other wing, i.e., holding it back sufficiently that it was difficult to attack. Like his father, he did not want the secrets to his success shared with the enemy, but he did not go to Frederick William's extremes in limiting its circulation. Moreover, according to Clausewitz, the oblique formation was less important in Frederick's success than his calmness and self-possession, and his firmness. These qualities made his troops believe him invincible.

Clausewitz also noted that armies were much smaller in those days, so that they had flanks which could be more easily attacked, and they were less mobile, less able to respond to surprises. Most important, Clausewitz said, Frederick always sought out a decisive engagement, then broke his enemy in a single battle.

Last, Clausewitz observed that Frederick always attacked his enemy's most fertile provinces, so that it was not necessary for him to bring supplies from a distance, but could instead feed his men and animals off the countryside.

Post-War Prussia

It is quite likely that Frederick the Great would not have become involved in another war. Certainly, not soon. The efforts he had demanded from his subjects could not be asked again. Nor was he by nature a lover of war.

Frederick had become a soldier to please his father; he had become an aggressor to strengthen the state. Now he wanted to enjoy life – to talk with intelligent and educated men (in French, of course), to compose music and to play his flute. He lived in Potsdam, his wife in Berlin. Not surprisingly, they had no children.

It does not appear that Frederick was gay. He once wrote that he liked women, but the enjoyment was not as great as the regrets. It was that he disliked everything about the wife his father had chosen for him, and he was as awkward around women as his father had been. In a state where discipline was everything, sexual morality was sternly enforced; and he had to be a model for the nation.*

He broke completely with one prominent aspect of his father's regime – making sport of educated men, ideas and high culture. Frederick demonstrated that a prince could be a great warrior and a practitioner of the arts of peace.

He also understood that no ruler could pay his troops unless the economy performed well and he was able to tax it effectively. That is, not

---

* Military duties were a good excuse for his neglecting his wife. There was always something that needed his keen eye and sharp judgment. Frederick understood how to make anyone grovel who failed to live up to his standards.

to tax businesses out of existence, but to give incentives and such assistance as would permit getting significant revenues. This money had to be in gold and silver, so that the mercenaries could be paid promptly with coins everyone recognised as having dependable value. Subjects would also be reminded by the portrait and coat-of-arms that their ruler was equally dependable. Political economy directed to this end has been called 'mercantilism'. No longer was it a universal point of pride for a ruler to know nothing of economics, though that attitude persists in western governing classes, media leaders and university faculties; perhaps that is why we call Frederick 'the Great' while denying that title to our modern leaders.*

Maria Theresa, Enlightened Monarch

Maria Theresa thalers became such a standard of excellence in coinage that they were used throughout the world until relatively recently – and early twentieth-century reproductions are still available at reasonable prices. She also became famous for reforms such as planting trees on the south side of roads so that her armies could march in the shade, while at the same time peasants would have branches to use for their grape vines.

By modern standards, however, she seems more autocratic than enlightened: she disliked Jews, she exiled Protestants to Transylvania and she crushed the Masons (so much for *the Magic Flute* if she had lived longer). She also curbed the privileges of the Church, ordering that no papal message could be circulated without imperial approval. On her deathbed she ordered that all troops be given a bonus of one month's pay – she understood the importance of buying loyalty.

She also never forgot anything. In the case of Frederick the Great, she never forgot Silesia, nor the humiliating defeats. She was determined upon revenge. And one way of working toward that was to marry one daughter, Marie Antoinette, to the future Louis XVI of France. That was one major step on the road to the Diplomatic Revolution that would make allies of Austria, Russia and France against Prussia.

---

* See page 289 below.

Chapter 11

The Old Regimes' Last Hope

The Seven Years War

Revenge for 1740

This war was a violent working-out of problems that the last great conflict had not resolved. There was no good reason for the war to begin in 1756, but once French miscalculations in North America were followed by British blunders, war in Europe quickly followed.

The French miscalculation was based on a belief that neither the English king nor British colonial governors would risk war just to remove a fort from the confluence of the Ohio and Monongahela rivers in western Pennsylvania; the intent was cut the Iroquois Alliance off from the Ohio country and to allow French Indian allies to return to rich ancestral hunting grounds. The Iroquois, however, demanded that the British act; and so, too, did colonial governors who anticipated that settlers would soon be moving across the mountains into what was perceived as a vast unoccupied region. In early 1754, after the governor of Virginia sent young George Washington to the fort's commander with a message to get out, the situation became complicated. When the French refused, Washington was sent back to establish a military presence nearby. There was a firefight about which Washington wrote, 'I heard the bullets whistle, and, believe me there is something charming in the sound.' A French attack on Washington's fort led to his surrender and, because he could not read French, he signed an admission that he had 'assassinated' a French officer (who had actually been tomahawked by one of Washington's Indian allies). This led to complications. After Parliament discussed the matter, it decided to send two Irish regiments to America. This ill-fated expedition was named for its ill-starred commander, Braddock, and became the opportunity for young Washington to demonstrate his talent for leadership. It also led to war with France.

One could easily call some of the Indian allies mercenaries. True, most had a great interest in the outcome of the war, but Indian customs meant that any individual who wished to sit out a particular war could do so. However, no Indian could do without European products – knives, kettles, cloth and, of course, the guns and gunpowder necessary to defeat rival Indians. French and British Indian experts emphasised the importance of presents and promises of booty for enlisting the 'savages' in any war. One might shrink from that name today, but to forget that almost all Europeans thought about Native Americans in primitive terms would be to misunderstand the military situation fundamentally. Some Indians went to war for the adventure – and to earn respect from their peers. But on the whole, the principle was No Money, No Indians.

George II was a passive king except for the family tradition of quarrelling with near relatives; formerly a highly rated general, he had led troops personally into battle, and he saw that his second son, William of Cumberland, had opportunities to distinguish himself. He allowed Parliament to govern – except in Hanover, where his family had ruled for time out of mind. It was Hanover which determined British policy at this moment – he insisted that Hanover be protected from French attack.

There was only one German state that could provide an army large enough and good enough to protect Hanover – Prussia, still ruled by Frederick II. Moreover, although Brandenburg-Prussia lay east of Hanover, the Prussian king also possessed valuable and strategic properties in Westphalia, right on the route French armies must use to reach Hanover. George's problem was historical memory – every Englishman knew that Prussia was a traditional ally of France, and every Prussian was equally certain that any future war would find his country on the side of France . . . except that France and Austria seemed to be in bed with one another. Given the marriage of the Dauphin, the future Louis XVI, to Marie Antoinette, that was literally the case.

Frederick II was acknowledged a master of military affairs, but he could not control politics. Normally, Austria was the death enemy of France, but now Maria Theresa of Austria put her desire to recover Silesia above her fear that France would annex more German territory along the Rhine; she concluded a treaty of alliance with Louis XV, then began to raise a army and collect allies. This was the 'diplomatic revolution' that should have destroyed Prussia nearly as thoroughly as the one that soon brought about the dismemberment of Poland.

England had hired 55,000 Russian troops to protect Hanover, but it was so clear that the empress of Russia, Elizabeth, hated Frederick, that it would not be possible to bring those troops to the Rhine.* Not that this mattered in October of 1755, when the empress declared that she would

---

* Elizabeth (1709–62) was the daughter of Peter the Great. A bright girl and a great beauty, he had wanted to marry her to Louis XV, but her illegitimate birth was too great an obstacle for getting her into the French royal family. In late 1741 she seized power in a

aid any power that went to war with Prussia! When Austria mobilised, so did Russia – though Elizabeth's troops did not move into East Prussia until 1757. Frederick faced France, Austria and Russia – the three great Continental powers – and possibly a host of minor enemies, too.

Why Elizabeth chose to do this is still debated. Thomas Carlyle, the nineteenth-century Scot lecturer/historian wrote in his *History of Friedrich II*:

> Fancy a poor fat Czarina, of many appetites, of little judgment, continually . . . beaten by the Saxon-Austrian artists and the Russian service-pipes. Bombarded with cunningly devised fabrications, every wind freighted for her with phantasmal rumours, no ray of direct sunlight visiting the poor Sovereign woman; who is lazy, not malignant it she could only avoid it; mainly a mass of esurient oil, with alkali on the back of alkali poured in, for ten years past; till, by pouring and by stirring, they get her to the state of *soap* and froth! It is so wonderful that she does, by degrees, rise into eminent suspicion, anger, fear, violence and vehemence against her bad neighbour?

Contemporaries speculated that Elizabeth had been infatuated with Frederick, then heard derisive remarks attributed to him about her. This fit well with her fading beauty, and her growing pride and extraordinary sexual appetite, but not with the brilliance of her mind, her practicality and the influence of her ministers. Was there an insult, a *bon mot* by the king quoted to her at the right moment? Even Carlyle, a worshipper of *the Great Man*, admitted that Frederick had a sharp tongue and wrote satiric poetry, and that he had insulted Louis XV's mistress, Madame Pompadour. Perhaps. But more important, Elizabeth was very ill, and she worried that Frederick would swallow up Poland as he had Silesia. She wanted her share – that is, as much as she could get.

Also, Elizabeth did not share her father's enthusiasm for the West, merely his mercurial temperament; she replaced Germans in her administration and army with ethnic Russians – the exception being the Baltic barons, who had proven to be both loyal and competent. Thus, Elizabeth's decision was almost certainly based on political calculations – that she could expand her empire farther into Poland-Lithuania. All this was betrayed to Frederick by a spy in the Saxon archives.

Frederick did not wait for his enemies to strike – in August of 1756 he invaded Saxony, knocking that potentially important state out of the war.

---

coup, then quickly made Russia an important force in European affairs. Until 1756 she had been anti-French; afterward, she saw only Prussia as a serious enemy – it was a competitor for hegemony in east-central Europe.

Dresden and Prague

Frederick found that Saxon king had prudently evacuated his capital, Dresden, and taken up a strong position on the western bank of the Elbe at nearby Prina, where the Austrian forces could come to his rescue. The Austrian commander, Maximilian Ulysses von Browne, however, found it impossible to move directly down the Elbe river – the intervening mountains, known as Saxon Switzerland, were easily blocked. Frederick ignored that route, crossing the mountain passes to the west. When he reached the Elbe, he confronted the slow-moving and incompletely mobilised Austrian forces. To his surprise, the ensuing battle was extremely hard fought – although the Prussians were victorious at the end of the day, the soldiers later said among themselves that this was not the Austrian army they had faced before.

Indeed, between the wars, the Austrian field marshal, Leopold von Daun (1705–66), had completely reorganised the imperial army. Taking personal charge of the infantry, he gave the white-clad infantry confidence; Prince Lichtenstein had similarly reformed the artillery. His cavalry was still not numerous, Hungary not having fully recovered from the Turkish occupation and the wars of liberation, but the Hungarians were doughty warriors, and Croatian light cavalry was equal to any horsemen in Europe.

Even more important, there had been a major change in the way that ordinary troops looked at war. When Frederick accepted the surrender of the Saxon army, he had assumed that he could simply absorb those regiments into his own army. That was the practice in the past.

Now, however, the Saxons began to drift away. There was no punishment which could prevent wholesale desertion. Worst, some of the deserters reformed their units and joined the Austrian army in Bohemia.* Frederick, not to be made a fool so easily, ordered Saxon prisoners put directly into Prussian ranks, where the simple soldiers and officers could guarantee their willingness to fight.

But patriotism could not be stifled. The Saxon units stationed in Poland by Augustus III (1696–1763) entered into what the official historians called *östereichischen Sold*, i.e., Austrian pay. They were joined in early 1757 by entire units that mutinied, then marched off towards Austria.†

---

* Saxons even today are proud of not being Prussians. The author remembers well driving from Prague to Leipzig in the summer of 1991, being among the first Americans to cross into Saxony from Czechoslovakia. Everywhere national flags were flying, with the symbol of East German Communism cut out, but just as prominently was the green flag of Saxony. It was quickly apparently how much the Saxons had resented the domination of East Berlin, which was seen as a continuation of the historical exploitation of Saxony, a centre of culture and learning, by the humourless and militaristic regime of the north. The palace at Pirna was memorable only for the porcelain collection and the friend who acted as guide.

† In 1758, when the Austrians announced that it could no longer pay these troops, the

Soon afterward Frederick invaded Bohemia again. It was an act of desperation – already French armies were across the Rhine, Russians were closing in from the east, and Austrians had advanced through Silesia within forty miles of Berlin. Under normal circumstances, he would have stayed on the defensive, but he learned that the enemy coalition was moving slowly, cautiously, each willing to let the others bear the costs of pitched battle. That gave him an opportunity to strike the Austrians first, disrupt their mobilisation and seize their supplies.

Frederick understood the numbers that he was facing. That made the typical slow advance and careful manoeuvring impossible – he had to knock at least one enemy out of the war immediately. He was, moreover, exactly the man to do this – there was nobody better at motivating and moving troops than he was, nobody more willing to take risks, nobody better able to assess the difference between risky and rash – a line indistinctly drawn and often hidden by the smoke of battle. Or, to paraphrase Clausewitz, in the fog of war.

Frederick pushed up the Moldau river to Prague. He was badly outnumbered, but he won several skirmishes, then fought a desperate battle just outside Prague.

Browne at the Breech

As the Prussians besieged Prague at the end of April in 1757, Browne led his men past the castle at Hradčany, down the steep slope, then across the ancient Charles Bridge and through the city to take up their assigned positions on the Zizka hills farther east (*Sterbohol* in Czech, now in the New City), where he supervised the digging of trenches along the rocky heights facing north. This position had been chosen by the Czech hero, Jan Zizka in 1420, when faced by overwhelming numbers of German crusaders under the Emperor Sigismund; Zizka's victory was surely remembered by the many Czech troops in Browne's army, but the main attraction for Browne was the steepness of the hills. Frederick, after looking at the Austrian position, chose not to attach head-on, but sought to envelop the imperial right by sending Marshal Schwerin on a swift march through the woods, with raiders to create a diversion on the other side of Prague.

What Frederick did not know was that once Schwerin's men came out

---

units began negotiations to join the Russian army. Because Augustus III honoured his promise to not allow his soldiers to fight against Frederick, the soldiers ignored him, and were joined by many volunteers. Units totaling 10,000 men accepted French pay. Many Saxon officers who made their way to Vienna were less lucky – many spent the war confined to an Austrian barracks. In vain Frederick demanded that all officers return to Saxony, on pain of the severest punishment.

of the woods, they would find themselves in a maze of fishponds and morasses. This slowed their progress so much that the element of surprise was lost. Browne immediately sent six regiments to occupy the Vitkov hill dominating the battlefield, then brought every man avail to fill in the gap between the formations; when this was accomplished he sent his rear units to the right to close the gap between the infantry and the cavalry. Browne's artillery, stationed on the hill, cut the advancing Prussians down like wheat as they slowly made their way forward. Schwerin, anxious about his troops' morale and shaken by the persistent cavalry attacks, seized a regimental colour and started forward, only to be killed instantly by grapeshot. Frederick coolly ordered the attack continued.

Browne, seeing the Prussians wavering, led his grenadiers forward in a bayonet charge. Seeing how well the attack was going, Browne rode over to the next line of infantry, urging more speed, and directing it toward the retreating Prussians; he was following behind the troops' rapid forward march when a cannon ball smashed his left leg. The news quickly spread through the army, some troops responding by attacking wildly without order or orders, others yielding to the reinforcements that Frederick had thrown into a gap that had opened – a subordinate refused to obey Browne's command to fill it, saying that Charles of Lorraine had told him to hold his position; moreover, even when Charles sent orders to move, the subordinate still refused because he did not know any of the messengers personally. The Prussians broke through or flanked the Austrian positions, then pounded mercilessly those still fighting. At length, the Austrian lines gave way in a mad rush for the city gates.

Browne's counterattack had failed, but the desperate conflict had rendered entire Prussian regiments useless for immediate redeployment; despite losing the battle, Austrian morale soared – the soldiers had stood up to the Prussians longer than anyone had expected. Browne's wound was given the usual incompetent treatment, but his frustration at having lost his chances for victory – both at Prague and his inability to participate in the great campaign shaping up – was too much for a body already weakened by ill health. Military historians believe that, had he been present at the subsequent battle of Kolin, Frederick the Great would not have been allowed to retire from the field unopposed – Max Browne would have insisted on an immediate pursuit and the destruction of the entire army.

Frederick's Star Sinks

The Prussian king had lost more men (14,000) than the Austrians (8,800) under his old enemy, but he had nevertheless prevailed and Browne had fallen. If the old Austrian general, Johann Baptist Serbelloni, had come up promptly to support Browne, Frederick would probably have been routed. But Serbelloni, who barely spoke German and was punctilious only in demanding respect for his noble Italian ancestry, could not be stirred to action. He heard the guns, but did nothing. The Austrians formed a defensive line on a row of hills to the east, at Kolin – a location they knew well from the previous year's war games.

At the ensuing battle, Frederick's troops finally had enough – they fell back from a hopeless attack, causing their king to yell, '*Rucker, wollt ihr ewig leben*?' (Cowards, do you want to live forever?) It made no difference. As the Prussian armies fell back toward their homeland, Frederick's enemies began to close in.

The most serious threat seemed to be the Russian army that had overrun East Prussia and was closing in on Berlin. Frederick was not worried, however, so long as his other enemies did not act after he withdrew troops from their fronts. The dilatoriness of his foe, as usual, worked in his favour. Still, the odds were greatly against him – 40,000 troops versus his own 25,000 (estimated figures vary considerably, but always with a significant Russian advantage).

Frederick was willing to offer combat partly out of desperation, but partly because he assumed that the fighting ability of the Russian troops was as low as it had been in past campaigns – relatively unskilled and prone to panic, dependent on foreign officers for even the most minor decisions.

His plan was to cut the Russian line of supply, thereby forcing either a retreat or a battle on his terms; perhaps the morale of the Russian soldiery would collapse. What happened was anything but. The Russians fought with dogged courage, refusing to break despite the punishing casualties. At the end of the long August day, Frederick had lost over 12,000 men; the Russians had suffered perhaps 21,000 casualties and been forced to retreat. Had the Russians a better commander, they would probably have prevailed.

As bad news flooded in, he met Daun at Hochkirch, in the Wendish part of Saxony. It was October 1758, toward the end of campaigning weather. Frederick had 40,000 men to Daun's 90,000, but he apparently believed that Daun would stand on the defensive, as was his custom. James Keith was less sanguine – according to Carlyle, he said that 'the Austrians deserve to be hanged if they don't attack us here'. Apparently, Daun felt the same way, first deceiving the Prussians by seeming to reinforce his fortifications, then leading 30,000 to the left and coming in on Frederick's right flank before attacking simultaneously all along the line.*

Keith's death in a failed counter-attack was the critical moment. Frederick ordered a retreat, which he carried out successfully, leaving

---

* Black, *European Warfare, 1660–1815,* says that Daun's attacks in columns here demonstrated that linear tactics were not the universal panacea.

over 100 cannon and 8,000 men on the battlefield. But he was not discouraged. According to Carlyle, he reassured one of his friends, citing a passage of the French playwright, Racine:

Enfin après un an, tu me revois, Arbate, Non plus comme autrefois cet heureux Mithridate, Qui, de Rome toujours balancant le destin, Tenait entre elle et moi l'univers incertain. Je suis vaincu; Pompée a saisi l'avantage D'une nuit qui laissait peu de place au courage; Mes soldats presque nus. . .

Visit me in a year, Arbate. No longer the happy Mithridates, but one whose destiny was always determined by Rome. Between that destiny and my uncertain present, I am overcome. Pompey took advantage of one night and left me little but courage. My soldiers are almost naked . . .

Or, as revised by Mozart's librettist, Vittorio Amadeo Cigna-Santi:

Tu mi rivedi, Arbate, ma quel più non rivedi felice Mitridate, a cui Roma lungamente fu dato bilanciare il destin. Tutti ha dispersi d'otto lustri i sudor sola una notte a Pompeo fortunata, a me fatale.

You will see me again, Arbate, but you will not see again that happy Mithridates, for whom Rome has long balanced his destiny. All has been lost, glory and sweat, in one night to Pompey, fatally for me.

Keith's body was plundered by Croats before being brought to Lacy, who is said to have wept in memory of their long friendship that had ended thus, their fighting in opposing armies.

Survival Against All Odds

Not even a military genius like Frederick could hold off the armies of the three greatest states in Europe. Russians came in from the east, Austrians from the south, and the French from the east. They overran East Prussia and Westphalia, and much of Brandenburg, eating all the grain stored by the peasants; they stole the draft animals, cattle, sheep, pigs and chickens. And the few men capable of military service that Frederick had missed were dragooned into their forces.

Starvation was averted only thanks to swamp-clearing programs Frederick had begun in 1747, right after the last peace treaty, creating large swaths of new farmland and planting them with potatoes. This crop was well suited to Brandenburg's sandy soil, and it was more difficult for occupying forces to harvest.

Frederick even lost Berlin temporarily, but he survived. *Durchhalten!*

(Persevere!) he cried, and his people responded. It had formerly been said that Prussia was an army with a country. Now the army and the people became one.

The Death of Elizabeth

Frederick received a Christmas present in early 1762 – the news required weeks to reach him – the long-anticipated passing of the Russian empress. She was succeeded by her idiotic nephew Peter III (1738–62), who was such an admirer of the Prussian king that he immediately pulled out of the war; he also hoped to obtain Frederick's help in conquering his father's hereditary duchy of Holstein, though why did needed such a small, distant land was clear to nobody. Frederick was thus saved from destruction – a miraculous event that Peter's wife, Sophia of Zerbst, better known as Catherine the Great, would never have allowed to happen. It did not take long for courtiers and officers to recognise that Peter was totally incompetent (as well as impotent and several other disadvantages to being a tsar with a future); they supported Catherine's *coup d'état* in June 1762.*

Catherine, realising how tenuous her hold on the Russian empire was, carefully avoided renewing the conflict with Frederick II – he was too dangerous a foe, and, should he inflict further defeats on the Russian army, she would be held accountable. Catherine was already too German for many nobles and churchmen, and it took time for her remarkable efforts at proving her loyalty and piety to be believed. This was especially difficult because she was simultaneously attempting to bring French culture and philosophy into Russia. While this was at least not German, it was certainly western, and hence suspicious.

Catherine, having grown up in Germany, understood the changes that Frederick and other Enlightenment rulers had made in their lands and in their armies; she would copy them – in her own fashion, one generally compatible with the wishes of her subjects. She made Russia a world power.

Peace

With Russia out of the war, Austria was soon forced to quit. France held out somewhat longer, despairing at reverses in both the New World and

---

* The coup was managed by Catherline's current lover, a liaison which had not bothered Peter, who had more interest in toy soldiers than sex. Peter was later murdered in prison, a crime that Catherine allowed to pass unpunished, and he was not even honourably buried until 1796, when his presumed son, Paul, carried that out to spite his late mother's memory.

India. Spain entered the conflict late, hoping to acquire Gibraltar, only to suffer defeat everywhere. Spain, as a British historian commented in 1741, was a sieve that could never be filled; the silver from the Americas flowed quickly out, but not before creating an inflation that made Spanish goods uncompetitive; its expensive bureaucracy stifled enterprise.

From this time on Prussia would be the dominant state in the Holy Roman Empire. Though the rivalry with Austria lasted well into the next century, there was little doubt that German patriots looked to Berlin rather than to Vienna for national salvation. Viennese might refer to Berlin as a '*Räubernest*' (den of thieves) for generations, but there was no question but that Austria was on a downhill course that became ever steeper.

Britain emerged from the conflict with the greatest colonial empire of all time. It also came out with an enormous debt, part of it due to the subsidies given to Frederick the Great. The efforts to pay off this debt without taxing the English nobility or reducing the pensions of army and naval personnel led directly to the American Revolution.

The French were left with an even greater debt, one that poor, befuddled Louis XVI made worse by going to war in 1779 on behalf of the Americans. This conflict, which had no point except to harm the British, left his state so bankrupt that he had to call the long-neglected Estates General into session. He then mismanaged the situation so badly that the French Revolution soon swept him from his throne onto the platform of the guillotine.

Aftermath

Frederick the Great shrank back from another great war. The strain of the Seven Years War – which he had not sought – was sufficient for him and for his nation for many years to come. He retired to Sanssouci, his appropriately named palace ('without cares') just outside Potsdam and enjoyed the life of an Enlightenment prince, composing and playing music, entertaining, relaxing, conversing. His repose was interrupted only in 1778–9, by the war of the Bavarian Succession, when he blocked a last effort by Maria Theresa to enlarge her possessions in Germany; it might have been a wider war if Louis XVI had not been drawn into England's contest with its American colonies; or if Frederick had possessed any interest in becoming Germany's leader himself – but he did not.

Maria Theresa went into mourning after the death of her husband in a carriage accident in 1766 while returning from the opera in Innsbruck; she was content to live her last years in semi-retirement and function as a somewhat detached enlightened monarch. In addition for doing what she could for her often unenthusiastic subjects, she hoped to modernise Austria in ways that would make it possible for her sons to take revenge

261

on Prussia. Her reward was, ultimately, the idolatry of her subjects, who came to see her as the mother of the country. That was appropriate for someone with sixteen children.

Joseph II, who succeeded his mother in 1780, paid little attention to his imperial duties. Instead, he concentrated on modernising and centralising (neither of which could be done without the other) his multi-national state. Such efforts would eventually provoke national reactions in Hungary, Italy and the Czech lands, but the few Austrians who were concerned about foreign policy worried more about what would happen if the Ottoman Empire collapsed and the vacuum was filled by Russia. But, truth be told, there were not many such people – life was good, and, when one could listen to Haydn and Mozart, drink coffee and wine, and eat well, why should one worry about politics? Vienna and Prague were not places for thinking about war.

The result was drift, and drift can be very comfortable. Who wanted more taxes, more conscription, more disruption of life? This was the age of Reason, the Enlightenment, and even those who had never heard the boom of cannons fired in anger, much less visited a field hospital, could understand that war had become unreasonable – properly trained troops would slaughter one another until it became difficult to tell the victor from the vanquished. Surely war was an artefact of the past, something that educated rulers would understand how to avoid in the future.

The Holy Roman Empire, thanks to the shift in the balance of power and Austrian disinterest, was now little more than a formal fiction. As long as there had been a national enemy – the Turk or the French – the empire had functioned more or less. Usually less. But now Prussia was seen ever more as representing Germany, with Austria being perceived as a strange mixture of nationalities that had little to do with people living along the Rhine. The princes of the empire were increasingly reluctant to contribute to the support of an imperial army that would not even march against the Turks and was now an ally of France. Nor did it contribute leadership. As Gagliardo notes, the army was now led by 'untutored and unexercised' Habsburg appointees who were 'parade-ground heroes and uniformed nonentities'.

Goethe, in *Faust, I*, has the appropriately named Frosch (Frog) ask:

Das liebe Heil'ge Röm'sche Reich,	Our dear Holy Roman Empire
Wie hält's nur noch zusammen?	What holds it together?

Voltaire was more biting, saying that it was neither Holy, nor Roman, nor an Empire. In fact, only a few decades hence Napoleon would declare it defunct, after being the centre of western European politics for 1006 years.

When the imperial armies were swept aside by the legions of the French Revolution, its soldiers became a source of mockery. When Bonaparte abolished the empire, Germans blushed, then began to search their deep souls for ways of redeeming their lost reputations. Beethoven, Schiller and Goethe were fine examples of the life of the mind and spirit, but pride was restored only by the Prussian army. At the Battle of Nations near Leipzig in 1813 Germans finally paid back their French teachers in the military arts, and Blücher's decisive contribution at Waterloo restored the Prussians' vision of themselves as the true bearers of imperial greatness. The K and K monarchy (*Kaiser und König*) was restored in Austria, but it was not the Holy Roman Empire. The motto '*Kaiser und Reich*', notes Gagliardo, was replaced by '*Deutschland über Alles*'. This was not an exchange that boded well for the future.

Henceforth, we can say, with some excusable exaggeration, the army *was* Germany. *There was no place left for traditional mercenaries.* Only for patriots.

Chapter 12

Mercenaries in Literature

This was an era filled with cultural change. Some would say cultural advances. Certainly, those of us who enjoy visits to castles, palaces, cathedrals and museums are pleased that our ancestors contributed their sweat and taxes in these useful ways as well as having their contributions go up in powder smoke and burning villages. Still, in all those places we see references to the military realities of the era – tapestries depict battles, with the commanders giving orders and, in the distance, ant-like masses obeying; portraits include men in uniform; music becomes somewhat less liturgical; a wider variety of instruments become popular (organs not lending themselves either to inspiring men on the march or being easy to move about); and in literature, there was the appearance of the first novels.

Grimmelshausen

Hans Jakob Christian von Grimmelshausen (1620–76) was fourteen years old when his native town of Gelnshausen in Hesse was destroyed by marauding troops. Orphaned, he became a mercenary soldier in various armies, ending up as a dragoon in a Bavarian regiment. His survival probably reflects his commanders' good judgment in taking him out of the ranks to do clerical work. Discharged at the end of the conflict in 1648, he married and began a career in the bureaucracies of various lords. Along the way he began the book that made him famous, *Der Abendteuerliche Simplicissimus*, alternatively known as *Simplicius Simplicissimus*.

The story begins with the young hero's town being sacked by soldiers, the boy escaping into the woods with his bagpipe. Henceforth, in his naïve simplicity, he drifts from one adventure into another, hardly knowing that they are adventures.

Among the dialogues is one between a nobleman and an old sergeant as to why only noblemen were considered suitable for promotion. The nobleman took umbrage to the accusation of class discrimination, pointing to individuals who have risen from the ranks; the sergeant, while acknowledging that it is hope of advancement which makes a common soldier do his best, said that in practice the nobles keep the door to high command firmly locked.

At one point Simplicius was captured by Croats, who had great fun with him, though their principal occupation was ransoming kidnapped children to their parents, selling stolen horses back to their owners, robbing, raping and occasionally (but only occasionally) looking for lice. Eventually, he escaped into the woods.

Tiring of his role as lute-player and beating bag, he changed into women's clothing, only to discover how difficult it was to defend his virginity (he was, after all, still a boy). His problem was not merely with the captain of his new company, or even just with the captain's desperately enamoured servant, but with the captain's wife! The wife, determined to have the pretty girl to herself, not sharing with her husband, often put her to work looking for fleas in the most delicate parts of her body. As the army broke camp, ready to fight the Swedes, he (she) was pursued into the woods by the stable boys, some intent on pleasure, others on watching, only to draw a large crowd that discovered, when he (she) was stripped, that she was no girl. This apparent effort at evading military service, or being a spy, landed him in jail.

On one occasion, while lying in wait to ambush a convoy, our hero saw a solitary man coming along, muttering to himself. Thinking that it might be a prince, out to view his subjects' lives incognito, he sprang out, pistol in hand, intending to rob him. To his surprise, the fool claimed to be Jupiter, trying to determine how to punish the evil men in the world and protect the good.

Our hero, more knowledgeable in the ways of the world by now, suggested that evil would triumph no matter what. Only the total annihilation of humankind would eliminate evil.

Jupiter antwortete: 'Du redest von der Sache wie ein natürlicher Mensch, als ob du nicht wüßtest, daß uns Göttern müglich sei, etwas anzustellen, daß nur die Bösen gestraft und die Guten erhalten werden. Ich will einen teutschen Held erwecken, der soll alles mit der Schärfe des Schwerts vollenden; er wird alle verruchte Menschen umbringen und die fromme erhalten und erhöhen.'

Jupiter responded: 'You speak of the matter like an ordinary person, as though you don't understand that we gods can arrange it for only evil men to be punished and for good men to be preserved. I will awaken a German hero, who will end it all with the edge of a sword; he will annihilate all crazed men and preserve and exalt the pious.'

The fool went on to describe how he would unify Germany, defeat the foreigners, occupy Constantinople and convert the Muslims, establish concord among the theologians, eliminate serfdom, tariffs and special taxes, and bring peace and prosperity everywhere. (One can see where this program would lead in the twentieth century.) The dialogue was interrupted by an attack of fleas – the tiny insects having complained that women were smashing them between their fingers rather than allowing them to die a more heroic death. Jupiter allowed them to live on him to see whether it was a bearable torment or not, then decided to send them back to women.

Tragedy and farce elbow one another in efforts to dominate the narrative. Our hero marries twice, learns that he is a nobleman by birth (a Scot, no less!), sees that the child of the serving woman looks like him and the child of his wife looks like the hired man, and a baby is left on his doorstep, with a note saying that it is his. He thus had to pay for three baptisms and a fine for adultery, a fine which was doubled because the Swedes ruled in the neighbourhood and he had served in the imperial army at Nördlingen.

A dignified escape came after his wife drank herself to death, their (her) son dying, too, and he made his way into the world of the water sprites, thence on tour of real and imagined places until he found himself back in his forest, where French, Swedish and Hessian armies were preparing to spend the winter.

A Swedish officer offered him command of a regiment – Scots being common in the Swedish army – and soon our hero found himself in Livonia, where he discovered that nothing was as promised; in fact, the regiment did not exist and everything his employer owned was actually the property of his wife. Going into Russia, he found that the war there had been concluded and soldiers were being dismissed; worse, refusing to embrace the Orthodox Church, he found himself trapped in Moscow, penniless, hungry and his every move followed by spies – moreover, he discovered that it was illegal to be an idler, with Siberia the fate awaiting the unemployed. Luckily, the tsar, learning of his military skills, hired him to make gunpowder. Distinguishing himself in battle against the Tatars, his blood-splattered clothes were taken away and replaced by new finery from the tsar's own wardrobe. Thus he learned that everything, everything, in Russia was owned by the tsar. Everything included the mercenaries who fought for him.

Happily, Simplicius was kidnapped by Tatars, sent to Korea as a present, passed on to the Japanese, then Portuguese merchants; in Egypt he learned to row under Turkish instruction until Venetians captured his warship. At length he was back in the Black Forest. In his absence of three years and three months peace had come to Germany.

He now reflected on life, and the advice of the Delphic Oracle, 'Know

266

thyself'. There was no joy without sadness, no peace without war, no good without evil. The world will lead us into evil lives, wear us down and destroy us. We have wants we cannot satisfy, pleasures that offer no relief, and successes which are but momentary. All that is good is a blessed END.

But there was a postscript, informing us that life as a hermit was unsatisfying, causing Simplicius to set out on an entirely new adventure! He was already aged, he says – over forty! – but nevertheless has many years ahead of him. Ironically, he spent most of these years on a desert island as a hermit. Peace had come to Germany, he learned, removing war, arson, murder, rape and plunder, but replacing them with new set of vices hardly less attractive. Asked by a Dutch sea captain if he was not afraid to die alone, Simplicius answered that he was not bothered by the absence of men, so long as God was with him.

The problem of how to be a Christian in an unchristian world is not resolved, but Grimmelshausen posed eloquently the dilemma of the average man, and he did it with humour, understanding and wit.

Tom Jones

Henry Fielding wrote *Tom Jones* in 1749. It became instantly popular for its impudent, even sarcastic portrayal of all classes of English life. In one chapter the hero almost found himself in the army that was marching against Bonnie Prince Charlie.

> The serjeant had informed Mr. Jones that they were marching against the rebels, and expected to be commanded by the glorious Duke of Cumberland. By which the reader may perceive (a circumstance which we have not thought necessary to communicate before) that this was the very time when the late rebellion was at the highest; and indeed the banditti were now marched into England, intending, as it was thought, to fight the king's forces, and to attempt pushing forward to the metropolis.
>
> Jones had some heroic ingredients in his composition, and was a hearty well-wisher to the glorious cause of liberty, and of the Protestant religion. It is no wonder, therefore, that in circumstances which would have warranted a much more romantic and wild undertaking, it should occur to him to serve as a volunteer in this expedition.
>
> Our commanding officer had said all in his power to encourage and promote this good disposition, from the first moment he had been acquainted with it. He now proclaimed the noble resolution aloud, which was received with great pleasure by the whole company, who all cried out, 'God bless King George and your honour'; and then added, with many oaths, 'We will stand by you both to the last drops of our blood.'

The gentleman who had been all night tippling at the ale-house, was prevailed on by some arguments which a corporal had put into his hands, to undertake the same expedition. And now the portmanteau belonging to Mr. Jones being put up in the baggage-cart, the forces were about to move forwards; when the guide, stepping up to Jones, said, 'Sir, I hope you will consider that the horses have been kept out all night, and we have travelled a great ways out of our way.'

Jones was surprised at the impudence of this demand, and acquainted the soldiers with the merits of his cause, who were all unanimous in condemning the guide for his endeavours to put upon a gentleman. Some said, he ought to be tied neck and heels; others that he deserved to run the gantlope; and the serjeant shook his cane at him, and wished he had him under his command, swearing heartily he would make an example of him.

Jones contented himself however with a negative punishment, and walked off with his new comrades, leaving the guide to the poor revenge of cursing and reviling him; in which latter the landlord joined, saying, 'Ay, ay, he is a pure one, I warrant you. A pretty gentleman, indeed, to go for a soldier! He shall wear a laced waistcoat truly. It is an old proverb and a true one, all is not gold that glisters. I am glad my house is well rid of him.'

All that day the serjeant and the young soldier marched together; and the former, who was an arch fellow, told the latter many entertaining stories of his campaigns, though in reality he had never made any; for he was but lately come into the service, and had, by his own dexterity, so well ingratiated himself with his officers, that he had promoted himself to a halberd; chiefly indeed by his merit in recruiting, in which he was most excellently well skilled.

Much mirth and festivity passed among the soldiers during their march. In which the many occurrences that had passed at their last quarters were remembered, and every one, with great freedom, made what jokes he pleased on his officers, some of which were of the coarser kind, and very near bordering on scandal. This brought to our heroe's mind the custom which he had read of among the Greeks and Romans, of indulging, on certain festivals and solemn occasions, the liberty to slaves, of using an uncontrouled freedom of speech towards their masters.

Our little army, which consisted of two companies of foot, were now arrived at the place where they were to halt that evening. The serjeant then acquainted his lieutenant, who was the commanding officer, that they had picked up two fellows in that day's march, one of which, he said, was as fine a man as ever he saw (meaning the tippler), for that he was near six feet, well proportioned, and strongly limbed; and the other (meaning Jones) would do well enough for the rear rank.

The new soldiers were now produced before the officer, who having examined the six-feet man, he being first produced, came next to survey Jones: at the first sight of whom, the lieutenant could not help showing some surprise; for besides that he was very well dressed, and was naturally genteel, he had a remarkable air of dignity in his look, which is rarely seen among the vulgar, and is indeed not inseparably annexed to the features of their superiors. 'Sir,' said the lieutenant, 'my serjeant informed me that you are desirous of enlisting in the company I have at present under my command; if so, sir, we shall very gladly receive a gentleman who promises to do much honour to the company by bearing arms in it.'

Jones answered: 'That he had not mentioned anything of enlisting himself; that he was most zealously attached to the glorious cause for which they were going to fight, and was very desirous of serving as a volunteer;' concluding with some compliments to the lieutenant, and expressing the great satisfaction he should have in being under his command. The lieutenant returned his civility, commended his resolution, shook him by the hand, and invited him to dine with himself and the rest of the officers.

At the meal Jones met a variety of officers. First a man who had received a battlefield promotion to lieutenant from Marlborough himself, but now, forty years later, was obliged to defer to inexperienced boys who owed their authority to family influence. He could have risen higher in rank had his beautiful wife made herself more approachable by the colonel, but he was not even aware of the reasons for his commander's refusal to favour him.

Then there was 'a French lieutenant, who had been long enough out of France to forget his own language, but not long enough in England to learn ours, so that he really spoke no language at all'. Lastly, there were the low-born sub-officers, who seemed equally devoid of learning, talent, taste and physical presence.

The meal deteriorated into a demonstration of ignorance, quarrel-someness and overly zealous drinking. Eventually, blood was spilled – that of our hero! This would ultimately spare him the need to accompany the army to Culloden. The duke of Cumberland's victory was as fresh in the minds of Fielding's readers as it is absent from today's, but both audiences have been able to relish Fielding's deadly comments about the military of his day.

Candide

François-Marie Arouet de Voltaire (1694–1778) was the most widely read of all the French *philosophes*. As a writer, no one could surpass either the novelty of his ideas, his compelling logic, or his wit. Though educated by Jesuits, he fell into the newly fashionable scepticism and freethinking to become a scourge to religious conformity, the pretensions of the aristocracy and the irrelevancies of university studies. In 1716 he was exiled from Paris for impertinence, then slammed in the Bastille for two years, without having learned anything beyond how to sharpen his tongue and to stay away from royal censors. He began to write history, a safer subject than satire, and in 1731 published his *Histoire De Charles XII*. Although the air in Paris became freer – Enlightenment thought was prevailing everywhere, even making inroads at the court – Voltaire went to Potsdam in 1750, left in 1753, then later settled in Switzerland. There it was safe for him to publish *Candide, ou l'Optimisme*, in 1759.

Candide was born in Westphalia, a simple young man of extraordinary naiveté (echoing, no doubt *Simplicissimus*), who was the servant of Baron Thunder-ten-tronckh. The servants suspected that he was the son of the baron's sister (perhaps inspired by *Tom Jones*) by a gentleman of the neighbourhood who could put on his coat-of-arms only seventy-one quarterings – insufficient for a proposal of marriage.

He was expelled from his lord's best-of-all-possible-castles (a joke on the currently popular theory by Leibnitz that God, being good, had made for humans the best of all possible worlds; hence the subtitle, 'or optimism') for conducting an experiment on cause and effect on the baron's daughter: if he touched her there, then what was the effect? Etc. Eh?

He encountered two soldiers, who, ascertaining that he was at least five foot five, recruited him into the Bulgarian army. However, tiring of the harsh treatment, Candide tried to take a walk, a swift walk away, only to be caught by four giants and placed before a court-martial. Given the choice of running the gauntlet thirty-six times or being shot, Candide demonstrated the superiority of man's reasoning ability by choosing to live, even at the cost of such a torture

In the slaughter of battle 6,000 men on each side were laid flat, after which each commander had a *Te Deum* sung, and Candide, who had hidden during the fighting, trembling like a philosopher, made his escape through a countryside filled with burning houses, corpses, ravaged maidens and orphans. Reaching a Bulgarian village, he discovered that the opposing army had done the same there. Soon he was in safety, in Holland, the most tolerant of all European countries, pleading for help, but a minister's wife, hearing from the second story that he did not agree that the pope was the Anti-Christ, dumped a bed-pan of liquid on his head: '*lui rèpandit sur le chef un plein … O ciel! à quel excès se porte le zèle de la religion dans les dames!*' 'she poured over his head a full pot . . . Heavens! To what excess does religious fervour carry women!'

The story continued, until by the final chapter Candide, the baron's now-ugly daughter, and various other characters settled down in the Turkish capital, where they could live out their days working and enjoying one another's company. When one of Candide's friends began listing the disasters that can befall the mighty:

'Les grandeurs,' dit Pangloss, 'sont fort dangereuses, selon le rapport de tous les philosophes: car enfin Églon, roi des Moabites, fut assassiné par Aod; Absalon fut pendu par les cheveux et percé de trois dards . . . Henri VI, Richard III, Marie Stuart, Charles I er, les trois Henri de France, l'empereur Henri IV? Vous savez . . .' 'Je sais aussi,' dit Candide, 'qu'il faut cultiver notre jardin.'

'The great', said Pangloss, 'are extremely dangerous, according to the report of all the wise men: for in the end Eglon, king of the Moabites, was murdered by Aod; Absalom was hung by his hair and pierced with three spears . . . Henry VI, Richard III, Mary Stuart, Charles I, the three Henris of France, the emperor Henry IV? You know . . .' 'I know as well,' said Candide, 'that we should look after our garden.'

This is the moral Voltaire recommends – that people 'tend their garden', leaving power-hungry and foolish lords fight over the inconsequential spoils of politics, intrigue and war.

No wonder Voltaire often quarrelled with Frederick the Great. No wonder he left the comforts of Potsdam after only three years in residence.

Bonneval

Voltaire may have been inspired partly by the legendary tales surrounding a French nobleman who had served in the War of the Spanish Succession, then in Turkey, and who was also a close friend of Rousseau and other Enlightenment figures.

In fact, Claud Alexander de Bonneval (1675–1747) lived a life that could hardly have been made more exotic by fictional exaggeration. He had served under Vendôme in Italy, then in the Low Countries, always with distinction, but his insolence toward the minister of war led to a court-martial in 1704; he fled the country to escape a death sentence. Prince Eugene employed him immediately, benefiting from his services at Malplaquet, then in the Balkans, where he was severely wounded. The political situation in Paris having changed, the charges against Bonneval were dropped; this allowed him to return home, where he married a daughter of Marshal de Biron. He then returned to Prince Eugene's service and was present at the capture of Belgrade in 1718; however, after being transferred to the Low Countries, he became a supporter of the constitutional rights of the citizens there (thus making himself unpopular with the Prince Eugene's governor). A court-martial sentenced him to death, but the emperor commuted it to one year's imprisonment, followed by banishment to Venice. He then went to Turkey, converted to Islam, and served in the wars against Russia. He is often credited with having contributed significantly to the Ottoman victory in the 1737–39 war against Austria.

His most important reform in the Ottoman army was to improve the units of grenadiers (*humbarajis*), whose duty was to hurl grenades into besieged forts and to service mortars. He also instructed in mathematics, which was a necessary skill for ranging mortars and artillery. Although the reforming grand vizier was removed by a Janissary revolt, Bonneval survived to open a military engineering school in 1733.

He was briefly governor of Chios, but, unable to avoid trouble, he was banished to an isolated post on the Black Sea. He was thinking of returning to France when he died.

A book with no basis in fact was printed in London in 1737: *Mémoires du comte de Bonneval, cidevant général au service de Sa Majesté Impériale et Catholique*. It was much in the tradition of Baron von Münchhausen.

Schiller

Johann Christoph Friedrich von Schiller (1759–1805) was born in Württemberg; his father being a ducal official. He enrolled in the military academy, after which he studied law and medicine, but his real love was the theatre, and his real talent writing. He became the principal figure of early Romanticism in Germany, the school of *Sturm und Drang* (Storm and Stress) which emphasised strong emotions and violent actions. His Wallenstein cycle, 1798–9, was instantly successful, reflecting as it did the tumultuous and conflicting politics of the French Revolution, and the potential for liberty and freedom. He later moved to Weimar to be near Goethe, only to die there prematurely.

In the prologue to *Wallensteins Lager* (*Wallenstein's Camp*) Schiller describes the great general's camp in 1634, half way through the Thirty Years War.

In jenes Krieges Mitte stellt euch jetzt	Imagine yourself a poet in the
Der Dichter. Sechszehn Jahre der Verwüstung,	middle of the war. Sixteen years of destruction,
Des Raubs, des Elends sind dahingeflohn,	robbery, misery have passed.
In trüben Massen gäret noch die Welt,	The world ferments beyond measure,
Und keine Friedenshoffnung straht von fern.	and no hope of peace is seen from afar.
Ein Tummelplatz von Waffen ist das Reich.	The Empire is a battleground.
Verödet sind die Städte, Magdeburg Ist Schutt, Gewerb und Kunstfleiß liegen nieder,	Cities are abandoned, Magdeburg Is ashes. Commerce and Arts are prostrate.

Der Bürger gilt nichts mehr, der Krieger alles,	The citizen is worth nothing, the warrior everything.
Straflose Frechheit spricht den Sitten Hohn,	Unpunished insults mock traditional customs
Und rohe Horden lagern sich, verwildert	And the raw hordes camp, wild,
Im langen Krieg, auf dem verheerten Boden.	Thorough the long war, on devastated ground.

By the second play, *Die Piccolomini (The Piccolomini)*, Wallenstein is discussing his fate with his chief lieutenant, Octavio Piccolomini. The time for choice has come, duty contesting with duty, self-preservation with obedience, friendship with oaths of loyalty. It is comforting to have no choice, no responsibility, he says, but eventually one must decide, and act. Wallenstein, now on a collision course with the emperor, believes that he can rely on his army – the soldiers' loyalty is to him. The retort is that such loyalty is only temporary.

In the third play, *Wallensteins Tod (The Death of Wallenstein)* the great general meets secretly with a Swedish emissary to seek an end to the war, telling him 'Austrians have a fatherland, which they love, with good reason. But this army which calls itself imperial, which is camped in Bohemia, has none. It is the garbage of foreign lands, possessing nothing but the sunshine that belongs to everyone.' And the nobles and officers, he is asked – this is a cursed crime without equal in world history, can they be relied upon? Those, Wallenstein responds, are mine unconditionally.

Wallenstein was, of course, mistaken. He had the spirit and belief in his own fortune to risk everything in a rebellion that would overturn the established order of politics and society, but neither his officers nor his men did. Wallenstein's genius could raise armies, train them, feed them and lead them to victory; but it could not persuade a mercenary army and mercenary generals to see the glorious future that awaited them if only they had the courage to act. Awakening that imagination was Schiller's goal – to make his generation understand the need to change their world forever. It was, after all, the era of the French Revolution. Why not sweeping changes in Germany, too?

The Three Musketeers

The equally unruly quality of the forces in France were caught vividly by Alexandre Dumas's *The Three Musketeers (Les Trois Mousquetaires)* and *The Count of Monte Cristo (Le Comte de Monte-Cristo)*. Dumas (1802–70) was one of France's most popular authors, mostly because of these two books that he wrote in 1844 and 1845, not for the other 250 he wrote using a stable of more than seventy assistants. His adventurous life included participation in revolutions, wars, intrigues, scholarship, being a patron of the arts, the lover of many women, and constant alternation between great wealth and poverty.

The Three Musketeers began in 1625, a year of crisis – nobles made war on each other; the king fought with Cardinal Richelieu; Spain fought the king; there were robbers, beggars, wolves, scoundrels. Ordinary Frenchmen fought the thieves, occasionally also the nobles and the Protestants, and sometimes even the king. The only person the citizenry did not fight was the king. Ah, such patriotism.

As the novel opened, young D'Artagnan, eighteen years of age, was taking leave of his father, who could give him little beyond advice to be courageous, to fear nobody except the cardinal and the king, and to behave like a noble. He was a Gascon, he was told, and a son of an honourable father, and, therefore, he should fight duels – with his sword – on any provocation.

D'Artagnan, our Don Quixote, followed that advice, taking smiles for provocations and frowns for insults. In the course of time he found himself in the king's musketeers, a hard-drinking, rowdy crew that missed no opportunity to cross swords with the cardinal's guard. There he met the jolly Porthos, the restrained Aramis, and the noble Athos.

Eventually this led to the famous oath, 'One for all, and all for one' (*un pour tous, tous pour un*). It is a marvellous summary of the mercenary spirit – everything for one's friends, no mention of the king or the state. Of course, our four friends are thoroughly loyal and completely patriotic – in strong contrast to their enemies.

The story becomes complicated, as is proper for a tale of adventure and romance, but ends with d'Artagnan discovering that Richelieu was not the enemy of the state that he had once believed. The English – the national enemy – were defeated, the Protestants beaten, and d'Artagnan, as an officer of the royal musketeers, could see that France and the crown were protected from all harm.

In the end, his best friend consoled him, '*Vous êtes jeune, vous, répondit Athos, et vos souvenirs amers ont le temps de se changer en doux souvenirs!*' (You are young, you are, replied Athos, and your bitter memories need time to change into sweet ones).

His three friends retired to private life, leaving d'Artagnan alone to pursue a military career. However, in *Twenty Years Later* (*Vingt ans après*, 1845) Dumas brings the four men together once more to save the king, and France!

For our purposes, we see in this novel an imagined regiment of the Thirty Years War – proud, semi-disciplined, quarrelsome, often inebriated and almost always politically naïve. Our heroes are loyal to one another, protective of the person and honour of their commander and king, and –

most important for us – individuals who stand out from the mass of faceless cut-throats and brigands that populate the Annals and Histories of the era.

Münchhausen

Baron Munchhausen's Narrative of His Marvellous Travels and Campaigns in Russia include stories that had been accumulating for a very long time. Real-life Münchhausens had been associated with sixteenth-century Livonia, but they had nothing to do with these stories of a fictional German mercenary; instead, the stories reflected travellers and adventurers' fascination with the exotic landscape of Eastern Europe. In the twenty-first century one is not supposed to remark that any oriental or semi-oriental nation was exotic, but it was nevertheless true.*

The author, Karl Friedrich Hieronymus Freiherr von Münchhausen (1720–97), served the tsar in two Turkish wars, then retired to Hanover, where he told wildly embellished tales which were written out by a family friend, Rudolf Erich Raspe (1737–94), and published anonymously in London in 1785 in English. It was such a sensation that it was translated into German the following year by Gottfried August Bürger (1747–94). Later, a further eight stories were added, but the authorship is not clear.

The most famous fictional exploits had the baron riding on a flying cannon ball. Another when the baron hurriedly sought shelter from a frightening winter blast, he hurriedly tied his horse to a post; when he came out in the morning, the weather had made a swift change to extraordinarily hot, melting the snow and leaving his beast dangling from the church steeple. The book quickly joined Swift's *Gulliver's Travels* and Voltaire's *Candide* as a popular imaginative masterpiece.

Cyrano de Bergerac

This popular play by Rostand was written in 1897, based on the works of a real playwright, Savinien Cyrano de Bergerac (1619–55), whose death by murder earned him a fame his works could not. Edmond Eugène Alexis Rostand (1868–1918) was a neo-Romantic whose work translated well and became best-known outside France for the 1950 movie starring José Ferrer that earned the actor an Academy Award and its less inspiring 1990 French version starring Gérard Depardieu, and *Roxanne*, a 1987

---

* The twenty-first-century reader is empowered to derive whatever message he or she gets from a text, no matter what the author intended. A reader is even permitted, under exceptional circumstances, to accept what the author did intend to say – in this case, that Russia was an interesting and exotic land.

adaptation by Steve Martin.

The play is set in 1640, a pivotal year in the history of France – the death of Louis XIII making his young son king. France is surrounded by enemies and wracked by internal dissension, the Spanish are pressing the siege of Arras, the key to Flanders. Only a few elite units are reliable, among those the musketeers of the Armagnac, who are, of course, most famous for their swordsmanship. The most prominent of their warriors is the long-nosed Cyrano, who can fight a duel and compose poetry at the same time. Cyrano, in the course of forcing a bad actor to abandon the stage for a month, quarrels with aristocrats who are hostile to royal authority. Thus the personal mixes with the political.

Cyrano is also deeply in love with his beautiful but insipid cousin, Roxanne, but he knows that his feelings can never be reciprocated – his face is too ugly, and she only admires beauty. Thus, while Cyrano cannot see past his nose, she cannot see past the flesh into the soul – until the last moments of the play, by which time it is too late for anything but tears. Whatever tears Roxanne fails to drop, the audience will supply – this play is for romantics who don't mind tension-breaking laughs.

Roxanne tells Cyrano that she has fallen in love with the most marvellous man in the world, building up his hopes until she remarks how beautiful her lover is. Cyrano, though crushed, permits her to continue, then even consents to her request that her lover, Christian – who has not even spoken to her yet! – be admitted into his regiment!

This is an extraordinary request, since the young man is a Norman, and all the men in the regiment were Gascons, fiery warriors from the south. Cyrano's reluctant promise to protect her love provides a following scene very useful for visualising a tavern full of soldiers, full of themselves, tankards flowing with ale, and Christian as sufficient in courage as he was deficient in brains. Christian, indeed, is brave on the battlefield, though too bashful to make an opening sally in the battle of the sexes.

The climatic scene, at the siege of Arras, provides sufficient cannon fire and swordplay for almost any stage. Also, more than enough bravado and boasting.

When the commander – the cardinal's nephew, and therefore not trusted by the Gascons whose numbers have been much reduced by a surfeit of combat and a paucity of food – visits the Gascon camp, he is met with hostile and insolent looks. Offended, he says:

De Guiche: *Vous ferai-je punir par votre capitaine?*
Carbon (the captain): *D'ailleurs, je suis libre et n'inflige de peine.*

De Guiche: Shall I have your captain punish you?
Carbon: It doesn't matter; I'm a free man and never inflict punishment.

De Guiche's revenge is to signal a spy that their position is the weakest in the defences, and thus the place for the Spanish attack. De Guiche's rehabilitation is that he takes his place among the ranks of those whose sacrifice will contribute to victory elsewhere on the battlefield. The fighting is desperate, Christian falls, the Gascons are shot to pieces, but there is no retreat, no yielding:

> Un Officier Espanol (se découvrant): *Quels sont ces gens qui se font tous tuer!*
> Cyrano (récitant, debout au milieu des balles): '*Ce sont les cadets de Gascogne,*
> *De Carbon de Castel-Jaloux;*
> *Bretteurs, et menteurs sans vergogne.*

> Spanish officer (taking off his hat in tribute): 'Who are these men who so love death?
> Cyrano (reciting, upright amid the gunfire): They are soldiers of Gascony,
> The company of Carbon,
> Fighters and liars without shame.

The fifth act, many years later, brings the play back to its beginning, and to the original Cyrano, who (as everyone should know) was murdered. A fatally wounded Cyrano visits Roxanne in her convent. No more need be said, but it is a guaranteed tear-jerker.

Modern Assessments

The public's long love affair with the concept of monarchy came slowly to an end in the twentieth century. Yes, kings survive today, sometimes as tourist attractions, sometimes to relieve prime ministers of troubling public appearances, sometimes to award Nobel Prizes. Crowns have even been restored, usually to assure the survival of democracy when threatened by ancient party rancour.

But the affection for royal families is dimming under the brilliant light of publicity. Most often this was the result of sensationalist newspaper stories – *paparazzi* are partly to blame, though tabloid sales demonstrate that the royals still have a deep hold on the public imagination. Sometimes, it was boredom, as in America, where the visit of the British royal family stirs neither interest nor anger. Today's Chicago mayor would not threaten to punch the Prince of Wales in the snout if he dared show it in the Windy City – the Irish have long since ceased to be a major voting bloc – and many Americans know nothing about his boys but everything about their most recent girlfriends.

Also to blame were gifted biographers like Nancy Mitford, whose brilliantly written tattle-tale best-seller *The Sun King* (1966) left Louis XIV and his family few shreds of honour, good taste or noble ideas to hide behind. Where Voltaire had emphasised Louis's encouragement of the arts, his defence of national unity and his promotion of national interests, Mitford gave us a series of mini-portraits. The Dauphine, for instance, shy beyond measure, preferred fat ugly women who bossed him around; and he did nothing to make anyone believe that he would be a good monarch. His only skill seemed to be hunting. What, we must ask, had Louis XIV done to create such a monster?* The answer: he had turned his education over to sadists who had beaten the last spark of independence and originality out of him. That, however, was not unusual for the era.

English boarding schools were hardly better. Wellington may have said, 'Waterloo was won on the playing fields of Eton', but surely few of the redcoats ever attended a public school (i.e., an elite private boarding school). The average soldier was lucky to be able to read.

There was never a love affair with mercenaries. But without them the literature of the era would have been poorer. We study our history, but we love our literature. And it is literature that forms the popular understanding of the past.

---

* Simon Schama has shown us that Frenchmen in the late eighteenth century saw their monarchs with little reverence – they mocked Louis XVI's Austrian wife, Marie Antoinette, with pictures showing her in pornographic poses.

Chapter 13

Summary

The Definition of a Mercenary

A mercenary of 1550 performed military service for pay; he usually supplied his own weapons and enlisted in a unit raised by a local entrepreneur – usually noble, but often not much different from a privateer. By 1650 a typical mercenary might be as interested in adventure as money, and princes were limiting their subjects' employment options. By 1700 most mercenaries served in regular army units, but the more important mercenaries were officers, often serving far from their homeland, often changing employers several times. By the French Revolution, national feelings were becoming more significant.*

We should think of some territorial rulers as mercenaries, too. After all, they did rent out their armies for wars in which they had only an indirect interest. The prince of Hesse most famously rented his army out to Great Britain for service during the American War for Independence. Certainly, we cannot talk sensibly about mercenaries without keeping their employers in mind.*

These generalisations are, of course, not true all the time or in all places. Generalisations are not intended to be more than efforts to make sense of otherwise bewildering masses of individual facts. But contemporaries were aware of the aforementioned changes and of the need to

---

* Geoffrey Parker, in *The Thirty Years War*, suggests that a decisive factor seems to have been the rulers' abilities (or inabilities) to raise money; without money, armies fended for themselves. Yet, the individual personalities of the rulers cannot be discounted. It is between these poles of determinism and free will that we have to explain the choices that people made and the ways that events played themselves out.

† Black, *European Warfare, 1660–1815*, considers the armies and taxation systems to be essentially private – individual entrepreneurs managed both systems, and private individuals, not the state, provided supplies and ammunition. The opportunities that war opened for advancement were largely limited to nobles.

avoid repeating the mistakes of the past. Most significant of those mistakes was allowing the armies of the Thirty Years War to get out of hand. In the next century rulers sought to maintain strict discipline and took great care to provide adequate supplies, so that soldiers did not have to forage – when soldiers were unsupervised, they were liable to commit crimes or even desert. Fortresses were more than strong points – they contained everything necessary for campaigns, including barracks, so commanders preferred to operate in their neighbourhood. Officers were expected to keep their troops in line, and to make them fight. When the French Revolution began in 1789, many of the royalist officers fled abroad. The initial poor performance of the French Republic's army against the invading Prussians and Austrians, even against units from Brunswick, Hesse and some organised by French exiles, seemed to confirm the widespread opinion that common soldiers could not fight without professional direction. Only in 1792, after the skirmish at Valmy, did it become clear that lower-ranking officers could be promoted safely, and later that this new class, once allowed to demonstrate its talents, would lead inspired troops in sweeping the old professional armies from the fields of battle.*

After the French Revolution, soldiers fought more for their nation than for money. But this great generalisation runs counter to many examples in this book, because some, perhaps many men, were already fighting for reasons other than money.

The best illustration that mercenaries preferred employers with whom they had much in common, or who could advance the interests of their religion and nation, were the 'Wild Geese', those Celts who lusted after opportunities to shoot or stab Englishmen. But their enemies were now British rather than purely English, with entire units of foreign soldiers fighting alongside the redcoats.

The Love of Travel

The Age of Exploration evolved into an Age of Travel. The motivations differed, the former hoping to increase the power and prestige of the monarchs, to bring the Church to the unsaved, and to enrich the discoverer. The traveller wanted only to go among strangers, to see places

---

* Britain is often presented as the exception to this generalisation. Black, *European Warfare, 1660–1815*, notes that the fortunes of professional armies varied greatly, first prevailing, then failing, when faced by popular armies. He attributes the success of the Revolutionary French armies to better logistics and greater numbers; the American Revolution had demonstrated that armies could overthrow the existing social and political systems, not merely strengthen them. The emphasis on expertise gave every advantage to men with an education, whether this was achieved at the new military academies or self-taught.

that were either famous or exotic, and to return home with stories and an increased knowledge of men and cultures.

Our instinct is to think of the upper-class leaders or the upwardly striving class of ambitious men, but for every noble on any expedition there were many more commoners. One must wonder what persuaded them to sail across vast oceans or tramp long distances. Was it only the money? Or was the some of the same motivations that inspired the pilgrim? Chaucer's pilgrims come to mind. Or Byron's *Childe Harold's Pilgrimage*.*

For those who could not afford to travel in comfort, there was always the army. Or, as in the recruiting slogan known to every American, 'Join the Navy and See the World'. In fact, the army would offer better odds for survival than a voyage around the world.

The soldier was a social outcast, anyway – except among young women excited by the uniforms and the thrill of meeting sexually aggressive and self-assured strangers. Why not escape the barracks, the increasing popular method for segregating troops from the civilian population and emphasising discipline? Why not sign on voyages of discovery? Or to serve in India and the Americas?

Political Evolution

The European world of the mercenary had changed significantly between 1550 and 1789. Whereas once it had been easy for young men of every class to choose among armies, by the eve of the French Revolution employment in foreign armies had been restricted largely to exiled nobles (who had a plausible excuse for serving a foreign master). Even then, such employment was becoming more difficult to find. Native aristocrats were monopolising the most lucrative positions of command, as Bonaparte learned when he graduated from the Royal Military Academy.

Reforms in the system came slowly. The semi-independent organisation of regiments, with officers buying positions and so forth, made more sense than relying on parliaments to authorise payments or deliver supplies promptly. Resistance to reforms was not mere obstinacy on the part of the military–feudal complex – it was based on practical experience.

Religion remained important, but it was less often used to justify political objectives; the sentiment was worn out by 1648. By 1715 the Scots were divided between Episcopalians and Presbyterians, with Catholics no longer of significance; but there was sufficient Jacobite

---

* Turberville notes that travel stories, whether real or imaginary, were highly popular, and not just among the educated classes. Parker, *The Thirty Years War*, warns against making volunteers into economic determinists. Motivations were multiple, sometimes trivial. Excitement and danger had their attractions.

sympathy for a dangerous uprising in protest of Whig domination and the Hanoverian dynasty. Sweden, described by Roberts as 'the Lutheran Spain', could do little after 1721 but look back nostalgically at its age of greatness and practise a dour pietism; later generations have largely forgotten both the glory and the suffering.

Europe had come together in fundamental ways. First, the peripheries – Ireland, Scotland, Russia, Hungary, Sweden – were now more joined to the centre;* second, the divided centre, after having run in parallel universes for a generation, became whole again; but, third, the Old Regimes – Austria, Spain and France – were giving way to the powers of the future – Britain, Prussia and Russia. France would have a spectacular resurgence under Bonaparte, then would once again lead the once great states on their way down.

The 'state' had grown more powerful, but we must be careful to remember that the statement attributed to Louis XIV – *L'État, C'est Moi* (I am the state) – though untrue had some grounding in reality.† Moreover, some of the greatest conflicts between dynasties and commercial interests still lay ahead. The national state was coming into being, with the army often leading the rest of society, but the nineteenth century fruition of that process still lay ahead. Enlightened rulers were in favour of this development for many reasons, not the least being that draftees could be paid less than mercenaries; and discipline enforced more fully.‡

Being a mercenary was less attractive now, too. Wages had declined significantly because conscripted foot soldiers were cheap, and looting was discouraged; it took relatively little skill to be a common soldier, the firearms being both simple and deadly, so that neither much training nor experience was needed to fill the ranks; and economies of scale made it both unnecessary and impossible to raise an army composed entirely of mercenaries.¶

Conscription – introduced by Sweden about 1600, Prussia in 1688, and France in 1778 – minimised the need for recruiting, while payments

---

* In Russia, for example, from the time of Peter the Great on, all members of the imperial family married Germans. One of these Germans became Catherine the Great.
† Barzun argues that if Louis ever made such a statement, he could not have meant it. No one knew better than Louis how limited his authority was. Moreover, 'Sun King' meant that he gave warmth and predictability to what had been a cold and chaotic kingdom.
‡ If an 'absolute ruler' had existed in reality, this process would have developed faster and more completely across all aspects of society, but Richard Bonney (his work covers a range of years that excludes most of Louis XIV's reign) reminds us that tradition, fear of change, dislike of foreigners and the accidents of human existence worked to impede it. Black, *European Warfare, 1660–1815*, sees developments in the state, especially in fostering education, leading to military innovation; the 'absolute' state did not yet exist, except to the extent the king could persuade the nobles and others to support him. In *European Warfare, 1494–1660*, he makes that case even more strongly. Thomson emphasises the use of law to reduce unauthorised violence.
¶ See David Latzko in a 2005 article on the web, 'The Market for Mercenaries'.

for wages, salaries, equipment and construction reduced some former military powers, such as Poland, to insignificance. States with the ability to raise taxes and borrow money rose; states without that ability sank.*

As appropriate to the age of the Enlightenment, when everything from God to science to society was subject to the scrutiny of logic, the military arts were codified and standardised. To prevent desertion and disorder, troops were kept in barracks or in camps, foraging was discouraged, and busy-work (drills, polishing buttons, more drills) kept the soldiers from thinking about mischief. This required the commanders to provide regular meals, reasonable housing, and suitable clothing. Thus, the commissary department became as prominent as the sergeants, and the tax collector ever more important. No taxes = no money = no food = no army.

Commanders were discouraged from engaging in combat. The normal attrition from disease was bad enough, without having 30 per cent or more of the men killed, wounded and captured in a few minutes of shelling by artillery, deadly exchanges of volleys and bayonet attacks. Armies were too expensive to be foolishly expended; good officers died even more predictably.

This implied that it was also foolish to release soldiers from service prematurely. Where once three years under arms was common, now it was twenty years or more. This made military service a profession not only for officers, but also for the common soldier. No wonder that so many men ran away, maimed themselves, entered the church or sailed to America.

With every small state maintaining an expensive standing army, rulers faced hard choices. How could they afford pleasure palaces – rude imitations of Versailles (and a few pretty good imitations!) – opera houses, art collections, academies of science, and attractive lady friends if they had to spend all their money on the army?

Or was it all a matter of power?† A desire to achieve a Faustian goal?

Faust

Johann Wolfgang von Goethe (1749–1832) was a philosopher, poet, scientist and government official from the Enlightenment into the

---

* Tilly sees a close correlating between warmaking and state formation, with capital providing the means for making war. Acquiring a monopoly on force meant disarming the general population. Parker, *The Military Revolution*, says that this is too simplistic, but in the broad sense still true – he suggests that instead of cause and effect, we should envision a double helix, with intertwined spirals interacting. Boot adds that no innovation confers more than a momentary advantage, but that states which fail to make the adjustments disappear, even if they were larger and wealthier.

† Roberts, in *The Swedish Imperial Experience*, noted that the 'Old School' had explained Swedish expansion as an effort to build a defensive shield around the kingdom, and that the 'New School' explained it as an effort to create a monopoly of Baltic commerce. Both failed.

Romantic era. His name is most often associated with his *Faust*, a long and difficult poem that he worked on for decades. The story is fairly simple: after selling his soul for vain knowledge, then bringing great harm to innocent people, Faust sought to make partial amends by building dikes to protect people who lived in fear of terrible storms – the model was Holland and Frederick the Great draining swamps and building canals – but his ambition could be accomplished only with the help of the devil. As Faust reached the age of 100, immensely rich and living in a fine palace, he was not fully aware that his profits from commerce were mixed with the proceeds of piracy. Moreover, he was not yet satisfied – the one criterion of his pact with the devil that kept him alive.

As he looked over his lands, he asked it if was all his. Yes, the devil responded, but Faust knew better: there was still one house belonging to an aged couple. 'Get it,' Faust ordered. And the devil did, burning it down together with the entire village and church. Murdered were Philemon and Baucis, who had befriended him when he first came to the coast; they were symbols of hospitality dating back to ancient Greece. This is how Faust rewarded generosity.

Faust was subsequently visited by four grey hags – Want, Debt, Care, and Need – and their brother Death. Care struck him sightless:

Die Menschen sind das ganze Leben blind.	Mankind is blind its entire life
Nun, Fauste, werde du's an Ende.	Now, Faust, you are, too, at the end.

Goethe's symbolism has stimulated reflection on mankind, mankind's fundamental drives, and God's purposes in the world. It might cause us, too, to think deeper about the role of power, politics and war today. Are we as blind as Faust, as blind as mankind was then? What will power do to us? Can we apply knowledge morally?

What Contemporaries Thought

Between 1806 and 1808 two German patriots, Achim von Arnim and Clemens Brentano, collected the folk songs of the 1500s and 1600s in *Des Knabens Wunderhorn* (*The Child's Wonder Horn*). Included in this was a poem that resonated well beyond the boundaries of the Holy Roman Empire. Italians, Frenchmen and Poles could sympathise with the verse:

Maikäfer flieg.	Junebug fly!
Dein Vater ist im Krieg.	Your father is off to war.
Die Mutter ist im Pommerland,	Your mother is in Pomerania
Pommerland ist abgebrannt.	Pomerania is burned out!
Maikäfer flieg.	Junebug fly!

The kings may have considered war a sport, a test of manhood, a necessary evil or even a bore, but our ancestors – at least the ancestors of most of us – saw it as the equivalent of a natural disaster. No, worse than a natural disaster, because floods and famine rarely take the males of the family away for years, burn the homes and tax whatever is left.

Mercantilism

We live in a global economy today. It was hardly different in the seventeenth and eighteenth centuries, though fewer people realised it – they drank their coffee or tea, with sugar, with few thoughts about how apples got into their dumplings (a worry that, legend tells us, helped drive George III mad). This global economy threatened life as traditionally led, and moreover, brought challenges that not everybody was able to respond to properly. As a result, then, as now, there were calls to protect the citizenry and the state from foreign competition. Not that European states were able to provide coffee, tea and sugar by domestic production, but those which could afford colonies could at least guarantee access to them at reasonable prices.

The Enlightened monarchs, proud of their logic, believed that possessing colonies would allow them to avoid paying inflated prices for foods and furs and other products from the New World, Africa, India and China, but also enable them to establish monopolies – then they could demand high prices. This led, not surprisingly, to wars that were both expensive and ruinous, and the passage of laws that benefited some of their courtiers, but not others. Thus ambitions to acquire military reputations, commercial fortunes, and bribes led one government after another into the blind alleys of lobbyists and nationalism.

There was also considerable worry about deficits, since rulers who did not repay debts promptly found that lenders would demand higher interest on loans. Rulers without hard cash could not pay their bureaucrats, much less their mercenary soldiers (who, unlike tailors, demanded their wages be delivered, or else). To get hard cash, ruler after ruler adopted policies we call *mercantilist*, that is, designed to assure access to important products and a favourable balance of payments.

Obviously, not every state can have a positive balance of trade all the time. The result was to discourage international commerce, which restricted economic growth and hampered entrepreneurs from new enterprises; by heaping one regulation atop others, the rulers hoped to smooth out economic uncertainties and inequalities for common citizens, though generally not for the aristocrats and the Church. However, since there were many more people clamouring for protection than asking for economic freedom, the rulers followed 'common sense' and imposed tariffs and other restrictions on imported goods, while encouraging products which would sell abroad.

First to denounce these practices were French *philosophes* François Quesnay (1694–1774) and Victor de Mirabeau (1715–89). Quesnay, the first of the economic philosophers known as *Physiocrats*, recommended a government policy of *laissez-faire, laissez-passer*, in short, hands off! Surprisingly, although Quesnay was at the court of Louis XV when his articles were published in the first *Encyclopedia* in 1756 and 1757, he was not consulted about economic policy; after all, he was the royal medical doctor, responsible for the health of Madame Pompadour, and what do such quacks know about anything? His principle, *Acheter, c'est vendre; vendre, c'est acheter* (to buy one must sell; to sell, one must buy) was too obvious for many learned minds to comprehend; those who set prices rejected his views that competition was the only way to determine a fair price and to eliminate a black market. Mirabeau was almost his only convert at first, but he was already well-known from his book *Ami des hommes au trait de la population* in 1756, then the *Théorie de l'impot* in 1760 – an attack on the taxation system that earned him a few days in a plush royal prison. Mirabeau had been reared for a career in the army, but his father had not been able to afford an officer's commission; hence, the son had begun to study law, then was greatly influenced by Montesquieu, later Quesnay, then the rapidly expanding number of Physiocrats. Known popularly as 'the friend of mankind' from the title of his most famous book, he died in 1789, after a long decline, just as his son was becoming famous as a reform leader in the movement that became the French Revolution.

An even more powerful voice was that of Adam Smith (1723–90), who published *Wealth of Nations* in 1776. He argued that free trade would set people free to produce more than before, and that this production would ultimately result in both greater wealth among the populace and greater incomes for the state. The 'invisible hand' would work better than all the well-intentioned state interventions.

These concepts led directly to the idea that political freedom was better that autocracy. The connection of free trade to freedom was not lost upon the authoritarian rulers of the eighteenth century any more than upon the authoritarians of today.

Smith's close friend, Edward Gibbon (1737–94), in his monumental *Decline and Fall of the Roman Empire* (1776–88) agreed with that sentiment. Why did the Empire fall? he was asked. He responded that this was the wrong question:

> The story of its ruin is simple and obvious; and, instead of inquiring why the Roman empire was destroyed, we should rather be surprised that it had subsisted so long. The victorious legions, who, in distant wars, acquired the

vices of strangers and mercenaries, first oppressed the freedom of the republic, and afterwards violated the majesty of the purple. The emperors, anxious for their personal safety and the public peace, were reduced to the base expedient of corrupting the discipline which rendered them alike formidable to their sovereign and to the enemy; the vigour of the military government was relaxed, and finally dissolved, by the partial institutions of Constantine; and the Roman world was overwhelmed by a deluge of Barbarians . . .

The vices of strangers and mercenaries. A strange sentiment for an English syncopate of royal favour who quietly voted for hiring Hessian mercenaries to suppress the liberties of American colonists. But who ever said that historians were wiser or more moral than the ordinary run of human beings?

The French Revolution

The decisive moment came in 1789. It was not that the French Revolution was inevitable. Simon Schama reminds us that the Old Regime was not a 'society doddering its way to the grave'. Quite the opposite. But there were problems.

The most serious was debt. The monarchy had raised taxes and borrowed money to finance its wars and extravaganzas. The public was willing to pay for wars – folk memory of foreign armies pillaging the countryside remained strong. But palaces and balls were visible signs of royal extravagance; and the scandal of the queen's necklace quickly led to stories spreading that Marie Antoinette was both a Habsburg whore and an Austrian spy. Tax-farming was inefficient and oppressive. Many sensed that a system built on buying and inheriting commissions and offices led to government by incompetents and playboys.

Nevertheless, the creation of a national army staffed by French nobles was a step away from competence – mercenary officers were expected to win, nobles preferred to parade. Preference for native aristocrats over colonial subjects, as practiced by Britain and Spain, would cost those nations the talent and loyalty of their subjects abroad. George Washington would have happily served in the British army, but the professional soldiers snubbed him (and every other officer in the colonial armies); this was the same experience that made Latin Americans hate the *Peninsulares* who held rigidly unto the tiller of the ship of state until Napoleon removed their dead hands. Americans on both continents were considered suitable only for rowing. And paying taxes. To collect taxes from the American colonies, the royal ministers and parliament overthrew traditional practices; by attempting to impose more direct government on the thirteen mainland colonies, they lost them.

France had lost colonies too, but that was not as much a setback as might be imagined, because colonies were expensive. Still, because almost everyone imagined colonies as great sources of wealth, they were good excuses for foreign wars. The expenses of wars, especially unnecessary wars such as the American Revolution, left Louis XVI swimming in a sea of red ink; and the example of a free people throwing out their king soon led to his swimming in a sea of blood.

The first European revolution actually broke out in the Dutch Republic, where the protests of 1785 against the king became open rebellion by 1787. The king of France, whose survival depended on suppressing such movements, lacked the money to intervene. The next steps were, in Schama's eyes, suicide.

The French people – and certainly French intellectuals – believed that instant and wide-reaching reforms would bring peace and prosperity to everyone. Instead, every community in Europe would be overwhelmed by war, taxes and military conscription.

The Lesson of the Wild Geese

Britain was relatively free of contesting armies after the War of the Roses, with the notable exception of the Civil War (1640-1649); the Glorious Revolution (1688) was glorious mainly because Parliament was able to maintain its dominant role in government without a bloody contest; it preserved the status quo. Ireland and Scotland were not so lucky. The memories of suffering following the Battle of the Boyne and Culloden were transported to America, to glow as fierce in anger the New World as in the Old. From 1745 to 1775 was only three decades.

The British penal laws that made Irish nobles chose between abject surrender (and becoming Protestant), sullen retirement to what remained of their estates, and exile, failed in their intent to disperse dreams of a successful uprising or dampen the smouldering hatred. Perhaps there was no policy that would have reconciled those who were so determined to resist the house of Hanover that they preferred serving in foreign armies, where they might have a chance to shoot at Englishmen. But no alternative policy was long attempted.

In 1775 Americans could look at Ireland, and to Scotland, to see what lay in store for them, should their revolution fail. To avoid this General Howe made repeated offers of reconciliation, which the colonists – aware that Parliament, not the general, made the laws – rejected. General Washington, determined to prevent a guerrilla war that would inflame the British military as such tactics had done in Ireland, insisted that the War for Independence be fought by his Continental Army, not by irregular forces such as has harassed the British on the retreat from Concord.

The wisdom of this policy was demonstrated in 1780–81 in the southern theatre, when warfare broke down into intimidations, reprisals, retaliations and retributions.

In the eyes of some modern historians 'Limited Warfare' was not as limited as the phrase indicates. This is true, but contemporaries had a good understanding of how devastating war could be. The more protection civilians and property had, the better.

What Was the Point?

Jacques Barzun has famously questioned our most basic assumptions about nation, race, class and culture. These combined to create 'the great illusion' that is leading western civilisation to self-destruction. The cosmopolitan world of yore began down this fatal road when king and realm turned into monarch and nation-state. Or so said Jacques Barzun. Nations are merely swept-together collections of diverse peoples, races are invented categories, and, paradoxically, mercenary armies were the last strongholds of true internationalism. Paradoxically, because wars achieve so little. Who can remember the causes of the great conflicts of the past? Or, for many young people, who cares?

Not everyone shares Barzun's beliefs, as the preface indicates. But it is a world-view widespread in circles which have rejected the 'realist' analysis of human affairs; and perhaps the 'idealistic' world-view, too. To find old-fashioned views about what drives humanity, one has to turn to the new nations of modern times, where recent history has often had an uncomfortable resemblance to the Thirty Years War or, for the more fortunate, to the nation-building models of eighteenth-century Europe.

———

It was suggested on page 251 that the individuals who composed our most important civilian elites are not well informed in economics and military affairs. Yet these groups have a tremendous self-confidence that, if given the power, they could manage our complex economic and intellectual world well.

Many of us are sceptical, because no one can quickly master the processes and learn the personalities that must be dealt with. Yet the belief persists that if only the most intelligent among us were given authority, perhaps in something resembling Plato's *Republic*, they could persuade people to put aside self-interest in favour of the common weal. This was certainly the view of the eighteenth-century *philosophes*, who believed that there were no problems which logic, science and good will could not resolve. Then they experienced with some dismay the reactions of rulers who, though seeming to grasp the principles behind a budget, could not understand why they could not continue to spend money as before.

Some of today's most intelligent people can be equally dense. In condemning all things military as evil, they are ready to turn power over to those most willing to use extreme measures. This is easiest to do when knowledge of economics and military history is superficial or altogether lacking.

———

We live in a world filled with economic, social and political turmoil, yet for the most part the readers of this book have known greater peace and comfort than almost any generation to precede them. If there is a lesson in this book, it is perhaps to feel relief that those days are largely behind us – except in vast areas of Africa, Latin America and the Middle East. A second lesson, perhaps, is how easily our settled lives can be upset.

We cannot do without armies today. Not without simply surrendering to bullies who decide that, if we will not use our money and manpower to defend the kind of world we want to have, they will put them to their own uses. Wherever organised armies are ineffective, and where we refuse to act ourselves, we should not be surprised if local leaders and local peoples hire mercenaries. Sometimes these mercenaries will be instructed to teach people how to defend themselves. Sometimes they are the tools of new dictators.

In Europe and America there is great mistrust of anything military. The reasons are too complex to discuss here, and there is no point to it. But the reality is that elected officials are very reluctant to put citizens and citizens' children in harm's way. In this they are little different than the rulers described in this book. Perhaps modern political leaders live longer and bathe more often, but they find it equally convenient to hire foreign mercenaries (sometimes calling them security services) or native ones (paramilitaries, militias) for conflicts in troubled regions.

If we cannot do without mercenaries, the challenge for us is to find ways to employ them rationally, so that they do more good and than harm.

Readings

Primary sources

Renner, Johannes, *Johannes Renner's Livonian History*. Trans. Jerry C. Smith.
Lewiston: Mellen Press, 1997.

Russow, Balthasar, *The Chronicle of Balthasar Russow*. Trans. Jerry C. Smith.
Madison: Baltic Studies, 1988.

Saint-Simon, Henri de, *The Memoirs of Louis de Rouvroy, duc de Saint-Simon,
Covering the Years 1691–1723*. Ed. Desmond Flower, New York: Heritage, 1959.

Arnold, Udo, *800 Jahre Deutscher Orden: Ausstellung des Germanischen
Nationalmuseums Nürnberg in Zusammenarbeit mit der Internationalen Historischen
Kommission zur Erforschung des Deutschen Ordens*. München: Bertelsmann, 1990.

Arnold, Udo, (ed.), *Die Hochmeister des Deutschen Ordens 1190–1994*. Marburg:
Elwert, 1998.

Asch, Ronald, *The Thirty Years War: The Holy Roman Empire and Europe, 1618–48*.
New York: St Martin's, 1997.

Ashley, Maurice, *The Glorious Revolution of 1688*. London: Hodder & Stoughton,
1966 and New York: Charles Scribner's Sons, 1967.

Barker, Thomas, *Double Eagle and Crescent: Vienna's Second Turkish Siege and Its
Historical Setting*. Albany: State University of New York Press, 1967.

Baxter, Stephen, *William III and the Defense of European Liberty, 1650–1702*. New
York: Harcourt, Brace & World, 1966.

Barzun, Jacques, *From Dawn to Decadence: 500 Years of Western Cultural Life, 1500 to
the Present*. New York: HarperCollins, 2000.

Benecke, Gerhard, *Germany in the Thirty Years War*. New York: St Martins Press,
1979.

Bengtsson, Frans G., *The Sword Does Not Jest: The Heroic Life of King Charles XII of
Sweden*. New York: St Martin's, 1960.

Berry, Lloyd, and Robert Crummey, (eds), *Rude & Barbarous Kingdom: Russia in the
Accounts of Sixteenth-Century English Voyagers*. Madison: University of Wisconsin
Press, 1968.

Black, Jeremy, *Warfare in the Eighteenth Century*. London: Cassell, 1999.

Black, Jeremy, *European Warfare, 1494–1660*. London and New York: Routledge, 2002.

Black, Jeremy, *European Warfare, 1660–1815*. New Haven and London: Yale
University Press, 1994.

Bonney, Richard, *The European Dynastic States, 1494–1660*. Oxford: Oxford
University Press, 1991.

Boot, William, *War Made New: Technology, Warfare and the Course of History*. New York and London, Gotham Books, 2006.

Braudel, Fernand, *Civilisation and Capitalism 15th–18th Century*. New York: Harper and Row, 1979.

Carlyle, Thomas, *History of Friedrich the Second, Called Frederick the Great*. New York: Harper, 1859–64.

Churchill, Winston, *Marlborough, His Life and Times*. New York: Charles Scribner's sons, 1968.

Collins, James, *The State in Early Modern France*. New York: Cambridge University Press, 1995.

Cracraft, James, (ed.) *Peter the Great Transforms Russia*. Lexington, MA: D. C. Heath, 1991.

Creasy, Edward Shepherd, *The Fifteen Decisive Battles of the World: From Marathon to Waterloo*. London: Richard Bentley and New York: Harper & Brothers, 1851.

Davies, Norman, *God's Playground: A History of Poland*. New York: Columbia University Press and Oxford: University Press, 1982.

Diess, Joseph Jay, *Captains of Fortune: Profiles of Six Italian Condottieri*. New York: Thomas Crowell, 1967.

Duffy, Christopher, *The Wild Goose and the Eagle: A life of Marshal von Browne, 1705–1757*. London: Chatto & Windus, 1964.

Ergang, Robert, *The Potsdam Führer: Frederick William I, Father of Prussian Militarism*. New York: Columbia University Press, 1941.

Faroqhi, Suraiya, *The Ottoman Empire and the World Around It*. London: I. B. Tauris, 2004.

Finkel, Caroline, *Osman's Dream: The Story of the Ottoman Empire 1300–1923*. New York: Basic Books, 2005.

Fortescue, John William, *A History of the British Army. Vol 1: To the Close of the Seven Years War*. London: Macmillan, 1910.

Gagliardo, John, *Reich and Nation: The Holy Roman Empire as Idea and Reality, 1763–1806*. Bloomington and London: Indiana, 1980.

Glozier, Matthew, *Marshal Schomberg, 'the ablest soldier of his age': International Soldiering and the Formation of State Armies in Seventeenth-Century Europe*. Brighton: Sussex Academic Press, 2005.

Goffman, Daniel, *The Ottoman Empire and Early Modern Europe*. New York: Cambridge University Press, 2002.

Grey, Ian, *Peter the Great, Emperor of All Russia*. New York: Lippencott, 1960.

Guthrie, William, *Battles of the Thirty Years War: From White Mountain to Nordingen, 1618–1635*. Westport: Greenwood, 2002.

Guthrie, William, *The Later Thirty Years Wars: From the Battle of Wittstock to the Treaty of Westphalia*. Westport: Greenwood, 2003.

Hellie, Richard, *Enserfment and Military Change in Muscovy*. Chicago: University of Chicago Press, 1971.

Howard, Michael, *War in European History*. London: Oxford University Press, 1976.

Hughes, Lindsey, *Peter the Great: A Biography*. New Haven and London: Yale University Press, 2002.

Ingrao, Charles W., *The Habsburg Monarchy, 1618–1815*. 2nd ed. New York: Cambridge University Press, 2000.

Karger, Johann, *Die Entwicklung der Adjustierung: Rüstung und Bewaffnung der österreichisch-ungarischen Armee 1700–1809*. Reprint: Buchholz: LTR, 1998.

Khodarkovsky, Michael, *Russia's Steppe Frontier: The Making of a Colonial Empire, 1500–1800*. Bloomington: Indiana University Press, 2002.

Kirby, David, *Northern Europe in the Early Modern Period: The Baltic World 1492–1772*. London: Longman, 1990.

Readings

Konstam, Angus, *Poltava 1709: Russia Comes of Age*. (Campaign Series no. 34) London: Osprey, 1994.

Kreem, Juhan, 'The Business of War. Mercenary Market and Organisation in Reval in the Fifteenth and Early Sixteenth Centuries,' *Scandinavian Economic History Review*, 49/2 (2001) pp. 26–42.

Langer, Herbert, *The Thirty Years War*. New York: Dorset, 1990.

Lynn, John, *The Wars of Louis XIV*. New York: Longman, 1999.

Macaulay, Thomas Babbington, *History of England*. London: Longmans, Green, 1898 and Boston: Riverside, 1899.

McKay, Derek, *Prince Eugene of Savoy*. London: Thames and Hudson, 1978.

McNally, Michael and Graham Turner, *Battle of the Boyne 1690: The Irish campaign for the English Crown*. Oxford: Osprey, 2005.

Magnusson, Magnus, *Scotland*. London: HarperCollins, 2000.

McNeill, William, *Europe's Steppe Frontier, 1500–1800*. Chicago: University of Chicago, 1964.

Maland, David, *Europe at War, 1600–1650*. London: MacMillan and Totowa, NJ: Rowman and Littlefield, 1980.

Massie, Robert, *Peter the Great: His Life and His World*. New York: Knopf, 1980.

Mitford, Nancy, *The Sun King*. London: Hamish Hamilton and New York: Harper & Row, 1966.

Mortimer, Geoff, *Eyewitness Accounts of the Thirty Years War*. London and New York: MacMillan, 2004.

Murphey, Rhoads, *Ottoman Warfare, 1500–1700*. New Brunswick: Rutgers, 1999.

Nelson, Walter Henry, *The soldier kings; the house of Hohenzollern*. New York: Putnam, 1970.

Parker, Geoffrey, *The Military Revolution: Military Innovation and the rise of the West, 1500–1800*. Cambridge: Cambridge University Press, 1988.

Parker, Geoffrey, *The Thirty Years War*. 2nd edn. London: Routledge 1997 and New York: Barnes & Noble, 1993.

Parker, Geoffrey, *The Army of Flanders and the Spanish Road, 1567–1659*. 2nd edn, Cambridge: Cambridge University Press, 2004.

Parvev, Ivan, *Hapsburgs and Ottomans Between Vienna and Belgrade (1683–1739)*. New York: Columbia University Press, 1995.

Roberts, Michael, *Gustavus Adolphus: A History of Sweden 1611–1632*. London: Longmans, 1953–58.

Roberts, Michael, *The Swedish Imperial Experience 1560–1718*. New York: Cambridge, 1978.

Saxe, Maurice de, 'My Reveries upon the Art of War,' in *Roots of Strategy: The 5 Greatest Military Classics of all Time*, ed. and trans. Thomas R. Phillips. Harrisburg, PA: Stackpole Books, 1985.

Schama, Simon, *Citizens: A Chronicle of the French Revolution*. New York: Knopf, 1989.

Schiemann, Theodor. *Charakterköpfe und Sittenbilder aus der baltischen Geschichte des 16. Jahrhunderts*. Mitau: Behre, 1877.

Schuster, O. and F. A. Francke, *Geschichte der Sächsischen Armee von deren Errichtung bis auf die neueste Zeit*. 3 vols. Leipzig: Duncker & Humblot, 1885.

Simms, J. G., *Jacobite Ireland: 1685–1691*. London: Routledge and Kegan Paul, 1969.

Spencer, Charles, *Battle for Europe: How the Duke of Marlborough Masterminded the Defeat of the French at Blenheim*. London: Weidenfeld and New York: Wiley, 2004.

Stone, Daniel, *The Polish-Lithuanian State, 1386–1795*. Seattle and London: University of London, 2001. Vol. IV of *A History of East Central Europe*.

Stoye, John, *The Siege of Vienna*. New York: Holt, Rinehart and Winston, 1965.

Strandling, R. A., *The Spanish Monarchy and Irish Mercenaries: The Wild Geese in Spain 1618–68*. Dublin: Blackrock, 1994.

Swift, Jonathan, *The Conduct of the Allies*. Oxford: Clarendon Press, 1916.

Szechi, Daniel, *1715, The Great Jacobite Rebellion*. London: Yale University Press, 2006.

Tanner, Marcus, *Ireland's Holy Wars: The Struggle for a Nation's Soul, 1500–2000*. New Haven: Yale University Press, 2001.

Thompson, Janice, *Mercenaries, Pirates and Sovereigns, State-building and Extra-territorial Violence in Early Modern Europe*. Princeton: Princeton University Press, 1994.

Tilly, Charles, *Coercion, Capital, and European States, A.D. 990–1990*. Cambridge, MA: Blackwell, 1990.

Tincey, John, *Blenheim 1704: The Duke of Marlborough's Masterpiece*. (Campaign Series no. 141) Oxford: Osprey, 2004.

Trevelyan, George Macaulay, *The England of Queen Anne*. London and New York: Longmans, Green, 1934.

Turberville, Arthur S., (ed.) *Johnson's England: An Account of the Life & Manners of his Age*. Oxford: Clarendon Press, 1933.

Tyerman, Christopher, *God's War: A New History of the Crusades*. Cambridge: Belknap Press, 2006.

Urban, William, *The Livonian Crusade*. Chicago: Lithuanian Research and Studies Center, 2004.

Urban, William, *The Teutonic Knights*. London: Greenhill and Mechanicsburg, PA: Stackpole Books, 2003.

Urban, William, *Medieval Mercenaries*. London: Greenhill and Mechanicsburg, PA: Stackpole Books, 2006.

Vale, Malcolm. *War and Chivalry: Warfare and Aristocratic Culture in England, France and Burgundy at the End of the Middle Ages*. Athens, Georgia: University of Georgia Press, 1981.

Voltaire, *The Age of Louis XIV*. trs by Martyn P. Pollack, London: Dent and New York: Dutton, 1926.

Voltaire, *The History of Charles the Twelfth, King of Sweden*. Philadelphia: Lippincott, 1865.

Watson, Francis. *Wallenstein, Soldier Under Saturn*. New York: Appleton-Century, 1938.

Wedgwood, C.V., *The Thirty Years War*. Garden City: Doubleday, 1961.

Wolf, John, *Louis XIV*. New York: Norton, 1968.

Wrede, Alphons, *Geschichte der K. und K. Wehrmacht. Wien, 1898–1905*. Reprint Buchholz: LTR, 1985.

Index